D1395138

HELEN WADDELL

A Biography

by

D. FELICITAS CORRIGAN

LONDON
VICTOR GOLLANCZ LTD
1986

First published in Great Britain 1986
by Victor Gollancz Ltd,
14 Henrietta Street, London WC2E 8QJ

British Library Cataloguing in Publication Data
Corrigan, Felicitas
  Helen Waddell.
  1. Waddell, Helen   2. Medievalists
  — Great Britain — Biography
  I. Title
  909.07′092′4   D116.7.W3

ISBN 0–575–03674–5

Typeset at The Spartan Press Ltd, Lymington, Hants
and printed in Great Britain by
St Edmundsbury Press, Bury St Edmunds, Suffolk
Illustrations originated and printed by Thomas Campone, Southampton

'It has ever been a hobby of mine (unless it be a truism, not a hobby) that a man's life lies in his letters. A much higher desideratum than interest in Biography is met by the method of Correspondence. Biographers varnish; they assign motives; they conjecture feelings; they interpret Lord Burleigh's nods; they palliate or defend. For myself, I sincerely wish to seem neither better nor worse than I am. I detest suppression; and here is the great difficulty. It may be said that to ask a biographer to edit letters is like putting salt on the bird's tail.'
(John H. Newman to Mrs John Mozley 1863)

'I am not prepared to admit that there is, or can be, properly speaking, in the world anything that is too sacred to be known. That spiritual beauty and spiritual truth are in their nature communicable, and that they should be communicated, is a principle which lies at the root of every conceivable religion.'
(G. K. Chesterton *Browning* 1903)

ACKNOWLEDGEMENTS

THE NUMBER OF creditors to whom this book is irremediably indebted lays the biographer open to the charge of being a mere setter of jewels not her own. The charge is freely admitted. I can only hope that the setting is not too unworthy of its gems. A list of those who have helped in little or much will necessarily be incomplete, but any catalogue must open with the name of Helen Waddell's niece, Miss Mollie Martin. With unconditional and unlimited trust, she placed in my hands everything pertaining to Helen's life, and she has never questioned a judgement; her first-hand knowledge of people and events has supplied crucial information, and her own pen added immediacy and veracity at every turn. I can only express publicly a gratitude that lies beyond words.

I thank all who have assisted me in specialist research, especially Mr W. G. Wheeler and Miss Mary Kelly of Queen's University Library who gave practical expression to their keen interest by sharing the fruit of their own labours, Mr Wheeler with information from the official history of the University, Miss Kelly with her professional decoding of George Saintsbury's cacography. Through the good offices of Father Peter Milward, S.J. of Sophia University, Tokyo, and the Reverend Colin Plumb of the United Reformed Church, the personnel of the Church of Scotland, both in Tokyo and Edinburgh, readily consulted their archives and with prompt courtesy gave me the exact data I needed; to these must be added the page of Japanese photographs taken by Sister Maria Regina Kageyama, designed to throw light on Helen's background and childhood. To Mr David Hall of Cambridge University Library, Helen Waddell's very knowledgeable bibliographer, I owe an ever-increasing debt; Mr Robin Lindsay helped me by the loan of letters from H. W. to Enid Starkie; Mr Mervyn Truran's erudite mind traced the vagaries of Madonella and her college for young damsels; Miss Penny Barnes cheerfully checked references to early numbers of *The Spectator* at the John Rylands Library; and at least once, Mr John Ginger's uncommon acquaintance with eighteenth-century social mores saved my feet from stumbling; Mr George Sayer, friend and biographer of C. S. Lewis, provided the only known references to Helen in C.S.L.'s letters.

Others have enriched the book with personal contributions: the Very Reverend Michael Stancliffe, Dean of Winchester, the Reverend Canon J. W. Poole, Miss Julian Allan C.B.E., Mrs Vivien Clarke. Miss Maude Clarke's nephew, Professor R. S. J. Clarke of Queen's University, Belfast, kindly allowed me the use of her letters and photograph, and Mr Seamus Heaney generously bade me use and re-use three lines that sadly he jettisoned and I happily salvaged from his poem, 'The Last Look' in *Station Island*. I shall take him at his word. By no means least, there remains to thank my unsalaried unwearied secretary, Miss Dorothy Goodwin who, for very love of Helen Waddell, patiently deciphered and typed hundreds of letters, and found only delight in the task.

Miss Livia Gollancz, my publisher, has shown enthusiasm and an unflagging interest from first page to last; to her, and also to the two members of my own community who brought to the reading of the script their own youthful vision and critical acumen, I offer heartfelt thanks.

Finally I acknowledge permission kindly given by the Syndics of Cambridge University Library to quote H. W.'s letters to Stanley Baldwin, and by the Librarian of Queen's University, Belfast, and Professor Saintsbury's grandson, The Rt Revd Mgr George Saintsbury, for the use of quotations from George Saintsbury's letters; acknowledgement is also due to the following publishing houses for the use of quotations from books issued under their imprint:

Constable Ltd, Helen Waddell's sole publishers during her lifetime, for passages quoted *passim* from *Peter Abelard*; Faber & Faber for the passage from *A Little Love and Good Company* by Cathleen Nesbitt, quoted on pages 55–6, and for three lines from 'The Dry Salvages', from *Four Quartets* by T. S. Eliot, reprinted by permission of the publishers. Quotations from letters by A. E. Russell are reprinted by kind permission of A. M. Heath Ltd.

F. C.

LIST OF ILLUSTRATIONS

CHAPTER I

NUMBER 25 NAKANO-CHO, Azabu, Tokyo, a house built after the Japanese fashion entirely of wood raised on piles a couple of feet above floor level, stood apart on rising ground, concealed behind a high bamboo fence. Flat-roofed single rooms sprawled in conscious irregularity, connected by stretches of wisteria-covered verandahs of dark beautifully-polished wood. Grooves on both inner and outer edges allowed for the smooth running of sliding screens or *shoji*, six or seven feet high, providing a paper wall of privacy by day, while at night heavy wooden shutters along the outer grooves sealed the house. It had its *kura* or fireproof apartment, built of very thick wood and clay, and its peculiarly constructed earthquake door to allow of escape in times of danger, when ordinary doors or shutters were liable to jam as the building swayed. The garden surrounding the house was even more romantic. Here a contorted tree-trunk, a huge boulder of unusual outline, large asymmetrical flagstones, terraces, flowering trees, a well of fresh water, and a stone bridge arched over a pond of goldfish — all most carefully planned on principles of contrast and emphasis — were a monument to the Japanese love of the curious united with an exquisite perception of beauty in single objects. In summer, violets carpeted the grass, and frail red, white and purple morning-glory trailed over every post. In winter, even the snows could not prevent the tiny black-branched plum tree from putting forth pink buds. Best of all, beyond the last outpost of the house, where an uneven flagged pathway turned a sharp corner into the dark shadow of pines, there stood a maple tree with deeply-furrowed corky bark, whose sheltering boughs would provide a window on Eternity to the spiritual eye of Helen Waddell, the child born in the city of Tokyo on 31 May 1889.

Modern Tokyo, graced today with no fewer than 79 universities, evokes an image of steel and reinforced concrete, world leadership in technological skills and electronics, workers unrivalled in textile, steel and motor industries, and a vista of roads, fly-overs and subways, all astonishing feats of engineering and planning. The result of post-war reconstruction and urbanization has been to make the city a sprawling monster of more than ten million people, sharing with New York the dubious honour of being the densest mass of human beings on the face of the earth. Very different was the Tokyo of a century ago. Between then and now Nature, with its cataclysmic earthquakes, typhoons, and cholera epidemics, is the sole common factor. What the earth-quake and fire spared of the buildings in 1923, the air raids of the Second World War levelled to the ground. Old Tokyo has virtually disappeared. Number 25 Nakano-cho has been replaced by the brand-new Roppongi 3-chome, in what is now a built-up area near the major restaurant quarter. There is no trace of the house which Helen Waddell later re-created with such artistry in her autobiographical collection of stories. The district of Azabu, however, much expanded of course, still houses the missionaries and diplomats — some thirty embassies are located there.

In April 1889, a few weeks before Helen's birth, Mary Crawford Fraser took up residence in the British Legation in Tokyo. Between then and the death of Hugh Fraser, her husband, in 1894, she sent home a series of letters published in 1900 with no fewer than 220 illustrations, under the title *A Diplomatist's Wife in Japan*. In vivid sparkling prose, she discusses assassinations, lepers, typhoons, Budd-hist sculptures, and the accepted customs of traditional life. The Tokyo she knew was ringed with shallow moats spanned by scores of solid bridges. She drove about in a carriage drawn by cream-coloured ponies; for refreshment, she was proffered a china dish piled high with maple leaves large and small, made in sugar, pink, crimson, green and orange, interspersed with autumn grasses and wild chrysanthemums; at a village fair, she bought up the stall-holder's entire stock of fireflies imprisoned in a black horsehair cage — a hundred 'Princess Splen-dours' as they were called. She carried them home, waited until all the household were asleep, crept into the Embassy garden and there, feeling like a white witch playing with stars, opened the cage and set the glowing things free. This gift of imaginative compassion for all beautiful living things was akin to Helen Waddell's, and Mary's 'land of leisure' like Helen's 'enchanted enclosure' remained enshrined in both their hearts for ever.

Helen Jane Waddell was the youngest of a family of ten, eight of them sons. Her father, the Reverend Hugh Waddell, had been sent with his brothers to an Irish national school, owned by priests and staffed by Catholics, before passing to Queen's College, Belfast, from which he graduated with honours. At the age of twenty-two, he entered the Presbyterian College, was licensed six years later, and then received a call to succeed his father as minister in the church of

Glenarm. He refused the call because he felt that his true vocation was to the mission field. British imperialism was just then at its height, and 'conversion of the heathen' went hand in hand with colonial expansion. So it was that in 1868, aged twenty-eight, the Mission Board appointed him to pioneer the evangelization of Manchuria; but after two years the harsh climate drove him home broken in health, and left him with a permanent malady of the throat. Possibly for the curative properties of sunshine and sea air, he was next drafted to Southern Spain to reopen the Presbyterian Mission. Before departure he married Jane Martin of County Down, daughter of a farmer and spiritually an ideal partner. It was in Spain that their eldest son Hugh was born. A century before ecumenism became the fashion, Hugh Waddell's immediate forebears and family had always mixed freely and gladly with their neighbours: there was nothing partisan or bitter about Hugh Waddell. But if the conversion of a Moorish Jew is well-nigh inconceivable, what shall be said of a Spanish hidalgo? Unwilling to spend a lifetime without winning a single recruit, as did a fellow-missionary among the Muslims of Mongolia, he applied at the end of his three-year term for a transfer: he saw no point, he said, in trying to 'convert' people who were as deeply Christian as himself.

Japan had opened its doors to the West during the 1860s, and although Ulster had acquired no foothold, the United Presbyterian Church of Scotland happened just then to need a missionary for Tokyo, the principal station of its newly-established Japan Mission. Hugh Waddell applied, was accepted, and in 1873 set out with his wife and child for the city which was to be his home for the next twenty-seven years. The difficulties confronting a Christian missionary were formidable. The Japanese were hostile towards any who would interfere with their ancient culture or religion. Let the West keep its formal logic, its abstract terms, its long words: the East would rest content with its age-long epigram, enigma and parable. The mechanism of the Japanese mind had never been touched by Greek thought, Roman law, or biblical concepts: that mind made no clear-cut distinctions but lived in a world of compromise, a no-man's land between any two absolute affirmations. Yet the isolation of the old order was about to disintegrate. During the last quarter of the century Hugh Waddell was to witness a mass of huge brick buildings in 'the foreign style' rise up in the centre of the city, and the beauty and elegance of native chest, brazier, screen and table give way to hideous German furniture. In the 1880s elaborate electric light standards would replace the traditional lanterns at the gates of the Imperial Palace, telegraph and telephone wires form a network throughout the

city, and tramlines succeed moats. With unprecedented speed, a small
nation in far-off Asia was to burst into a major power in the world's
economy.

Visits to Europe and America in 1871 by Japanese officials had
resulted in the displacement of two million samurai, and the
announcement in 1872 of a system of universal education, prelude to
the promulgation of the Japanese Constitution of 1889. Although
with great reluctance Christianity had been legalized in 1873, the very
year of Hugh Waddell's departure for Japan, there seemed to be no
opening for the reception of the Gospel, and no practical work had
been done. (Catholic missionary endeavour since the time of St
Francis Xavier had been a heroic tragedy.) Born educator that he was,
Hugh Waddell at once recognized the Japanese thirst for knowledge
and on 10 June 1874, soon after his arrival, he opened a day school for
children in the Western part of the city. The school grew quickly in
size and importance, gave him access to parents and, little by little, he
won their confidence and esteem. For ten years he never took a
holiday. Assiduously he read, he talked, he studied the language of the
common folk, and from pupils, pilgrims, ricksha porters, he imbibed
the racy colloquialisms that spiced all his teaching and gained him
renown as pastor and catechist. From the outset he was troubled by
the thorny problem of adaptation: how present the doctrine of the
Trinity to minds steeped in the Buddhist or Shinto tradition? In
October 1876 he was appointed to translate the Bible into Japanese,
and with his Chinese missionary experience behind him, opposed
some of the commonly accepted terms for the Godhead: 'He was a
staunch advocate of "Ki" for the word Spirit instead of "Rei" the word
used in Bible translation and in speech. He would say *Sei-ki*, instead of
Sei-rei for Holy Spirit. He held that *Rei* taught pantheism, while the *Ki*
was the personal spirit.'★ Precisely because the Christian revelation
must seem strange and indigestible propaganda, he sought, among the
Japanese peasants living under conditions not unlike those of their
ancestors of five hundred years earlier, a simple language and homely
metaphor that would evoke response. His children would later tease
him over his propensity for pilgrims: 'Pilgrims had a fascination for
our father, as for us,' Helen was to say. 'We very often found him
lounging at the tent door, and talking in his drifting fashion, what he
called "brushing up his colloquial".'

★*Proceedings of the General Conference of Protestant Missionaries in Japan
held in Tokyo 24–31 October 1900* (Methodist Publishing House, Tokyo,
1901).

Meanwhile his own children had come in swift succession. Six boys — Hugh, Jimmie, Martin, Sam, Charlie and Tom — were followed by Margaret (variously called Maggie, Peggy, Meg or Bun), two more boys, Billy and George — and lastly Helen. All but the eldest were born in Tokyo and, thinly clad and barefoot, or at most sandalled, they prided themselves on being Japanese 'born and bred' as opposed to the pathetic English and American foreigners who invaded their territory arrayed in stiff white collars, tailormade suits, and shiny black boots. But if the difficulties facing Hugh Waddell in his apostolic labours were formidable, what shall be said of his domestic problems? One's heart goes out to his wife, who had to bear what was possibly the heavier burden. Jane Waddell was said to be as zealous a missionary as her husband and, in spite of a family running into double numbers, to possess a heart 'big enough to hold a presbytery', to quote a fellow-missionary. From 1880 she must often have been left to cope alone, for Hugh was constantly absent for long stretches in the out-stations he had founded in the province of Idzu, and on itinerary visits throughout Joshiu. A letter of twenty pages, written in his large clear script, survives to illustrate the bond between husband and wife.

G. K. Chesterton has observed that nothing is 'too sacred' to be quoted: parody of the sacred is alone to be feared. The two letters to be quoted, one from husband to wife, the other from wife to husband, admittedly fall into the category of the sacred:

> Idzu,
> Kamagori,
> Rendaiji Mura.
>
> Thursday afternoon   1st December 1889
>
> My dearest Jenny,
>   Your welcome letter was waiting here for me when I returned a few hours ago. I was away from Rendaiji since Monday. I need not tell you how delighted I was to see the old address which I used to wait for when in Spain in other days. I think I was quite as anxious today to hear from you as I was even then, and you know what that means. As of old I waited until I got my clothes and things put to right before I ventured to look inside, enjoying the thing all the while just as the boys do their apples before they eat them. When I opened it I was very glad to find one from Hugh, and quite his own one too. I must send him one tonight in turn for it. I need not say how delighted I was to peruse yours. I have read it twice already, and I suppose I shall repeat the same until I get another one from you, which I hope will be soon. . . .

The letter goes on to describe mission personnel and progress, looks forward to his return the following week, longs for that reunion, and is subscribed 'With love and kisses to wife and wee ones, and thanks for all your prayers. I am your own Hugh.'

All ten 'wee ones' were living with their parents in Tokyo. As sons of a missionary the three elder boys evidently felt it a duty to preach in season and out of season. Years later, after a long walk with Martin, Helen recounted this incident:

> We sat on the heather and I told him scraps of Japanese verse, and he told me stories of what he did when he was little in Japan: one delightful tale of visiting a little Japanese house, a solemn unauthorized trio, aged from seven to ten: and the extraordinary gratification of their hosts. They inspected the foreign children very minutely, being especially intrigued by their hair, and hailed every remark with profound reverence. Jim was a fervent evangelist at that age, and pointing severely to the Buddha on the Butsudian, denounced the worship of idols with great fluency. And the dears, instead of being angry, bowed profoundly, and set the Buddha into a cupboard. Now did you ever know finer manners than that?

In a characteristic passage, Helen was to recall her own training in prayer:

> Most children are taught the Lord's Prayer, and just a word or two of prayer for their own people by name. Should they be more 'particular'? I believe we get a habit of 'lumping' our sins when we are little that it is hard to get out of. And also a selfish way of praying. Here as nearly as I can remember is the kind of thing I prayed for when I was little:
>   'Our Father, we are sorry for the wrong things we did today. Help us to be better tomorrow. Forgive us for being cross and thinking all the time about ourselves. Bless all the people who are sick and the people who are sad, and come to them if they cannot sleep. And bless the people who are hungry and poor, and help us not to be selfish any more. And make us all good. For Christ's sake, Amen.'

But the mother who first taught her small daughter how to pray, was ailing. Throughout 1891, Hugh noted with growing anxiety his wife's lassitude and general indisposition. 'It was not easy to live in Japan in those days,' George Braithwaite, one of his colleagues, was to tell Helen years later. 'The year that I went out was somewhat terrible. That summer they died in hundreds. One could not walk in Asakusa without meeting the carts of the dead. It was cholera. Your father had his wife and children, but every day he went amongst the dying.' In the circumstances, Hugh Waddell finally applied to the Central Committee in Edinburgh for compassionate leave of absence from Tokyo in order to take his sick wife home. The Synod refused his request. He was able to accompany her and all the children only as far as Canada to stay for a short time with his only sister Mary and then, to save money, he travelled steerage back to Yokohama leaving his family to reach Belfast as best they could.

There Mrs Waddell settled at 84 Clifton Park Avenue. A large photograph taken in a Belfast studio — to reassure Hugh in Tokyo? — shows Jenny surrounded by a corona of five tall teenage boys, three small imps posed on tiger skins in the foreground, Meg standing sentinel on her mother's right, while a golden-haired baby Helen nestles on her mother's lap, head against her breast, tiny right hand linked into the encircling arm. Although artificially posed, the group is strikingly focussed on the mother. There is complete unity. The figures are in close contact with one another, the eyes direct and unafraid, hands (often so indicative) relaxed and unselfconscious, and in a protective gesture one of the elder boys has placed his hand on his brother's shoulder without the slightest embarrassment. It is evident from the only letter that survives, that the whole family were under the same roof; to pass any comment on the contents would violate the sacred:

84 Clifton Park Avenue
March 28th/92

My own dearest Hugh,

Here I am again on Monday night writing you after having the washing all finished up. I got your last letter on Saturday night. Oh how glad I am when your letter comes in. Two or three times I have noticed it how your letter just came to cheer me up when I needed it.

We are getting on as usual. You good darling what a nice letter you wrote me — I wonder shall we indeed be together again. Hugh dear, isn't it a wonder how we can live apart as we do. I try to battle every lonely feeling away and say if possible 'It must be' 'it ought to be' as it is. I hope God may bless us much more abundantly seeing that we have not our earthly head of the house with us. I hope He may be more than a father even to the children when you are away from them.

The children have been telling you about George's eyes. Poor wee fellow I was quite alarmed about them especially one night when he could scarcely open them. But I am thankful to say they are almost better now. Poor wee laddie he made no ado about them nor has been cross. He is the favourite in the house. And the baby is a dear nice wee girl but truly a little yaka mashii★ the mother's daughter. You know she is so smart hardly like a child in many ways. I have great times hunting them all to their lessons. I do hope they may all do well. If they as you say were all Christians how nice. I shall write the little Noda boy as soon as I have time. But Hugh dear what a busy time I have. I cannot keep up the mending. I find I have really

★*yaka mashii*: a noisy nuisance.

not the time but I do my best. Now the long days are in and the baby does not go to sleep so early and this gives me less time still. Be sure and thank Seki for her kind enquiries poor soul it brought the tears to my eyes the kindheartedness of her.

So many people leaving Japan. Hugh dear what changes since you and I first set foot on the shores. How many have come and gone since then. . . . Give my kindest congratulations to Mr and Mrs Wada on the new addition to the family and at any time when it would be appropriate to do so give my Yoroshiku's* to the ladies of the congregation and tell them I shall never forget their unmerited kindness to me.

I told Mrs Lyons that you wanted them to write you and I think they will. Just before I began this letter I took a race up the street to see them after the youngest four were to bed. All well. Lyons is at work every day and so I hope all may go well with them now. I like Mrs L. very well but after the experience I had with Miss Grey I try to be careful — for believe me it is not good to get too intimate for fear of a leak. But as I say many a time I take a slip round after dark when the little ones are to bed and the others at lessons and stay ten minutes sometimes and sometimes perhaps a little longer but not much as my work of some kind awaits me here. Besides I do my best to keep my own house and find my consolation in my own home. The cough I wrote you about is going away. The cold always weakens me and I am so slow to shake it off and so prone to catch it. I am getting old Hugh dear hide it as I may. I am afraid my charms won't be many when you come home. But you must just think of me at my best! What a nonsensical letter Jenny is writing this time you will be thinking as you read this.

10 p.m. almost you will be sleeping by this time. If I could only just gaze at and imprint fond kisses on those lips so often pressed by mine how nice. Oh is there such joy in those for me yet.

I would like to peer into the future and wonder if I shall ever be in Japan with you again. But I hope if it be my path of duty to stay and *not* to go that I may be enabled to do so. I have been wilful all my life it is nearly time I should give it up but it is hard sometimes to 'pluck out the right eye'. Hugh dear ask for guidance and help both for your own self and myself and our dear children that we may all be led aright all be helped in the right path that has His blessing upon it for oh dear it is easy deceiving one's self in going and doing the wrong way.

I did not go up to see my mother. The snow and cold came back so but I may go some day. If so it is just possible my next letter may not be so soon with you so do not be uneasy. It is a pity of my mother. W. is not steady he stopped for a little but the last accounts I had were not good. My poor old father's prayers are they not to be answered for him. Many a time his life has been miraculously saved surely by a providential watching over him but he seems to take no advising. Mrs Waddell in her letter said about

*Yoroshiku: best regards.

Willie — that she did not know where he had gone to nor perhaps would not for a long time. He left London but where no one knows amongst his friends. It's sad about him. This drink oh what a curse one does not realize the danger of tampering with it or tasting it at all.

Now I must say good night I am very sleepy but I persevere and would finish this letter. When you are praying for me ask very specially that my hot temper may be healed also that I may have wisdom and grace to fill the seat of authority God has now placed me in to His glory and praise. This seems to be so far beyond me but with God we are told all things are possible.

Kisses kisses love and all endearments from us every one and surely surely from your own loving wife.

Jenny Waddell

The hardship of life in the mission field, the fatigue and responsibility of her new task, and the grief of separation from her husband made Jenny an easy prey to the epidemics that ravaged not only Japan but the ports of Great Britain in the closing years of the nineteenth century. Shortly after writing the above letter, she fell desperately ill. To reach Hugh quickly was impossible. Marconi did not shake the world with his radio signals across the Atlantic until 1901, and in 1892 mailboats could take three months to reach Japan. Yet somehow word of Jenny's grave condition did get to him, for extant letters of introduction to notable Presbyterians in New York asking for help to speed him on his way are dated 16 May 1892. Little did he know that his wife was already dead. The laconic death certificate states that on 11 May 1892 at 84 Clifton Park Avenue, Jane Waddell aged forty-two years, wife of Hugh Waddell Minister, died from Typhoid Fever twenty-one days and Endocarditis twelve days, Sara Thompson of 26 Allworthy Avenue being present at her death.

No records survive to tell the exact date of Hugh Waddell's arrival, but when he reached Belfast it was to find his wife dead and buried, and his youngest child lying in a coma. Jenny had died just three weeks before Helen's third birthday and the babe had fallen victim to her mother's deadly disease. Human effort was unable to rouse her until, distraught with grief, her father summoned her back to life, speaking to her urgently in the Japanese tongue she had been accustomed to since birth. At once she opened her eyes, recognized the father she was to worship, and returned to earth to gladden his sad heart.

'I do not think that any man that came through what he did would ever again be light of heart,' George Braithwaite told Helen. 'You remember that when the Board of Missions refused to allow him to come home, when your mother was ailing, and there were all the little children. He took her to America, and when he came back to us he lived in the Japanese quarter in lodgings. I remember sitting with him at supper, and as we talked there was nothing on the table but bread, and water, and sometimes milk. There was not any butter. It was a hard life.

'But he was Irish to the last. I remember how he kept us laughing sometimes. But he did not show every man his heart. I saw, years ago, the crest taken by an Indian missionary: it was an ox, and the motto: "For service, or for sacrifice." That is how I think of your father. We say, "The Lord is my shepherd", and it is a word of great comfort. But there is the other side. For why does the shepherd guard the sheep?'

Home merely on compassionate furlough, separated now by death from the support and perfect companionship of his wife, and by oceans from the scene of his life's labour, Hugh was faced with the difficult decision of his own and his family's future. There can be little doubt that had a call to the Irish Presbyterian Church reached him then as it had done in 1867 before he went to Manchuria, he would have accepted it and stayed in Belfast. But 25 years' absence had made him a stranger in his own land, and no call came. He therefore took what was surely the only sensible course: he remarried. A woman's care for his four youngest children was essential. On 15 September 1893, his forty-eight-year-old cousin, Martha Waddell, became his wife. A photograph taken at this time provides a nice foil to that of Jenny with her brood. There is no real focus in the second photograph: Papa is there as being the central link in the family, and is balanced on the other side of Meg by a delicate Dresden china figure, charming, alert, thin-lipped and intelligent. The grouping in both photographs is similar, but the differences are subtle and profound. In the second, the ten children are decidedly more elegant: they are no longer merely neat and clean, they are positively smart — Meg and Helen in dainty lace collars and rucked bodices, the boys in neckties and waistcoats adorned with watch chains. The figures stand further apart, no one clings to or protects another. A winsome little Helen, half-huddled against her father's knee, comes nearest to physical contact, although her sidelong glance at the camera suggests that she is suspicious of things. Sadness and fear lurk behind the eyes of the three elder boys, hands self-consciously folded or stuffed in pockets, partly no doubt owing to adolescent growing-pains but also to a desire to assert independence. In assuming her future responsibilities, Martha Waddell did not lack courage: however fragile in appearance, her tiny hand could rule with a rod of iron should need arise.

Having now settled his family under its new governing head at Glandore, Cavehill Road, Belfast, Hugh had no option but to return alone to his work in Tokyo as soon as possible. This he did at the end of that year, for in the spring of 1894 he was sending letters to his little daughter, treasured for life in a packet labelled in youthful script: *Letters from my Father.* In essence they do not differ from the kind any fond father would send to any engaging small child of his, but incidentally they throw a significant light on Martha Waddell's skilful handling of her formidable charge. The smart little *yaka mashii*, as her own mother had called her, was soon sending Papa pictures and printed letters by every post. 'Mother says you blow me a great many kisses across from Ireland. I am very glad to hear that you and Willie and George and the others are so good children and that you make Mother so happy. Your little bird is still with me and tells me of you every day. I hope to keep it with me until I go back to you again. It has still the nest and eggs. Mother tells me how you wait at the foot of the stairs in the morning with your arms open for her to take you in her arms. Jesus wants you to come to Him that way also every morning, and He will take you up in His arms and bless you. I send you a little leaf out of my garden, with kisses on it for my own little Helen from her loving father, Hugh Waddell.' Years later in a letter to her sister, Helen was to pay tribute to the woman to whom she owed her early upbringing: 'She was a very tender mother. I think I'd have starved for love if I hadn't had her when I was little.'

Meanwhile back in harness in Tokyo, Hugh Waddell was coping with problems sufficient to daunt the stoutest heart. What some of them were may be gathered from his letter of controlled but bitter recrimination to the Secretary of the U.P.C. Missionary Board in Edinburgh. The benefactor who shared the hospitality of her roof was Mrs Robert Davidson, whose husband had preceded Hugh by three months in the Japanese mission field. The letter is sent from the Davidsons' house:

> No. 6 Akashi cho,
> Tsukiji, Tokio,
> Japan.
> April 16, 1895

Dear Mr Buchanan,

In regard to the arrangement for my rent, I regret that the Board did not see their way to approve of the plan suggested. I only asked the same amount as would be needed today were my family here with me. The custom of the Japan mission on the field was to do as I was doing. I was and am paying for house rent for my family at home about 350 yen or £35 per annum. This left a balance of 250 yen or say £25 for a house here. For the present I was gaining this sum by the kindness of a fellow-missionary who knew my difficulties and wished to help me. Had I rented the house from her and paid the rent and got a receipt for it, the Board could not claim such a gift. . . . Now if I had been hoarding up the money of the Board and seeking to enrich myself by this means there might be some show of justice, but I told you that I was hardly able to make ends meet. I am living in a fashion I have never done in my life before. I did without a fire the whole winter and many a cold day and night I had the word of God say, 'The workman is worthy of his hire'. When I joined the Board to come to Japan I made no stipulation as to terms. I trusted in the honour of the Church that called me to make all reasonable provision for me and my family. I have simply sought for food, raiment and house accommodation for myself and family and the ordinary education of a family of my own rank in life. I have wrought night and day to fit myself for preaching the Gospel to this people — and in all this I have only done what was my duty to do as a missionary of the Board. On the other hand, I did not imagine that I would find myself in debt after 20 years of hard toil. But today I am in debt one hundred pounds or nearly so, and since 1891 I have spent on my family, in addition to my income from the Board, some £250 received from other sources, and had not God sent this money to me I might have starved. My poor wife toiled night and day to keep her children clothed and nourished, and she died burdened with a load of cares and sorrow which a little more consideration of the Board might have done much to obviate or lessen. The decision of the Board to make Mr Davidson take his furlough when he did not want it, and to forbid me to take mine who did want it, I can never forget. The misery and sorrow caused by that decision to one now at rest I shall never forget. And now I warn you if my health fail or the health of my family from lack of proper housing, food or clothing, on you and the Board will rest the responsibility. May I also remind you that a missionary in the Dutch Reformed Mission with a family to support as large as mine and circumstanced as mine is, would receive £200 per annum more than I am at present in receipt of.* Just before my wife died, a kind family of your own church sent me £50. I wrote home to my wife telling her the glad news: she wrote back full of gratitude, and said, 'Take care of it for God has meant it for some special purpose' — I little dreamt at the time that it was to be spent in connection with her own sad death. God has from time to time thus supplied my wants, and I feel assured he will not forsake me now, though at present I see no way should you cut off my allowance for rent . . . I have no other resource left but to ask the Board to grant me an increase of salary. If the Board cannot entertain the proposal, please find from them whether they are prepared to send out my wife and children on the same terms as we were allowed when I brought out my family before.

*In justice to the United Presbyterian Church of Scotland, it should be pointed out that their records show that in 1899 the Reverend Hugh Waddell's salary was £350 for the current year, a not-inconsiderable sum according to contemporary standards, but seemingly insufficient to support two establishments and educate eight sons.

The sequel makes it pretty clear that his request was refused, for he took swift action. In April 1895 he moved out of the Davidsons' hospitable home, rented lodgings payable by the Board, in September acquired 25 Nakano-cho, Azabu, a house large enough to accommodate his family, asked leave to make a swift visit to Belfast, set his affairs in order, and then return to Tokyo accompanied by wife and children. This he did in the early months of 1896, and had booked the return passage for Mrs Waddell and the four youngest children on the German Lloyd's vessel leaving on 25 May when, on 12 May, a bombshell shattered his plans. A letter from the U.P.C. Mission Board in Edinburgh informed him that they no longer required his services in Japan. Extracts from the seventeen-page reply, sent by Hugh Waddell on 20 May 1896 from 23 Lower Easter Street, Belfast, to the Reverend James Buchanan in Edinburgh show his spirited reaction. He opens with a Pauline-like defence of his ministry:

God, who led me to Japan as I believe, and gave me the power to acquire the language, also blessed the simple preaching of the Word to the Conversion of many souls, and today I see a Japanese Christian Church organized, and I think I can say without boasting that God has employed me to build in that Church in company with many dear fellow-labourers from all Christian lands. My mission work has not been a failure, and if God has thus used me, the Board need not wonder if I hesitate to accept a decision which would be a recall from Japan.

Now when I came home, I told the Board the difficulty I was in about my family and how much they needed a father's care. Should I return to Japan I must leave six of my children at home and take four out with me. Now I am happy to say that my brother-in-law the Rev. John Waddell has kindly consented to take the two youngest into his family and train them up as his own children, and the four elder boys I have arranged for by having them to live in Belfast with my brother, who has taken a house sufficiently large for them and his own family. Then in regard to the four I purpose taking out with me, the Board has intimated in the last Minute that I must pay for their travelling expenses . . . I ask for no favour; if the Board think it just to make me pay, I shall do so. In regard to my own passage money to and from Japan I am prepared to refund it to the Board should they decide that I must do so. I may also add that I have given up my house in Belfast, disposed of my furniture, and already prepared in part the outfit for Mrs Waddell and the four children.

I come now to a second reason. I think the Board does me a grievous wrong when they dismiss me against my own wishes, making provision for me only for one year and a half. If I had any sure prospect of getting settled at the end of that time the case would be different: I found that to be impossible on the ground that I was too old, and had been too long abroad in the Mission field. I am fifty-five, and twenty-one of these I have spent in the service of the U.P. Church. I came among you a perfect stranger, from a different Church and a different country. I did not doubt your good faith. I went as your missionary for life to Japan, and I did not suppose you would cast me off in my old age or leave me to want. But if you carry out the Minute before me, you leave me to starve a year hence as far as any provision on your part is concerned. I hope you will therefore see that I am shut up to the course I have taken in refusing to accept the proposal of the Board, and respectfully ask you to reconsider my case and allow me to return to Japan as I have proposed.

Japanese and Scots alike supported Hugh Waddell's request to resume the work which he alone could do; the Board relented, and the next boat to leave Glasgow for Yokohama numbered among its passengers four children with their missionary parents. The highly intelligent quartet at once captivated the boat's third officer, a young German named Ludwig. 'I've still fragments of the things he gave us,' Helen recalled during the First World War. 'I don't suppose the boy had much, but he simply emptied his pockets on us four at every port — Turkish delight and coconuts and fans, and he spent all his spare time playing with us. He wrote to us for years, and was answered in a quadruple letter. Then one of his letters wasn't answered, and we lost his address.' Helen was then just seven, but her memory reached back much further. To the same correspondent, she saw herself aged three with a passion for spring-cleaning: 'We'd once a dear old servant, when my father was left helpless with ten on his hands: and on top of all her work she used to come upstairs and find that my wicked self had turned out all my belongings and left them on the floor to be tidied: only weary in well-doing at that stage, and departed to play itself. And she put them back and never said a word.'

A child of Helen's abnormal sensitivity must have divined and shared the anguish of the painful months that preceded the family's return to Japan, but she seems to have wiped it away from the table of her memory. The next five years were years of untold happiness, spent in the daily companionship of her adored father, and hoarded for ever in her heart:

My father was a sinologue and saint, the Vicar of Wakefield turned Chinese scholar [she wrote]. Looking back, the creative memory to me is the murmur of my father's voice, the pacing up and down the verandah in the early light and the household still asleep; the Psalms in Hebrew, the New Testament in Greek, the Lord's Prayer in Japanese.

Japan was in her blood. It remained far more than a memory and, while she scarcely ever spoke publicly of the Japanese milieu that had moulded her, its effects on her attitudes and thought can hardly be exaggerated. At twenty-nine she would tell a close friend:

I can't write about facts tonight. It's too like a Japanese night, and my brain is drugged with all sorts of memories and sounds: one of the nights when scraps of verse drift past you, and your heart goes after them, like the lights on the tiny ships that go floating down the Japanese rivers, taking the spirits of the dead to sea.

> As when a soul laments, which hath been blest,
> Desiring what is mingled with past years,
> In yearnings that can never be expressed
> By sighs, or groans, or tears.
>
> Because all words, tho' culled with choicest art,
> Failing to give the bitter of the sweet,
> Wither beneath the palate, and the heart
> Faints, jaded by its heat.

These early years spent in Tokyo happen to be richly documented by none other than the two sisters concerned. The family of six had settled into the house already prepared for them. A thickish exercise book survives stripped of all binding, inscribed in Hugh Waddell's handsome nineteenth-century copperplate:

> Maggie Waddell aged 14 from her father:
> About 20 past 2   January 25 1898
> Address: 25 Nakano cho, Azabu, Tokyo, Japan.
> Book for 'special' things. All private.

Meg was not exactly a methodical diarist — she often leaves a large space for the interesting entries she never made. She records the weather, the daily menu, her reading, visitors, she summarizes long sermons and is in everything the dutiful elder daughter of a Christian missionary, until a gurgle of sudden laughter or an unconscious poetic insight gives birth to a creative phrase that leaps right out of the page. To this source-material must be added Helen's four completely autobiographical stories written expressly to meet the desire of Dr George Pritchard Taylor, for 42 years a missionary in India. After her own father, his was the most potent spiritual influence in Helen's life, and it was his sensitive loving questioning that led her to unveil what otherwise we might never have known. She began by writing in the first person, but soon abandoned it. 'I felt that "I" made the story too self-conscious,' she explained to Dr Taylor. 'Now, it's one Elizabeth: you know, Elizabeth is by common consent the name that would best have suited me: because on the rare occasions when I have dignity and state I would get it in full, and all the other times I would be Betty.' To her father she usually gave the Japanese title *Sensei*, an aureoled word signifying a scholar and master especially beloved — perhaps the Hebrew Rabbi expresses its nearest equivalent. Of the four children, Meg, Billy, George and herself, Meg and George rarely appear: the action is centred on Billy and Helen, with an occasional sub-plot featuring Kate Lascelles (whose actual surname, as Meg's diary reveals, was Larges), an American playmate from the big red bungalow opposite their house, who was not a bad sort until she reached George Washington and Bunker Hill in her studies, when she became unbearable. Why, one may ask, did Billy alone retain his own name and figure so prominently? The bond of affection between Meg and Helen was broken only by death; no shadow ever clouded their relationship: 'We two are rather like a tree that forked so near the root it looks like two trees, but in the earth there's only one,' as Helen put it. George, the future presbyter, favourite and favoured, was angelic; Billy, a doctor like three of his brothers, was an archangel a little damaged. Then, why Billy? In a letter to Dr Taylor, Helen was to write:

> Away at the back of my mind I am seeing a glimmering of what I think my *real* book will some day be. I have been thinking a good deal of Billy: the ugly mouth and the most beautiful smile I ever saw: the queerest mixture of sensuousness and imagination, spirit and flesh, religion and devilry. And I suddenly knew that some day I was going to write of Billy the child — all the promise that flickered out. The richest thing in my life has been Japan — outside books, I mean. I can put all myself into Billy, for he *was* like me. It will be a child's East, with its delight and its strangeness and its sinister breath: I know from things I remember that Billy saw that sinister evil side of it with half-attraction, half-repulsion. The book will end, I think, with the boy suddenly diving back from the rail where he was waving goodbye to my father in the little sampan, because he was ashamed to cry. You know, Billy and Geo came home to school alone: a Japanese ship with a kindly English captain and a sneering devil of a Scottish engineer.

That book was never written. Urged by her correspondent, she produced four short episodes which, as her letters prove, were actual: 'After Strange Gods'; 'Kwannon of the Single Grace'; 'The Doorkeeper of Buddha'; and 'White Iris'. This first decade of Helen Waddell's life may be summed up in three lines from Seamus Heaney:

It is a paradigm
of dream and watchfulness,
the exact gaze of silence.
      'A Cart for Edward Gallagher'★

At seven, she may not have been articulate — the statement admits of doubt — but she could certainly feel and understand. The knobbly bark of the maple tree in the garden of her home provided a natural step-ladder for bare toes, and she would climb into its branches to 'write things in her head'. Out of sight of verandah and roof, cradled in its boughs, she could see nothing but blue and the sharp delicate etching of the young leaves. 'A young green is the youngest thing created — it's far younger than rosebuds and there's more of the unearthly, more of heaven in it,' she was to tell Dr Taylor. 'You can liken young girls to rosebuds, and they *are* sometimes, but there's nothing like young green leaves outside Paradise.' Perched in her gazebo, she may have glimpsed heaven through open doors, but she was also cudgelling her child's brain over the anguish of the struggle in time. At eight years of age, she knew the whole of the *Letter to the Hebrews* by heart; the verse she quotes in a letter to Dr Taylor recurs constantly in her later writing, and was the germ of the most hauntingly beautiful of her Japanese stories, 'The Uttermost Isles': 'One remembers one's childish pondering over the strange refusal of the intimate sure sweetness of return to this world of sunlight and trees in the text, "Women received their dead raised to life again: and others were tortured, not accepting deliverance, that they might obtain a better resurrection."'

Alive to everything Christian within her own home, she was equally alive to everything Japanese outside it. She had been confided to the care of a Japanese nurse with shaven eyebrows, blackened teeth, and a funny old face that creased into a thousand wrinkles at the questions showered upon her by the August's honourable little ones. Did she black her teeth to save brushing them? No; they were blackened when she married, so that no other man would find her good to look upon. But wouldn't her husband like to find her good to look at? He never thought of that, she replied. She was far too courteous to correct the child by pointing out that, to a Japanese, thick eyebrows 'like hairy caterpillars' gave the face an unpleasant boldness, and unblackened teeth were like peeled caterpillars and gleamed

---

★An early version of the poem that appears as 'Last Look' in *Station Island*. These lines do not appear in the final version.

horribly when a woman smiled. Was she going to climb Fujisan with
the pilgrims? A burst of laughter. Fujisan was not for women to climb:
it was far too holy for that. Girls? What were girls? A girl would marry
a husband and worship his ancestors, but if she didn't produce a son,
then her husband should divorce her and marry a wife who would
give him ten sons. Helen took it all in. Wasn't she the equal of Billy
and George? It was a challenge that was to recur in an acute form: why
was woman not man's equal?

Her nurse had mentioned hairy caterpillars, and a hairy caterpillar
was the serpent in Helen's paradise. She never conquered her fear: as
she later admitted to Dr Taylor, the sight of one aroused in her
physical terror:

> There are things one is afraid of with one's mind, and things one is afraid of
> with one's body. Elizabeth knew the things she was afraid of with her
> mind. Not the lizards who lived a hot darting life in the stones round the
> pond. Elizabeth loved them, especially the young ones, with the blue-
> veined transparent feet. Not the rats, who romped over the wooden
> ceiling, nor the 'heli', the house-snake, who reduced their population and
> exercised among them a benevolent despotism. Of one thing she was
> afraid with her body. Once, she watched her brother gardening and was
> conscious of an unfamiliar coldness on her feet. She looked down and a red
> earthworm crawled up between her toes. For long enough it was one of the
> things that Elizabeth saw in the interval when one lets oneself slip down
> the steep places which end in sleep, and it roused her shrieking.
>
> But there are worse things than worms. Elizabeth had never seen them
> until the summer that she went to the hills, and she and Kate Lascelles
> played together on the verandah. It came along one day, three slim inches
> of it, barred with black and orange and green, a strange phosphorescent
> green. It hooped itself as it came, and the long body rippled through all its
> length, arching and straightening alternately. And it came as if it knew that
> it was coming. It was the first time Elizabeth had known the physical
> sickness of fear. Kate Lascelles opened her eyes at her. Hairies? They were
> nice soft furry things. They wouldn't do you any harm. Elizabeth watched
> with a strained wordless horror while the high-pitched American voice
> assured her that there were heaps of those things, that Karuizawa was
> swarming with them, that the trellis over at Elizabeth's house was just
> thick with them. Elizabeth sat under the trellis that night with the purple
> wistaria hanging from it like black grapes in the moonlight, and thought of
> those other things that lay under its leaves and hooped themselves along its
> stems.
>
> With the extraordinary perversity of childhood, Elizabeth came to make
> pets of them. Kate and she kept them in chocolate boxes, with an arch cut
> in the sides — it was Elizabeth's idea, this refinement of terror — for the
> thrill at the sudden sight of the abhorred head, and the slow heaving of the

gorgeous body through the narrow passage. Kate and she raced their pets against each other. Elizabeth had trained herself to a certain dreadful pride in them, a shuddering familiarity. She even captured and fed on vine leaves one creature, the biggest even Kate had ever seen, of whom even Kate was a little afraid, breathing more freely when his magnificence was restored to his prison. It was the third day of his captivity: Elizabeth and Kate kept house. It was Kate who screamed and pointed. Elizabeth's eyes followed that quivering finger. The beauty had escaped. He was on her frock, climbing, with that strange deliberate relentless advance which Elizabeth had learned to fear most in the world. Looking down at him so near, he had grown bigger: she saw the points of crimson in the hideous head: with every swift loop he was nearing her face. The whole world reared and sank again in ghastly circles of green and orange: then mercifully went black. . . .

Lizards, rats, house-snakes interested Helen, she was completely at home with the birds, animals and reptiles who shared her secrets, but at eight years of age her closest friend was a toad who never moved. Again, to Dr Taylor:

He was older than the other toads, and perhaps he was stiff. He lived under the verandah where the earth is never wet; it is dry and white and flaky, with a smell that one forgets when one grows too tall to be at home under a roof two feet high — Elizabeth was eight but she was small and thin. No one knew where his hole was. He had never been seen going or coming; he was squat and motionless, or else he was not. He sat beside the great half-hewn stone from which one stepped out of the garden into Sensei's room, the last outpost of the great house that zigzagged in single rooms and stretches of connecting verandahs across the garden. It was like him to choose the last verandah. One turned the corner sharply into a shadow of pines; at noon to come here was to find darkness. It was best after sunset, the little space between sunset and the dark, when the things that have been beaten all day by the strong shafts of heat take breath again. It was then the Toad came out, and sat, and looked before him. Elizabeth came out too, for there is a madness comes with the dewfall when one must dip and swerve with the swallows; the Japanese old women say the Spirit is in the heels. But always when it was spent, she came and sat beside the Toad. Sweet violets grew beside the posts of the verandah, and Elizabeth smelt them in the dusk, and wondered if the Toad did too. She thought not. He saw and heard, but she did not think he felt, or cared to feel. Once, greatly daring, she put out one finger and touched him very lightly. His back was rugged and hard and cold. He did not stir; he sat and looked before him. Elizabeth was ashamed and sorry. It was as though she had shouted in an empty church.

She never spoke to him, not even that day to apologize. She was intimate with the lizards and talked to them all day long. But with him speech was superfluous, and impertinence. And because she had divined it, she vaguely felt that he was not ill-pleased when she came to sit beside him. It was his impassivity that held her. It was a great thing to sit so very still. It was not ignorance, nor apathy; she knew that he saw her, heard her breathless coming. But always he had the same steady regard. He had a wide mouth like all frogs, but it had not their fatuous wisdom. There was something about him self-contained, remote, tolerant. Afterwards when Elizabeth saw the great Daibutsu at Kamakura, she had a curious sense of the familiar: yet the stillness of the Toad was more compelling. The massive countenance of the Buddha is the countenance of the man who has achieved indifference: the Toad had the unsought directness, the eternity of the symbol.

In order to escape the heat of Tokyo, the Waddell family used to spend the summer months as guests of fellow-missionaries, either up in the hills or in what was then the straggling seaside village of Kamakura on the Pacific coast. From the eleventh century the ancient city of Kamakura had been the centre of government and military power of old Japan, until civil war and tidal waves swept away almost every trace of its former glory. At the end of the nineteenth century, it was no more than a little rice-growing hamlet. The place was pretty well bare except for crumbling temples guarded by sacred groves of purplish-pink cryptomerias, their tall cedar-like branches curved into a kind of seven-branched candlestick bursting at the tips into myriads of tiny green-gold feathery fans. For imaginations like Helen's and Billy's, it needed no iron tongue of midnight to strike the hour of faery. They trod the region Elenore from morning till night, found it in the long flight of stone steps that led up to a two-storeyed gateway and abruptly ended there, or again in the three moss-grown torii of grey stone standing in silent desolation before the once-famous and now empty Shinto temple of Hachiman, god of war. But there were two shrines in Kamakura which still attracted large pilgrimages: one, the great Daibutsu erected in the thirteenth century, the largest bronze statue in the world, a figure from head to foot alive with profoundest suggestion; the other, the temple of the goddess Kwannon the Merciful, the golden image standing in the darkness of a jealously secluded shrine, Kwannon of the numberless arms who 'sits by the stream of time and listens to the prayers of the world'.★

The children were well acquainted with Buddhist and Shinto temples, with their sacred groves, lavers, stone lanterns and empty rice bowls. Hugh Waddell deliberately encouraged his children to share in the life around them. One summer, he took them to the great

★Kamakura is no longer a straggling seaside village: it is once again a glory of modern Japan.

temple at Shiba where the Shoguns lie buried and, while he looked on and smilingly quoted Greek poetry, the old clean-shaven priest had graciously given them sweet cakes from before the very altar and then sent them into the sunny courtyard to feed the doves with crumbs of the sacred bread, before leading their father into the dim recesses of a vast library to display some of its treasures. Hugh Waddell never preached to his children: he set the pattern himself. They watched him repeatedly bowing as horizontally as his European back would permit, noticed how slowly he always lifted his sun-helmet at mention of the Emperor, courteously waiting for the prostrate Japanese to rise before going on to speak of the Christian God, Joh Te, the Heavenly Emperor.

Their summer holiday at Kamakura brought them into close contact with the surrounding peasantry who thronged there on pilgrimage. Whatever the motives of the chattering bands — whether religious devotion, desire to see the cherry-blossom, or keep a lover's tryst — the walking tour offered a delightful escape from a somewhat uneventful existence. While their father 'brushed up his colloquial' the Waddells mixed freely with the groups of white-clad pilgrims in their wide bason hats, kimonos tucked into girdles, pilgrim-club emblazoned in huge black characters across their backs, and it was they who taught Billy that Kwannon the Pitiful, the faithful powerful mother, never refused a supplication made to her under the special title, 'Hito Koto Kwannon' — the Kwannon of a Single Grace — but that the petition must never be made twice under penalty of a refusal. Now, Billy was secretly longing for a white rabbit with a pink nose that twitched. No use, he felt, applying to the blue-green Daibutsu, to that fifty feet of towering bronze sitting on his broad stone platform, exposed to sun and storm through six centuries since the tidal wave of 1494 swept away without a trace the temple that had been one of the wonders of Japan. Much better try Kwannon, goddess of mercy. The pilgrims had taught him the invocation. There and then Billy stood, fingers in ears, eyes screwed tight, while his small sister stood by in tense sympathy. Finally Billy opened his eyes, blinked, searched in every direction, and said flatly: 'I said I'd pray it a hundred times, and I've done it. I knew it would be no use anyway!' He thought deeply and concluded that there was only one solution: Helen and he must go on pilgrimage to the actual shrine, enclosed and guarded on the hill behind Amida Buddha.

They were staying in a bungalow built wholly of wood, fitted with an earthquake door, the whole shack fastened down with iron rods to prevent the frequent typhoons from lifting it bodily. That night, Billy presents himself fully-dressed, lowers Helen's mosquito net, and invites her along. Her weak protest, 'They'll hear you opening the shutters' is answered by a tug at the bar and a challenging, 'If you're afraid, you needn't come.' Within a few minutes, two little figures are padding along the silent road that leads them in half an hour to their goal:

> Through the gateway glimmered countless steps among the pines. Under the black sweep of her great temple roof a half-burned incense stick sent up a faint spiral of smoke into the moon-steeped air. Billy knelt, clapping his hands together softly. 'Hito Koto Kwannon,' he began; then the memory of Sunday morning in the little church at Shiba came upon him, and he went on fluently in Japanese. Somewhere behind the grating the Goddess of Mercy stretched out kindly arms. 'Humbly we beseech thee' — he had caught the very cadence of Mr Wada's voice. . . . The rapid utterance stopped. I opened my eyes and looked. Billy was staring at the shrine, his mouth still open, his eyes wide and blank. There was a moment of terrible silence. Then he turned to me.
>
> 'I've forgotten,' he choked, 'I've forgotten the Japanese for white rabbit.' The minutes slipped past us, one by one. The silence in the courtyard came nearer and nearer. And still we stood, straining in a sore dumb agony. With a sudden jerk, Billy turned and faced the shrine, his head held high.
>
> 'A WHITE RABBIT,' he finished in English, very slowly and authoritatively, as one speaks to a foreigner, 'A WHITE RABBIT.' There was not any sound within the shrine. After all, Kwannon does not always work by miracle. Tomorrow it would come. The Kurumaya-san would bring it from the station in a basket, nibbling cabbage leaves. And at least we had routed the silence of the courtyard. The tide was far out when we came from under the tunnel of the pines.
>
> There came no white rabbit. Possibly Kwannon, although a goddess, does not understand English.

'I wonder will someone ever be able to write of the world as it appeared to him — or her — at say eight years old?' Helen once asked Dr Taylor. 'Two things — yea three — I never do if I can help it: clean my own boots (shoes, but no matter); scrub wood; and clean silver. And when I was little, the one dreadful thing about being a servant seemed to me the washing of a porridge saucepan.' Meg's diary, begun when Helen was eight, affords an insight into life at 25 Nakano-cho. Unconsciously, it also betrays the diarist's beautiful, self-effacing loyalty, as in her non-committal entry: 'Cleaned silver and rubbed tempers the wrong way — ended by reading *All's Well that Ends Well*.' Not a word of complaint about an obviously obstreperous little sister. But while the reader of Meg's artless diary cannot help but feel admiration for its attractive author, the Japanese nurse's question makes itself insistently heard: 'Girls? What are girls?' Two by two the Waddell boys were to return to Europe to train for a future in the Church, medicine or commerce. Meg and Helen were left to attend a mission school for an hour or two daily. Were they both apprenticed as Presbyterian ministers' wives-to-be, or was it simply that, like many another father, theirs enjoyed his daughters' company? Whatever the reason, although their education was not much attended to, like Mary Lamb they also were tumbled into a spacious closet of good English reading. Foremost of course, as became daughters of the manse, stood the King James's Bible, read from first page to last every year and committed in chunks to memory. Every evening one of the family circle read aloud to the others — Calvin's Letter to M. de Rochefort, Shakespeare, Bunyan, Burns, Scott, Tennyson, Harriet Beecher Stowe. 'Tell me, don't you love the Latin hymns of the Middle Ages?' Helen asked in 1917. 'The first time I read *Uncle Tom's Cabin* I must have been about nine, and the clearest memory I have of it is the "veneration" that came on me when I came to the three lines quoted from the *Dies Irae*:

> Recordare, Jesu pie,
> Quod sum causa tuae viae:
> Ne me perdas illa die.

It was partly sheer reverence for Latin — which I don't believe I ever lost — and partly, I like to think, because there is enchantment in the very words.'

To an unknown correspondent who had consulted her about his projected mediaeval subject, she wrote on 2 October 1935:

Do forgive the delay: I was away from home, and distracted by arrears when I got back. It's an enchanting subject you have chosen.

My infancy was spent in Tokio, so that I missed the kind of book that is given to youngsters by aunts at Christmas. But the first I remember reading (which doubtless explains my bias towards the Middle Ages) was a child's version of *Reinecke Fuchs* in English. I don't know the title: and anyhow the book had no back to it. But the text was inspired: and so were the illustrations, above all of Reynard in his more devotional moments, pacing the cloister.

The next was Brer Rabbit: I knew it also by heart: how much of its bland cynicism remained with me I do not know. The third was *Ivanhoe*: I can still remember 'In that pleasant district of merry England which is watered by the river Don . . . ' Friar Tuck was my first Falstaff: and Brian de Bois Guilbert so absolute a hero that I had no patience with Rebecca who, you may remember, was about to hurl herself out of the turret window as he advanced: this seemed to me at the age of seven excessive. The fourth was a book I did not read for years, but the title of it was, I think, the master-title of my youth: *The Confessions of St Augustine*. It was partly the sound of the name, which is a singularly noble one, and partly because my father, who was an absent-minded scholar, offered me ten shillings if I would read it through. It was not earned in his lifetime: but the book was regarded with veneration.

Those were the beacons: but there were also things like *The Secret of Adam's Peak*, about the valley in Ceylon where the elephants go to die: and all the good jungle of stuff that was in the *Boy's Own Paper* of the nineties. My father used to pick them up, shabby bound volumes in blue and gold, in little secondhand bookstalls in Tokio, and bring them to his ravenous brood.

Helen's father, scholar and sinologue, had one weakness which his small daughter was quick to spot. In the letter just quoted, she has not given him away by betraying the fact that often, below the surface of the mind centred on Christian catechetics to the Japanese mentality, he was absorbed in the last number of the *Boy's Own Paper*, and was secretly watching the sunrise over the steaming river flats of Bangkok, speculating as to why Dr Gordon Staples, R.N., messed his best cruises by having curly-headed girls on board, and wondering anxiously whether the next instalment had yet reached Iijima? Deep in Hugh Waddell's heart dwelt the boy eternal, and his life and the lives of his sons and grandsons were to be punctuated by the weekly arrival of *B.O.P.* First published in 1879, *B.O.P.* was launched by the Religious Tract Society to provide reading for boys that would inculcate lofty social and national values, and brought stirring contributions from writers such as Talbot Baines Reed, R. M. Ballantyne and Jules Verne. *G.O.P.*, the *Girl's Own Paper*, edited by a man, presented the socially-desirable image of the boy's sister with big dreamy eyes created by good digestion, plenty of exercise, and a bath of pure cold soft water every day of her life. No wonder *G.O.P.* petered out in 1901, whereas *B.O.P.* lingered until 1956. It was *B.O.P.* that became Helen's sobriquet; with eight brothers, she was hardly likely to opt for *G.O.P.*, especially as she loathed cold baths. When years later she responded in Belfast to a young nephew's demand for a brand-new navy blue and gold annual of *B.O.P.* for a Christmas gift, her mind travelled back to Tokyo, and she wrote of evening walks with her father after the business of the day was done:

If some of us hanker after the old bottles, and would cheerfully retire into captivity with a *Boy's Own Paper* under either arm, it is for sentimental and adventitious reasons. For those which I have in mind were exposed — a fate that would have pleased some forgotten contributors not ill — in a little second-hand bookshop kept by one Iijima, near the canal which they call Sendai's Sorrow. It was a very disreputable side street that led to nowhere; yet one foreigner at least in Tokyo was never known to pass the mouth of it successfully. 'We won't go tonight', he would say indifferently, scenting it from afar; but one observed a gradual crab-like motion sideways as he neared it. His pace slackened; at his feet the little street dived into twinkling darkness; halfway downhill the paper shutters of Iijima glowed with a moth-eaten radiance. There was still a ritual of hesitation to be gone through before he sat him contentedly down on the creaking *étalage* and laboriously unlaced his boots, while Iijima within, crouched like an anxious spider, protested the unworthiness of his vile mats to receive so much as the defilement of so learned feet. Iijima was the complete shopkeeper; he had that air of having kept the good wine until now, which is the incommunicable mystery. And so next morning more worm-riddled Chinese litter would lie about the floor, débris of the quarry whence the great work on the Interpretation of the Trinity was to be hewn. But if a tattered '92 or '97 in tarnished blue and gold had come with it by way of *apologia*, his household had no repinings.

All, that is, except his Griselda-like elder daughter who would commit her sighs solely to Maggie Waddell's book for special things, all private:

> May 10th   The Crown Prince's wedding to Lady Sada-ko, she aged 17. Had terrible time dusting Chinese books. The Boers are getting it now. Papa turns at beef and takes very poor meals. Last night biggest earthquake since we came to Japan.

It is noteworthy that the second Mrs Waddell rarely appears either in daily life or in written accounts. She was content to fulfil her role of missionary's wife with competence, charm and modesty, to support and never to overrule Hugh's education of his children. She seems to have left Meg to deal with servants and the ordering of meals: she was not interested in the provision of food at any time, more's the pity. Far too often Meg's diary records: 'Threw off 3 times last night. Got up feeling very sick. Mother ate horrid oyster. Threw off. Sick. Bed. Earthquake for two minutes.' Polluted water and food reflect little credit on Martha Waddell's control of the household, and yet it was a happy one as any random excerpts from Meg's 'special things. All private' bear witness:

An old time-table
Rise   5 or 5.30
5.30–6   Read Bible, Do a few sums.

6.30   Lay table

6.30–7 Dust parlours and knit

7 or 7.15   Breakfast

After breakfast   Prayer 8.15

March 2nd 1898   Helen reading *The Young Giant*. (Don't feel quiet in my mind about Christ.)

March 3rd   George learning history. Helen writing Coral Island about what they did on Monday. Willie did nothing.

March 6th   Read Numbers 8, 9, 10 and part of 11. Went to school at 1 p.m. Learnt about French Revolution. Felt better. Opened new tin of Bologna sausage. Helen only ten more pages to write in her storybook.

March 15th (Tuesday)   Got up, Helen and me, about 6 to 6 a.m.

June 22nd (Wednesday)   Rose about 3 a.m. Off to Karuizawa to Mrs Davidson — 6 hours in train, through 26 tunnels.

July 18th   Afternoon Mrs Gooderham called and had a talk, then in sailed Mrs White all ablaze in low-necked short-sleeved white kind of ball dress.

July 26th (Tuesday)   Sad news. Papa thought over Willie and George's future and proposes to send them by themselves to Ireland to Aunt Mary of Ballygowan. Papa left for Yokohama to see about it. Papa saw Nord Loyd [sic]. Prices raised. Not settled. Oh Dear!

July 27th (Wednesday)   Got up at 15 to 6. Read 1 Chron 24, 25, 26, 27. Had bacon for breakfast. We are in such money troubles. Poor Papa. What shall we do! How much money have I? About twenty-four sen (6 pence). Not much. Oh! have we no friends? The Boys at home seem to have no hearts. They will be sorry when Papa's dead. I will never never forget poor poor Papa. Jinricksha man drunk. Lying naked.

July 29th (Friday)   Got up at 5.15. Letter from P & O came. No reduction for Willie.

August 9th   I want to improve myself but have no time. I want to learn French, Latin, Geography, Grammar, Botany, History. Is there any use improving myself? I will do all my duties *well*. There is a great deal in that word. There is 9.30. I must go. WELL, amen.

August 12th (Friday)   Helen had bad night. Dr Kitajema came. Said she was bilious.

August 13th (Saturday)   Helen stayed in bed till breakfast. I read 1st and 2nd Job to her. Bathday. Had beef soup for dinner. Helen loves it. Cold bath. Mended George's coat and partly trousers. Willie and George in bath. Now about 8.30 a.m. Helen's stomach gives her spasms of pain. Mother applied flannels wrung through hot water which eased it a little also rubbed her and gave her essence of ginger on sugar. She took a little brandy in milk. Went to bed as usual.

August 20th (Saturday)   Awfully itchy [sic]. Took cold bath. Lumps like flea-bites all over me. Spread quickly. Weals along my arm. Read

Esther 8, 9, 10 and Job 3. (I read 2nd and 1st chapters before.) Rash came on my face. Willie said unkind thing and I cried.

By way of prophylactic, Meg worked through *Job* for a whole week and later drew up a list of resolutions of cobweb soapsud permanence: 'I am 15 and must really begin to study harder. Oh dear. I am behind for my age. I know English History, little of Geography, little of Arithmetic, write pretty well, not much of Grammar, I'm afraid. Something of Composition. Nothing of foreign languages. Oh dear. I must begin to study Latin. I must read my Bible more. I do not know much about God. God help me to progress in everything. Pretty good at Dictation. I hereby promise that I will only take an hour of reading on weekdays, do my knitting, sewing, and everything diligently well till end of week.'

On one level, the regime was Spartan. Sympathy reaches out to the elder sister, longing to study yet obliged to mother the siblings, to hem pillow cases, patch chemises, darn her brothers' pants, accompany hymns at Mission services, and pick up what crumbs of knowledge she could. Her diary abounds with references to Papa going without food and Mother's lying a-bed while she, for all their indigence, was left to deal with an astonishing number of servants: 'We dined on scrubbing-brush soup and beef. Took out plateful of beef that had been boiled, roasted and par-boiled to Sneg.' No wonder they all so frequently 'threw off'. But the diary can rise far above the domestic scene and reveal fascinating glimpses of images and contours stored away in the memory of the child who would recreate them later in *Lyrics from the Chinese*. Here is Meg's entry for 16 January:

Walked home in moonlight. Helen and I ran ahead, skipping downhill. Stopped on bridge to admire view. One side, the dark mud of river, here and there sparkle of water, dark leafless clumps of bushes, and above the beautiful full moon in the starry sky. Other side dark, dark, twinkling dots of light in houses and the hum, restless but subdued, of a semi-invisible multitude.

Here is Helen's re-telling:

> I saw the marsh with rushes dank and green,
> And deep black pools beneath a sunset sky,
> And lotus silver-bright
> Gleam on their blackness in the dying light
> As I passed by.*

Lyrics from the Chinese XVII.

Meg recounts the number and nature of Japanese New Year orna-
ments — a lobster, an orange, a ring of rope, ferns and tufts of straw
hung over doorways — she listens to Helen reading aloud *A
Midsummer Night's Dream*, passes to Tennyson but 'we do not think
him equal to Shakespeare', and finally records that although the world
is white with snow, the plum tree has burst into blossom. 'There was a
plum tree in the garden in Tokio', Helen would one day write to Dr
Taylor, 'that came out almost in the snow — a tiny pink plum tree
with black branches. Did I ever send you one of the unpublished *Lyrics
from the Chinese*? I kept it back because it was sophisticated and self-
conscious beside the earlier work, but rather pretty in its way:

> Last night the east wind blew with bitter rain,
>   And stripped the wood and strewed the branches far,
> And all the little river boats swept in,
>   And wrecked them high above the river bar.
>
> Yet all night long beside my winter pane
>   This old uncared-for plum tree slept alone,
> And now spreads out its branches, gaunt and grim,
>   Clean washed and glittering in the early sun.
>
> A few half-drowned buds show faintly pink,
>   And their small fragrance smote upon my heart.
> A better painter might think scorn of it,
>   But their faint laughter is beyond my art.

And Number I, perhaps the best-known of the published Chinese
Lyrics, recaptures the walk taken by Meg and Helen along the river
bank: 'River gurgling and splashing,' Meg writes. 'In places branches
met overhead. Path tumbled away in places. Very perpendicular. At
last came to open. Had to cross big stones of river, roaring and
splashing. No bridge. Did so very tremblingly.'

> The gourd has still its bitter leaves,
> And deep the crossing at the ford.
>   I wait my lord.
>
> The ford is brimming to its banks;
> The pheasant cries upon her mate.
>   My lord is late.

It is fascinating to discern in the ideas, experiences and reactions of
the child Helen, the larger patterns of her adult life: the self-revelations
of her youth strikingly foreshadow the mature woman. Not for a

quarter of a century would she suddenly pass from her bed in a Paris hospital into the person of the aged Abbess Heloise, steeping her nuns in Abelard's theology, but at eight years of age she was already identifying herself with her favourite characters. In an instant she could become the Jew Isaac's beautiful daughter, passionately loved by Bois-Guilbert, the Knight Templar. She later told Dr Taylor:

> At sunset the bells in St Andrew's Cathedral rang for evensong, and Elizabeth climbed the maple and leaned against the trunk, listening for the first clear shattering note, breaking the yellow light of the afternoon like an oar-blade dipping into bright water and rising with a scattering of drops. All things fresh and green and young belonged to the carillon. Even Mr Whitford who was the curate of St Andrew's and came to see Sensei, was fresh and clean and young, and Elizabeth admired him in the detached manner of childhood until one day he came upon her gardening, and she fled from him, being barefoot, and dishevelled and self-conscious, and he gave chase and was insolent in capture. Elizabeth had just read *Ivanhoe* and was temporarily Rebecca, and this is not the manner in which Rebecca received advances. That same evening he sealed his damnation. For passing the verandah he caught sight of the Toad where he sat in his obscurity, and paused before him interestedly. Then he stooped and poked him with his stick. Elizabeth felt a curious sensation of drying inwardly. The Toad sat and looked before him; looked at the white-trousered legs of the Church of England, into them and through them. Mr Whitford laughed self-consciously and said 'Funny old chap.'

Siegfried Sassoon opined that experience intensely absorbed in youth provided material that possessed special qualities of aliveness, impetus, and creative richness when it was afterwards commuted into literature by some mysterious fusion of craftsmanship and emotion. Did Helen Waddell ever forget or forgo such experience? The Toad, for instance, reappears in Helen's retelling of The Story of Jacob the Supplanter in *Stories from Holy Writ*. In flight from Esau, Jacob reaches a tiny cave, rattles a stick through it for possible snakes, and finally creeps in. 'His old friend the toad was sitting in one corner of it, but he did not croak or move. . . . Then the dew fell, and the dust smelt the bitterer for it, and the toad came and sat at the mouth of the cave. Jacob spoke to him and scratched his back, but the toad took no notice of him.'

To the eight-year-old child, the Toad might indeed have symbolized the profound differences between East and West: he felt no emotion whatever in the presence of 'the cloth', the carillon, the pseudo-Victorian Gothic cathedral with its air of wealth and display: his preference was for a life of simplicity. A day or two after Mr

Whitford's social call, as Helen lay feverish and wakeful during a
sultry dark night, she heard 'a strange boom that seemed to pour into
the emptiness of the night and fill it with sound, mournful and
dominant. She knew it for the temple bell at Uyeno, five miles across
the sleeping streets, the great bronze bell that the priests of the night
vigil strike at dawn. There was no repetition of it, like the hurrying
ripple of the carillon. There was a finality about the single stroke, the
symbol One became audible in sound that had an echo of the Infinite.
Elizabeth lay and heard the quiet flowing back again and, listening,
remembered the Toad. This was the sound for which the Toad must
wait. This was his world, that began with twilight and ended with the
dawn.'

The toad's was not the only world to begin with twilight and end
with dawn. Sometimes Billy's did. Perhaps realizing that his days of
freedom were numbered and the school-discipline of Campbell
College drawing inexorably near, he became ever more daring.
Scenting its danger, he makes up his mind to explore Hanarisan, the
Mount of Snakes, visible on the skyline of Karuizawa where the
family are on holiday. 'We are going to do pilgrims,' he announces
one afternoon in lordly tones to Helen. 'To do it, you mustn't put on
your sandals.' When she wiggles her toes rather anxiously, 'That's
you!' he mocks, 'and you practising early Christian martyrs at home!'
He yields magnanimously to her weakness — she may wear sandals.
He provides two pilgrim staffs, his own surmounted by a snake's
head, and together they set off across the moors where sharp swordgrass tears at their bare legs. On and on they go, yet the nearer they
approach, the further the Mount of Snakes recedes, until even Billy
decides it more prudent to turn and make for home. As the sun goes
down, the children trudge doggedly along filled with unspoken fear.
Suddenly they stumble, reach the brim of a hollow, and stop dead:

> They had come upon a Japanese burying-place, a few grey stones, rough-
> hewn and oblong. They lay scattered here and there, and they were few,
> half a dozen at most, but the sunset was on them and on the short white-
> bleached grass, and in the midst the glory that had held them — a clump of
> white iris straight and slim, the intense white radiance of its full-globed
> bloom shining distinct against the old grey stone and the glow in the dry
> grass. They stood motionless, not in fear: simply that the natural soul of
> beauty in them was for once satisfied. Billy's eyes were fixed on the
> immaculate splendour below him. He took a step.
>
> 'Billy, you can't,' cried Elizabeth. 'It's stealing!' Her deep little voice
> rose to its highest note on the e. But Billy was already in the hollow, and
> his knife was out. Three he cut, and scrambled back to her. 'One's for

you,' he said handsomely. 'You can carry it if you like.' It was held out to her with Billy's famous smile. He bore his aloft like a lamp.

Safely home, the children place their treasures in an old earthenware vase, set it in the gap of the shutters opening on their verandah, and highly satisfied fall asleep. But not for long. Helen is suddenly wide-awake and terrified, with a terror quite different from the awful night when Billy and she took home a bowlful of crabs which they left overnight on the verandah. A noise of small and stealthy goings-on somewhere in the dark startled the children out of sleep, only to find when light filtered through that the crabs had gone in dreadful procession round and round their beds. But now, panic-stricken, Helen listens. Is that a bird crying out, or is it true what Sanagi-san said, that a lost soul cries in the bird? Oh, why won't Billy wake up? Billy is fully alert, and Billy is afraid. He bounds out of bed, reaches the verandah, and takes hold of the white iris. 'Gomen nasai, Excuse me, I did not know. You shall have them tomorrow, as soon as it is light,' he says — and when Helen finally drops off to a troubled sleep, she is in Billy's bed, firmly clutching a handful of his pyjamas.

Before sunrise, they are up and out to fulfil their promise. As they strike the road, they see shadowy figures dressed in white moving slowly down a path, carrying a rude wooden coffin. Led by an old priest, they are chanting prayers for the dead in a broken monotone. They are jinricksha porters — the funeral has to be so early because their day's work lies ahead. Then come the mourners, an old man with two children hand in hand. That is all. 'Come on, it'll make it look bigger,' Billy urges, and then, after a long silence, 'It's O Riku san.' Billy and Helen knew him. All summer he ran between the shafts of his ricksha, trotting stout foreigners up and down the Karuizawa roads, until he strained his heart. That was the end. The sequel must be left exactly as Helen has told it:

So the foreigners had heard of it and come. After all, O Riku san was not to be forgotten in his death. The old man's glance fell on the white iris, white for sorrow, and the light grew brighter in his eyes. O Riku san was indeed to be mourned as he should.

The daylight had broadened, but the moors were still grey when they reached the hollow. The kindly coolies had come after sundown and made all ready. It does not take very long to bury a Kurumayasan. 'Namu Amida Butsu! Namu Amida Butsu!' droned the old priest, as they covered up the little shrine with the dry tangled sods. . . .

It was all over: all but the placing of the offerings that were to cheer the soul as it fared on its way to the *meido*, the shadowy land of the dead. The Kurumayasans stepped back, as though giving place to the stranger. A little awkwardly, Billy knelt and laid the white iris on the sods. The Kurumayasans grunted inarticulate approval. Then O Ji san stumbled forward, fumbling in his sleeve for the little packet that he laid on the grave. It was a roll of rice carefully wrapped up in seaweed, a great delicacy among the hills: but it looked very small and very poor in the still grey dawn: sorry comfort for one who must take a long journey.

And something of it must have struck O Ji san. He had begun the time-old prayer for the dead, the cry for their safe keeping that is the same in all ages; but even as he spoke his eye fell upon his poor provision, and the thought of O Riku san's disappointment smote his heart. He stood for a moment irresolute, looking at it: then on a sudden he was on his knees, his shaking hands outstretched.

Perhaps that was why O Riku san was so very lean. Perhaps that was why O Riku san was going to the *meido* so soon.

There broke from Billy one great rending sob. With a blind rush he was at the old man's side, and tumbling into his astonished hands whatever was in two trouser pockets. It was more than usual, for the two had been saving for weeks to buy the little white owl down in Daiku san's, the carpenter's, and had got the sum, all but two *sen*, last night. But O Ji san was already on his feet.

'No, Little Honourable One, no,' he said, bowing with his old-world Japanese courtesy. 'O Riku san will understand . . . he will understand.'

'Take it,' cried Billy unashamed. 'It will buy him hot *mame*, and *kobu* — and bran cakes. And he will soon, oh soon, be at the *meido*.'

O Ji san wavered. Then raising the money to his head in the old graceful fashion, he bowed low. 'The Little Honourable One is very good,' he said gravely. And Billy fled.

Billy the child, 'the queerest mixture of sensuousness and imagination, spirit and flesh, religion and devilry,' had been Helen's summing up of this brother of hers. It is debatable whether any school could have provided an education comparable to that which, Rousseau-like, Billy gave Helen during these most formative years: no social prejudices or distinctions, no intellectual pressures, no cut and dried theories; simply the lively curiosity of two superb artists in the making, left completely free by their enlightened father. Their father was something of a puzzle to his four children. On the one hand, with his head buried in tomes filled with little strokes all of different lengths and curves and at different angles, he spent hours making copious notes for his work on the Trinity; and he filled them with awe as, bareheaded in the early sunlight, he paced the upper verandah every morning, murmuring the Psalms aloud in Hebrew to catch the cadences, and rising to a chant when he broke into the Gospel in

English. On the other hand, he could meet a really serious appeal to reason and common sense with cascades of infectious laughter. For instance, they had been given two sen to squander on a box of chocolates with a Parisian lady on the lid, but in order to reach the dim, cool interior of Kameyasan's shop which stocked everything from tooth-powder to tinned salmon, they had to cross a bridge where women went to wash rice. It consisted of a single plank over a stream that gushed down from the mountains with a gluck and a gurgle, and it swayed deliriously when Helen was in the middle, and George jumped on the other end. Maternal orders in council had forbidden them to paddle there, because there was a lot of broken crockery and if you cut your feet, you'd get lockjaw. Barefoot, Helen and the two boys gleefully descended and carefully cleared away every scrap of blue earthenware, dragged their father down by way of a Royal Commission on Public Safety, and implored an All Clear. Instead of giving it, he stood convulsed with laughter which was intensified that evening when they returned, in wrath and grief, to complain that Mrs Kameya had smashed the bowl in which she washed her rice upon that very spot. Their father's humour was incomprehensible and irresistible.

The high jinks of the four children were brought to an end when, in the spring of 1899, Billy and George were sent home to Ireland and placed in Campbell College, then flourishing under the headship of James Adams McNeill. Founded in 1894 to provide 'a superior liberal Protestant education', it specifically admitted a limited number of clergymen's sons at reduced rates. C. S. Lewis considered it in 1910 'very much what the great English schools had been before Arnold. Every boy held just the place which his fists and mother-wit could win for him.' Meg and Helen were left behind in Tokyo. 'Girls? What were girls?' When Meg received her first letter from George, and there was nothing for her from Billy — who may have been too busy exercising his mother-wit and fists on his companions at Campbell College — she went up and in a fit of deep and rare despondency cleaned Billy's room, as if it were echoing her own cry for his presence. Then she took her pen and dashed off in her diary a few delightful sketches: Helen skipping; Helen in the maple tree absorbed in a book; a figure standing on its head, labelled 'George's Calesthenics'; all four children hurtling 'down the peak'; George and Billy performing acrobatics on the swaying plank-bridge; and her father, curiously resembling the sculptured head of Socrates.

With the boys' departure and the consequently depleted household, the two girls became their father's constant companions, and Meg's diary noticeably more detailed:

May 6th (Sunday)   At 2 went in rickys to park, Papa preached. Many came and listened attentively. No disturbance at all. Several times they smiled. Instead of listening, Helen and I wandered about. We went up to see the great bronze figure of Buddha, reached by twenty stone steps. Before him was a great wooden money-chest, a box for incense sticks, and several flowers. He is sitting, hands joined, knees bent. Enormous height and hollow. Opposite him on another hill was a huge bell rung by a man, who banged it at intervals with a beam. This resulted in a deep solemn mournful musical sound. Coming down from this, we descended thirty steps to visit a fox temple. It was rather small but had little pillars for itself. The outer room was shut off from the inner by a lattice door. Here was placed a table with several little painted images representing foxes. On either side of the table was a large yellow fox image. The room was hung all over with lanterns great and small. We saw a man worshipping the fox. He knelt on a matting between money-box and table, bowed his head, clapped his hands many times. At last took a dark box from the table, shook it, turned it upside-down, took out a long thin piece of wood, which he seemed to read. Did this three times, then bowed and left. The real fox lived, not in the temple but in a hole not far from it, approached by several torii and a paved walk. A little money-box was hung up before the hole. The man, dropping a cent or two into the hole, prayed, clapped his hands, bowed and withdrew. We retraced our steps to the service and remained there for the rest of the time. We left at 5 for home.

For once, Meg has said nothing about Papa's sermon, not even that it was dull. There is a contemporary word-painting of Hugh Waddell holding an outdoor service in Uyeno Park, a place much patronized by the Japanese. It is written in an English as quaint as the preacher's 'colloquial' of which he was so proud. Its piquancy is heightened by the realization that its author, a Mr Sakamoto, would be dressed in his own dignified costume consisting of the *hakama*, wide silk trousers pleated like a kilt, beneath a graceful kimono of soft grey or brown, covered with a large dark-blue cape, and that he shuffled along on wooden sandals worn with *tabi*, strong snow-white cotton gaiters. The vehement European must have contrasted oddly with the Buddhist priest in white kimono and stole, seated cross-legged on the edge of his platform in the preaching-hall, smiling and talking away in a low clear voice, using no gesture whatever:

On Sunday afternoon I went out from my house to take a walk. It was in early spring. The North Wind was blowing cold when I arrived at the Uyeno Park. There were few abroad in the Park. I rested under an old oak tree. Whilst I was resting I heard a voice in the distance. Looking round to see where the sound came from, I found the voice to be of Mr Waddell, the Park Lecturer. He was preaching close to a tea-house. As it was a long time since I last heard him I went forward to listen. The audience consisted at first of about 14 or 15 people, some apprentices, some nurse-girls, also gentlemen and merchants. The pulpit was a little way from the road, near to it were two benches under the oak tree, covered with mats. Behind Mr Waddell stood a small organ, at his left a signboard which bears an inscription written thus:

A Lecture on Christianity, by Mr Waddell and Mr Yaraihara,

on his right a stand on which was placed a sheet of music containing the hymn to be sung. There were two men beside him who seem very cold as they sat on the bench. This completes the arrangement for the lecture.

The robe of Mr Waddell was a frock coat as usual his necktie was black and broad. He looks to be of the age of sixty: his hair is white as snow, his face as red as ink: his countenance differs from the ordinary European, his face is flat: nose is not high: eyes partially hidden by the eyelids: his eyes are glittering under the over-arching eyebrows. No one can look at his eyes without being impressed by a feeling of reverence. The man resembles in appearance the statue of Socrates. An historian told us Socrates was not handsome: neither is Mr Waddell; but his countenance and his zeal and earnestness in preaching like to Socrates is a strange coincidence. If we can induce another point to the resemblance already noted it must be said that Mr Waddell deserves to be reverenced as the Sage or Socrates of this day.

I feel sorry the number of the audience was so small. Notwithstanding this he however was preaching as sincerely and earnestly with his curious Japanese as if he were preaching to an audience of hundreds of thousands. As I stood there the sermon was half over. His tall figure growing more solemn, his strong voice more clear, looking up to heaven he pointed up to the top of the oak tree and said 'What is it makes the large tree grow? It is the heat and light of the sun. Nothing but sun can make it grow. A hibachi of air cannot make it grow. If we wish to make a noble man, God is necessary. Idols and Buddhist priests are of no one — what is absolutely needful is God in heaven.'

When he said this two or three spectacled young men standing behind me said in a low voice 'His grammar is not correct.' 'No foreigner can use properly the participles in Japanese grammar.' 'But he is very honest.' . . . 'We must go.' . . . 'Wait a little, let us hear him longer.' Mr Waddell went on with skilled gestures and postures with his sermon. 'A parent protects his children, and behold young boys who come up to Tokio away from their parents do not study diligently, drink wine and go to bad places. They become degraded, simply because their parents cannot protect them.' The hearers all at once laughed a little because of his curious illustration. 'The same reason those who do not believe in God act badly, gamble and steal, but those who believe in God are protected by God: therefore they are kept in the right way. God can see in the dark. God is to be feared.' At this time the number of the audience increased so that I who was in the outer circle at first found myself soon so surrounded as to be in the inner part of the circle. Some people passed on, others came, and still the audience increased. Mr Waddell said moreover 'Christ took upon him the sins of his people. He answered for them, became their surety. A parent answers for his child, an emperor is responsible for his people. When China was defeated the man sent by China with proposals of peace — a German — was repulsed, because of his imperfect qualification. Next came A Cho in Kaii. He also was repulsed for the same reason. At last came Li Hung Chang. The Japanese government recognized him because he was the supreme officer of the Chinese court. He made peace for his nation. Christ redeemed the sins of the people of the whole world. Christ is sinless, Christ is the parent of his people — an affectionate parent.' The audience was as quiet as the earth after rainfall.

Mr Waddell after ten more minutes suddenly changed his tone and lifting high his Bible he said 'Men must trust upon God. Those who would trust in God must read this book.' These words were the conclusion of his sermon. He then awkwardly bowed his body and saluted the audience. He descended from the pulpit. The semi-circular multitude began to move but the majority of them were still standing there as if they expected something more would follow. Mr W. was wiping the sweat from his brow while he was speaking with the Japanese man who attends him; in the same time, the other young man began to play on the organ — he had on a simple garment and simple Japanese trousers. He was a little pale, and bending his head and half closing his eyes began to sing this song, 'Jehovah is my Shepherd'. His voice was not high, but he sang nicely, as we hear the showers falling on the olive tree in the Palace of Olympias. The music soothed us. When the music ceased Mr Waddell began to make his preparation for the homeward journey. He first put on his overcoat, next he wound round his body a long black cloth in length more than ten feet. What did he use the cloth for is a question. Perhaps it may be a protection from cold, but for whatever purpose it is quite curious. His body is increased in roundness by this winding round of the cloth till it became like to a drum. He then putting the Bible under his arm and saluting his companion started away. He passing the right side of the oak tree went his way in the middle of the path, went towards the 'Hiro-Kogi'. The two men who were with Mr W. cleared the place, and carried the organ by jinricksha. The wind was blowing and fallen leaves were whirling. The dust was flying in clouds.*

To Hugh Waddell's prominent eyes, snub nose, broad nostrils and wide mouth reminiscent of the Greek philosopher might be added the Socratic merriment, the Comic Spirit, and the deep conviction of a divine mission. It was not only Mr Sakamoto who was struck by the resemblance. Years later in a letter from Paris, Helen wrote to Meg

*From the Waddell family papers.

that her landlord, Monsieur Farre, 'was looking at Papa's photograph one night. "C'est Socrate." And then he said what so many people have about him, "Tres pur". It isn't just our word pure — it's the sense of living unalloyed.' The two words sum him up exactly. At the turn of the century he had completed 27 years' missionary labour in Tokyo. From January 1900, Meg's diary referred increasingly to her father's bouts of sickness covered by the generic term 'flu. As the months advanced without definite improvement, he was granted leave of absence to return to Ireland to recuperate. On 7 July he, his wife and two daughters bade a temporary farewell to Japan and, with Mr Pickwick and Mr Snodgrass for entertainment, travelled home via Vancouver. On board ship, Meg made jottings about the passengers, and concluded: 'Last but not least comes Miss Helen. She is in fine spirits especially after tea, when the soda gets in her little heels. She keeps me busy keeping down the fizz but otherwise is remarkably good and docile. The mornings are the worst with her. I always know when she is feeling not exactly tip-top. She hates to get up so early (7.30!), feels so dull all day after. Doesn't see the use of bathing every day. Tires one, less time to snoodle. Feels so shivery after it too, has a headache. Then I begin to laugh — at this, she laughs too, and all is over.'

Among Helen's tattered papers there is one entitled 'Retrospect'. It opens: 'It was a habit of our youth — the two brothers and the two sisters who made up the tail of a family of ten — to dispute endlessly how many times each of us had been round the world. I, the least of them, cut a poor figure in these global calculations with only one and a half to my credit: and as the first voyage was at the unobservant age of one, my elders refused to count it. The last journey was in the autumn of 1900, when my father was sixty and I eleven.' That journey was 'last' in more than one sense: it marked the end of Helen's enchanted childhood and the enclosed world of Old Japan. No records survive to locate the exact birthplace in Tokyo of the nine Waddell children: beyond all doubt it has been swept away together with 25 Nakano-cho, the paradise of the youngest of the ten. Chōrōha, the Presbyterian church Hugh Waddell did so much to found, was merged after the Second World War with other Protestant groups into the national Nihon Kyōdan, the Japan Union Church. But in spite of the throngs of pilgrims and sightseers armed with the latest Japanese cameras and transistors, in spite of the immense skyscrapers that punctuate the skyline and dwarf the beautiful old buildings of the Meiji period, in spite of the standardization in spelling and pronunciation of shrines of gods and goddesses, the pine-clad bay of Kamakura still stands where the Pacific breaks in soft thunder on the white sand, and the massive figure of the great Daibutsu, symbol of Enlightenment, sits alone under the open sky as he has sat for centuries, with half-closed eyes, drooping figure, quiet hands, and air of repose, behind the altar adorned with giant lotus and bronze lanterns. This was the Japan that moulded Helen Waddell and, to a certain degree, caused her to lead a double existence, one in the mind, the other in the heart. She never forgot this 'richest thing' in her life.

In childhood she had often been carried in a *kago*, the large wickerwork saucer suspended by ropes from a bamboo pole slung across the shoulders of two coolies, one in front, one behind. As they walked, swaying ecstatically, they chanted what Helen later considered the loveliest street-song in all the world. Possibly she thought so because throughout the stresses of her life, its magic could transport her in a flash to her heaven-haven:

> *Song of the Kago Men*
> I go to the house of the Beloved,
> Her plum-tree stands by the eaves,
> It is thick with blossom.
> How do you go to your love's house?
> On the wings of the night wind.
> Which road leads to your love's house?
> All the roads in the world.

CHAPTER II

IDEALLY, AS ONE door shut upon a Japanese childhood lined with fairy gold, another should have opened into a romantic garden of tryst and youth. It was not so. The transition was bleak and bitter. Tokyo, whose open gutters were strewn in April with cherry blossom and crept in July like some death-dealing serpent, had given way to a city that prided itself on its unique system of sewage disposal; Tokyo of the wooden houses and paper shoji, of lotus flowers and pungent pines, of exquisite courtesy and age-old etiquette was replaced by a city of bustling busyness that saw itself in terms of citizens of the wide-flung British Empire, law-abiding, church-going, self-helping, thoroughly prosperous and progressive; the massive Daibutsu of the half-closed eyes and quiet hands had to yield to the Victorian Economic Man. Instead of stone lantern and ruined temple, the emblematic City Hall, modelled on the Capitol at Washington, stood mathematically centred in neat rectangular plots, guarded by City Fathers frock-coated in stone, large feet firmly planted on Irish soil — theirs by divine right of conquest — from which sprang carefully tended beds of red geraniums and blue lobelia and white alyssum, floral proof of civic loyalty to Union Jack and British crown. Of course, that is not the whole story. At the turn of the century, Ulster was both challenging and inspiring: poets, painters, sculptors and music-makers abounded. W. B. Yeats, then in his mid-thirties, had spent his childhood in Tullylish, and his poems and plays were pouring from the press; young men were producing plays of the Irish countryside; the opening of the Ulster Literary Theatre of which Helen Waddell's brother, Samuel Rutherford Mayne, was a founding member, beat the Abbey Theatre to it by a fortnight. There was a wholesome intellectual ferment which a girl gifted with sensitive antennae was bound to feel and appreciate.

Upon their arrival in Belfast, in the late autumn of 1900, Hugh and Martha Waddell settled with the children in a rented house, 6 Glandore Gardens, off the Antrim Road. An immediate problem was to put the two girls to school. The closely-knit Presbyterian community — largely doctors of divinity, law, medicine, or linen lords — had made ample provision over half a century for the education of their children. Helen's parents fixed their hopes on Victoria College for Girls, a school which rivalled in distinction its counterpart, Campbell College for Boys, already a family preserve. Founded in 1859, six years after Cheltenham Ladies' College, Victoria College offered an education far in advance of its time. Although city-bound, the casement windows of the imposing stone structure in the Crescent opened upon wide lawns and tennis courts; there was a well-stocked gymnasium, a spacious lecture hall and, best of all, to a staff-list of able women-graduates, drawn from Dublin, Belfast, Girton and Paris, the early records add the names of no fewer than nine outstanding men, one of them a noted musician who, anticipating educational theory by half a century, initiated choral singing and music appreciation.

Meg and Helen duly presented themselves for an interview with the foundress of the school, Mrs Margaret Morrow Byers (1832–1912), a woman whose majestic and forbidding front concealed a heart of singular tenderness, especially towards daughters of the manse. Not only was their sparkling intelligence more than likely to compensate for empty pockets, but Mrs Byers herself, married at nineteen to a Presbyterian missionary in Shanghai and widowed with a baby son before she was twenty, had graduated in the school of hard experience. She recognized ability when she saw it and, after making generous financial concessions, admitted both girls to the Intermediate Department for students between the ages of ten and eighteen.

So far, their education had been erratic to say the least. Seventeen-year-old Meg, now expected to work for a degree, lacked even a smattering of algebra or French. According to herself Helen, aged eleven, was 'an outlandish little creature with an amazing vocabulary, most of it Sir Walter Scott's.' Years later she spoke of the deep humiliation she felt at her own backwardness — she could not work out the simplest division sum. Before very long, however, she was talking blithely of differential calculus and conics, and the teachers of Mathematics and English Literature were struggling one against the other to secure this prize student. She was placed in 'Honours Junior' among girls all older than herself. A small group of close friends, Cathleen Nesbitt the future actress, Helen Forbes the most beautiful girl in the school, and Meta Fleming the best-loved, immediately opened their ranks to admit Helen Waddell, the most intellectual, and the trio became an inseparable quartet. Unlike their brothers, the girls did not become boarders, for the school was within easy reach of home. Their future seemed happily assured.

When in July 1900 Hugh Waddell bade a hurried farewell to Tokyo, it was not because he intended to retire, far from it. After months of recurring sickness, he had simply applied for an early furlough, thinking to recover more speedily in his native air and return to his mission with health restored. He was just sixty years of age, bursting with plans, and eager to complete the work of his life, *The Interpretation of the Trinity to the Chinese Mind*. With 27 years' apostolic labour behind him, and his ten children's future now pretty well assured, he could reasonably look forward to a little more leisure for study and possibly a little more affluence. These dreams were shattered by a letter which finally caught him up. Written on 21 June 1900, it informed him that in the previous month the Synod of the United Presbyterian Church of Scotland had decided to discontinue the mission he had founded in Tokyo. As for the future? As he already well knew, dismissal meant one year's salary, and beyond that, nothing. The prospect was hardly one to cure a sick man. His life savings amounted to exactly £800 which would yield an annuity of a mere £40. In addition his travelling expenses for freight and luggage for the homeward journey had cost £44.6s. 3d., whereas the Mission Committee restricted the grant to a maximum sum of £16. His appeal to headquarters in Edinburgh elicited this response from the Reverend James Buchanan on 6 February 1901:

I am sorry you have written in the way you have of our Foreign Mission Committee's action in the matter of your allowance for luggage etc. Such a statement will, I fear, prejudice you in the eyes of the Committee. I am glad you called attention to the fact that you still have two children who have not been on the Education Fund. In making up the calculation about your salary it was supposed that your two children now on the list were your youngest children. No payments were made on behalf of Margaret, or rather the payments which under a mistake were paid in her name were really for one of her brothers. Allowance for two girls from 6th to 31st July 1900 at £5 per quarter £1.8.3d Do. for half-year to 31st Jan 1901 £10. Do. for Feb. & March £3.6.8d = £14.14.11d.

Shelving further correspondence, Martha took her husband off to recuperate at Ballygowan, a beautiful old house in the gift of her family, leaving the four children — Billy and George had rejoined their parents — in Glandore Gardens under Meg's gentle command, ably seconded by Bella, a beloved servant. No one suspected the gravity of Hugh Waddell's condition. From Ballygowan, Martha sent her charges a regular series of medical reports, moral exhortations, and domestic injunctions. Early in June she wrote:

> Papa sat out yesterday evening until after seven o'clock. I read him some of Thomson's *Seasons* today. The roses are coming into bloom, the peonies with their bright colours are beautiful amid the shrubs, the Woman is working in the garden. Papa is greatly pleased, dear Maggie, that you are getting on so well. He says you and Helen will get your reward, he is proud of his BOP-POP being head so long. He says tell Willy and George to keep following out his instructions in all things so that they won't have to be ashamed on his return. He is pleased to know they stand so high in their class. Maggie dear will you tell Bella I would like her to give a rub each day, or at least every other day, to the fender and the fire irons in the drawing room to keep them nice, they would soon discolour. I rubbed them every day when I was at home. I wish she would get the woman to come a day and clean the windows and wash the rooms. [After further directions about laundry, the letter concludes:] Papa says please give our love and kind regards to Mrs Byers. Ever my dear ones, Your loving Mother, M. Waddell.

This letter must have been followed almost immediately by a crisis in Hugh's condition and a hurried return to Glandore Gardens for, in her well-thumbed copy of devotional readings, *Daily Light on the Daily Path*, Martha Waddell has entered under June XX: 'Belfast. On this day 1901 a short time after seven o'clock evg my dear Hugh was not for God took him. His wee wife Martha. "We asked life. Thou gavest him length of days for ever and ever."' In his Will, Hugh Waddell had drawn up a list of his property, adding: 'All the above I give and bequeath to my wife, Martha A. Waddell for her own support and enjoyment, and for the support of my four youngest children, as my wife may see to direct, as long as these children may require such aid'; and he thereupon appointed her their legal guardian.

Mid-June had brought the children to the eve of summer holidays. While the Will was in probate and there was business to settle, Martha despatched the two girls to her brother and sister at Ballygowan House. To Helen, now aged twelve, Ballygowan like Tokyo was situated a mystic seventy miles away beyond all confines of latitude or longitude. Aunt Minnie, arrayed in a white gown sprigged with lilac in the fashion of forty years earlier, always had a warm welcome for the children, while Uncle Hugh, like Claudian's Old Man of Verona, lived his life in his own fields, reckoning time in terms of flowers and crops, and pottering about among massive trees he had known as saplings. The beautiful seventeenth-century house set on a hill among a charmed circle of trees was a children's paradise. The house was reached through a door in the wall which opened into a secret garden, a riot of roses, rhododendrons, snowberries and sweetbriar, divided by boxwood hedges. A threshold of broad uneven flagstones gave on to the uneven flagging of the hall, where all day long the reflected light of trees wavered on ceiling and mirror, like the rippling of green water. To the east, the Mourne Mountains were etched against the skyline, and beyond the garden gate lay mile upon green mile of the quiet County Armagh. Such a setting should have brought peace and healing to an overwrought child suffering the anguish of bereavement. But Helen never did anything by halves: throughout her life, deep emotion took heavy toll of mind and body. Death had robbed her of her dearest possession on earth. Her reaction was violent. She underwent a crisis of despair.

Her haven was the library. Here the small, thin, sad child could escape even from Meg, and browse to her heart's content. But it was precisely here, between the pages of the rows of books bound in half-calf, that The Destroyer lurked. The family had owned the house since the days of the Plantation of Ulster. 'Each generation had left its jetsam behind it,' Helen would one day record, 'the snailshells of theology in which it had sought shelter from the white radiance or the balefire of the eternity of its individual vision.' Relentlessly, one after another, the authors disputed predestination and election, the human will and the essence of faith. In Pyke's *Persuasives to Early Piety* she read of the young lady with great gifts of mind and heart who, by attending an evening party, quenched the Spirit and died in dreadful agony of soul, certain that she had sinned against the Holy Ghost, the sin that can never be forgiven. Helen's inner rejection of a Puritan theology of such savage intensity was brought to a head by Samuel Rutherford's *Triumph of Faith*: its interpretation of life, solely in terms of conscience and will, thicked her blood with cold. All she knew was that her whole being cried out for love and beauty: if religion did not involve her whole self, she would have none of it.

She returned to Belfast, a rebel. Soon after the new term opened, there was further upheaval. Upon Hugh Waddell's death, the General Assembly granted his widow the statutory allowance of £37 per year; the Scottish Education grant might very well be withdrawn, and the yearly income from investments would not go far to provide food, shelter, clothing and school fees for the next ten years. In this contingency, the Waddell sense of duty asserted itself and, although struggling to establish themselves in medicine or commerce, the elder brothers agreed that they must give the siblings what they themselves had received. Hugh and James guaranteed the two boys' fees as boarders at Campbell College; Martin and Charles promised to support their sisters. The elder boys had scarcely known their stepmother, and the little they knew they didn't like. Friction had broken out almost immediately. Released from her subordinate position and her husband's gentle and magnanimous influence, Martha Waddell was now absolute; the seniors could make no arrangement without the sanction of the tight-lipped custodian of their own brothers and sisters. Smouldering resentment burst into flame. When as spokesman Martin interviewed their stepmother, so many sparks flew that all future communication had to be carried on through the family lawyer, R. T. Martin, first cousin to his own mother, Jenny Waddell. Difficult Martin was often to prove, but he had a seeing eye that made him tender towards another's pain. Clearly he had been observing, and was not too pleased with what he saw. In a letter of September 1901 to R. T. Martin, who was also Martha's legal adviser, he stipulated that his contribution 'be used in clothing my two sisters in a ladylike and fashionable manner'; that Margaret go to Anderson & Macaulay's, or Robinson & Cleaver's to 'see for herself, and ask the dressmakers about fashions and fit herself out for school, as I can appreciate a girl's feelings when not perfectly dressed'. The chivalrous plea tells its own story.

The lawyer's response was uncompromising — there must be no interference from outside in the upbringing of the children, no conditions imposed, no demands made: Martha Waddell was their legal guardian. His letter continues:

> It is obvious the boys can only go to Campbell College provided that you and your bros undertake absolutely their support, supply their outfit and settlement in life, including their maintenance during vacations, and that you pay her £35 per annum towards the support of the house until the girls can provide for themselves. In case the above proposals be not agreed to, there seems to be only one course open to Mrs Waddell: viz —
>
> 1. Remove to a smaller house
> 2. Dispense with a servant
> 3. Send William at once to business
> 4. Let George be educated in a National School until ready for business
> 5. Let Maggie be put to teaching, or any form of business, to procure aid towards her support
>
> With all this the utmost economy will require to be used in regard to food and clothing. However painful it would be to be compelled to take this course, Mrs Waddell must face it, rather than sanction any arrangement which would be contrary to the intentions of your father regarding herself personally.

Clearly Martha Waddell's government of her charges would be founded neither on compromise nor barter. The concluding phrase of the letter veils a threat: Hugh Waddell had left any money he possessed to his wife 'for her own support and enjoyment'. Significant also is the fact that in this ultimatum, Helen is passed over in complete silence, her very existence ignored. Was her future already tacitly settled — to attend upon her stepmother unto death?

At the cost of considerable self-denial, the brothers honoured their pledge. Billy and George remained as boarders, Meg and Helen continued as day-scholars, at their respective schools. The family had to move house of course and exchange the more imposing 6 Glandore Gardens for 19 Cedar Avenue, Helen's home for the next twenty years. Branching off the main artery of the Antrim Road, the street was then situated almost on the outskirts of the town close to the tramline terminus: there were no green leaves, no gardens. The thin red-brick house stood in a long corridor train of thin red-brick houses, each with a few inches of white pebbled earth in front, and a genteel little railed-in balcony outside the main window of the first floor. In Sir Thomas Browne's phrase, the house was animated with the soul of a porwiggle or tadpole, and Helen hated it with a perfect hate. Holidays brought a welcome respite from the daily grind, for the three youngest boys — Tom, now a medical student, Billy and George still schoolboys — not only enlivened things with their pranks, but even dared to set at defiance their guardian's virtuous maxims of gentlemanly conduct. All three were crazy about football. When Tom, who would one day play for Ulster, received a maternal injunction to give up so rough and noisy a game, he did not mutiny: he merely went upstairs, slung his football boots round his neck, slid down the drainpipe, spent a glorious afternoon on the field and towards evening returned to shin up the pipe, regain his room, and make his appearance in the drawing-room well-groomed and weighed down by innocence.

The boys fared better than their sisters. For most of the year school provided the two girls with their only escape. In her autobiography, *A Little Love and Good Company*, Cathleen Nesbitt has drawn a pen-portrait of Helen shortly after her father's death:

> Helen Waddell and I used to walk home from school together, sharing our growing delight in poetry and our first religious doubts. These doubts, combined with our intensive reading of Darwin and Huxley, led us to discard *all* religions, though we admitted 'from the heights of our mental superiority', as Miss MacWhirter used to say scornfully, 'that there was great poetry in the Bible and in the Koran'. What little prigs we were; we

could not wait to announce that we were 'no longer Christians'. One day Helen and I, passing a Roman Catholic cathedral on our way home from school, decided to go in. We had never been inside a Catholic chapel. We were deeply moved and impressed by the magnificent ritual. Helen even made the Sign of the Cross as we left. 'It's strange how difficult it is to throw off old superstitions,' she said when we were outside. 'I almost expect the Lord God to hurl a thunderbolt on our Protestant heads for consorting with the Scarlet Woman.'*

The story is illuminating. Paradoxically, the strict religious framework of Victoria College contributed powerfully to Helen's rebellion against orthodoxy. Naturally enough, the school's literary idols were Milton and Bunyan, interpreted by the able English mistress of whom Cathleen Nesbitt writes: 'The most exciting class was that of Miss MacWhirter who taught history and literature and, like Miss Jean Brodie, had her little group of "special girls" of whom Helen Waddell was the bright star.' Helen read voraciously, but with her theological background and training she also read critically. It was at this time that she reached the firm and lasting conclusion that she liked neither Milton nor Bunyan, however magnificent their poetry and prose; she was even prepared to tomahawk all the stern old fathers of the Puritan tradition. Fresh from her fight with Apollyon in the person of Samuel Rutherford, she saw in them all the same steel-cold preoccupation with ethics to the exclusion of sense and imagination. The Puritan attitude to letters, she argued, was that of a policeman watching a crowd, taking cognizance only of the 'disorderly'. In autobiographical letters written ten years later to Dr Taylor, she charts her own progress from the age of twelve. 'You know my heresy concerning Milton — which I have never found any one, on reflection, to disagree with yet: that he is the least ideal of our great poets: gross in his thought of women and of love: originally of an exquisite sensuousness that degenerated, thanks to a certain hardness and egotism in his own character and the "iron" of his age, into sensuality.' So much for Milton, but it was Bunyan's *Pilgrim's Progress* — the book which has been translated into 108 different languages — which evoked her fiercest hostility. With evident relish she repeated J. B. Yeats's re-creation of Shakespeare's characters in terms of the Chief of Sinners: 'Hamlet he would have had "Mr Facing-Both-Ways"; Juliet "Mistress Bold Face" or "Carnality"; Romeo "Mr Lovelorn"; Macbeth "Mr Henpecked".' Her Father in God was at first outraged, but he had to face the fact that she was obviously sincere. The series of

*Cathleen Nesbitt: *A Little Love and Good Company*, Faber, 1975.

letters on Bunyan reveal two contrasting poles in her own mental and spiritual make-up, and for that reason are important.

She begins by asserting that she finds *Pilgrim's Progress*

a dangerous and misleading document in religion (wicked, perhaps, but a grave conviction of mine), in its absolute lack of recognition of the Person of Christ, and the mechanical entrance into the way of holiness. That wicket-gate haunted my childish mind for years. There is terribly little spiritual religion in Bunyan to me. Even as a child I was awfully disappointed that Greatheart did not turn out to be the King himself. One person in the story I miserably identified — Ignorance: and it was with myself. Tell me, is there anything in all Bunyan equal to that one sentence of St Augustine's — 'Thou didst touch me, and I burned for thy peace'? Some day I think I'll compile St Augustine's prayers: 'Too late have I loved thee, Beauty so old and yet so new.'

Her next letter turns away his wrath with a soft answer:

I am sorry I put it so badly about Bunyan. I never dreamt of saying he was unorthodox. It's not that he misrepresents Christ's *Person*: it is that he ignores the *Perpetual Presence*. It's the absolute lack of mysticism that makes the book barren to me. I don't think you quite took my meaning about the wicket-gate. I do not think, with you, that it is the 'decisive act of choice'. If Bunyan meant that, he abused one of Christ's most gracious metaphors. Surely it means Christ himself? Bunyan may have meant that — I think he must: but he gives no faintest indication of it. He quotes 'Strait is the gate', but not the illumination of that hard saying that St John gives: 'I am the Door'. Christian condemns Ignorance because he came into the Way down a little crooked lane, not through the wicket-gate. I don't think the sternest theologian could have done that, unless with the thought in his mind 'No man cometh . . . but by Me'. But my grudge against Bunyan was that though I believe he had Christ's metaphor in his head, he made it so mechanical. It was years before I realized it.

I am afraid I speak bitterly about the book, but it was never gracious to me, except the glorious bits. I always felt the 'doctrine' behind it; I always felt that I was Ignorance, that I had come down a little grassy lane instead of through the wicket-gate — whatever that mysterious process of conversion might be. It was childish but it haunted me.

I can't help feeling that the Christ of the *Pilgrim's Progress* is the 'Byzantine Christ'. I read a wonderful Russian novel once, 'The Death of the Gods': a study of Julian the Apostate. And the thing I've remembered longest is his dread of the Christ in the altar-piece, with lightnings in his hand, throned on clouds. Once, he came on a little neglected country chapel, with a rude altar-piece, dating almost from the Apostolic Age: a Shepherd with a lamb in his arms. He did not think the two could be the same. You know, I think it was that remote majesty that drove the fearful to pray to Mary to intercede with her Son. They had forgotten the reality of the Incarnation.

I do sometimes speak 'wild whirling words' of people like Bunyan and some of the straiter Evangelicals, but it's because they made things very hard for me when I was a child. You will say it is the merest truism to say that 'Christ has a different way with every soul who comes after Him, just as in the days of his flesh' — but the realization of that infinite accessibility was the profoundest astonishment of religion. It's a surprise to me yet.

Of course it was my own fault. But you see I'd have been racked, I think, rather than have spoken about those things to any one. I just turned them over and over in a very miserable little brain. It's terrible to think how much a child can suffer. And the reticence of them — I'd have *hidden* rather than risk being questioned. Embarrassment can be agony when one is twelve.

Her long letter closes with a typical retraction:

I have finished the evening over the *Pilgrim's Progress*. And I have come on the story of Mr Fearing and a sentence on the last page from Mr Standfast: 'I have loved to hear my Lord spoken of, and wherever I have seen the print of his shoe in the earth, there I have coveted to set my foot.' And I take back everything!

What then has become of the 'atheism' so blatantly flourished before the eyes and ears of Miss MacWhirter's English class at Victoria College? The plain truth is that it never existed. In the library at Ballygowan she had stumbled on an antidote, revealed to no one, not even to Meg. As she was exploring the shelves, she happened upon two books, the *Confessions* of St Augustine, and a volume of mediaeval Latin hymns. In them, as she admitted later, she discovered the God of Beauty and the 'wingy mysteries of Divinity' with passion enough in a single line to bankrupt whole anthologies. The conflict between the masterful logic of Calvin and John Knox's theological thunders of her Presbyterian background, and the magnetic pull of the 'European thing', dates from 1901 when she was twelve: it was never fully resolved. With her usual subtlety she was to project this collision between incompatibles on to Ballygowan House itself:

The century of its building was Puritan; the century of the Penal Laws its maturity: it is a countryside inveterately Protestant. The nearest Catholic chapel is at Tullyorier, a shabby chapel and in no way venerable: but when the feeble voice of its bell comes across the bog on a still evening, the house listens with a sort of angry and thwarted devotion.

This youthful crisis of faith branded her soul: she could never forget or ignore it. Years later, at the height of her powers and fame, she summed up those months after her father's death in a rare letter of self-revelation to Meg:

> This morning in bed I turned to *Daily Light*, and read the thing for August 9th. It brought back the days in Ballygowan when I was in most bewilderment, and when I used to read this small book in a kind of aching despair. I suppose that phrase 'broken cisterns that can hold no water' and St Augustine's 'Thou hast made us for Thyself, and our heart is restless till it finds rest in Thee' are almost the deepest stains in the blotting paper which is my mind. I don't believe it was ever fear that moved me, even at twelve. It was a kind of homesickness — what some French writers call the 'nostalgie de l'infini.'

Helen was expert in concealing her deepest feelings. She gave no outward indication of her inward turmoil. Schoolfellows recalled her as the girl with the twinkling merry eyes, 'one with the inhabitants of the legendary Tir-na-nogue, the country of the ever-young'. Even among those who taught her, there were some who considered her a clever little butterfly, able to toss off amusing but completely shallow verse. This facile idea is belied by the evidence. She was not what she seemed. A photograph reproduced in Cathleen Nesbitt's autobiography depicts the celebrated quartet of Honours Junior — Cathleen, Helen Forbes, Meta Fleming and Helen Waddell. In sharp contrast to the smiling charm and silken elegance of the other three, all obviously older, Helen Waddell stands in deep mourning, a grave and intense little figure. The face arrests attention, with its snub nose, sensitive mouth, cleft chin, and eyes that peer shortsightedly through thick lenses, under a mop of dark curls. The Socratic snub nose, inherited from her father, was an object of family derision. She was not photogenic: 'Our dusky sister from Alabama — a cross between Helen and a pug' was the family description of a youthful photograph. In a mischievous letter written with schoolgirl gusto from the house of Waddell cousins, Helen paid off an old score:

> Many a time I've thanked heaven that my father was a Reid, not a Waddell. The Waddells are lean and high-nosed and terribly touchy. Do you know the kind of people who have never been in the wrong all their lives? They have an unshakeable complacency, 'justified' in everything they have done. I'm a scrambling untidy black crow, for I always know when I've put my foot in things. Muriel has the finest nose I ever saw, an exquisite thing, which made me feel base-born whenever I looked at it. Also she has the most supercilious upper lip — you know mine in the photos — well hers is the same, but with a regular curl at the left side. Finally, her voice has a tired note in it that makes you feel you and the world you live in are 'so inconsiderable that the mind freezes at the thought'. Do you wonder

that for ten minutes I sat and hated her (also remembering the fact that she wears threes in boots), and then she started growing on me. And yet when she looks at you with her curious mouth half-smiling and a gleam of family Puck in her face, you think you fairly love her. There was a most gorgeous tea — chicken and tongue, and all manner of home-baked things, five home-baked cakes.

Not all her Waddell relatives were given so summary a dismissal: two, both ordained ministers, were especially dear, her uncle John Waddell, and her cousin Jimmie Mulligan. 'I loved my uncle John, and he returned it in full measure and running over. I was mortally lonely those years and hard up' — it was this uncle who warmly welcomed her to his beautiful house, and eased her bleak existence. As long as Meg remained at home, Helen was even allowed to accept his invitation to stay for a weekend. As his manse was within a stone's throw of Cedar Avenue, it afforded its teenage guest a chance to chronicle small beer and regale Meg with bulletins dropped through the letter-box by hand. The unformed girlish script and high-spirited contents of one such bear witness to its writer's frolicsome youth:

> Antrim Lodge, Antrim Road
> Tuesday

My wee Waddly,

How are you getting on in the distressful absence of your loving sister? It's not half bad staying at the Manse. Maggie and Jeannie are really very decent, being as gracious and chatty as they could be.

You needn't fear that Jeannie will outshine you. Her dress is a crepe-de-chine, green but ugly. The shade is rather too dark, I think, for such light material. The bodice is trimmed with puffs of white silk down the front, and the skirt is not one half as pretty as yours. There are no flounces. Meg has blossomed out in Muslin, rather a pretty lavender-fawn striped material, and the sleeves are fashionable style, full at top, caught in at the elbow, and then full again.

Mrs Elliott, pretty with fair fluffy hair, has a very strange laugh, ending up with a wail like a child in whooping cough. She is very lively though, and I like her. Mrs Irwin is the wet blanket. She is Scotch, and has attended Assemblies since she was twelve years old. She talks in a precise sort of tone, and Mrs Elliott lapses into meek silence when she begins to speak.

Bob Elliott is a very jolly fellow, but 'the handsomest man in the Assembly' looks ghastly. I don't believe he is half well.

I expect we will have a good deal of croquet. The Elliotts are croquet enthusiasts.

Auntie and I are sleeping together. Your sympathy is urgently requested. All the same it's not half as bad as I thought. I keep well over to my side, and she doesn't take up as much room as one would expect from casual survey. She is really a very decent soul, Meg, and I like her well.

I wonder would Mrs Irwin and John hit it off well.★ Last night she said to John — 'How did your wedding come off?' 'Oh,' said John, 'it isn't on yet!' 'What, what!' from Mrs Irwin. 'I suppose', said John hastily, 'you mean the Greenock wedding?' 'Of *course*,' retorted Scotchy, and her face was a study in thunder clouds.

I saw them all off to the garden party, Mrs Elliott in her wedding dress (cream silk, I think, and an overskirt of lace, most splendiferous to behold), Mrs Irwin in violet figures, Jeannie in green, and Meg in her muslin. I tell you they were a swell mob in earnest. All the Robinson girls and mamma Robinson toddled down the road in fearful grandeur a few minutes after, with the attendant spread of obsequious ministers.

The grub here is splendiferous. All the bestest chayney, and the presentation taypot etc in full force, while there is a huge centre bouquet in the lamp-vase contrivance posted on a gorgeous centrepiece wreathed round with trails of flowers. Your humble servant is so overcome that she can hardly eat. There are little slices of bread rolled up in the napkin, and Matilda in starched (though toothless) state, stalks round with the vegetables. The dignity is only slightly marred when, as today, she nudges Miss Jeannie's shoulders, and murmurs, 'Aw, Miss Jeannie, it's you that doesn't know what's good for you' as she passes on regretfully with the slighted potato dish.

The ministers have desecrated the study with their pipes, in spite of Harry's conspicuous notice posted on the bookcase:

Smoking strictly Prohibited. Penalty — Smoked bacon
N.B. This rule to begin and end in smoke.

I have had some grand spells at reading — Barrie's Margaret Ogilvie, Hearts in Exile, and Sandy. Hearts in Exile is splendid; Sandy is middling, not bad at all. I am too lazy to write any more.

I have a rare story for you. Sir Robert Anderson gave a reception when he became High Sheriff. Sir Dan Dixon was there, and took the ladies to supper. 'What'll ye have, ladies? Champagne? Here waiter, champagne!' 'Oh sir, this is a teetotal concern,' whispers the waiter. 'Eh what? Lemonade then, 3 lemonades!' Then turning to the ladies, 'Boys, but it's the quare surprise my stomach'll be getting the night!' That's one of John's.

Helen used to liken herself to the Grand Old Duke of York: 'When we are up we are up/And when we are down we are down.' Faced with any ordeal, she would be prostrated beforehand beneath a dead weight of incapacity and dread that usually vanished in the brilliance of performance. Like many a younger sister she thought Meg, six

★Uncle John's son, John, ordained in Bangor in 1902, married in 1907, was brother to Harry, Jeannie and Meg.

years her senior, so much more accomplished, so much easier of approach than her gawky adolescent self. One of her letters at this time tells Meg:

> You have the gift of sympathy — unless in those moods which do come upon us both when we go round like the oft-quoted melancholy clam with its shells shut up tight — and you have the gift of pleasantness. You may not know it, but you have the kind of face that when you smile makes other people want to smile too. And when you're cheerful there is the note of the springtide in your voice. If you were blessed with a voice like mine, like a grandfather clock, its deeper notes being as John of Bangor once said, the very thing to 'lead in prayer', you'd soon find the difference.

Little is recorded of Helen's schooldays beyond her brilliance at mathematics and English. In 1917 Dr Taylor sent her *The World of the Unseen*. She already knew the book well and told him: 'It had a peculiar charm for me because of my mathematical training, and because of a marvellous sketch that I read when I was fifteen — the experiences of a circle that knew only two dimensions, and how a third was revealed to it by means of a sphere. But when it tried to tell other men what it had seen, it was indicted for heresy and madness.' English not Mathematics was her predominant passion, and her early love remained. When Dr Taylor asked her to choose books for India, she explained her choice:

> The wee books go to you tomorrow: *Virginibus Puerisque* and *Memories and Portraits*. I am haunted by a fear that you may have them, but I risk it. Stevenson is one of the people I cannot criticize — like Sir Walter Scott. *Ivanhoe* was almost my first novel: I read it about nine, and he translated me into a kingdom. For which reason I shake hands with Stevenson when he says, 'Walter Scott is out and away the King of the Romantics.' But *Virginibus Puerisque* I read about fifteen, just when one is beginning to think, at least in the speculative essayist way of thinking. *Aes Triplex* and *El Dorado* are not ill reading at fifteen, while the second and fourth parts of the title-essays were a revelation — not in religion, but in the science of living. One takes truth and disillusioning very hard at that age, and there are bits of those essays that I clung to so desperately then, that now they have about them the sentimental value of the spar on which you came ashore. There's hardly a page in either of the books that hasn't a sort of palimpsest effect on me.

At the age of sixteen Helen went down with a severe attack of measles, but that was slight by comparison with the trial that awaited her at seventeen. Meg had always been her inseparable companion: she had never envisaged life without her, for were the two not 'like a tree that forked so near the root it looks like two trees, but in the earth there's only one,' as Helen had put it. Meg had passed from Victoria College to the 'University House' as it was called — Queen's was not founded until 1908 — where students qualified for the B.A. and M.A. degrees of the Royal University of Ireland. In answer to Dr Taylor's enquiries about Meg's scholastic attainments, Helen replied:

> It was in my head that I *had* told you: that I haven't is simply proof of this peculiar grace about Peggy, that her degree is the last thing you think about. She took it in 1906, the B.A. Pass of R.U.I. in Mathematics, French and English. She never was at Queen's but she made the 'University House' of old V.C. a very cheerful spot. Nobody ever doubted Peggy's very delightful brains: but they remember with most affection her attendance in the 'kitchen', which was an unofficial Junior Common Room. Peg never worried overmuch about what they call in biographies 'the usual academic distinctions'. She came home from Japan so late that it never occurred to her to work for a degree in honours. You see, to begin French and Algebra at seventeen means not very easy going. And, considering that, to go through without a hitch and have one's degree at twenty-two was sufficiently astonishing. You would not have wondered at my omitting to mention Peggy's *scholastic* career, if you had *seen* her just then, and I am heart thankful she never had to teach — it was a sorry outlook.

A family conclave of cousins and aunts, analysing Meg about this time, agreed that she wasn't what you'd call pretty, but there was a fascination about her, a kind of witchery that swept you off your feet, while her gift of sheer gracious fooling brought a breeze of laughter into the dullest company. She evidently bewitched John Dunwoodie Martin, her own mother's first cousin, Minister of Magherally in County Down. Separated from Meg by a whole generation, he had two formidable rivals for her affection: a much younger colleague in the ministry, and an equally young businessman. By upbringing of course she was in her element in clerical company, so that with great equanimity and deliberate choice, she accepted 'J.D.'s' proposal of marriage for the sole reason that she loved him. They became formally engaged on 26 July 1906, during her final year at College. Desolate and sick at heart, Helen sought solace in *Daily Light* where the Scriptural passage for the day — the call of Abraham to leave behind all the dear and familiar things of home to go into the far country of his new inheritance — gave her strength to face the inevitable parting. In September of the same year, immediately after her final examinations, Meg was married and was on her honeymoon when the degrees were conferred.

If the seventeen-year-old accepted the fact of her sister's marriage, she found it difficult to accept her brother-in-law. Time, closer acquaintance and experience of his sterling qualities were to mellow her attitude, and she ended by appreciating and loving him deeply. For some time however she nursed resentment: she felt he had robbed her sister of youth, that Meg's was a life without any spring in it. J.D., as he was invariably known, owned Kilmacrew House in Banbridge, a remote eighteenth-century stone-tiled farmhouse, standing in about 120 acres of wood and arable pasture. In her prefatory note to *Stories from Holy Writ*, Helen has described it as 'an old whitewashed house in County Down, its three feet thickness of wall sunk in ivy and in apple orchards, but with the silence of the bog behind it, where at night one could sometimes hear the drumming of the snipe'. Yet Meg had far more to do than simply admire its natural beauty and entertain her husband's guests. Kilmacrew was a farmhouse; life demanded of its mistress immense courage and vitality to cope with the household, the livestock, and the endless preparation of meals for family and farmhands. It was all very well, Helen decided, for J.D. to be a visionary and dreamer, exercising in pulpit oratory his Shakespearian gift of metaphor and phrase, but his wife needed iron strength, and her sister was only a daffodil head. There were days when Helen did not love John.

From a letter addressed to 'My dear wee fat-head', it is clear that Helen was spending the end of that eventful year at Ballygowan, only a few miles away from Kilmacrew:

I'm writing for Auntie to say that 'they will be very glad to see you in your own home'! We'll be with you as early as possible, provided that there won't be such a hard frost that the horse couldn't walk. I'm simply reminded of you at every turn. I'm writing with the old 'jet black ink' bottle that we bought three years ago — it's nearly done now, and has to be set up on its end — and I'm wearing the little blue skirt that you resurrected so often, same wee brass buttons and baggy seams. I wanted to go out this morning so Auntie suggested Aunt Jane's 'elastic siders'. I went up and fished them out, and when I looked at the funny little demure broad toes, and thought of the gay little Lothario that pirouetted in them, I nearly howled — on the wrong side. I'm going to walk into the old post-office today — all alone! And our old orchard — too bare of leaves now for privacy, and the dog, a wee bit fatter but as gamesome as of yore — oh noctes coenaeque deum! Eheu fugaces! Do you remember the day I spouted all those 'for the last time' — and we missed the train?

I'm sleeping with Auntie in our old long room. And I opened the old secretary — all the same, down to the blotting paper that dried J.D.'s love-letters. Och, do you remember the first you wrote him? Och, I can remember you sitting scribbling at the old desk half-dressed with your bare fat arms and the candle-light on your golden hair. Haw! I'll write a pome on it, dear.

> A grass-grown orchard, and a moss-grown tree,
>   The glory of the sun-steeped air,
> Hone of the reaper, and a drowsy booming bee
>   And the gold of Margaret's hair!

> A long low room, and the twilight of the night,
>   The gloom of an old secretaire,
> Fair flushed face, and the yellow candle-light
>   And the gold of Margaret's hair!

★   ★   ★

> A windswept orchard, and a leaf-stripped tree,
>   Brown rotting leaves and the chill dank air,
> Wind in the branches like the wailing of the sea.
>   Ah! but Margaret was fair!

> A long low room and the twilight of the night,
>   Love-letters dead in an old secretaire,
> Red dying embers, and the ghostly pale moonlight,
>   Ah me! for the glory of her hair!
>   (Ballygowan, January 1907)

The year that followed Meg's marriage was naturally the hardest to bear: Helen hungered for the society of young companions. She spent her holidays as she had always done, but the old secretaire was altogether too evocative of the past. 'Do you remember what happened this time last year?' she asked Meg. 'I can just see yourself coming out of the dark and the rain into the lamplight, with your eyes blazing like stars, and your wee face glowing, and the whole of you seemed to be thrilling with electricity. Do you remember that rose on the dear wee blouse, that was stole from the Kilmacrew laurels. I'd have kept it as a relic, more than your wedding-dress.' And then she gives herself away: 'There is a great quiet here — and oh, I wish the sun would come out, for the trees make *such* a shadow.'

Short rare visits to Kilmacrew emphasized the indubitable fact that Meg's life was now fulfilled, whereas hers was empty: 'I have a crow to pick with you — a black crow. What for did you not turn your head to see the last of me? I hung out of the window and near bawled myself hoarse and wagged about like a lunatic — and there were you with your innocent face jogging peaceably down the hill with your eyes riveted on the beastie's ears — quite childlike and bland, and as unconcerned as if you had just dumped a sack of turnips. Mebbe it was just as well, for I was overcome with such a violent irritation that it drowned the pangs of parting.' The letter ends on a minor cadence that hints at unspoken discords: 'Mother was glad to see me, and there is a great peace upon us. Meg dear, I'm glad I'm home. I needn't have been so afraid. I think we understand each other pretty well, and next year will be a good year. And once again, I am glad to be home. Somehow I needed to get — readjusted. And I'm feeling uncommon cheerful.'

It was true that for years there had been mounting tensions between Martha Waddell and her two charges. She observed their mutual love and understanding with growing resentment, and so contrived to separate the two that it was an actual adventure to get out for a walk together. Helen yielded in order to preserve harmony: Meg's womanly dignity was long past the age of tutelage. Now that she was free of its shackles, she was clearly indignant at any affront to her liberty. A letter of 1907 shows Helen studying her sister with a very penetrating gaze, and going out of her way to kindle Meg's sympathy for their stepmother:

I have been thinking about you a good deal, and the word that is borne in upon me as the Highlanders have it is this — 'How is it that ye have no faith?' I think you would get through life easier if you believed that people cared for you half as much as you care for them. Mind you this, people are always fonder of you than you give them credit for, and remember likewise that people very seldom mean to be as nasty as they are. If there's one thing about Mother it is this — she doesn't change. If Mother likes you once, she likes you everlastingly. She was awfully pleased that you have asked her. I never knew, but it had hurt her a bit that you hadn't for so long. Meg, it really frightens me sometimes when I think of the heart she spends on us two, and the sorry return she gets. For sometimes I think she sees how much you count with me — and it hurts. And then you know what a treat it is to us two to get by ourselves — sometimes maybe we aren't as tactful as we might be. I don't suppose you remember *Weir of Hermiston*, and the row between father and son, but there is one sentence in it that haunted me, and curiously enough I came on it just after your letter. 'Who are we that we should know all the springs of God's unfortunate creatures? We are all *incompris* — only more or less concerned for the mischance: all trying wrongly to do right; all fawning at each other's feet like dumb, neglected lapdogs. Sometimes we catch an eye — this is our opportunity in the ages — and we wag our tail with a poor smile.'

It's thundering mightily, and I must trot upstairs to wee Mother. Thank God — I mean it — that at least you and I have wagged our tails in unison. Don't be disappointed that I am only going to you for the week-end. It will be very short, but you are to forget *how* short as soon as I arrive,
    Only we'll talk awhile, as children play,
    Without tomorrow, without yesterday.

The schoolgirlish script, written on rough 6½″ by 4″ sheets torn out of a cheap notebook, is that of Helen at eighteen: the letter's astonishing maturity recalls her own mother's report that the two-year-old babe was a dear nice wee girl but so smart, hardly like a child in many ways. Indeed, hers was an insight that takes most people a lifetime to acquire. Not that she was ever a precocious prig: high spirits and self-mockery enliven every letter, but especially delicious are her irreverent asides on the worthy wives of the clergy:

> While I was at the Adairs, Mrs Irwin came to pay a parochial and I was introduced, and she looked at me over her nose (it's a good distance) and said she had heard of me. Well, I may be conceited, but I think she had something pleasanter to look at than I had. As for manner — my dear, she vowed at the beginning of her ministry that she didn't mean to be the commonplace minister's wife. She isn't — count your blessings, name them one by one, and remember gratefully that you are like other men, or 'femils'. Shouldn't wonder but that she is a great success. But if you'd been built that way J.D. would have disposed of you quietly in Ballowly Bog. And you'll agree, as I expect, that he'd be right in such an act — but this is not for Sunday.

The year 1907 was marked by three notable events: her matriculation and farewell to Victoria College; the birth of the first of Meg's four sons who, with their sister sandwiched half-way, were to be the joy of her heart and the occasion of some of her most moving prose; and her sudden passage into adulthood when her favourite cousin, Jimmie Mulligan, 'the proudest and most sensitive of the whole connection', asked her to spend Christmas in his manse and look after his three small boys, while his sick wife wintered in the sanatorium at Banchory. 'I think Jimmie never forgot that fortnight,' she wrote years later. 'Even then he could talk to me — forty-five and eighteen. Night after night in the Groonsport study, eighteen darning endless stockings, and patching endless small trousers (I'd found a six-months' accumulation in the wardrobe), and forty-five smoking endless pipes and glowering into the fire, and making another up with "It's a shame to be bothering you like this, but you're such an understanding kid!"'

The understanding kid had already been singled out as a prospective bride while still at school. 'Curiously enough *my* first lover was a friend of Meg's husband — a Professor of Hebrew,' she told Dr Taylor. 'I met him at Kilmacrew the year after she married, when I was just eighteen, and he about fifty-five (he thought I was fourteen).' She is referring to Professor F. Moore of the Free Church of Scotland College in Edinburgh, a man of deep erudition, who talked to her in shy, hurried sentences, wooed her in top hat and frock coat, and spread under her feet his fair dream of making her mistress of the beautiful property in Tyrone, inherited from his mother, where he spent his vacations. True to his high calling, he had modelled its garden on the Garden of Eden and outlined for Helen its many charms: the orchards planted with peach and apple trees for the sake of their blossom; the river that glided and wound with innumerable twists and turns through his little estate, providing him with Adam's prerogative of giving names, a different one to each island and promontory. Mesopotamia lay between two rivers, and beyond that the Prairie, the size of the Kilmacrew drawing-room; one patch, known merely as the Upper Garden awaited — Helen? — to glorify it with a loftier designation. Then there were the dogs: his two favourites, Pluto, and Proserpine, the others bearing the more commonplace names of Philistine gods and Assyrian goddesses. 'The Professor', to give him his invariable title, was to haunt 19 Cedar Avenue for years but, however gladly Martha Waddell might have accepted this second clerical son-in-law, Helen was resolved never to marry a man so much her senior. 'It's bad for a man to be a bachelor fifty years' was her uncompromising verdict, after refusing his offer of marriage with a 'No' that he realized was irrevocable.

In the summer of 1907 she left school, but instead of going up to Queen's at once, she decided to spend a year at home studying Mathematics under a Mr Harvey, who held his classes at Victoria College. Whereas she had no rival in English, Latin or French, she had not yet mastered to her own satisfaction the Maths and Experimental Physics required for the first year's University syllabus; behind the decision lay also the nagging self-reproach of leaving Martha alone for most of the day in order to achieve her own academic ambition. So she set to work for an entrance scholarship, glad to postpone her departure for another year. As always, regular reports were despatched to Meg at Kilmacrew, the 'Majesty' referred to being Helen's nickname for Miss Anna Matier, headmistress of Victoria College: 'Mr Harvey says we have got on fine. I am at present toiling painfully through determinants and the uncanny "species quadrilateral", and I have trimmed the old geranium hat of gorgeous memory with an old blue ribbon and some velvet, and it looks — as her Majesty remarked this morning — quite fascinating.' Accomplished needlewoman as she was, Helen was just as likely to ask Mr Harvey whether he approved of her geranium hat as to discuss the species quadrilateral. This unicorn among the cedars would discomfit, bewitch, infuriate and enthral most of her professors in the years to come. Clearly Mr

Harvey was no exception for, on the eve of the examination, Helen sent Meg a final statement of progress:

> I'm working harder than ever I did afore, and I hope ever will again. I take every evening at it, and some of the afternoon, and I'm growing to hate it fervently. Oh dear, surely I deserve that bloomin' scholarship. I get the rarest letter from Mr Harvey that ever you did see — I'd written to him could he give me a few final licks into shape before October 28th, and got a prompt reply from London, where it seems he's now coaching. 'Dear (but sinful) Miss Waddell', was the opening, and he goes on, 'As you may see by my address you may gang your ain gait to distinction now: you can no longer play like the grasshopper or whatever it was, and then roll over all the burden on my shoulders.' So he meanders on for four pages, had the cheek to call me 'a little vagabond', and finally ends up: 'Now if there be any good in you, search for it, and see that you get that scholarship. If you do not, or cannot, may you get your deserts at once instead of waiting till the next world.'
>
> I was all alone when I got it, and as I read I roared and then ramped at the man for his cheek and almost tore my hair in rage — only it was very nicely up, my second day, and I refrained. Yes dear, I'm now a lady growed. My hair began on top, and now goes up and down like a barometer according as it is voted becoming or otherwise, but like the barometer it has stayed persistently at the nape of my neck for two days — the combined influence of Mother and Aunt Minnie making higher flights unpopular.

In the autumn of 1908, the sinful little vagabond went up to Queen's University, Belfast, on a scholarship awarded *summa cum laude*.

CHAPTER III

In 1908 THE newborn Queen's University, Belfast, was small, self-conscious and self-contained. To anyone accustomed to swarming hosts of undergraduates, and impersonal red-brick seminar techniques as opposed to Oxbridge tutorials, the direct contacts and close friendships formed between staff and students at Queen's in the opening decades of this century must come as a pleasant shock. No matter what their field of study, they all resembled one large family and, in a sense, that is precisely what they were. The explanation of this phenomenon is to be found in the historical background of the College.

Until 1845 Ireland had but one University, Trinity College, Dublin. Founded in 1591 on the site of the Augustinian monastery of All Hallows confiscated under Henry VIII, its avowed aim was to conquer Popery and establish a Protestant nation — a somewhat tough proposition. In 1633, in an effort to speed up the process, Laud, Wentworth, and the Provost of Trinity, William Chappell, introduced new Anglicized statutes, inaugurated fresh acts of repression against Catholics, and imposed on the protesting Fellows a completely English style of life modelled on Oxford and Cambridge. In the century that followed, Trinity reached its peak of expansion and achievement. It saw the graduation of men who are its glory: Jonathan Swift 1667–1745; George Berkeley 1685–1753; Edmund Burke 1729–97; Oliver Goldsmith 1730–74; Henry Grattan 1746–1820; and Theobald Wolfe Tone 1763–98. With the exception of 'poor Poll', these sprang from the ranks of ruling Anglo-Irish Protestants, yet were all alike Irish patriot-agitators: they fought for liberty, free trade for Ireland, the reform of the land laws, and the granting of Catholic relief. The limited success that attended their efforts was pretty well cancelled out by the Act of Union of 1800, which ushered in a century of political and economic upheaval. By the early nineteenth century, Trinity had become not only an exclusive but also an expensive Protestant stronghold.

In 1845, in an endeavour to meet widespread demands for universal education and to conciliate opposing interests amid the complexities of Irish politics, Peel carried through Parliament an enlightened measure for three purely undenominational colleges, styled The Queen's Colleges, to be set up at Belfast, Cork and Galway. Dr Russell, President of Maynooth, and Dr Murray, Archbishop of Dublin, gave the plan warm Catholic support, but it was fiercely opposed by Dr Cullen, Primate of Armagh. His attitude was not so obscurantist as may appear; the Presbyterians shared his misgivings. The Colleges were to be British Government institutions, likely to be affected by every change of administration; moreover, their proto-type, the English University system, was inextricably bound up with the Established Church, which hardly existed in Ireland. Events soon proved that such fears were not groundless. Before Peel could carry his scheme into effect, he had been succeeded in office by Lord John Russell who, despite perfectly lawful remonstrance, appointed an almost completely Protestant professorial staff to an almost com-pletely Catholic student body at Cork. In the unlikely event of obtaining an acceptable deal from a politician of Russell's calibre, and in face of the disturbing tide of liberalism and anti-clericalism sweeping over the universities of Western Europe as a whole, the apprehensive Irish bishops torpedoed Peel's proposal, forbade Catho-lics to attend the Queen's Colleges and — painful fiasco! — invited John Henry Newman to found a Catholic University in Dublin.

As far as Belfast was concerned, the Catholic withdrawal simplified matters. The Northern town was in a much stronger position vis-à-vis the British Prime Minister than either Cork or Galway, for the simple reason that 90 per cent of its citizens were Presbyterian, and the Established Church a mere cipher. From the outset therefore Pres-byterianism was the dominant influence at Queen's College, Belfast — a fact duly recognized by the English government. For thirty years from 1849, the year of the opening session, until 1879, the College was governed by an ordained minister, the Reverend Pooley Shuldham Henry, first in a long line of Presbyterian divines, ably seconded as Vice-President by Thomas Andrews, a scholar of European repute. Under the guidance of two such men, it was natural that the College should forge strong academic and theological links with the Scottish schools of Edinburgh and Aberdeen rather than with Oxford or Cambridge. In spite of the seemingly favourable winds, all was not plain sailing. As early as 1845 vigilant eyes had discerned breakers ahead. Forebodings were justified when, in 1879, a series of national expedients — notably Lord Beaconsfield's establishment of the Royal University of Ireland — came dangerously near to making shipwreck of Peel's project. According to this new scheme, the Royal University was a purely examining body with its headquarters in Dublin; its professorial staff were to draw up syllabuses and set examination papers throughout the land for candidates now empowered to obtain external degrees, irrespective of any College membership. In other words, it strongly resembled the Open University of the 1980s. Naturally this seriously threatened the intake of the three existing Queen's Colleges, where the decline in numbers led to general anxiety about the future. This thoroughly unsatisfactory state of things prevailed until 1908, when the dilemma was happily resolved with the passing of Augustine Birrell's Irish University Act. The Royal was to be replaced by two universities: the National, situated in Dublin, with constituent Colleges in Cork and Galway; and Queen's of Belfast, now raised to independent University rank, with Senate, Chancellor, and President. At this point, the Catholic bishops withdrew their veto, and the new foundations at last fulfilled Peel's high hopes of providing for all a strictly non-sectarian higher education.

For Queen's, the year 1908 was an exciting time of transition: everything was in a state of flux during the rites of passage from College to University; neither Faculties nor Chairs were clearly or finally established. Numerically, the student body fell short of five hundred, divided among the four Faculties of Arts, Science, Medicine and Law. There were as yet no halls of residence, no mechanism so to speak of full university life, but there was an amazing vitality and sense of purpose, an intellectual rigour and vigour permeated at its best with a deeply Christian outlook that marked the Queen's students of those years for ever and aye. This was the University that admitted Helen Waddell to membership in October 1908, and trained her in the mental discipline so evident in her scholarship and unique power of expression.

During her first year, Helen followed three courses: English Literature and Language under Professor Gregory Smith with Robert C. Ferguson as assistant-lecturer, and Algernon Okey Belfour, Lecturer in English Language; Mathematics under Professor Alfred Cardew Dixon; Latin under Professor Robert Mitchell Henry. All three professors were quick to appreciate the penetration, capacious intellect, and personal charm of the new student, and each coveted her for his Honours school. An extant letter to Meg sketches the daily round:

> Queen's is as usual, except that Gregory Smith's wife is dead, and we have had his big-nosed assistant, Ferguson, for a week on end, and are awfully tired of him. He's a conceited big thing, and he stands with his big heels sticking right over the edge of the platform. It is fervently hoped that he'll

follow them some day. Dixon's Maths make me lead the strenuous life —
but I'm getting along as well as the rest of them. He has started a wee class
on Thursdays for practical work, from 2 till 3, but it's a pity to miss a good
thing, so I'm staying for it. Henry is also threatening us with a Virgil class
on Tuesdays — but the gods forfend! My dear, he set your poor wee sister
to read in the honours Latin class: I did not know that a Waddell could feel
shy, but I know it now.

Years later, in a letter pleading that Meg's eldest son be given a pre-
University year to prepare without stress for an Honours degree in
Engineering, Helen wrote:

I lay out for a year, do you remember, working for an Entrance
Scholarship in Maths, and it made all the difference when I went to college.
The worst of it was that Mr Harvey coached me, not alas for Entrance, but
for First Arts Honours conics and such, with the awful result that the plain
mathematics of the paper terrified me — I always was a duffer at the
straightforward things — and I clean lost my head. I think I was 13th out of
the 14 candidates. But at the end of the year, the man who is now Belfast
City Surveyor and I were the two from Queen's who got Honours in
Maths. And just to show the Providence in things, I gnashed my teeth over
what seemed a lost year, but it just held me back to be in time for the new
English degree — it was started just as I finished 1st Arts — you remember
how Gregory rejoiced over filching me from Dixon. And a year sooner
would have had me bound to Mathematics — always a struggle. 'There's a
divinity. . . . ' The things I've raged over are the things I thank God for
now.

In 1909 the new Charter of Queen's was put into effect. As a result
of a considerable increase in the British Government's financial grant
to the University, the professorial staff was augmented by the
establishment of additional Chairs. From being Professor of History
and English Literature from 1905 to 1909, Gregory Smith was now to
occupy the Chair of English Literature solely, a position he would
retain until 1930; A. O. Belfour was appointed to the Chair of English
Language. One of Gregory Smith's first acts was to engage Professor
Dixon in battle over Miss Waddell's future: was she to adorn the
Honours school of English or Maths? To the other's lasting resentment, victory fell to Gregory Smith, who thereby saved Helen from
the unthinkable fate of spending the rest of her days in pursuit of the
cold and austere beauty of mathematical truth.

Helen was not displeased. 'Had the first lecture with Gregory
yesterday,' she reported to Meg, 'and oh, but it was peaceful to hear
the mellow Oxford voice of him discussing the contrast of Marvell
and Pope in satirical verse.' For the remainder of her life she would

acknowledge that to no one was she so indebted as to Gregory Smith. Years before she encountered Charlemagne's Court circle, Helen shared their propensity for playful nicknames. She blandly informed the Professor of English Literature 'hereinafter to be called Gregory' so she said, that his christening was evidence of verbal inspiration. No other name could possibly suit him so well. It had a flavour of state and scholarship about it, and conveyed him so much more adequately than his patronymic. So her guide and mentor lost surname and rank to be elevated to the papacy as Gregory the Great, except on those occasions when his impassivity, remoteness and oracular wisdom recalled the massive bulk of the Daibutsu in Kamakura, when he became the Buddha. Once, in an outburst against his calm unconcern, Helen told him that he made her feel like a puppy barking at the Sphinx, but she had to admit his baffling charm. All the same, she knew perfectly well that his air of indolence masked his strong support as he steered her course, convinced that one day she would fulfil his high hopes.

George Gregory Smith (1865–1932), born at Edinburgh, had graduated there at nineteen years of age, spent the next eight years at Balliol, returned in 1892 to lecture in Edinburgh for thirteen years (where George Saintsbury became his colleague and friend), was an examiner for the Royal University of Ireland 1906–9, and lived his last twenty-five years in close association with Queen's, Belfast, first as Librarian 1905–9, and finally as head of the English school from 1909 to 1930, when he retired to London in order, so he said, to be near the theatres. His long academic career at Queen's coincided with that of his greatest friend, William StClair Symmers (1863–1937), pathologist and bacteriologist, scholar and scientist, ever reckoned one of Belfast's most illustrious citizens, and the most admired and loved figure on the campus of Queen's from 1904 until his retirement in 1929. 'The adorable Symie', like so many of her associates, gladly joined the ranks of Helen's friends and admirers. There is gravity as well as gaiety in Helen's admission: 'I've frequently said, laughing, that I shall marry no man whom I do not like half as much as I do Professor Symmers, but there is truth in it too. He is big and radiant and kindly, with a massive head and beaming spectacles, one of the far travelled men who have the simplicity of children. He is as critical as Gregory, but infinitely kinder, and his "humanity" in every sense is an abiding joy to me. And if I had been Mrs Symmers, I would certainly have done what she did, even though Professor Symmers at five and twenty may not have been as wholly charming as Professor Symmers at fifty.'

The truth is that Queen's had transformed Helen: she had become suddenly and amazingly happy. She found many schoolfriends already there. Of the Victoria College quartet, only Cathleen Nesbitt had gone her own way to win dramatic fame in Granville Barker's Shakespeare revivals; Helen Forbes, the most beautiful girl in the school, was now ruler and arbiter of fashion, coveted partner at all Queen's dances; Meta Fleming of the speedwell-blue eyes and radium-like spirituality, living up to her sobriquet of Greatheart, later supplemented by the title 'our Lady of Perpetual Succour' (odd how the papist influence of the Redemptorists in Clonard Street made itself so speedily felt), was preparing herself in secret for a missionary career by a brilliant performance in Modern Languages. With Helen's generous co-operation, she was also quietly regenerating a rather moribund Christian Union — between them, they would sweep it to the foremost position among College societies. Akin to Meta Fleming in spiritual quality, and even closer to Helen in intellectual gifts, was Maude Clarke, only daughter of the four children of Canon Clarke of Carnmoney, a parish on the outskirts of Belfast. Three years younger than Helen, she went up to Queen's in 1910 to read History under Professor F. M. Powicke. The two families had long been friends, although Maude had been educated at Alexandra School, Dublin. Maude was as much Meg's as Helen's, Helen sister to Maude's three brothers, and the rectory of Coole Glebe a place of safe anchorage. 'It was an old house as bare as Argo, full of echoing uncarpeted passages, and great low-ceiled rooms,' Helen wrote to E. L. Woodward. 'All its richness was in its multitude of books, and in the walled garden on the southern slope, looking across the Lough to the delicate sea-coast of the Ards.'

The friendship with Maude Clarke was undoubtedly the greatest of Helen's life. She has painted her in a few vivid strokes: 'Maude comes in', she wrote to Dr Taylor, 'in a rose costume and furs; she has a distracting trick of lifting one soft tail and stroking her face with it, and looking like a very little black cat. Sometimes one sees only her eyes and a slowly circling tail.' The interaction of the two minds is fascinating. In a simple form, it may be seen in their contrasting attitude towards the gipsy encampment that lay close to Coole Glebe at the foot of the Antrim hills: Maude hoped to be captured and held up to ransom like a Crusader; Helen crept into the gipsies' own skins. 'I came back from Carnmoney with five gipsies this morning,' she reported to a friend, 'and felt a little like that great lady in the old London ballad who went off with the raggle-taggle gipsies-o! They were so good-looking, especially the grandmother: the finest *old* profile I have ever seen, and a marvellously tender mouth, and they were all worshipping one baby — men and women both. They didn't care who was in the train: it was the aristocrat's indifference — they were among an insignificant and barbarous people. They made me feel provincial and suburban.'

To Dr Taylor, Helen analysed the difference between Maude's mind and her own in more technical terms:

> She has an extraordinary mind: I think she forgets nothing, and yet she reads enormously: but it's not chaos. It's just as though the creative intelligence brooded above the mass. Is it Shelley's phrase, 'the shaping spirit of the imagination'? That's mine, as much as it's good for anything. Maude's is Matthew Arnold's 'the imaginative reason'. Add to that, in talking, not yet in writing, an unerring gift for words. She is the most original talker I know, and the most effortless. I've never heard her use an adjective that wasn't the expression to the last nuance of her thought, yet she never seems 'precious'.

So much for her women friends. But at Queen's, in spite of having had eight elder brothers, she was moving for the first time into a world of men where, free to some extent of her stepmother's dreary moralizing, she found herself the lodestar of a brilliant group: Billy Lynd, younger brother of Robert the essayist, and Maude Clarke's brother Brice, both medical students, and J. M. Barker, future missionary to Manchuria among them. 'Brice was talking about you last night,' was Maude's parting shot one evening. 'He thinks you are very wonderful. "Maude," he said suddenly, "think of the hundreds of clever men there must be in England who don't even know there's anybody like Helen in the world."' He may well be the central figure in the ballad *Il Penseroso*, composed under Helen's blotting-paper to while away a boring lecture:

> I wander lonely as a cloud
>   About the lonely quad,
> And one by one they come to me
>   And ask me why I'm sad . . .
>
> I was a naughty medical,
>   I did not love to work,
> But since the night she danced with me
>   I never want to shirk.
>
> But now that dream is over
>   And she is gone away,
> Because in Arts the lectures
>   Stop on the 10th of May.

Later, in a letter to Dr Taylor, she recalled a garden-party in May: 'I was feeling very wicked and very gay, and beguiling a nice medical — and suddenly realized that he was going to fall in love with me. It is a sensation at any time but when one is just nineteen — I think he did fall in love with me: but as he had done it several times before, and was to do it several times after, you are not to be sorry. Especially as I didn't fall in love with him.'

The garden was known as 'Symie's Garden', a little lost pleasance (now buried beneath a wing of the U.V.F. Hospital) that its owner, Professor Symmers, made over for several years to the women students until Riddel Hall, the hostel overlooking the river, came into being. Here they could escape from lectures and city pressures to watch golden and purple crocus break in the grass, read aloud William Morris under the apple tree in blossom, or simply chat against a background of flowering lilac or blazing rhododendrons. It was Helen's custom to spend the last half-hour in this little fenced-off paradise before returning to the gardenless Cedar Avenue. 'I used to lie on the grass and think to myself

"Who doth ambition shun
And loves to lie i' the sun" —

and wish it were me. I always have that little garden in my head when I hear William Morris's

"I know a little garden close
Set thick with lily and red rose."'

Evidence in plenty goes to prove that Helen was besieged by admirers, especially at the students' weekly dances. A high-spirited letter of self-mockery tells Meg all about it:

I'd give my boots to see you and get telling you all about Thursday. I wore my blue dress and Helen Beatty told me when it was all over that I was an undoubted success. And Mr Cowper asked me for the first six dances at the next, and Mr Lynd for the next six and the supper dance and to see me home. However as I told Mr Cowper I couldn't give him more than three unless my intentions were serious. But Meg the holy joy of the thing is that said Mr Cowper is the same B.Sc. with the eyeglasses and the supercilious mouth that Helen introduced me to at the Toney reception — don't you remember me bewailing to you about the way he watched me talking to McCartney and the dislike in his critical eye? and judging therefrom that the swanky and brilliant men were not for me? Well when he came up I looked at him in frank amazement and as he said afterwards with a 'What on earth am I getting now?' despair in my eyes. And when the time came I was in a shaking funk, with the result that I lost my head and he leant against the wall and writhed with laughter about half a dozen times before

we got once round the room, after which he said that if he was going to
waltz with me I might hold my tongue for he couldn't do two things at
once. And the devil entered into me and I looked in his face and said
solemnly, 'I like you, Mr Cowper.' But there are shadows on my lot: Lally
McThwaine did not ask me to dance with him though he made faces at me
all evening. George Cowper said he would go round and thrash Lally
McThwaine next morning. Most of the men I was introduced to at the last
were in hospital (I don't mean from the effects, but as pups), however I got
13 out of 14 dances and was booked for four extra. Billy Lynd landed in
from another engagement about half-past ten and saw me up to Helen's.
He said that he had had a most miserable evening and that he wouldn't give
Norman more than 9d for the dance ticket instead of 1/3, and that he
wouldn't have given him the 9d except for the dance he stole. It is all very
sad.

Whether tickets cost the lordly sum of 1s. 3d. or merely 9d.,
dancing demanded some degree of elegance. As children, Meg and
Helen in their dresses of sober serge and black boots, with home-
made rag dolls, had contrasted cruelly with their silken-clad
schoolfellows on dainty tip-toe clasping the prettiest dolls in the
world. Nothing much had changed. The tension evident in some of
Helen's letters at this time can easily be traced to her scant wardrobe
and the difficulty of providing herself with suitable clothes. An
S.O.S. to Meg reads: 'I wonder *would* you lend me the embroidery
on your dress? This stuff won't go round, and in the daylight it
doesn't match a bit. Don't if you'd rather not — now I mean that —
and I will quite understand.' That appeal was followed by: 'Do you
know what it is like to dress yourself side by side with a young
woman in soft pink satin and real lace and a gold necklet? And this
imp wished that someone would tell her that her dress was pretty
and her shoulders white — but nobody did.' Yet she was not such a
failure as she would have Meg believe, for another letter refers to her
dress as being 'the softest, daintiest thing you would want. Kathleen
and Maud White were dressing with me, and I shuffled into it in a
corner, and when I came out they both stopped dressing and said —
My word! It was not my face, dear, oh no — but they had never seen
my "pluffy" neck before and they said it was a pity I couldn't wear
evening dress regular to breakfast. It was rather depressing as Maud
said with great truthfulness that she had never thought I was pretty
before. Meg, as you love me don't leave this lying about but burn it
— if I weren't writing in such a hurry I would not be making such a
fool of myself. Many thanks for the combies — I put lace round the
top and ran blue ribbon through it: they were a great comfort to me.

Everybody was in evening dress and I came to the conclusion that it makes a man either a genius or a fool, in looks I mean. It would have taken more than evening dress to have made geniuses out of some of them. It wasn't that they weren't clever, I don't mind that, but do you know what a man is like when he is "stockish"? I thought maybe it was my fault and was too lazy to care, but I saw some others sitting out and such solemn irreproachable demeanours, about as vivacious as their tombstone chests.'

The austerity natural to Helen from childhood could deny her everything except beauty, and beauty she loved in every form, whether in people, nature, dress, furniture or literature. She herself was not 'beautiful' in the accepted sense: friends who loved her have even described her as 'faceless', yet she undeniably exerted a fascination felt by all who ever met her. Artists such as Paul and Grace Henry were anxious to fix her unusual colouring on canvas. 'Cornflower blue is peculiarly my colour,' she told Dr Taylor. 'Rose is barred to me, because my colouring is too gay without it. Maude says I am a baby about colours. This was when I set up a new pair of evening shoes before me and contemplated them ineffably. But they were nice. They looked as if they were my great-grandmother's, black brocade with green vine-leaves on them, and very high brocaded heels. I don't think I'm really extravagant but I do love pretty things. Professor Symmers once settled me in an armchair just where the light fell on my dress — a lovely shadowy blue and roses one — and then he sat down unabashed to contemplate it.' The same letter records a visit made to her former headmistress, Miss Matier: 'Madame eyed me: the next I heard of it was a cheque for five guineas and a command plus entreaty to go to Lowry's and buy me a respectable garment. That little lady would like to dress me in a Field-of-Cloth-of-Gold manner, and feed me on curds and cream, and marry me to the Prince of Wales. She told me once that I did not know how much I mattered to her: and that is why I can let her do things like this. The result is an exquisite Shantung silk coat and skirt, a deep creamy yellow: very soft and full, with a broad sailor collar. And with it — this *was* extravagant — an enormous black hat, almost untrimmed except for a tiny patch of blue.' The imagination all compact that was later to breathe on the men and women of the Middle Ages and make them stand on their feet, living beings, was exercised even on old clothes: her obstetric hand could bring forth beauty from a ragbag. An invitation to dinner in a hotel with Dr and Mrs Symmers sent her into a panic — she had nothing to wear: 'Very sulkily I fell to the reformation of a faint heliotrope dress in a shining crepe,' she wrote to Meg. 'I cut down the neck to a deep V, put on fluffy frilling like what the small boy wears in Millais' *Bubbles*, sashed it with black satin from Mother's goods-box, and fastened the white frill with a spray of pink sweet-pea. And when I had put on a pansy evening cloak, and a black Spanish lace scarf over my head (the sweet-pea glimmered through it most divinely), I sat down on the edge of Mother's bed and said — "I *do* like my clothes!"' Quiller-Couch tells the story of a sulky naval cadet swept away by a laughing girl escaping from her many suitors for the opening dance of the season's ball. In answer to Q's teasing, the young man blurted out almost in tears: 'It isn't her beauty, sir. You saw? It's — it's — my God, it's the style!'

Helen Waddell undoubtedly had style. The first to acknowledge it was Gregory Smith: he never underestimated her gifts. As soon as he had been given autonomy in 1909, he set about the formation of a School of English, based largely upon his thirteen years' collaboration with Professor Saintsbury at Edinburgh. The urbane sardonic Balliol man, in temper and mind an eighteenth-century Atticus, conceived of a liberal education as being, in part, a fellowship of minds akin to Addison and Steele's Kit-Kat Club. He therefore summoned Helen — already his right-hand ally in all things — pointed out to her that Queen's oldest club, the Literary and Scientific, was now outmoded, asked whether the time was ripe to divorce Arts from Science, and proposed that the newly-enfranchised English School set up its own club. That was all. He left the rest to her.

Max Beerbohm has observed that undergraduates owe their happiness to the consciousness that they are no longer at school. The nonsense knocked out of them at school is all put gently back at the university. Certainly students everywhere and at all times are much of a muchness: it was with a smile of recognition that Helen was to meet the goliards of the twelfth century in Paris and Orleans: she already knew their Belfast counterparts. So it is that she reported as usual to Meg:

Our first meeting is to be next Friday, and Gregory is to read us a paper. I had to interview him and ask him to be patron, and he talked to me for nearly an hour and was a duck, a word I never thought I would apply to him. He suggested that this thing be called the 'Tatlers Club', and added maliciously that he meant no personal reference. And finally asked me to come to him in any difficulty, which was nice of him, as I had been compelled to make it very plain that we didn't expect our patron to come to all the debates. He seemed a trifle tickled at the time, but Mr McCartney (who I had to ask to be President) told me afterwards that he was intensely amused at the secretary's frankness. But I have eaten, drunk, and slept the

Tatlers Club for two weeks, and I'm already wishing it at the bottom of Belfast Lough.

During that fortnight, she published a skit on the engineering of the Club in *Q.U.B.* — *Queen's University Bulletin.* In it, the secretary finds she has invited no fewer than three eminent persons to be Vice-President, and each has signified acceptance. A pessimist suggests the Club be styled The Ephemerals, a superior person, The Babes in the Wood. When, to salvage her injured dignity, the secretary pleads she must catch a train and promises to write up the minutes of the meeting for *Q.U.B.* under the heading 'Genesis', the pessimist invites her to complete her job by writing up the sequel for next month's issue under the heading 'Exodus'. All the same, Helen had put a great deal of work into the preparation. The patron had been warned not to brood over every meeting — she admitted to Meg her fear that he would be like the elephant who found a deserted nest of eggs and sat on it with the tender admission: 'I too am a mother!' In addition to Professor Gregory Smith, the board of directors consisted of P. McCartney, a Classics Don, as President, A. O. Belfour, Vice-President, and Helen Waddell from the rank and file. The stage was set for a brilliant official opening of the Tatlers Club in February 1910. On condition that Meg would not read her letter aloud to anyone under pain of having her younger sister branded as a lunatic, Helen sent her an account of this first session:

Queen's was in a state of 'Sturm and Drang' all last week, and all over these unhappy Tatlers, or rather over that fool McCartney who, to our sorrow, we had elected President. There was an audience of about seventy. Gregory sat and beamed in his wonted chair, with the sheep on his right and the goats on his left — namely, Mr Belfour and Mr McCartney. There was some speculation at first as to which was the goat, but events speedily cleared that up. For McCartney got up to deliver his Presidential address, and about half-way through began slanging the Literary and Scientific, the oldest Society in Queen's, and this in his most offhand Oxford Manner. He meant it as a sort of burlesque, flinging down the gauntlet — or so he said afterwards. But as it happened, there wasn't a man there who didn't belong to the Lit. and Sci. and I sat and felt the atmosphere behind me getting electric — and I made agonized faces at McCartney which he was too short-sighted to see. And Gregory sat and buried his face in his hands and tried to look as if he were not laughing. It seems when he got McCartney out, he said very briefly — 'Well young man, you've done it now! just you look out for next Q.C.B.' Gregory knows his Queen's.

The men sat very quietly on to the end — but once outside there was a Bust. And there is an article going to Q.U.B. that will shrivel the young Don from Oxford — and I'm very much afraid will shrivel the Tatlers

with him. And two days after, a letter came to 'the Secretaries' that made
my flesh creep. It was from the Vice-President of the Lit. and Sci.
cancelling his membership — a most Burke-like piece of stately dignity —
reminding the Tatlers that 'it was sometimes easier to criticize a record
than to beat it', and ending, 'Might I urge upon your Committee in your
own interest and that of the University the advisability of some immediate
step which will make clear once for all the place which academic etiquette
holds amongs your ideals.' The unhappy Secretary gasped for breath and
promptly despatched the gage of battle to McCartney with a very brief and
very cold statement: 'Unfortunately your audience was largely drawn
from the Lit. and Sci. and this somewhat unpleasant manifesto exactly
expresses the general atmosphere. May I see you tomorrow at twelve?'
You can guess I was pretty mad, after all the bother I had to get the thing in
working order, and have him just smashing it at the start. But I was
beginning near twelve to get sorry for the chap, for the letter was an awful
slap to a man who prided himself on Oxford 'form'. I needn't have wasted
my sympathy. The wretch was in a state of unbounded amusement
except, he said indulgently, for the annoyance to myself. But he thought
he had better resign — and as one or two of the men had told me it was the
one thing that would save the Society, I heartily agreed. He said his sole
regret was that he had given me any vexation about it, demanded that a
general meeting should be summoned to receive his resignation next day,
and finally assured me that indeed he would be good — but there was a
twinkle in his eye that I did not understand.

Friday came, and the room was full — for the news had gone like
wildfire. We had all gone looking most unfeelingly gay but, faith, it didn't
last long. McCartney came in, in his gown, looking thinner and more
delicate than ever (he is an Anglo-Indian), and sadly mounted the
platform. And then with a patient dignity of martyrdom made a most
complete apology to the outraged Society, and handed in his resignation.
Anything more painful I never listened to, people's faces were getting
absolutely tense with strain, and still that weary voice went on — the
wistful submission of a man who had failed. At last he sat down with his
head sunk over the desk like a man disgraced, and one by one they got up
to implore him to take back his resignation — and he listened and never
raised his head. He smiled sadly once or twice but that was all. And all
around me the girls were saying, 'Ah Helen, you must have been far too
hard on him. He's far too sensitive to be shown that letter' — and so on, till
I was nearly in tears myself. Meta Fleming declared it was the most pitiful
thing she ever heard; even Miss Lewis said she could hardly sit through it,
and the entire meeting stamped applause when the final appeal was made.
McCartney rose to his feet again and gravely and gently asked for time to
consider. And the mob streamed out slowly and sadly until he and I alone
were left. I stayed, for I wanted to soften what I had said, or what I *thought* I
must have said to bring him to this. He waited till the room was clear and
then he looked me in the face and said — oh, the divil! — 'Didn't I do that

well?' Meg, if you can't imagine my feelings, I can't explain them. There was me sitting for an hour in a perfect agony of remorse and pity, and the wretch laughing in his sleeve the whole time. It was diabolical, but oh it was clever. And angry and all as I was at being hoaxed, I couldn't keep from laughing while that fiend went on describing his sensations — and finally ended up with 'Do you mean to say I took you in too?' And he went off to his room with one burst of laughter — though we saw him going through the hall a little later with a face like a virgin-martyr. He bound me not to tell anybody of course, but I feel sometimes as if I'd burst with it. I hope this has not bored you to death, but I'm laughing yet.

The secretary of the Tatlers was young and very merry, but she was also very wise, and harmless folly went hand in hand with stern study. She possessed in a high degree that talent, ability and genius which the magisterial voice of J. H. Newman declared to be the raw material that it is the business of a university to cultivate. At the end of her second year at Queen's, Helen reported to Meg:

Thank goodness the class exams are over. In my last, we were told to compare Shakespeare and Ben Jonson, on which I could have written for a week. The day before, Gregory returned our essays. Well, as he once phrased it, I usually pursue the even tenor of my way along the A, and had given up all hope of a rise. He read out the 17 names in alphabetical order — my miserable self coming last. The only First Class at all was Ella Fisher, A –, 'a good essay, gracefully written,' says Gregory approvingly. Internal curses from me, being like the Turk too fond to rule alone. Then a weary waste of B, B –, B – –. Then, 'Miss Waddell'. Pause. 'An exceptional piece of work . . . an original treatment . . . in fact, one of the best essays I have ever read . . . and I have judged it worthy of the highest mark to be given — A + .' He ended up, 'By the way, if some of you have time, you might read it for yourselves, not merely for the matter — it has *literary merits*.' If they were not nice, they would poison me, but I sat in the exam yesterday and wondered what it would feel like to drop from A + to B – .'

D. H. Lawrence has observed that it is surely the English who are the *nicest* people in the world. It is amusing to find Helen's paddy roused when she met that niceness head-on. A Miss Caldwell there was, who 'had the most self-possessed manner I ever saw, and a neat complacent English face — and no matter what Gregory would say about anything I'd done, she would come to me and praise my "very nice" paper with a calm patronage that made me want to flatten her nose with my very Irish fist.' Pugnacity however was not part of Helen Waddell's make-up: she could not deny her brains, but her sense of proportion, her diffidence and modesty preserved her from any self-assertiveness or exaggeration. There were times when Gregory Smith had his work cut out to restore her lost self-confidence. 'Cheers, cheers, cheers,' she told Meg, 'I was seeing Gregory and feeling dismally that he would be a glad man the day he washed his hands of me. He believes I'll do something yet. He said something about "a young woman of my ambition" and I said "I'm not a particularly ambitious person". "You have reason to be," says Gregory very quickly. "But I'm not going to tell you what I think of your powers." I had said that my thesis was a desperately small piece of work and very superficial. And Gregory looked at me and straightened his mouth. "Dear me, but you must be ageing terribly!" And then he gazed out of the window . . . "After all, we are more wonderful even than chickens. . . . " I looked at him in blank amazement, and he proceeded to tell me about an essay of Samuel Butler's in which he marvels that six weeks will leave a chicken prepared for the responsibilities of life, whereas it takes three and twenty years to make a curate.'

Several essays from Helen's undergraduate years survive: all bear her authentic stamp. Small wonder that so stern a critic as Gregory Smith had to salute them as literature. One, entitled *Arcady*, covering seventeen pages of girlish script, was written in three days: its theme can be heard re-echoing throughout her mature work, from her early Preface to *Lyrics from the Chinese* 1913, to her last public appearance when she delivered the W. P. Ker Lecture in 1947. The essay opens:

> There is a book some day to be written — though now that R. L. Stevenson is dead, I know not who will write it — upon the inwardness of children's rhymes. Therein it will be shown that the problem of that Simple Simon, who went a-fishing for to catch a whale, when all the water he had got was in his Mother's Pail, is in its essence the problem of Richard II: even, according to certain commentators, of Hamlet, Prince of Denmark. And there is another rhyme, of an import rather poetic than psychological, which is more haunting than many greater lyrics, for this is the burden of it:
>
> > 'How many miles to Babylon?'
> > 'Three score and ten.'
> > 'Can I get there by candlelight?'
> > 'There and back again.'
>
> It seems that they do not sing it now, that it has been supplanted by a more popular and more prosaic variant, wherein the questioner demands the road, not to that most pagan and princely city, but to no less respectable a place as London Town; while the answer has none of that fine indefiniteness which chanced on three score and ten, a mystic number, which only in mathematics is equivalent to the result of multiplying ten by seven. It is the

kind of answer which one expects from the school of Benjamin Franklin, and the author of 'Self-Help', and all the other authorities on How to Succeed in Life. For hearken:

'One foot up, and one foot down
This is the road to London Town.'

Now, one foot up and one foot down may be the road to London, and to many other desirable places, but it has never yet taken any man to Babylon, which is the less to be marvelled at when it is remembered that Babylon is one of the chief towns of Arcady: and that Arcady has never yet been secured within any parallels of latitude or longitude.

Not, at all events, since the days when, in the map of the world, the pink of the continent faded distractingly into the blue of the sea, with the magic legend, 'Undiscovered Territory' upon its neutral tinting. Or the greater days when a notable prisoner paced the parapet of the Tower at sundown, seeing visions and dreaming dreams of a land that reflected the glory of the sunset, an El Dorado of which Manaos was the capital, where a man might find wealth, and find again honour; and the seaman, outward bound, and dropping down with the tide, turned to wave a greeting to that eagle broken-winged, and saw Sir Walter Raleigh, as the world has since seen him, a gallant and ill-fated figure, black against the glory of the sunset. And when the dreams were put to the test, and the 'Destiny' sailed westward, a sorry ship and a ruffian crew, and found there neither gold nor glory but dishonour and death, then might men talk no more of El Dorado: the west had lost for ever its enchantment. . . .

Helen then passes in quick review some of Arcady's main cities — Camelot, Samarcand, the city in Illyria, Venice, the forests of Arden and Sherwood, regions that nothing artificial can touch and yet live. But beyond lie other forests whose very names are incantations: Ascolot, Lyonesse and Broceliande with their immemorial sequence, Launcelot, Pelleas and Pellinore. Here she pauses, and one hears the voice of the twelve-year-old Helen rejecting Milton the Puritan while mourning his all-too-brief sojourn in Arcady, when he was tempted by the Arthurian epic. There are some, she says, who knew John Milton in the days when 'the old strewn roses charmed, the old strange road was mad with song' for him, and they have never ceased to mourn for his sudden departing. 'For they heard him pleading with the nightingale when all the woods were still —

"Whether the Muse of Love call thee his mate
Both them I serve and of their train am I:"

they had heard the joyous pagan chanting of the sixth elegy through all its sonorous Latinity, on the glory of wine and the glory of song; and though it be great heresy they had rather heard Milton the Pagan Greek singing of

"such sights as youthful poets dream
On summer eves by haunted stream"
than Milton the English Puritan justifying the ways of God to men.'

It is not perhaps without significance that *Arcady* was written in the spring of 1911. Increasingly Helen was being driven in upon herself, forced to become herself a dweller in Arcady. 'I want you sometimes so badly,' she wrote to Meg, 'specially when I come tramping solidly up Clifton Street on my "long sea-way home". Lizzie and Ruby Crawford and May Bamford are in digs together this year, and like it awfully. Wouldn't it be rare good fun? Each girl takes her turn at housekeeping for the week, and keeps accounts, and at the end they divide by three. I had a lengthy screed from Meta inviting me for a week-end if I wouldn't come for a week. However Mother doesn't like the idea of me visiting there. There ain't no use getting riled, I suppose, but there is a pain within me that is not in my tummy.'

Why the pain? Because Martha Waddell was quickly developing into the merciless stony-hearted stepmother of the traditional fairy-tale. The fragile charm and tender graciousness of her bearing towards outsiders masked a self-centredness that wanted to separate and sour any affection not directed primarily to herself. To her, laughter and the love of friends, however dear to Helen, were not worth the wear of winning. First to fall under the ban was Cathleen Nesbitt. The playhouse was to be equated with the brothel; the theatre was a frivolous flim-flam unworthy of a Christian and, if Helen valued her soul's salvation, she would steer clear of common actresses — the order went forth: all communication with Cathleen, who was so *simpatica*, must henceforth cease. Helen did the wise thing. She saw Cathleen, explained, met with perfect understanding, and the gulf of silence left their friendship intact until it was resumed years later in Oxford. The jealous eyes then turned on Meta Fleming. She was too possessive, made too many demands on Helen's time, drew her away from her neglected and ailing mother. No longer was Helen free to enjoy a rare weekend in Meta's home at Loughry, a house of wide spaces, kindly ways, and lavish grace, that stood beside a stream marked with stepping-stones evocative of Japan.

Finally and inevitably of course the jollity and game, the luxury and riot, feast and dance of the weekly ninepennies at Queen's could not be tolerated by so rigidly righteous a guardian of morals. It would have been much easier to bear, and possibly a way out could have been devised, had Helen revealed to close friends the domestic situation, but intense loyalty sealed her lips. An unwonted outburst to Dr Taylor, which even then did not tell the whole truth, explained just how successful Mar's tactics had been:

It began in my second year at College, when her eyes suddenly seemed to give up. I just dropped things, committees and tennis, I couldn't in decency be away all day, and read all evening, and the poor wee Mother alone and ill. I got into the habit of never, unless for something tremendous, going out in the evenings. She simply told me that my duty to her was as great as my duty to other people. There was no sacrifice she would not accept from me without so much as seeing it was sacrificed at all. That has been the cruelty of it. If she had ever said when I refused opportunity or pleasure for her, 'Dear, it was good of you,' I'd have counted it less than nothing and vanity. She has seen me refusing an invitation and crying as I wrote, without a shadow of misgiving, saying in a little while with absolute complacency, 'You may be thankful you aren't motoring this dirty afternoon'. She disliked my dear Meta inveterately. It grew almost to hatred because Meta persuaded me to become President of the Christian Union. She went to India: every letter I wrote or received from her was the occasion of such bitterness that in the end I wrote at odd moments by stealth. Meta had a sore heart many a time, and I never could explain the reason—I hardly admitted it to myself. She tolerates Maude because Maude, thanks to her own bitter experience (Mrs Clarke was for years in the house when Maude was growing up, and never quite sane, in a strange egotistical sort of insanity), has been infinitely wise and very patient.

In her *Testament of Youth*, Vera Brittain has declared that Maude Clarke 'remains an enigma which time is unlikely to solve'. The faint air of desolation that haunted Maude Clarke's beautiful face sprang from this personal tragedy. As Helen put it: 'To come upon her walking in the spring rain on the Antrim hills was to see Persephone come back from the dead, but with the knowledge of the kingdoms of it in her face.' Maude was a consummate diplomat. Determined that the door of Cedar Avenue should not be shut against her, she deliberately 'called in' as often as possible, 'but in that ten minutes', Helen recorded, 'that fresh cool air of the other world, the almost colourless world of the *actus intellectus*, blew on you, fresh from things that bubbled slowly, and you went on your way recreated.' Maude's daring even went so far as to trade on Mar's fondness for her missionary past; she wrested permission for Helen to accompany her to a matinée performance at a Belfast theatre. Helen the eight-year-old—for so she at once seemed—had to share the rare experience with Meg:

Och, but I wanted you Friday week. There was a Chinese play at the Opera House, and Maude begged for me and the matinée and I got it. And it was funny enough as it was, but if I had had you with me, we would have squealed. It was exactly the kind of humour that appeals to our curious but rather simple minds: everybody who died on the stage went up to heaven by a wooden ladder which the property-man held securely, all but the wicked dwarf who was half-way up the ladder when the property-man caught his eye, and jerked his head downwards. The dwarf took the hint. The property-man followed you about with a paper rose if the scene represented a garden, and at intervals you smell it. Sometimes you go to smell it when his arm has grown tired, and this annoys you very much, but the property-man does not mind. When you are going to be killed the property-man gives the executioner a sword out of the property box, and sits down and reads a wee Chinese paper — you see, he is supposed to be invisible. If you want to hang yourself, the property-man holds a fishing rod arrangement which is a weeping willow, and you swing on the end of it, and then the fat smiling chorus rises and says blandly, lest there be any mistake, 'He hangs himself' — and all the time the Chinese musicians sat in a little alcove at the back of the stage and kept up the quaint wee twanging and stringing that you would near give your soul to hear again.

Maude might visit Helen with more or less impunity: for Helen to return the visit to Coole Glebe was an altogether different proposition: 'Wild rush to see how much I can get written before Mother demands — "Surely you are not writing to Maude all this time?" Just got a card to ask me for tennis and tea on Saturday, and a promise to see me home — also to help at her stall at the Church Fete on June 27–29. I am refusing Saturday, but going to her on Thursday and Friday of the Fete. Meg dear, when will I have an orgy of accepting invitations instead of refusing them?'

'E si poco vivuta, che ancor son giovane' — she had lived so little and was still so young. Helen quoted these words — so poignantly true of her own life — in 1921 during her lecture in Oxford on the Elizabethan theatre, when discussing Robert Wilmot's *Tancred and Gismund* (1591). As in childhood, was she identifying herself with her heroine Ghismonda who, hungering for life, revelling in her freedom from the cloistered existence of her salad days, and newly-conscious of her own power of attraction, rose in rebellion against Tancred, the father who idolized and thwarted her? Only too well was Helen acquainted with

> the image of the emptiness of youth,
> Filled with the sound of footsteps and that voice
> Of discontent and rapture and despair.

At twenty, her dancing days were ended. For the next ten years she would be forced along a steep and stony path of self-renunciation,

sustained for the most part by a deep Christian hope that found
constantly-repeated expression in George Herbert's

> Once more I smell the dew, the rain,
> And relish versing.
> O only Light!
> That I am he
> On whom Thy Tempests fell last night.

There was one oasis in this dry and thirsty land: Kilmacrew. 'This is
the kind of house where no one ever knows the date of the month,' she
wrote to a friend, 'and there is a smell of turf fires everywhere, the
kind of house that pedlars still come to, because it is so far off the road,
and I bought yesterday very strong white linen for pillow cases, and a
man at this moment is trying to persuade my sister — I can hear the
murmurs at the door — to buy some new gadget for her chickens. I've
just caught, "An' if ye could see the look on the faces of them
chickens." There isn't any place in the world where I sleep as I do here.
Because it is in a hollow, and it has been a wet summer, the trees are
deeper and the roses have grown in great masses and the ivy nearly
meets across some of the windows. My brother-in-law won't have it
cut, and I tell him he will soon be living with the Desert Fathers.'

But better than all the roses and all the chickens were the children
who rose with the lark at 6.30 every morning and pranced in the hall
with clogs on, while one as high priest sang an incantation in which
the only articulate phrases were

> 'O come and see
> The Big Bum-Bee'.

I think of Sydney and Jack sometimes when my life seems one long wall-
paper of exam questions. And wee Margaret Mary is as the dew of the
morning — think that's the name of a whiskey brand, but no matter. Poor
wee soul, I can see Sydney's thin little legs and the eager face. 'Don't let
him shovel too much coal,' as Belle used to say, 'he's only gristle.' As for
Jack, I lay my hand upon my mouth. But after all, Meg, think how they
must have had to smack Napoleon Buonaparte and William Pitt, and
everybody but George Washington. Those yelling fits must be an
experience to live through. Would there be any use in leaving him to 'find
himself'? — for somehow there's a certain exhilaration to the devil in you
in provoking your parents to smack you: it's more gratifying than being
ignored. You will tell me you can't ignore an engine shriek of 50 h.p. I am
growing into a Maiden Aunt.

This description of Kilmacrew from Helen's pen is certainly not
more graphic than a letter, undated as usual, from the mistress of the

house; recounting the saga of a week's spring-clean enlivened by an invasion of the family's clerical connections. So few of Meg's letters are extant that a rare discovery cries out for quotation as showing the gay insouciance, the homeliness and the Irish charm of a true native of the fabled land of Tir-na-nogue, who put a spirit of youth in everything she said and did, yet was to prove under bitter trial that she could endure precisely because she could laugh:

Kilmacrew.
Banbridge.
Sunday.

My dearest Imp,

A terrific spring clean and many interruptions sums up my existence since I bad you farewell that Tuesday. Today is my first breathing space and I have not gone either to church or Sunday S. I felt the effects in a kind of general ache — almost like influenza — and have just spent today paddling about. It is a gorgeous day, just a riot outside, and everything so green and new — 'tis a pity that weeds don't always stay young — even nettles and docks when only three inches look fresh, pleasant and innocent. We had some for our vegetable today and they ate rather like curley greens. Helen, this place is a welter of pleasure on a day like this. Our wee wired run at the hall door is a perfect mass of wallflower bloom, and when you sit by the window or on the door slip the perfume is delicious; it always reminds me of a bright sunny day at old Glandore when I was keeping house and there was always a most delicious mixture of sunlight and wallflower and paint and a delightful feeling of things happening. I suppose it was a spring clean time too, but I always have that funny uplift somewhere about my inwards when I smell the wallflowers. But to come down to ordinary, I can hardly begin to tell you all that has happened — it is really a kind of nightmare to me. Did I tell you of our papering the kitchen, and how, in the middle of it, this Sat. week, Geo. arrived in — well of course I stopped. George Brown was papering, and 'twas well I did, for we had hardly got a cup of tea over us when R.T. and Edith arrived — she looking eggs for preserving. Well I hadn't any but was to get some for her for following Saturday also some from Mrs Rabbits. We spring cleaned like mad, but as we were doing the nursery and J.D.'s room fresh, ceiling whitened, walls papered, we could get in no speed, especially as our paperer was a desperate bad hand at the business. All well so far till Thursday — picture front with all the details of three beds, and contents of J.D.'s wardrobe adorning myrobella and laurel, a big feather bed dumped on our garden seat, the famous straw triangle straddling the cement walk, and a terrific washing waving on line and hedge inside; children revelling in mortar dust — stairs one inch deep — upstairs absolutely impassable with cots, jugs, books, paints etc and the bathroom the receptacle of all the odds & ends imaginable, chambers ad infinitum, and a big torn blanket huddled in one corner where Jinnie had pulled it out and left it when picking the white clothes for the wash: picture all this and us in the middle of it, then also picture poop poop of a motor, two ladies & a baby. Helen, I can say no more. There is a white heat smoulders inside me when I think of it — Edith and K.D. —— !! and Miss Dunwoodie the lady governess!!! It is past comedy truly, but fortunately they could not turn on account of our pleasing friend the dumped feather aforementioned, till Jinnie was haled out to remove said obstruction. I slipped on my black skirt and by miraculous work managed to clean Mary and Charlie before a pleasant shrill voice 'Where's Meg' comes through the kitchen door. Meg emerges, half dried Charles in one hand, werry rough and suspicious looking paws herself, and very uncertain and rather bewildered at the best solution for such an advent. Uv coorse I got them tea, and they gathered daffodils and K.D. clumped down the orchard in gaiters to feed the chickens, and Jack paid her gallant attentions, and lady help followed afar, even with byre, and exhibited a pair of ankles at sight whereof Jinnie and I retired below the range of view of the kitchen window and clasped hands. It made up for a werry little. But I was all coming to pieces and K.D. remarked in childish treble — 'Oor blouse is unfastened' only for politeness there was more than me blouse unfastened. At tea they talked in that idiotic way, innuendo, about Maisie and some Major, and I did not listen. They stayed about an hour and a half, and then made off. I just changed my skirt and started again — Jinnie and I papered till nearly eleven, for Geo. B. is a perfect fool — wrinkles no word for his papering. At eleven Geo. turned up, had been preaching for Scott, I had forgotten somehow all about it. He tramped upstairs to find me poised on three bricks and a pillar. Geo. was rather mad I think that we were in such confusion. All men think women like spring cleaning. I was in a very frisky mood somehow, and described most vividly our adventures — but oh, such a day, and such a finish — but Geo. did not seem to relish the fun.

Friday we wound up our dust as well as we could, and Saturday we darned and cleaned up as usual. Geo. left on Sat. evening. I did not feel too well, just tired and not hungry, and today the thought of S.S. and church was too much so I pottered about at home. I got the old cretonne with the red border and put it on the rocks in the far orchard, and I just lay there, with my head on my folded arms, and listened to the cheery wee birds. I like the blackbird, he is a lazy singer and has a pleasant lack of hurry and bustle, and he ended up each sonnet to a lady love called 'Chitteree'. Everything was nice and leisurely, only then a hen yelled out she had laid an egg, and scared everything away. Just like Peter on the lee shore when wreckage is strewn up, for the wind could not blow more than the tops of my broom, and the sun warmed the backs of my legs in a most soothing and comforting way, and there was just enough nice dry moss to be soft but not damp, and just below me a hen had laid five nice brown eggs under a broom bush; and there was no mortar and no walls, just clean, green, pleasant grass. And now I must close. I'm all right again tonight. The

warm sun and the orchard cured me, and this week should see most of
our cleaning done.

Yours as ever most faithfully, and with a big hug for wee Mother.

The ancient Bun.

The concluding paragraph of a bread and butter letter from Helen
to Meg, thanking her for the weekend spent at Kilmacrew just before
she was to sit for her Finals at Queen's, distils the very essence of the
place and aptly summarizes Meg's high-spirited account of the
vagaries of her household:

> I've been trying to get a metaphor for my feeling about Kilmacrew; the
> stir and the cheerfulness and the upsettingness of it. It's a bit like a magic
> lantern with the slides gone wrong so that when you expect to see the
> water coming down at Ladore you find the family bath-tub. But a magic
> lantern hasn't enough open air about it — suffice it that when you put
> your penny in the slot, which means buying your week-end ticket, you
> are not sure whether it is going to be Violet soap or Bull's Eyes, but
> you'll feel all the time that you are out on the spree. Whenever I want to
> throw things at my destiny, I remember this last week-end, and say to
> myself that having that, I possess many things. It has gone into the House
> of Quiet with some of the perfect hours which no man can take from
> you.

In 1911 Helen graduated B.A. with First Class Honours, and
remained at Queen's for a further year in order to complete her
studies for an M.A. This demanded the submission of a thesis.
Whether she was free to choose her subject, or whether it was
imposed, is not clear: more than once, she certainly suggested
Thomas More as its theme, but each time Gregory Smith vetoed it.
'It won't be Sir Thomas More,' she reported in a letter. 'Gregory was
so heavily against it that I became perverse. I said I *would* do it, if
only for the pleasure of meeting him in Purgatory and saying, "I did
it".

'"You won't meet me in Purgatory," said Gregory, with what, as
I pointed out, was unwarranted assurance. "Oh, I'll be there all
right," says Gregory easily. "It's *your* whereabouts I'm thinking of."

'"You suggest. . . ?"

'"The *Limbo Infantium*", says Gregory.

'But maybe some day I'll edit More's *Pico della Mirandola*, with an
introduction on Neo-Platonism. That would be fun.'

One is left longing for the might-have-been, for the tapestry of
260 years that Helen with her capacity for allusion and correspondence could have woven, had she strolled down Cheapside, past

Milk Street where More was born in 1478, across to Bread Street almost directly opposite where Milton was born in 1608, and along to St Giles's, Cripplegate, where Thomas More's father married Agnes Grainger in 1474, where Oliver Cromwell married Elizabeth Bourchier in 1620, and where Milton was buried in 1674. She never abandoned hope of working on More, as a letter to Dr Taylor shows: 'I see in The Times a note on the manor-house of the Colts — Jane Colt was Sir Thomas More's first wife, and it ends with a reproach — the indifference of the nation to one of its greatest. There is no critical edition of his English works, no collection of his letters. Can you see my hands opening and clutching? For I have always loved him. Curiously enough, I'd thought of him for my thesis.'

In the event, the subject of her M.A. thesis was *John Milton the Epicurist*. Her conception of Milton as man, scholar and poet was all of a piece from girlhood, when she rejected his dogma, until 1942 when she translated his *Epitaphium Damonis*. In so doing, she made peace and amends by making his grief on the death of his friend Charles Diodati in 1638 the expression of her own on the loss in World War II of Jack and George Martin, her nephews.

The pages of her handwritten manuscript, scattered, unnumbered, and difficult to piece together, are sufficiently coherent to give a fair idea of the general plan. It is interesting to see the early Helen Waddell: the brilliance is there but the prose is occasionally lumpy, mannered and self-conscious. She has not yet reached the easy command of language, the spontaneity so strikingly evident in all her later writing. For all that, her treatment throughout shows an amazing maturity of judgement. There is one puzzling and curious fact about the loose sheets of the thesis: they are annotated quite unmistakably by Professor George Saintsbury, whose pencilled and well-nigh indecipherable scribblings adorn the margins. Saintsbury, Gregory Smith's old friend from Edinburgh, was the visiting professor and external examiner at Queen's when Helen graduated. In a testimonial, he wrote in 1917:

> I have known Miss Helen Waddell for the last seven years: my acquaintance with her having been originally made by examining her for the B.A. degree of the Queen's University of Belfast in 1911. I noticed at the time the altogether exceptional ability and originality, as well as knowledge, shown in her papers: and the impression was deepened by her work for the M.A. degree which also came before me subsequently. For appreciation of literature and power of expressing that appreciation it would be difficult to find a superior to her. . . .

The opening chapter of the thesis displays a complete sureness of

touch in its penetrating analysis of the difficulties confronting any
biographer, and Milton's in particular:

> Think how little we know of each other, the pathetic shifts at understand-
> ing, the infinite possibilities of misconstruction even when the man is in
> life and eager in explanation — and you think yourself into a humour when
> all biography seems an impertinence; an unfavourable one an outrage. All
> men have suffered more or less heavily: except perhaps when they have
> been allowed to speak for themselves, and the biographer becomes but a
> skilful scene-shifter. But this may never be done with Milton, for there is
> the added seeming-impossibility of judging him on his merits. In this
> instance, the influence of politics on letters cannot be disregarded to
> Milton's eternal loss. . . . It is not so much the effect on Milton: it is the
> effect on his audience. It does not matter whether we are Whig or Tory,
> Royalist or Roundhead — what does matter is this, that the Milton of the
> middle period wrote the *Eikonaklastes* and the *Animadversions*, and the
> *Defensio Secunda*. It is a sort of infected area, and it taints our perception of
> him, do what we will. In a very literal sense, it is impossible to write or
> read a biography of Milton without sympathizing with Mr Dick's
> unfortunate obsession: it is very hard to keep King Charles' head from
> unwelcome apparition. He died, it may be, with his 'singing-robes' about
> him; but they were stained, if not with the life-blood of his King, at all
> events with the mud of controversy, a stain less poetical, and harder in the
> cleansing.

When, from biography, she passes to Milton's poems, perennial
storehouse of study for the girls of Victoria College, Belfast, her mind
immediately presents an unresponsive and glazed surface, and the
voice of the twelve-year-old rebel browsing among the books of
Ballygowan House comes across loud and clear:

> 'Paradise Lost' is what we were wont to call in the days of our youth a
> 'Sunday book'. This is psychologically and historically the reason for the
> unpopularity of John Milton. He comes before the bar in those Sessions of
> the Poets which every sufficiently youthful reader holds at intervals, only
> to find the jury hopelessly prejudiced. Not that it ever returns an
> unfavourable verdict. It has not the courage. John Milton is too eminent a
> person. But it damns with its praise: it convicts him of Moral Sublimity
> and Austere Grandeur, and sentences him to isolation for life.
>   Being a Sunday book means that you set him on a shelf by himself, along
> with, say, the Pilgrim's Progress; banish him at once from the cheerful,
> graceless fellowship of the ungodly, who bear you company throughout
> the week, the 'rakehelly rout of ragged rhymers', ragged as far as the
> covers go, which but bespeaks their greater popularity: a stout unwieldy
> Shakespeare, a well-worn Byron, a still more well-worn Scott, an
> atrocious English translation of 'Monte Cristo' and 'The Three Musquet-

eers'. John Milton is on a shelf by himself, and there he is likely to remain. For as once was said of the higher walks of Theology, most of us sit down on the edge of the holy ground, under pretext of taking off our shoes.

This was altogether too much for Professor George Saintsbury to whom *Pilgrim's Progress* was the embodiment of Burke's *On the Sublime and Beautiful*. Of course he was totally unaware of the child whose mind had been haunted for years by the wicket gate. There are pencil underlinings beneath 'along with', 'banish' and 'cheerful' in Helen's second paragraph, and the margin is glossed: 'P.P. one of the cheerfullest bks in the world.'

But, being Helen Waddell, she cannot maintain a negative stance for long: her powers of sympathy and compassion force her to enter into the man himself, to ignore both Johannes Miltonus, set for the defence of Parliament, and John Milton, author of *Paradise Lost*, and search out 'Milton — Mr John' as he was called in the catalogue that kindled Dr Johnson's wrath. This she does with notable skill:

One grows weary of the broad divisions, of the drama in three acts which is supposed to represent his life. It doesn't represent it: what does go to the making of it are the stray impulses stirring in the blood when he wrote the 'Song on May Morning'; the dreams of his future masterpiece as he sat over the 'Trinity' manuscripts on sunny mornings in Aldersgate Street; the vision of liberty that swept over him, as over Coleridge long after, quickening his pulses 'like a wind from the sea'; the long hours of depression, so pathetically dreaded — 'the weight of an immeasurable discouragement'; the rare moments of uplift at the thought of his great sacrifice; the heart-burning when they gibed him because he was blind, and because he was unpopular at College. We have had enough of generalizing, we want humanity: not the stately sonnet on his blindness, but the exceeding bitter cry —
      'O dark, dark, dark! amid the blaze of noon,
      Irrecoverably dark!'
That, read it as often as you will, can never lose the sheer physical shock of pain with which you first came upon it. . . .

The eighth and final chapter of the thesis, entitled *Civitas Dei*, is a deeply-moving exposition of Milton's last years. Yet throughout, one is conscious of a note of special pleading which seems to be that of Helen the Presbyterian herself. She recalls Milton the boy-priest, fired with childish zeal to spend his life in the holy places of the faith, to whom music was a passion only equalled by his turbulent love of liberty and free speech. How then did he come to desert the Church? In a passage of noble prose, she sketches Archbishop Laud's work of restoration in Lambeth Chapel after its desecration under Elizabeth I, when the stained glass was dashed from the windows, the Communion table dragged into the centre, the Crucifix in the East window smashed beyond repair — and in the midst of the desolation, the archbishop with his own hands helping to repair and restore:

> In truth, there are less pleasing objects for contemplation than that ungainly little figure, toiling at his labour of love: and the light falls from those same stained windows with something of a transfiguration on the eager hands, those same old hands that are to be stretched through prison gratings in benediction over Strafford's doomed head.
>
> But John Milton stood without, with unbowed head. Something in him revolted at all that splendid state. Is it simply a concession to the temper of the age . . . that having gone one mile with the Puritan party in the demand for freedom of thought, he will go with them twain in their hatred of ceremonial? In dealing with so strongly-marked an individuality as Milton's, it is as well to keep 'environment' and 'the influence of contemporary opinion' as much out of one's mouth as possible. Milton did that which was right in his own eyes, without fear or favour. 'A man may be heretic in the truth,' he writes in his imperious pride, 'and if he believes things only because his pastor says so, or the assembly so determines, without other reason, though his belief be true, yet the very truth he holds becomes his heresy.' And so to Milton the splendid pomp of liturgy and ceremonial are the trappings, tawdry and tarnished, of an outworn paganism, the half-broken mould of a spirit that had long since fled. 'How have they disfigured and defaced that more than angelic brightness, the unclouded serenity of the Christian religion, with the dark overcasting of superstitious copes and flaminical vestments. Tell me, ye priests, wherefore this gold, wherefore these robes and surplices over the gospel? Is our religion guilty of the first trespass, and hath need of clothing to cover her nakedness? What doth this else but cast an ignominy upon the perfection of Christ's ministry, by seeking to adorn it with that which was the poor remedy of our shame?'

To this passionate indictment, H. W. adds the acute observation: 'It is still an affair of aesthetic judgement, the temper that would prefer Aphrodite rising from the sea to a Madonna robed and crowned.' And then, the schoolgirl who daringly dipped her fingers into a holy-water stoup, made a large Sign of the Cross, and lost herself in the pageantry of a High Mass in a Belfast church, and the woman who, all her life, felt forced to return to St Augustine, the mediaeval hymns, and the Latin liturgy in order to slake her spiritual thirst, ends on a note of tender understanding of the Puritan poet's *Psychomachia*, as the fourth-century Prudentius called it, that 'Battle of the Soul' which poses an eternal problem to the artist: 'There is no fight with dragons,' as Helen has put it in *The Wandering Scholars*, 'but the harder problem, the strife between Beauty and Beauty, the one destructive of the other.' She draws her argument to a close in cadences that remind one almost inevitably of the organ music that Milton himself so loved:

> Death is nearing him. It matters little, the Saturnalia of Charles' Court, the licence of the stage, the Prelatry that is scourging the Nonconformists with scorpions instead of whips, to this man to whom the night winds are already bringing
> 'Murmurs and scents of the infinite sea.'
> And yet, as he nears his end, something of the appeal of the venerable church comes upon him, and in his last published writings he speaks of the church from which he had gone out in anger, with something of the tenderness of a son. Rumour had it that he died a Catholic, and though that could never be with John Milton, it may have gained some colour from this strange new tolerance for his own Mother-church, the retreat on that assured authority which has seemed as the shadow of a great rock to many an undisciplined and weary spirit.

Her work completed, the Other Helen rose uppermost. 'I want to smell the old fields and chop onions for you at dinner and lie on the bed and shudder at Sydney's step on the stair — and I want to hear him say "Hi Auntie" and feel him on top of me:

> "Lay this earth upon thy heart,
> And thy sickness shall depart."'

There was a shadow over Degree Day: it had no fizz, since Meg was unable to be present, for the birth of her fourth child was imminent. On the strength of her brilliant performance, Queen's offered Helen a research scholarship. This was the Isabella Tod Memorial Scholarship tenable for three years, awarded in rotation in the Faculties of Arts, Science and Medicine to the woman candidate obtaining the highest place in the examinations. Its value, payable in three annual instalments, amounted to £9. No wonder that George Saintsbury in *Oxford Sixty Years Since* wrote of academic emoluments 'unworthy of a brick-layer or a window-cleaner, but such as in those benighted times gentlemen of breeding and more than some education were very glad to accept.' And women also sixty years later.

Gregory Smith was loth to lose Helen, but she deferred any decision on the expenditure of the princely sum until the reopening of the academic year: 'The one thing I'm thankful for at this minute', she told Meg, 'is that I haven't got to choose my subject till October. I think Gregory's fearfully pleased — you see, this is the first time the Studentship has ever been awarded. He wanted me to go to London and the British Museum — but I put my foot on that.' The letter concluded:

I do not want to do Research. I do not want to write anything more for ever and ever Amen. I want to eat gooseberries and talk in an *un*-intellectual manner to Sydney and Jack. You made my mouth water.

> Who doth ambition shun
> And love to lie ' the sun,
> Seeking the food he eats,
> And pleased with what he gets —

which is maybe more than Sydney's da will be when I am running the shanty and you laid by the heels. Hurry up, and have a long long summer. I had an enthusiastic letter of congrats from Harry: 'In you the Waddell intellect hath flowered, and reached its apogee.' I knew you would roll that last word under your tongue, and you'll use it in impossible conjunctions. Be awfully careful of yourself these days, my darling, do.

CHAPTER IV

WHEN QUEEN'S AWARDED Helen Waddell the 'Isabella Tod Memorial Scholarship tenable for three years', Professor Gregory Smith had suggested that she study at the British Museum and prepare a manuscript for publication — possibly from one of the lesser-known Elizabethan dramatists. This vision of unhampered freedom for scholarly work must have appeared to Helen the more entrancing since, in that same year, Maude Clarke, who had graduated with First Class Honours in History under Professor F. M. Powicke, had won the first scholarship in the Lady Margaret Hall examination, and was preparing to go into residence in the autumn of 1913. But Helen's vision fled before reality. As the summer months passed and the time for departure drew near, the gloom of Cedar Avenue deepened to such black despair that she was morally forced to change her plans and search for an alternative to Gregory Smith's proposal. Soon, she was writing to inform Meg of the cancellation of her plan to go to that London which, in the Scottish Dunbar's phrase, is 'of townes A per se':

> Will you be glad or sorry that I may not have to go to London after all? Gregory has hit on a subject — or rather I hit and Gregory approved — that I can get all the books for here. The reading will be something enormous, but it's a fascinating thing — and Gregory is *almost* excited over it; says it's absolutely fresh.
>
> Mother is like a different person since. It was getting like a kind of big black tunnel before her, worse luck; as for me, life has suddenly fallen flat, but with a pleasing flatness. It's worth it, to see her so happy. 'Parsimony of pain, glut of pleasure, these are the alternating ends of youth' — and as I told Gregory, London wouldn't have been glut of pleasure with someone in the background who counted the minutes from your outgoing till your incoming. And the gods will be good to me and take me some time, and let me go to the theatre every night . . . And I have settled down upon 'parsimony of pain'.
>
> It was about a week ago that Gregory sent for me, he being just home. He has been ill all summer, 'in the hands of the surgeons' as he said, and looks ten years younger and twenty years thinner, and he has shaved his moustache, and it has left him a mouth a little like the Earl of Shaftesbury's. I watched it with a kind of fascinated interest — it was like being introduced to a new

man, and I'd fall in love with him tomorrow if I got the slightest encouragement.

I have lured him into the first 'personal' remark I have had from him. He was in an uncommonly gamesome mood, had been shut up for days with a cold, and I think he was heart glad of somebody to make him laugh. Well, I propounded my subject, which is: 'Woman as a Dramatic Asset' — in other words, the evolution of us, the Eternal Feminine in fact, from Noah's wife in the Miracle Plays (as Gregory pointed out maliciously, Noah's prime comment on her gave the pitch for our later appearances —'Lord, but women be crabbed aye!') down through Portia and Cleopatra and the naughtiness of the Restoration to Bernard Shaw's Candida.

And Gregory rose from his seat. 'An excellent subject . . . absolutely fresh.' By this time he was tramping up and down. And then he sort of twinkled: 'And an excellent subject for *you*. . . . You have a good many of the qualifications. . . . ' He was gazing out of the window, but I knew by his back that he was laughing. And be it counted unto me for righteousness, I did not ask him what the qualifications were.

Meg, it makes up for London, for it is a subject that will be an abiding joy to me. And Gregory says it is certain of a publisher.

As it turned out, none of the research carried out by Isabella Tod's scholar was ever submitted to a publisher. It remains in scattered hand-written sheets of prose, bubbling over with humour, originality, and amazing breadth of scholarship. One complete chapter of eighteen pages, entitled The Thynge Herself was evidently planned to be the opening jeu d'esprit:

'Hast thou aught written there of the feminine gender?' said Diabolus Primus to Diabolus Secundus, as they fared together up Watling Street. They were carrying brief-bags, for it was the Day of Judgement when, as every medieval playwright knew, it was the duty of the smaller devils to appear as junior counsel for the prosecution. 'Yes,' said Diabolus Secundus with feeling, 'more than I may bere of rolles for to render.' This is the expression, rather more genial than usual, of the prevailing sentiment of medieval drama.

For the medieval playwright was a person without illusions. 'I always bless God', said William Morris, 'for making anything so strong as an onion.' It is the ideal temper in which to approach the grosser half of medieval literature. For though there are standpoints from which that literature will seem a
              'garden close
      Set thick with lily and red rose',
it was a walled garden, and on the other side of it the medieval bourgeois planted sage and onions, under correction from the great voice of Jean de Meung. Medieval drama is an alien growth from the red rose of the

Lancelot legend, or the white mysticism of the lily of the Graal: it sprang from a ranker soil.

For the drama is the expression of the bourgeois spirit in letters, the spirit that first became incarnate in Jean de Meung though it has since had many avatars, being indeed the strongest force after that divine impulse of which the Olympians are begotten. Classical drama had more exalted progenitors: 'Comedy rolled in shouting under the divine protection of the Son of the wine-jar.' But medieval drama had the bourgeois to its father, and for the centuries of its minority he was 'sole lord of the theater'. The thirteenth-century bourgeois slept too heavily of nights to be wakened by any dawn-song, the 'aubade' of exquisite suggestion; the prose epic of the Graal was too high a history for any but the Seigner of Cambrien and Messire Jehan, Seigner of Yule; but in drama, the bourgeois heard his own voice, saw himself 'put for it robustiously'. Laughter held both his sides when Noyes Wyffe obeyed with emphasis the Latin stage-directions, and Noah rubbed his head and said 'Marry, this is hotte!' And when Adam warned all men against trusting the woman and the Devil,

> The one more than the other . . .
> The sister and the brother,

he had his audience with him. Lyric and epic may be the lords spiritual and temporal of letters; the drama is the third estate.

Drama, the woman and the devil, the sister and the brother, were much in evidence in the writer's own life just then: for two years past, Helen had been wrestling with the devil for her brother's body as well as his soul,

> Mors et Vita duello
> Conflixere mirando.

To Meg, Helen wrote at Christmas 1912:

I'm sure you've been wondering that I didn't send you the socks and the address for Billy, but dear, he turned up on Saturday morning, could stand the place no longer. Do not worry about him, for even Dr Irwin is content that he has left, and says he is looking splendid, and that the one thing is for him to get into work at once. He was miserable at Haydock — nothing to do, nothing to think about, nobody to talk to but morphia maniacs, or regular lunatics, and he says he was just getting morbid. You needn't be afraid of his going back to the drug. I was talking to him by himself for a bit, and he speaks of it with a kind of shudder, says he is glad, *so* glad, to be cured, to be a man again, and that he would never have left the place only that he was afraid of it, for his will was getting weaker instead of stronger, and he was wild for something to do.

We'll have to pray for him desperately, but I am in great heart about him. He is trying to get a hospital somewhere but he says he will take the first job that turns up, so long as it isn't a cargo boat with too much spare time on board. He will never face that again. And he has set his face to the

Indian Medical, and Dr Irwin is encouraging him. He and I have a catchword to heart us and we shout it at each other parting — 'January 1913' — which is the first exam he will try for. I told him how it was you hadn't written at Christmas — and he smiled his old smile and said he knew all right.

Worry, according to Meg, melted Helen like snow. In a strange way, Billy was her counterpart and her letters over the next two years show that this brother of hers, who was more like a son, was never far from her thought. Her work began to suffer and, as she was putting nothing down on paper, she looked round for excuses: she felt she should read the entire literature of Europe before tackling the question of Romantic Comedy; the paragraphs were already marshalling in shadowy battalions but she couldn't bring them into action yet awhile. The time and place were unpropitious. 'It is utterly impossible to do it,' she explained apologetically, 'unless you can trust to the lightness of your hand. It's like making paste for pies. And that is really why it progresses so slowly.' Yet one can already discern *The Wandering Scholars* in faint outline, and the ground was undoubtedly being prepared for lectures on the mediaeval mime which she was to give at Oxford in 1921. At the time, however, she grew dissatisfied with the whole theme. 'The research subject I chose,' she wrote to Dr Taylor, 'the development of feminine interest in drama, is not big enough. Working at it, I found I was continually leaving it for a much finer thing — the discovery of love as a dramatic subject, almost *the* dramatic subject. Now the book will be the study of the slow change from the medieval distrust of it to the Neo-Platonic ideal of men like Sidney and Spenser. It's just a fragment of the great battle between the spirit and the flesh. What I have written won't be altogether wasted; some of it will be recast. Curious how one gets the whole history of man's thought of love in Shakespeare alone — the scholar's impatience in Love's Labour's Lost, the idealist's revolt in Hamlet, the sensualist's revolt in Troilus, and for The Tempest — well, you'll have to read Sir Arthur Quiller-Couch on that.'

Under Gregory Smith's direction, she was already tracing the origins of the Liturgical Play as a dramatized form of the liturgy, adapted for the pivotal festivals of Christmas and Easter. To Dr Taylor, avid for every scrap of her work, she quoted a passage based on the usage of Mont St Michel that might have been lifted straight out of the books she published more than a decade later:

For the last three days of Holy Week, the extinction of the lights at Matins flung the cathedral into darkness, and symbolized the dying of the Light of the World: but while the third nocturn was being chanted on Easter morning, four of the brethren vested themselves, and one clad in white concealed himself in the Sepulchre of the dead Christ, while the other three, habited like women and 'stepping delicately, as those who seek something,' came up the aisle. The great question and answer,

'Quem quaeritis in sepulcro, O Christicolae?'

'Jesum Nazarenum crucifixum, O caelicolae',

had long been familiar in the antiphons, but one can imagine the thrill of the simple congregation when the challenge first rang from the very Tomb itself. It was a fine instinct that chose the most dramatic moment of the history of the faith: and the resurrection of that instinct in the Church that had sworn its extinction is one of those ironies which the Comic Spirit is never weary of contemplating.

'I found I was continually leaving it for something finer.' Helen was to do precisely that all her life, as her unfinished papers and unfulfilled hopes testify. During her first year of research, she did publish a book, but not as a result of plodding investigation. The 36 poems of *Lyrics from the Chinese* were chanced on by happy accident; they blinded her with sudden illumination and fixed her future. Naturally Meg was the first to be told of her discovery:

I am just fresh from Gregory, and he was positively excited, and as for myself, I'm 'lepping' —
Do you remember the old shelf of 'Chinese Classics' by James Legge D.D., Trubner & Co., London and Hong Kong — the very name of it is an incantation — I've worked beside it for years and dipped into most of them, dull dogs enough, chiefly sayings of emperors and sages. . . . Well, it happened on Tuesday. I had sickened my very soul over Jean de Meung and yearned for anything, by way of dry disinfectant. And I reached out to the familiar shelf, and something guided my hand to one of the volumes I had never opened before. It opened itself at

'The gourd has still its bitter leaves'

the first of the lyrics that I send you, and I found that I was reading the prose translation of odes that were 'sung at the court of Loo in the 29th year of the Duke Seang' — in the sixth century before Christ, when Confucius was eight years old.

My breath came thick, my head swam round — for I know buried treasure when I see it, and not even the Reverend James Legge's awful and literal prose could hide the freshness of it. And in ten minutes I had written this. I'm going to give you the prose first. By the way, it's the cry of a woman who has turned her back on marriage for the sake of love.

The gourd has still its bitter leaves
And the crossing at the ford is deep.
If deep, I will go through with my clothes on,
If shallow, I will do so holding them up.

> The ford is full to overflowing,
> There is the note of the female pheasant.
> The full ford will not wet the axle of my carriage.
> It is the pheasant calling for her mate.
>
> The boatman keeps beckoning,
> And others cross with him, but I do not,
> Others cross with him, but I do not.
> I am waiting for my friend.

I do not think you will be disappointed in the lyrical rendering of it
—it deserves a page to itself:

> The gourd has still its bitter leaves,
> And deep the crossing at the ford,
>   I wait my lord.
>
> The ford is brimming to its banks;
> The pheasant cries upon her mate.
>   My lord is late.
>
> The boatman still keeps beckoning,
> And others reach their journey's end.
>   I wait my friend.

I did about half a dozen more and sent them to Gregory last night. He
saw me in the library today and came for me straight. I was expecting a
'Very pretty . . . quaint . . . but I think you had better finish your serious
work first, and then you might do something with them.' As a matter of
fact, my 'serious work' is apparently thrown to the winds. 'Have you any
more?' was his first demand. 'Here, come into my room for a minute.' So I
went. He was rushing to his lecture, but he was for once roused. 'Go on
with them? Certainly — by all means.'

Seven lyrics re-cast in twelve hours called for no alteration
whatever, and within a week, she had added another twenty:

I have seen Gregory, and I am to work on the lyrics until I have enough to
fill a book, get them typed, 'and then I'll help you to hawk them round',
says Gregory with his slow smile.

'And I may drop the pre-Shakespearian woman just for a little?' says
Helen Jane eagerly.

Gregory remembers that he is Professor of English Literature:

'I was just thinking when I got your MSS this morning that she was rather
in the background. And' — his gravity is portentous — 'if these lyrics of
yours hadn't been so exceptional, I am afraid you would have heard from
me today.'

Meg, that man is a joy to me.

'What about the title?'

'Lyrics from the Chinese?'

'Very good,' says Gregory. Then a flash crosses his very impassive countenance. 'I've just thought of one. I shan't tell you.'

'*Please.*'

'How about "Chunks from China"?' — And I think they must have heard us laughing in the library. He went through every one of the twenty, criticizing and appraising. But my triumph came when he came to one I had hesitated about sending him. It was too elaborate, I thought, for the old simplicity. But I knew it was a musical thing — how musical I didn't know until he began reading it aloud in his wonderful voice. And he lingered out the lines till before he knew he was chanting; three-quarters way through he found what he was doing, looked horribly embarrassed, and finished in a voice absolutely toneless. This is it:

I saw the marsh with rushes dank and green,
And deep black pools beneath a sunset sky,
And lotus silver-bright
Gleamed on their blackness in the dying light,
    As I passed by.

And all that night I saw as in a dream
Her fair face lifted up
Shine in the darkness like a lotus-cup,
Snow-white against the deep black pool of night,
    Till dawn was nigh.

In an incredibly short time Helen had assembled 36 poems, annotated them, added an exquisite Introduction written in prose of great distinction, submitted the book to Constable who accepted it at once, and had the satisfaction of seeing her first publication issue from that eminent house before 1913 was out. She dedicated it to her father, and sent the first copy to Meg with this inscription:

Here's in token of the day
You and I will go away,
You and I alone;
And on some soft summer night
Through the dusk and candlelight
Enter Babylon.

'The Chunks' as they were invariably called gave Helen immediate standing. 'Like "Sonnets from the Portuguese" may not "Lyrics from the Chinese" serve to disguise a new and powerful poet?' James Douglas asked in *The Star*. Within a couple of months the book had sold a thousand copies, and the publishers were receiving applications for leave to set the songs to music. (At home in Sussex, a

twenty-one-year-old Alec Robertson initiated his series of eight
settings with 'a very smooth and flowing melody' moving to 'faster
and brighter' over brilliant horns, to a dying fall marked dreamily
pppp. He completed his compositions as a young Army officer in India
in 1915.) Helen's brother Sam, actor and dramatist, executed a
triumphant *pas seul* in Donegal Place when he informed Martha
Waddell that 'A.E.' — George Russell — had reviewed them and they
were the talk of Dublin. Success brought a certain solace to Helen in
her loss of Maude Clarke, who had gone up to Oxford a few months
previously.

Three letters from Maude to Helen have been preserved. They
demonstrate more powerfully than any analysis their extraordinary
meeting of minds. Written in large bold clear script, the letters bear no
date and address no person, except the earliest which is headed
'Dumfries 2.10.1913.' All three are written on lined sheets torn out of
an exercise book; the first describes her circular tour en route for
Oxford:

I am writing to you because you hinted I wouldn't. Also I don't want to
write to my Father.

It wasn't very interesting last night. The sea was painfully calm and I
was thus robbed of my chiefest pleasure which is to look the embodiment
of enjoyment when every one else is longing for the final shipwreck.

Just one thing happened which may amuse you. As soon as the boat
started I went to the upper deck where it was gloriously windy and
established myself in a corner to contemplate at leisure the blackness of the
water and the churned-up foam. A few minutes later this retirement was
invaded by a presuming party in an overcoat, chaperoned by the voice of a
gentleman. I think he was an officer. Anyway he had a glimmering of
strategy for he took up a position which entirely blocked my retreat from
the corner. The following dialogue perforce ensued:

'It is nice and dark up here.'
'Very dark.'
A perceptible pause.
'Far nicer than on the lower deck.'
'Much nicer.'
'There aren't nearly so many people.'
'Not nearly so many.'
Another pause.
'How nice the searchlight looks.'
'Very nice.'
A very long pause.

Then I looked up and discovered the invading force had retreated
silently and in good order. It was quite amusing when we came to

Stranraer and I descended into the glare of electric light to speculate which of the half-dozen young men who eyed me unobtrusively had been so dismayed by my emphatic manner of assent.

The story is true.

Carlisle

I have just concluded a most exciting hour at Carlisle. Of course this morning was an undiluted horror. In the end, or at the end of my courage, I lied generously and bolted by a ridiculously early train. So I had to put in an hour at 'bonnie Carlisle' while awaiting the Newcastle connection.

And it was an exciting hour. I shoved my luggage into the expectant arms of a porter and extracted from him a promise to produce it at the Newcastle train. Then I made for the Cathedral, and spent fifteen minutes there gloating over the colour of the east window. I prowled round the Fratry for another ten minutes. Mercifully there is no crypt to tempt me. The castle proved to be out of the question so I cut along for the best second-hand bookshop. The vendor proved to be a delightful person. I explained that I had a minute and a half to catch an imperative train, that I had money to spend, that I wanted books of the genuine kinds — chronicles, law books, first editions. In a flash I was in the midst of wonders. A Renascence Plutarch in nine volumes — glorious Greek type; Black's Tasso in two white vellum volumes; 'The Clergyman's Lawbook'; Newcastle's letters. I made a hasty selection. The book man made a rough calculation. I hurled the money, also counted roughly, at him and fled incontinently for the station. Now hear the sum of my treasure. Algernon Sidney's 'Discourse of Government' — a first edition. Sir Philip Sidney's 'Arcadia' — slightly imperfect but at least a 16th century copy. This is for you if you are very good. 'Ecclesiastical Documents', Camden Society. 'The Pylgrymage of Sir Richard Guylforde to the Holy Land, A.D. 1506', also Camden Society. Now tell me quickly that I have the book-lover's flair.

I got the train, in fact I am in it at this moment, but there is one man in Carlisle who feels that he has entertained an angel by no means unawares.

at 5 Beauclerc Terrace
Sunderland

You can reward my efforts with a letter to this address.

The neuralgia is a little better today.

Yours
Maude.'

When she finally reached Oxford, she was by no means pleased with what she found, and despatched this very Irish letter to her sympathetic compatriot:

Lady Margaret Hall
Oxford

Were you angry because I did not write or did you guess why? Never in my life have I felt so incapable and inarticulate. This time I think the fault is in my stars. Briefly I hate most of the people and I am hustled by the system of work.

Two essays a week for Miss Lodge, and I am producing such abortions that she is frankly puzzled. She asked me on Thursday if I detested the constitutional side of history — which conveyed her meaning to me quite adequately. Two essays a week for Mr Penson, my economics coach. I don't worry about their quality but they take up an abominable amount of time.

And the irony of the thing is that my lectures are fascinating and infinitely suggestive. I go home from them raging that I must waste my time over these miserable essays. Up to this I have not been able to read for a single lecture. I am furiously angry. If I say anything to Miss Lodge she will insist upon my spending three years instead of two at the degree course — which would merely prolong the agony. I may remark that every one here writes two essays a week for each tutorial. So there is no escape from that senseless system — absolutely the worst thing in the world for me.

I wish I could convey the spirit of this place. It is like a girls' school where there is an excellent understanding between pupils and teachers. The air is heavy with deference to authority in any form. The third year students reverence the dons . . . the second year students reverence the dons and the third years . . . the first year — well, there reverence is boundless. They grovel. Etiquette has them fast in its net. Fifty times a day I have to remind myself that I am not here to be bullied. You know that I am by nature submissive.

Tomorrow I am going to make a declaration of Independence. I shall ask Miss Lodge for an order to read in the Bodlian [sic]. The library here is appalling but it contains all that I want for her wretched essays. I should like to entrap her into saying that I must not work for my lectures. No one here does work for them. They are voted 'no use for schools'. Damn!

I should like to tell you about those lectures. Mr A. J. Carlyle lectures on the theory of Feudalism. His knowledge of the Middle Ages is enormous. He began his course by saying that the two great barriers to the understanding of medieval society were the Renaissance and the Romantic movement. The one for its contempt, the other for its idealism. Yesterday he was tracing the idea of personal loyalty through the medieval epic. The literature for the subject is infinite. I also go to Mr Austin Poole's lectures on Anglo-Saxon diplomatic. I am the only person attending that course — it does not pay for schools. He is teaching me how to criticize the form of documents, how to date them, how to detect a forgery. It is fascinating work.

Do you realise my condition of shamed irritation?

I don't think I can write any more tonight. It is very late. Anyway I have cleared the ground. I will write later on in the week. Yours, Maude.

Since so little is known directly about Maude Clarke, one of the most brilliant women in the Oxford of her time, perhaps Helen

Waddell's biographer may be forgiven for including Maude's third letter — like the first, it bears no address or apostrophe and plunges at once *in medias res*:

It was a very good letter. Perhaps I will answer it tomorrow. Tonight I must merely relieve my mind in hope of winning sleep thereby. You remember my intention to work at the medieval study and influence of Aristotle's 'Politics'. Well, since I came up I have been having a glorious time working at the subject. All week I was in a state of exaltation about the fascinating people who wrote about it. I felt I was discovering. Tonight, just half an hour ago, I picked up Barker's 'Political Theories of Plato & Aristotle', a book I had never the energy to read, intending to glance indulgently at his bibliography. Something in the Index caught my eye and I found, horribile dictu in the Epilogue, ALL MY STUFF. Helen, it isn't even his own. He casually quoted from Sandys' 'History of Classical Scholarship'. How I cursed! All my people — bar one little one. Albertus Magnus, Dante, Gilles de Rome, Siger de Brabant, Marsiglio of Padua are mentioned categorically.

The really funny part of it is that this afternoon I was thinking a little complacently that Mr Barker was the one person I would like to show my essay to. I knew it was the sort of thing he would like to do.

What should I do? I have worked for a fortnight at the thing. I am tempted to go on, read all the medieval political people again and write on a theory which is perhaps true — that the 'Politics' were too secular and too unacademic for the medieval scholar. Politics is in a limbo between Art and Philosophy. That is why it so seldom comes to its own. It is a big subject after all, involving the whole question of the value of political theory and its relation to literature & theology.

I am purely shooting this at you as it comes to me. Tell me what you think about it. At least sympathize with me for my bereavment [*sic*].

In spite of the intolerable load of work, the Lady Margaret Hall scholar kept an observant eye on Blackwell's window display to report on the progress of the Chunks. The glad day dawned when she was able to inform Helen that two prospective buyers had been unable to obtain it, since all the copies were sold. Cheered by a sense of achievement, Helen entered upon 1914 in a spirit of sober optimism. Edward Arnold, the educational publishers, had engaged her to supply four books of fairy tales — 51,000 words in all — for children seven to nine years old, at a total payment of £39. Her ambition soaring, she also embarked on a play, *The Spoiled Buddha*. Meanwhile Gregory Smith was watching the rising of the star with gratified contentment. 'The Chunks are selling marvellously. Sir Hiram Wilkinson is taking one to the Chinese ambassador,' Helen told Meg. 'Gregory is his very nicest about it, and wants me to send one to

Professor Saintsbury.' Hitherto the almost mythical figure of George Saintsbury, professor of rhetoric and English Literature at Edinburgh University, distinguished critic and historian with more learned books to his name than anyone could count, had been known to Helen only as her external examiner in finals at Queen's. On 19 June 1914, Gregory Smith invited Helen to a dinner-party at his house in order to meet the friend and collaborator of his early academic work in the School of English. 'It was from Liverpool I started on a June night, with a horrible cold, and a sense of overwork,' Saintsbury recalled later, 'and hardly the faintest premonition of what was going to happen.'

At this point one feels impelled to beg pardon of Saintsbury's shade, to apologize to the man who so often expressed scorn of 'the disgusting and most idle controversy' that often followed publication of letters, and made people of taste pray that nothing biographical should ever be published about themselves. As a letter-writer, Helen ranked him with Walpole and Lamb, and considered his letters quintessential to an understanding of the man. Let that be the present writer's defence. He was to ask Helen's leave to destroy the bulk of her letters for, 'though there is nothing that any one might not read, there is a good deal that they don't deserve to.' Happily some of hers escaped the holocaust, and a fair number of his to her remain to puzzle the expert palaeographer. His cacography, he explained, was a purely physical thing, the power went out of his right hand after scarlet fever in childhood, leaving his wrist unsupported. In *A Second Scrap Book*, having written of his very bad sight and a malformation of the hand that made his script an astonishment and a hissing and a curse to all mankind, he added a characteristic footnote probably meant for Helen: '"No *man* can read it", as De Quincey says of something else. But oddly enough, women sometimes can.'

As one would expect of such a man, there is not a trace of the fatuous or foppish in his letters; they scintillate with flashes of wit, literary allusion and playful fancy moving lightly over a groundwork of deep understanding and affection which thinks in jest and feels in earnest. After their first social contact in 1914, Helen and G.S. — whom she usually referred to as 'the Saint' — were to meet face to face only once more, in 1931; yet his influence over her mind and outlook was perhaps even more profound than Gregory Smith's. 'I don't mind confessing — such is my both excessive and infinite folly,' he wrote to Helen, 'that *the* two great men of letters to whom I should like to think that I stood as a mere infinitesimal fraction to a vast integer of somewhat similar material are Donne and Swift.' Did Saintsbury see in Helen a counterpart of Swift's Stella? He was 44 years Helen's senior and devoted to his invalid wife, his two sons and small grandson, who all figure in his letters, but he met any imputation of old age with a chuckle: 'I am old enough in body — and I always was "a melancholy man" in a way but I have never been less than twenty or more than five and twenty in the not-body, a word by the way that I never saw anywhere — did you?'

In an appreciation after his death, Helen drew a parallel between him and Donne:

> Both were of high pride and in their youth of towering ambition, and both were checked and frustrated of what they had judged to be their vocation. . . . Both were denied security and reputation through the best years of their manhood, and found in place of them a passion and mastery and exultancy in living that glows to the last twilight of their day: and in the end, when they had come to their strength without it, they had honour in all men's mouths. Saintsbury's five times repeated failure at Oxford to obtain a fellowship cost him something more than the initial sharpness of humiliation — leisure for an absolute exactness of scholarship, even though it was more than made up for by his depth and range. . . . He married young: he had Prospero's island of enchanted lawn at the beginning of his life instead of at the end, and all his years were transfigured by it: and he was supremely his own master.

From their first moment of meeting at Gregory Smith's table, Helen and G.S. had responded to one another as iron to the magnet's breath. They invented an elaborate game called 'Samarcand' — spelt indifferently with a c or k — geographically situated 'dans la Bokhara' but quintessentially abiding only 'in the imperishable recesses of fantastic memory (as somebody once said) & that memory is indivisibly & inextensibly yours and mine. Is it not so, Quintessence whom at various times they have called Helen?' His request for her photograph met with a blank refusal: let him think of her only by candlelight, as he had seen her at Gregory Smith's house:

Sep. 24. 1914

Madam,
    (I may not alas! call you 'Dear') Inconstancy has been granted as one of the privileges of your 'rebel sex' as the poet so justly calls it — also cruelty. But while the inconstancy has no limits the cruelty should have some. You are doubtless aware (indeed the fact has been made the basis of venerable jokes) that the Society for the Preventing Cruelty to Animals publishes lists at intervals of the nature & number of the cruelties it has avenged — as thus:

'Cat   — Putting walnut shells
        on feet of   /'

To this list will now be added
'*Professor* (aged)   Refusing photograph to   /'
    I trust *this* abomination will be, & will remain, unique in the annals of
inhumanity! It were idle to reiterate the other stock charge of want of logic.
Otherwise I would ask how you ensure my 'only thinking of you by
candlelight' through not sending me your photograph? The connection, I
trow, is excessively anaesthetic. . . .
    P.S.
    But it would have been so nice to look at you by candlelight! I love
candles & always use them — in two mighty candlesticks rising from the
floor. You might have been held between!
    P.P.S.
    My eyes & my heart don't live in cat & dog fashion. My eyes tell my
heart what to love, & my heart tells my eyes what to delight in.
    (Stap my vitals, if that isn't pretty!)
    P.P.P.S.
    'I was nice to you.' Are you nice to me?

Battledore and Shuttlecock needed no photographs: the impression
each made on the other was never forgotten. Helen had left Gregory
Smith's house on that memorable night at 10.30 p.m. expressing a
wish, as she did so, that the 10.30 limit could be extended to 10.30 a.m.
The reciprocal attraction had been exciting: Saintsbury had found her
good to play with? In answer to her teasing, he was later to recall:

Beloved and Fair,
    You good to play with! oh Heavens!
            'Some plays with some: some will with
                                others be
        Sometimes: — all times, all plays, all
                                ways, with thee!'
You don't know who wrote that: I think it was the Judicious Poet: & I fancy
he prided himself especially on the 'Sometimes'. If you think of it it is really
a great thing logically, metrically (some-times) & poetically. Our plays
have alas! been limited to a certain amount of writing & a tiny but seraphic
one of talking, hearing, seeing & even (Laus Deo —) the smallest but still
very effective *feeling*. For even the banal handshake *sometimes* establishes
the electric circuit; & when your gracious shoulder touched mine & set us
off (*though you did not know it at the moment — don't say you did*) straight to
Samarcand — there was no doubt of it. But if your still more gracious wish
to substitute 10.30 a.m. for 10.30 p.m. had come off, *how* we might have
extended the play! Well, well! in such a case 'on [pourrait]★ peut être de

---

★The square brackets indicate an editorial guess: the original is indecipherable.

bonne [faire rage de] plaisir' to adapt a favourite quotation of mine (I am not sure I have not inflicted it on you before) the context & origin of which it is not lawful to mention, as Theocritus observes. . . .'

And when she saucily asked whether he'd like to submit her to another *viva* as at Queen's in 1912, he replied: 'Did I wish I had *you* for a viva? The words are divisible into as many meanings and treatments as would make a folio of Scholastic Philosophy — & to every book & chapter & section & clause & so on there could only be appended the most unscholastic response "Oh didn't & wouldn't & shouldn't I!"' As for the charge of affectation which, so she told him, had been levelled against her: 'Well I ought to be a judge. Now I never thought for one second of your being affected on that unforgettable evening at Gregory's. I shouldn't have minded if you had been: but you *weren't*. You are Helen Helenizing in Helenity — yourself & nothing else. For which let us thank the Lord!'

She never experienced the slightest difficulty in Helenizing in Helenity, but what of the research scholarship that had so far nothing to show for it? Saintsbury added his voice to Gregory Smith's in urging her to go up to Oxford. Helen's mother's cousin, the lawyer R. I. Martin, had already come forward with an offer of substantial help — an act of generous reparation for having ignored the youngest child of the family in the dry all-too-legal proposals he had put to her brother Martin and the elder boys, after their father's death. 'He was my mother's cousin — my *own* mother,' Helen informed Dr Taylor, 'immensely prosperous, very legal in manner, and rather too much given to "bossing" his whole connection, but he is one of the kindest men I know: his good deeds are endless, and at least as many are done in private as in public. . . . He is very much interested in me, but I baffle him. He wanted to send me to Oxford — at his expense: and though he has forgiven me for refusing, he still thinks it a piece of incredible obstinacy and folly.' It was all right for men to talk, but the old nagging problem remained: could poor wee mother be persuaded to let Helen cross the sea and pledge herself to academic study for a whole three years, when she could scarcely let her out of her sight for an afternoon's golf, once in three weeks? She said so. At this, Gregory Smith gave up the struggle. He had quoted Saintsbury to her, and unbent so far as to admit that he had never met either man or woman who could equal her in scholarship. If her study and research were to close now, it would be a loss not only to herself, not only to her subject, but in fact to the world at large. His plea was unavailing. 'Well,' he said heavily, half to himself, 'it means your career will be literary, not academic. You've shut the gates on that.'

Looking back, Helen saw herself at this time as 'an undisciplined eager grasping thing — desperately hungry to live,' and summed up her experience in a passage from Hugh Walpole's novel, *Fortitude*: 'It is a trifle sententious, this quotation, but it's good. It's the four countries a man passes through, before he knows fortitude. First, the country of *Lacking all Things*: second, the country of *Possessing all Things* — more making shipwreck here than in the first: third, *Losing all that which you have*: fourth, and most terrible, *Knowing what you have missed*. If a man has that knowledge and faces it without murmuring, he has won his soul. That is a free translation of what he says. I like it. For usually one thinks of "knowing what you've missed" as a sort of irremediable canker of one's mind: it's a relief to think of it as a challenge to your courage.'

Fortitude had stamped Helen Waddell's life since 20 June 1901, the day of her father's death, and it was deepened during the years of young womanhood by a spiritual ascesis far surpassing the exercises of any monastic novitiate. She was to look back on the decade of her twenties as an interplay between negation and enrichment: in the final analysis enrichment won, so that to Hugh Walpole's four countries she would have added a fifth — *Knowing what you have Gained*. The testing gave her a lasting philosophy of life. Suffering and negation, she would argue, are necessary if life is to be whole; failure to give the bitter of the sweet is a refusal to face life, a selfish desire for enrichment without the anguish of the struggle. A cry, drawn from Hezechiah's prayer (Isaiah 38), runs through her letters and published work, and sums up the pattern of her life: 'O Lord, by these things men live, and in all these things is the life of my spirit.' Nevertheless the gains were tremendous. A mind such as hers needed the razor-blade sharpness of masculine intellects like Gregory Smith and Saintsbury — these men were a university in themselves, and they gave unstintingly. No one could have profited more.

For Helen 1914 was a momentous year for, in addition to one 'Saint', another saint entered her life to penetrate it at a completely different and more profound level. The Reverend George Pritchard Taylor, M.A., D.D. (1855–1920), for five years the recipient of weekly letters from her, was born in the Gujurat Province of India, graduated from Queen's, and in 1877 sailed for India again where he worked as a Presbyterian missionary until his death 43 years later, returning to Europe only twice, in 1890 and in 1914. During his second visit he preached at the church frequented by the Waddells, and was afterwards invited to their home. His experienced eye and almost feminine intuition summed Helen up very exactly. He repeated his visits and before bidding a final farewell, he asked Helen with great tact and delicacy whether she would allow him to provide a small annuity to enable her to buy books to ease the problem of research. Happily married but childless, he made no claims whatever: he merely asked her acceptance of £80 a year. She cut it down at once to £60, but his ingenuity devised all kinds of extras and, for the first time in her life, she was 'affluent'. Their beautiful relationship is an idyll: his very selflessness made its own impact, and she responded with the pent-up love of her deeply-affectionate nature:

As if you hadn't overwhelmed me enough, you say in that adorable little aside, that the pounds are to be guineas. That was what touched me most nearly. It's the tenderness of you in little things that makes me feel sometimes as if I could say my prayers to you. I want to tell you — I think it will please you more than anything — that you have somehow helped to 'justify the ways of God'. For once or twice I have wondered if I were right in giving up Oxford for what Gregory thought an unnecessary scruple. It didn't seem possible to vex my Mother and leave her alone. He warned me that I had ruined myself as far as academic high places went, but that it probably meant my life was to be literary, not academic.

I felt inclined to agree with him. But when I began the siege of the magazines, when I published the 'Lyrics' and found they would bring me in something like tuppence a year paid quarterly (I am not really fair to Messrs Constable: they have given me, I suppose, about £15); and when 'The Spoiled Buddha' came back from six editors, I grew a little afraid. Though I held to my soul Stevenson's assurance — I wonder if you know it? — 'So long as men do their duty, though it be greatly a misapprehension, they will be leading pattern lives; and though they may never come to lie beside a Martyr's Monument, they will find a safe haven somewhere in the Providence of God' — all the same I began to think it might have been 'greatly a misapprehension'. And, under five and twenty, one does not want a Martyr's Monument: and even the promise of the 'safe haven' is not as gracious as 'the haven where we would be'. Now do you see what you have done? And are you content?

He was more than content. From his return to India until his death, their unfailing weekly letters braved submarines and the hazards of war: they survive, a rich mine of biographical material. While his letters testify to his spirituality, culture, courtesy, and sheer human lovableness, it is a measure of Helen's versatility that, in addition to meeting him as an equal in discussions of mediaeval Latin hymns, doctrines of grace and election, problems of biblical exegesis, the Irish question and Rabelaisian buffoonery, she could also measure up to a letter such as the following, from this Master of Experimental Science:

> I notice that Hinton (the Fourth Dimension) calls the simplest fourth dimensional figure (the figure that a cube traces out when moving evenly in the fourth dimension) a 'tessaract'. Sometimes he spells it 'tesseract'. This term is new to me, but it's well to know it as being the fourth dimensional correlate of the three dimensional 'cube' or of the two dimensional 'square'. I think I'll send you my proof — just from analogy — that a rotated tesseract rotates about a plane.
>
>   . . . When dealing with four dimensional bodies one feels transported if not right into Alice's Wonderland, then into the very precincts. Lewis Carroll, you remember, was mathematical Tutor at Christ Church. Can it have been his mathematical studies that flowered into those delightful surprise stories of his?

The giving was not on his side alone: how much her letters meant to him is clear from the opening lines of his letter of 15 April 1915, written from the Stevenson Memorial College, Ahmadabad, of which he was founder and Principal:

> Helen dear,
>   It wasn't till this morning the mail came in — a day late — but your sweet letter is far more than worth all the agony of the longing and the waiting for it. The reading of it from beginning to end was a pure delight, but the sweetest part of it was at the close. My heart gave such a throb of joy when I read that tiny postscript: 'My father, I do love your letters'. Do you know, at times I've felt so timid about writing you them. I've been almost tortured with the fear that I had been presuming more than I ought, & possibly more than you wished, upon the goodness that accepted me as your father: but those kind words of yours are blessedly reassuring to me & comforting. To myself it has been all along such a joy, a joy quite unspeakable, to know that you consent to be a daughter to me; and I do so wish and pray that I may be to you all that a father ever can be to the best and dearest of daughters.

The weekly letters were being constantly delayed or lost, and lives disrupted, by the World War. Helen frequently refers to meetings with the 'young pups' of her College days — some of them never to return — resplendent now in naval officers' uniform, among them her two brothers Charlie and Tom. Billy, who for two years or more had been a ship's doctor, volunteered at once for the Medical Corps but was rejected; George was exempt as being on the eve of ordination to the Presbyterian ministry. As a family, the Waddells spoke to one another of the deepest spiritual realities with enviable ease. George had evidently revealed to Helen his deep distress over the suffering occasioned by the war. Her reply contains the germ that was to grow, mature, and burst into the unforgettable scene in *Peter Abelard* when he rescues the screaming rabbit from the trap. For that reason it must be quoted as it stands:

> Christ's Passion, if we believe it at all, was simply the Passion of God. The Atonement is a fact of eternity as well as of time, and Calvary was the eternal suffering of God made manifest for a few hours in mortal flesh — the suffering that the sin of the world always has inflicted, and will inflict to the end. And to realise it ever so little, remember the people who are taking the war hardest — poor J.D. heartsick over Roumania, make that knowledge and that sympathy infinite, and you begin to understand Gethsemane.
>
> But that suffering has no redemptive effect unless we choose. It's like letting the men die for us in the war, and never taking it to heart. You hear people say, 'But what if at the end of it all, the world is no better than it was before it?' I suppose it's up to us. Their suffering is 'vicarious': but it rests with the people they die for whether or not it shall be 'redemptive'.
>
> Remember that anything in Christ's life has infinity at either side of it. He is 'the Lamb slain before the foundation of the world' — the eternal travail of God . . . God omnipotent, but limited by his own creation, because He has made creatures so like Himself that to coerce them would be to take his divine gift from them — the free spirit of man.

George was to be ordained in 1915, and Helen watched him emerge from the chrysalis stage with pride: 'George looks beautiful in his new suit,' she told Meg. He had been called to Donoughmore in Co. Down and, in addition to planning the furnishing of his manse, his younger sister was busy plying him with brilliant suggestions for sermons, all of which he took in good part: 'I wonder how it is the things you write seem to catch one about the heart so much,' he wrote to her. And then, true son of his father, he added, 'But Helen, Cairncastle and the sea, that place had an air of its own. I don't wonder Papa was a missionary, for if I'd stayed much longer there I do believe the far-off call would have come to me.'

It did come, but from a quarter no one expected. Following upon ordination, he held his first Communion service, the solemn 'Sacrament' of the Presbyterian assembly, on 13 June 1915 at Donoughmore. The theme of his address was the psalmist's 'He knoweth our frame, He remembereth that we are dust':

> . . . We know, in our own hearts, how easily *we* forget. There are places of which we have said, 'If I forget thee, O Jerusalem!' — but life has brought us to new cities, pleasant havens, and the memory has dimmed:

and it is only perhaps a sudden breath of new-mown hay or the smell of the burning whins, that wakens the old crying in our hearts.

Aye, and there are people we thought we could never forget: lives that we have seen go down into death, and that seemed to take half our lives with them. But the graves fill up with the dust of the years, until some day you come on his name in some old school book, or you find a shell that you and he quarrelled over when you were children together by the sea, and the memory of him comes in like a flood, and you cry again — 'I am distressed for thee, my brother Jonathan.'

'Children together by the sea' — Billy and himself playing on the white sands of the Pacific coast near the shrine of the great Daibutsu at Kamakura? Billy held 'in remembrance'? On 16 June, three days later, Helen wrote to Dr Taylor:

I can only write to you a very little. Dear, do not break your heart for me, but I had bad news this morning. It is my brother, the one just older than I am, the George that you said was called for you. He died very suddenly last night of heart failure. He had gone to the South on Monday to stay for a little with Eileen's people — he was engaged to her. He was so dear that I think Christ looking upon him loved him. And we cared for each other so much that nothing can take him from me. . . . My father, it was a perfect death — to go straight into God's love from the dearest love he knew.
'The good, the better, and the last the best,
This is the order of the Master's wine.'

Her letter of the following week completed the natural sequence of events:

My Father,
. . . They sang the twenty-third psalm at his burying — a great company of them; the men who liked him so, and sang it to 'Martyrdom'. I chose it instead of the Burial Psalms, because it is a psalm of the living, and not of the dead. And when they came to
'And in God's house for ever more
My dwelling-place shall be,'
the peace of God came down upon the house. And I was satisfied at last. It seemed to take away something that was crushing my heart.

The evening that they brought him home was the hardest. I know now what made Abraham pray that he might bury his dead out of sight. The coffin lay there on the velvet pall with the flowers heaped round it, and I knew that George was inside it, dead. I did not feel him near me any more. I could not even remember him. And I lay that night and thought of him, but it was George dead that I thought of, lying under the flowers.

And then — I think one writes some chapters of the Bible in blood — I seemed to be living the eleventh chapter of John.

Jesus said unto her: 'Thy brother shall rise again', and Martha answered — I know now how drearily — 'I know that he shall rise again at the resurrection at the last day.'

Jesus said unto her, 'I am the Resurrection and the Life. He that believeth in Me though he were dead, yet shall he live, and whosoever liveth and believeth in me shall never die.'

'Believest thou this?'

Martha said unto him, 'Yea, Lord.'

And so I fell asleep.

The sun shone on him for his burying, just as it had shone for his ordaining. All his brothers had come to him: the four men that he cared for most, all ordained within a few months of him, came that morning and stood round him in a sore dumb agony; they took the last lift. And Meg and I watched him go out into the sunlight; it was as if he went out on a great wave of love. . . . Meg and I brought him a cross of white iris, with blue iris at its heart, and we hid our card in it, because the message was for his own self. 'I thank my God upon every remembrance of you.' He was no saint, my father, he was terribly human. But in one thing at least he was Christ's man, and that was his heart. He's in every verse of that thirteenth chapter of Corinthians. . . .

I can't write to you about your last letter. Your love comes round me like a shield.

To allay his anxiety, she added reassuringly: 'My father, I am not unhappy. I think the Valley of the Shadow is a little like the Valley of Humiliation, where Heartease grew.' After the funeral, she went straight to the sure refuge of Kilmacrew, and from there sent Dr Taylor a little poem with an explanation of its provenance:

It was the Sunday after he died, and I went out into a sunny green field with my nephew Charles, and saw the first wild roses. It was the sharpest thing that ever happened to me. These things belonged to him somehow. It would have seemed easier if he had died in winter. And days after, someone in the train had a great basket of red roses, and it wakened again. You will understand now what went to the writing of this:

> It had been easy to wind you
> Your winding sheet of the snows.
> What have I done that I find you
> Dead in the heart of a rose?

I have just seen a little snap of Geo, taken at the door of his Manse. It was one of the boys who was down seeing him, and snapped him the June morning before he went South. It's the great old house thick with ivy, such a promise of peaceful habitation in it, only that the windows are blank and empty. And the boy who was never to live in it is in the doorway, too small for me to see his face, but just the easy way he used to stand, with his great height and the long legs. And there is such a promise of summer about him, the grass on either side of the path high to the knee, and in it masses of poppies and tall white daisies. It was so like his life — on the doorstep of a house untenanted.

And it's good to remember looking at it, 'In my Father's house are many mansions.'

A whole year was to pass before she could bring herself to tell Dr Taylor why George, speaking as young David, had been distressed for his brother Jonathan. She was contributing to *Daybreak*, a children's magazine, the biblical events that would be published in 1949 under the title *Stories from Holy Writ*. On 30 May 1916 she wrote:

Did I tell you that I had read at last *A Service of Angels*? It was just before I fell to writing Jacob's vision of the 'traffic on the ladder'. I had never 'taken much account' of angels before: but I love the thought of them now. It fills the empty places that ache with their own beauty; and I am so much — by necessity — 'the Cat who walks by Himself' that I'll find them good company. It is nice to think that the beautiful 'old things' weren't scattered and exiled by the Nativity. (I always bore Milton a grudge for that.)

One I have always seen — George. 'It was impossible that he should be holden.' And I have sometimes wondered if he isn't in quest of that other brother, the Billy of 'White Iris', until he find him. For Billy — I never told you before, for I did not want to distress you when it was near, had lost his way. I wonder if you ever read Stevenson's 'Old Mortality' — the last paragraph on his friend who 'somewhere on the high seas of life, with his health, his hopes, his patrimony, and his self-respect, miserably went down.' It was drink in that case: with Billy, drugs. And he died fighting, but it was a hard fight. 'Derelict', he once described himself, with his funny twisted smile, 'Dangerous to navigation'. It was so hard a fight that when the end came so easily and the sea took him, we felt that God had been merciful. George and he were together always when they were little. Billy was not more than six months dead when George went to find him.

I was just twenty-two when I found out about Billy. After that, his death was easy. But of them all, he was the most — lovable is hardly the word, for George was that — and yet lovable *is* the word, for there was always a sort of half-whimsical tragedy about his gaiety, and Geo's was too spontaneous for that. He had an ugly mouth, and when he smiled it took the dearest curve I know.

You will see why those books you asked me to get, with their promise of 'some better thing' even for people like Billy, meant more to me than you knew. I don't know why I say 'even like Billy', for he was maybe

nearer God than the people who justify themselves, or the people who
have been fenced, like me, and sin unnoticeably.

Writing of Billy leads her to tell her correspondent of her current
research — an article on Chinese poetry that she intends to call 'The
Hyacinth Fields' (G. W. Massingham was to recognize at once the
style and accomplishment of the unusual contribution, and publish it
as his leader in *The Nation*):

> I was working at a Chinese article this week, and digressed to two Japanese
> lyrics — one, a mother's lament for her little son.
> > The hunter of dragon-flies
> > Today how far away
> > May he have gone!
> and another,
> > Being tired
> > Ah the time I fall into the inn.
> > — The wisteria flowers!
> There is a world between them, but they are alike in this, that they have
> captured the moment, blotted past and future into the eternal Now. Those
> two lyrics have a poignancy for me that they would hardly have for other
> people. I sent them in a letter to Billy, telling him that he was sometime to
> find me a *kakamono* with a hidden bay between two headlands, because he
> and I would be small children in pith helmets, playing there to all eternity.
> It missed him at one of his ports, and came back to me from the Dead
> Letter office. He never got it. And I never see that lyric about the hunter of
> dragon-flies that I do not remember him. And remember on the heels of it
> that he may not have gone so very far.*

The death of her two brothers was a watershed: she herself realized
that the current would now broaden and flow in a different direction:
'Somehow the sea went out with him, and the tide hasn't come in
again, and I am waiting and filling up in some fashion till life comes
back,' she told Dr Taylor. 'I have a curious feeling that I've come to
the end of something. End of Book I in fact. Life before seemed such a
gay little road straggling up hill, and now it has suddenly flattened out
and one is walking on the level. What helps to emphasize the end of the
chapter is that there's every prospect of Gregory Smith's departure.
Saintsbury has resigned, and the papers are unanimous in naming
Gregory as his successor. I shall miss him worse than I like to think.
For he was my literary Father-Confessor, and I think both of us

---

*Billy, a ship's doctor, was standing on deck during a violent storm, when he was
suddenly washed overboard and drowned. There was no question of suicide.

enjoyed the relationship. He was so perverse and indolent and kindly, and his criticism was of an extraordinary "*fine*-ness"'. He hadn't Saintsbury's breadth, nor his humanity, but he had more subtlety; and after six years of intermittent strife — in the matter of feminism in the University and other minor feuds, I have to admit a baffling charm. He was one of the best-hated men in Queen's, and knew it. I remember his chuckle of appreciation when I told him of George's metaphor for him, his "glacier motion". But the people who knew him well enough liked him extraordinarily, and I'll miss him for that reason, as well as for sheerly utilitarian ones. I suppose it will be good for me to "gang my ain gait" — but it has helped to make me feel suddenly old: not "elderly", just quite grown-up.

'Which reminds me of the adorable Charles. Charles is three, and we call him the Saga, because he sings wordless melodies all day long, if he happens to be playing in loneliness. He had denied that he was to be a big man when he grew up — I was baking when his sister, Mary Margaret, aged five, brought the charge, and Charles turned to me — "What is you, Aunt Helen?" Aunt Helen puts the bread into the oven and straightens herself. "I'm a big woman Charlie" — "ARE NOT" says Charlie loudly. "Aunt Helen's a girl" says Mary Margaret. — "IS NOT" says Charles. "Is just Aunt Helen" — which was very comforting.'

She was 'filling up in some fashion' until life should pulse once again in her veins, clutching at little bright things like a baby catching at furniture, to save herself from collapse. Everything in her world seemed in disarray. George Saintsbury was busy dismembering his marvellous collection of books before going South. Gregory Smith was looking forward to Edinburgh with a fair amount of confidence, and Helen sent to Japan for a little Buddha to present to him — a sort of colophon as being the Buddha's latest reincarnation. It was at this point that Maude Clarke came forward with a suggestion that Meg, Helen and herself should go away for a few days. On 12 August 1915, Helen wrote to Dr Taylor an account of their odyssey:

> Dear,
>   It's before breakfast, and the sun is shining, and I had a perfect day. That is why you were not written to yesterday. Maude and I have found a house to stay in that came out of a book. It is awfully difficult to believe this morning that it is really there. We had hunted the country all over for a hole to hide in. Every place was either full up or else it was spoiled by people who liked us and would take pity on our loneliness and ask us — for breakfast and dinner and tea. And we both

wanted dead isolation, with Meg for a long weekend to play with in the middle.

We were desperate. We were sick of writing to addresses and at last Mother said — 'Go down for a day to Larne' (Larne which we despised) 'and see for yourselves.' We went, chastened. We walked along the sea front patiently, and the sun went in, and it thundered upon us and rained as I never was rained on in my life till we had to laugh. Very far away round the coast I saw a house just at the sea, with miles between us. 'You needn't,' said Maude grimly, 'that's not the kind of house that lives on "Apartments".' But I was perverse, at any rate the walk would dry us. To sit down then would mean rheumatic fever. So we progressed, and our waterproofs caught at our ankles and we were exceedingly dejected, and never a little white card with 'Apartments' was to be seen. Except one house, a town house with a dining room recently vacated by a Navy man who smoked Three Castles, and with green linoleum covered with pink roses, and all the windows shut. But it was clean. Maude was so wet that she was weak. We said we would write. While Maude talked, I sniffed. And when I got her out I said that I would sit in a cottar's house in Glenarm and look at the sea through a single pane of glass before I would contemplate that linoleum for my daily food, and be pervaded by — drains. And we walked and walked and were just dry when it thundered and rained again. This time we took refuge in an archway that smelt evilly, and a cow and a calf eyed us resentfully and tried to evict us, and then stood with their heads in shelter and their backs in the rain and looked at us with mournful eyes, until the smells drove us forth, and they took our places with great satisfaction.

By this time all houses were behind us — nothing but sea and rain and rocks and a forlorn path at the foot of the cliffs and that solitary house on the point. We were near it when we saw a path up hill to the road. 'We may as well take it' said Maude drearily, 'there's no use going to that house'. But I was very perverse (which must be a sort of collision of 'persevere').

We had to climb up to get to the gate and then climb down again. There were many steps, the wooden shelving kind, and there were dripping fuchsias and a tent in the garden — and the ground fell straight to the sea. And it had stopped raining. And Maude grew more hopeless with every step. And then we saw the little white card.

And *such* 'Apartments'. A great old clean house with shallow stairs, and a sea wind blowing through it. And our sitting room an enormous drawing room with a deep window seat all round the bay, looking out to sea — a nice old shabby golden-brown room that would seat about fifty, and will only have to hold three. Huge old-fashioned sofas, deep ones, and armchairs, and cushions on the window seats; and such wide deep windows. To look at the bedrooms was a formality. We have one each, huge double-bedded rooms, again window seats, and again the sea. And it's *ours* — for £3.

We're going next Wednesday, and Meg with us. And Maude and I are going to write a novel together — but more of it when I've time.

Dear, about the boy's funeral. You are so dear to be concerned. But his brothers are settling that, and none of them are poor. But it was so utterly like you.

CHAPTER V

LARNE ON THE Antrim coast, staring over an Irish Sea alive with floating contact-mines as well as fish, was not white-sanded Kamakura where Kwannon the Merciful sat by the stream of time listening to the prayers of the world — there was nothing godlike about Larne. In any case, mountains not seascapes were Helen's natural setting.

> 'Thy justice is like mountains great,
> Thy judgements deep as floods' (Psalm 36.6).

That proved, she told her clerical cousin at Howth, that God's justice had the kindness and divinity of mountains, whereas his judgements had the mystery and inexplicable cruelty of the sea. Most ingenious, he replied, and countered with the Hebrew text: the amateur exegete quailed before Hebrew and sat down. Nevertheless on Wednesday 18 August 1915, Larne had its points. Martha Waddell's act of unprecedented generosity in acceding to Maude Clarke's request was not lacking in self-interest. She may have wanted to obliterate the remembrance of the painful scene she had caused in refusing to allow George's coffin to rest in the front room of the house in Cedar Avenue: the incident had driven Helen to the verge of hatred and, for once, she may have filled her stepmother with fear. However that may be, no company could have been more welcome and health-giving than Meg and Maude, no task more therapeutic than collaboration in the writing of a novel.

On 15 August, exactly two months after George's death, Helen penned her usual Sunday letter to Dr Taylor:

> I told you last time about our novel. You will not think I am shirking the other work, my father? For I simply can't do it yet. Your mind has to work up to a certain heat before the thing illuminates. I was just about beginning to write when George died. And it's incredibly difficult to rake the ashes into a glow. Gregory advised me to leave it, and when I told him, half-laughing, about this idea for a novel, he jumped at it and said it was the best thing I could do. It would amuse me, and keep my hand in — and possibly be very profitable. And the subject especially delights him.

The name of it is 'The Taming of the Shrew'. She isn't really a shrew —
she is a very adorable young woman, quicksilver and eager and intolerably
exacting; married — for her sins and doubtless his — to the most academic
and conventional of critics. You'll have to wait for the rest until you get the
novel. But the first chapter is written, and Maude and I will have a glorious
week. We want it finished before she goes back to Oxford in October. If it
ever reaches publication it will be anonymous, simply '*The Taming of the
Shrew* — a Collaboration.' And it isn't only a skit. It has been dawning on
me for years that it's no good asserting your individuality and being an
aggressive person; it seems to hold good everywhere that to lose one's life
is to find it.

Peggy comes tomorrow, and on Wednesday we three go to our house.
The people are quite cheerful about giving us dinner at seven, and they
look as if they could cook. Can't you imagine us, after being out all day in
the sun (it has rained consecutively for seven days, but no matter), eating
an enormous dinner, and then settling down on that cushioned window-
seat to write out the second chapter. One sees nothing but the sea from that
window, and next week the moon is to be full.

I wrote a teasing letter to Saintsbury, and told him about our house, and
its general remoteness and its candlelight, and demanded that he should
attend us there, and be our third collaborator. This morning brought me
six illegible pages of regret, and a very genuine offer: 'I need not in plain
prose say that if I can do "the cricket on the hearth" business in any way I
am, as in all others, at your service.' It will be good to have him, for I
believe he has read and remembered and reviewed more novels than any
man living.

At the end of the 'blessed lazy week' spent in Larne, Helen reported
progress:

The first book of the novel is finished, and we are breaking ground for the
second. Meg is going to take a photo of us and call it 'The Collaborators' —
me bunched in a corner of the sofa with the writing-pad on my knee and
scowling, Maude full length in an easy chair with the eyes of a seraph.
Maude talks but she will not write; only it is really the most wonderful
talking in the world.

The two practitioners of the 'arts babblative and scribblative'
reacted upon one another like scissor blades, snip, snap, snip: this may
possibly explain why the action progresses after the manner of an Ivy
Compton-Burnett novel, mainly by dialogue. The principal characters are unmistakable: Dr Edward St John, distinguished Shakespearian scholar and critic, *alias* Gregory Smith; his close friend
Taverner with an unspecified 'R' for initial, *alias* George Saintsbury;
St John's wife, Elizabeth ('Elizabeth is by common consent the name
that would best have suited me'), *alias* Helen Waddell; her beautiful

mocking confidante Anne Delahide, nicknamed 'Egypt', *alias* Maude Clarke. All four would cut fine figures in a republic of letters. Transposed into an eighteenth-century key, both matter and manner might have come straight out of Jane Austen, the *Tatler*, or *The Spectator* — perhaps in the form of a 'countercheck quarrelsome' from Miss Mary Astell flung in the face of no less fearful a personage than the terrible Dean himself.

To savour it to the full, it is perhaps best to approach the novel as one would a complex crossword puzzle, for analysis suggests that it is an intricate network of recondite allusion, a highly-accomplished academic game written, one suspects, for Gregory Smith's and Saintsbury's delectation. Not for nothing was H.W. the disciple of two such mentors; not for nothing had she made a special study of the Restoration period; not for nothing did Saintsbury regard himself as 'an infinitesimal fraction' of Jonathan Swift. Indeed, a letter of violent protest from Saintsbury makes it clear that although she laid no claim to be Stella, Helen had teasingly compared herself to Vanessa, the woman who smothered Swift with her unwelcome affection:

> Vanessa? I hope not. I loathe her. She was a cat — not a Heaven cat, a cat of Freya all wings & love like some cats but a hell-cat — a cat in the sense in which women use the word — a whining, tell-tale creature who kept on pestering when she wasn't wanted.

When Helen and Maude put their two heads together to concoct a story, it is clear that tracts of half-related reading began to drift into combinations, and shared convictions grew luminous and shone through the action as it took on shape. 'Crossword clues' might run somewhat as follows: In *The Peace of the Augustans*, a work Saintsbury was engaged on at this very time, with Helen much in mind, he discusses Addison and Swift's handling in the 59th and 63rd numbers of *The Spectator* of 'that eminent feminist Miss Mary Astell, otherwise "Madonella"' (the anagram 'Stella' must surely be pure accident?). Now the collaborators' novel first entitled *The Taming of the Shrew* was altered without more ado to *Discipline*. Had Saintsbury put them on the scent? Mary Astell (1668–1731) was the author of *A Serious Proposal to Ladies* (1694) 'to erect a monastery with a double aspect: a retreat from the world, and an institution of discipline to fit us to do the greatest good in it.' Part II of the same work, published in 1697, was dedicated to Princess Anne, daughter of Anne Hyde, first wife of James II. 'Only connect,' murmurs E. M. Forster. . . . Anne Delahide? And Edward St John? In a letter to Stella of 1710, Swift writes: 'I was this morning with Mr Secretary St John, and we were to dine at

Mr Harley's alone about some business of importance.' The reference
of course is to Henry St John, later Viscount Bolingbroke, Secretary
of State and associate of Robert Harley, Earl of Oxford, head of the
Tory ministry, with whom Jonathan Swift allied himself as chief
political writer. (Both Gregory Smith and George Saintsbury were
ardent Tories.) As for R. Taverner, were the authors tilting at his love
of the Anglican liturgy and the Authorized Version of the Bible,
whose extraordinary merits he never ceased to laud, and to applaud
'the utter shipwreck of the elaborately foolish attempt to revise it'? For
Richard Taverner (1505–55) was responsible for 'Taverner's Bible'
which appeared in 1539 under the patronage of Wolsey. Furthermore,
the all-Tory Brothers' Club founded by Henry St John at the
inspiration of Swift 'to advance conversation and friendship and assist
deserving authors' may well be the mental background of the stage-set
for St John's and Taverner's exchanges in H. W.'s novel.

There are also echoes of Jane Austen as, for instance, in the choice
and use of names: Elizabeth — the vivacious Elizabeth Bennet; Aunt
Catharine — the other aunt, Lady Catherine de Burgh; in Edward,
Anne and Taverner, the foils; in the library scenes, the arch-
playfulness and all-pervasive feminine psychology, and in the change
of air and place of action that leads to the dénouement. But the
characters are not second-hand: they are drawn in the way Helen
herself thought; she repeats the very phrases and incidents to be found
in her letters when writing of Gregory Smith and Saintsbury. In
addition to all this, the sheer beauty, sharpness, audacious fun, the wit
and grace of the writing, could issue from no mind or pen but Helen's
own. As for the erudite references, they simply add to the fun and
deepen the enjoyment in much the same way as a reading of Joyce or
Eliot. The story itself is slight; when completed, it only amounted to
36,000 words, about one third of the ordinary length of a novel at that
time.

Finding the labour of doing nothing insupportable, after three years
of marriage to an anti-feminist husband she fears and scarcely knows,
Elizabeth St John plans to smash his shell of urbanity and courteous
contempt, and to establish the rights of all women as well as her own
autonomy. She joins a group of militant suffragettes, hurls a brick
through a draper's window in Oxford Street, spends that night with
her associates in a police-cell, figures prominently in press photographs of the culprits, and is handed over next day to her husband
who, in perfect silence, goes surety in twenty pounds for his wife's
good behaviour while Taverner, like a shaggy St Bernard, looks on
with aching sympathy, infinitely admiring and protective. On her

The Rev. Hugh Waddell

Hugh's first wife, Jane (Jenny) *née* Martin.
They were married in 1868.

The Waddell family. Helen is the baby on her mother's lap.
George is in front of her, and Billy is on the right.

25 Nakano-cho, Azabu, as it was in 1982. The address has been renamed 18 3-chome, Roppongi, Azabudai, Minatoku, Tokyo. The 'street improvements' were made in 1967.

The Daibutsu at Kamakura

The temple Zojoji, close to where the Waddells lived in Tokyo

The Waddell family with their new mother. The front row shows
(*l.* to *r.*) Billy, George, Helen and Tom. Back row (*l.* to *r.*): Sam,
Jimmie, Hugh, Martin, Charlie. Meg is in the centre.

Helen and Meg in 1906

Meg's wedding to John Dunwoodie Martin. Helen is sitting in front of her brother-in-law.

Maude Clarke, 1925

Helen as a young woman at Queen's University

Helen with three of the Martin children

Helen in the 1920s; the formal photograph on the left was probably taken to send to Dr Taylor

Left: Number 19 Cedar Avenue

Above: Helen in the Mourne mountains

Below left: Professor Saintsbury

Below right: George Gregory Smith

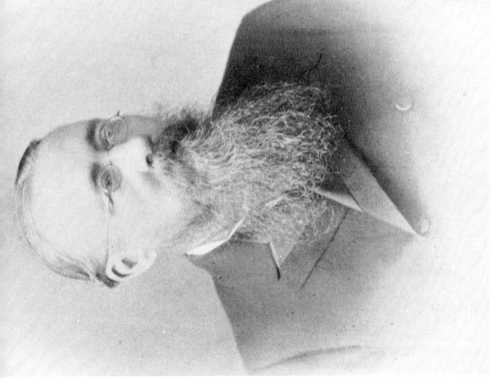

The four older Martin children
(*l.* to *r.*): Jack, Charlie, Mollie, Sydney

Kilmacrew House

return home, Elizabeth feels with fierce resentment that her husband has banished her as before to the nursery:

> If she could hope for any understanding from him, she could humble herself, admit her incredible folly. But she had none. Of one thing one could always be sure with Edward: perception without intuition. He had the finest critical faculty she knew; his mind was like an agate knife-edge; not, like Taverner's, blunted with humanity. He could not help seeing things exactly as they looked. He would see what she had done and every humiliating circumstance of it, but he would see it on a flat surface. He would never know why she had done it. He would not even try to know. One does not trouble to comprehend inferior intelligences, instinctive motions. Was that what had driven her to the Women's Movement: a personal reaction? 'Self-assertion. And enthusiasm. And insincerity?'

Whatever the reason, she has failed to dislodge him from his pedestal: he remains as glacial, impassive and inaccessible as ever. But Edward St John's wife is by no means an un-idea'd girl. She next indulges in the sport of having the engineer hoist with his own petard. The wife of the well-known Shakespearian scholar publishes a learned dissertation supporting the Baconian theory of Shakespearian authorship, which at once attracts the attention of reviewers:

> 'She's got us all,' Taverner tells St John. 'First there's myself, the one, two, three, Big Bow-wow manner. Then there's Bradley . . . and lastly you, the *Ironia*.' He flicked over the pages. 'Oh, the bad, bad puss! She's caught the Whigs bathing, and gone off with their clothes . . . but why did she ever publish?'
> 'It might' said St John dryly 'be a manifesto. I thought the Suffrage phase was chiefly contagion.'
> Taverner wheeled. 'Did you tell her that?'
> St John knit his brows.
> 'I don't think so,' he said slowly. 'I did say she mustn't do it again, I said it was silly.'
> 'And so she vindicates her intelligence!' Taverner sat down heavily, and the two looked at each other with a glimmering smile.

For the first time in her experience, Taverner is critical of Elizabeth's action: he even hints at treachery on her part. Dismayed, she suddenly sees herself as the woman who has shouted in the market-place, the woman without reticence, and her reaction is immediate flight — not only from her husband, but from herself. She proposes to Edward that she spend the winter with her Aunt Catherine in Devonshire, he courteously assents, and she departs. She endures the new surroundings for a couple of months until the atmosphere and assumptions of an ultra-Victorian household prove intolerable, and she runs away again. This time she goes to the other extreme. She accepts an invitation to membership of a group of merry youngsters who regard themselves as the nucleus of a Society for the Realization of Life, and gather for an Easter so-called house-party at a hotel in St Kevin's, three miles from the Lizard. In due course she despatches a frantic telegram to Anne Delahide to get her out of it: 'It's the Hollow Land, and my flesh is crying out for honest cynicism; what you would call Destructive Reality.' Anne's noble response: 'St John delirious, calling for you' releases her with honour unstained. Craving at last for Edward's honest cynicism and resolved to be good, Elizabeth returns home only to find her husband on holiday and the house empty. Drifting from room to room, moping and aimless, she is confronted with an Edward she does not recognize — one who has replaced the Van Eyck over the fireplace with an Irish landscape of turf-carriers against a blue line of hills, who has been deep in 'Samson Agonistes' not Shakespeare and, more puzzling than all else, is at present thoroughly enjoying a fishing adventure with the unexalted. He finally returns. The bantering irony of his greeting freezes the warm welcome on her lips, the meal passes in an interchange of social niceties until, taking the initiative, St John informs her that, thinking she would be absent much longer, he has planned to go to Bayreuth in the summer for the Wagner Festival. This is the last straw. She will be known as 'Dr St John's wife' no longer. Anne is leaving for Italy in a fortnight: she will accompany her, they can take a Henry James Palazzo in Rome, live there happily ever after, and so eliminate Edward as he has eliminated her.

She finds her friend deeply immersed in a folio of Anthony Wood, telling of the mischief that befell Merton by having its first married warden thrust upon the College.

'Anne,' she said abruptly, 'I'm not going to live with Edward any more. He makes me feel like a puppy barking at the Sphinx.'

'But why bark?' Anne's interest was strictly academic. 'Do you expect it to sit up and take notice?'

'I've stopped barking. . . . And I've stopped even being vivacious. It's Edward. He has taken all the things. He talks. You know what he used to be like between two women at dinner — torpid. And now he's a Social Success.'

'The Relapsed Bachelor,' murmured Anne. 'This is going to be even better than the Bacon-Shakespeare divorce. The ground of separation that Dr St John usurps the conversation. And the case would turn on whether Conversation or Conduct is three parts of life. Dr St John would have

Matthew Arnold. All the same, I think you could make out a good case.'

'I wish,' said Elizabeth drearily, 'you would be serious.'

Anne leaned back on her pillows and looked at Elizabeth mildly.

'What are your plans?' she asked with gentle interest.

'I'm going away with you next week. I'm going to live with you.'

Anne started upright.

'But I wouldn't live with you for anything!' she said in consternation.

Elizabeth sat motionless, gazing with wide hurt eyes.

'For week-ends, Elizabeth,' said Anne coaxingly. . . . She leaned forward, laying her hand on Elizabeth's arm with her inimitable Early Victorian gesture. 'I love you, Elizabeth,' she said softly, 'but I cannot marry you.'

Elizabeth stirred. A smile was twitching at the corners of her mouth. She rose and surveyed Anne deliberately.

'I think,' she said slowly, 'I would hate you, if it weren't for the shape of your face.'

On 9 January 1916, just before Maude Clarke returned to Oxford, Helen wrote to Dr Taylor: 'This week has been very good to live. I was never working at such speed before, and the novel is within two chapters of the end, and one of them is practically written. The last chapter is what they would have called in Greek tragedy the "reconciliation", and all day — Sunday as it is — scraps of sentences have been swimming into my head. It is the final passage of arms between Elizabeth and St John, and a lot depends on it . . . I do want you to like the novel. Bits of it *ought* to be true, for the writing of them tired me so.' And a week later: 'The novel is finished. The Egyptian and I hammered out the last paragraph on Friday afternoon, and then lay flat upon the eiderdown of the Egyptian's bed and said "We are very wonderful". The Egyptian is Saintsbury's name for her, and it suits her better than anything else.' To anticipate a probable objection from Dr Taylor, she explained: 'The book is something of a protest against cocksure analysis. I fancy more people than we think have a window open to the east. As for the ending, I asked Peggy, teasing, what she thought St John did. "I *know* what he did," said Peggy positively. "He made a grab for Elizabeth." I think he did myself. But we liked to leave a lot of things unsaid. And only to suggest what Saintsbury called "the delectable dawn".'

With title altered to *Discipline*, the finished product was now subjected to George Saintsbury. When asked to deliver judgement on her work, he had already warned her: 'I shall read the thing in cool blood and tell you what I think of it. I really believe that as a critic I *can't* lie. "You find it easy, Sir, in other relations" say you, gathering the purple amice round your virgin form.' And then, with his amazing encyclopaedic knowledge he informed her: 'You know a certain Mrs Brunton had the impudence to anticipate your title exactly 100 years ago? Oddly enough I have just been writing in my French novel book a demonstration that novels ought as a rule to be long because novelists are *not*, as a rule, clever enough to make them short. But you are clever enough for anything — such a "Play-*girl* of the West" . . . as never was, I believe, before: and never will be again. There! G.S.'

Saintsbury was not a man to mince words or offer insincere flattery and, as Helen told Dr Taylor, he had reviewed more novels than any man living, a fact that makes his reception of *Discipline* all the more telling. By this time he had left Edinburgh and was temporarily living in Southampton where he was born and later buried. Written on 24 March, his letter is headed:

Eve of Our Lady   Polygon House
1916   Southampton
Elizabeth Regina,

It is excellent. I have not read a better short story since Sir Henry Cunningham's *Wheat and Tares* which appeared about sixty years ago. And I don't think I'm prejudiced — if I am it's the first time I ever have been — in criticism.

Of course if I'm not prejudiced I'm to a certain extent 'biased'. I don't mean by the Taverner part though that is uncommonly complimentary but by the Elizabeth part. You have put so much of yourself into it that reading it one enjoys *you* — slowly. Yes: it *is* good. . . . There is Meredith in it but 'Meredith improved': and there is no Henry James in it, thank Heaven! Indeed there is not much that is not purely yours — unless it is the Egyptian's.

'One thing I have against thee' as St John says (the other). Why do you call *this* St John 'Dr'? No men who know ever do that except physicians, the peculiar & almost extinct kind of lawyers called 'proctors' & doctors of music. At least no Oxford man does. But this is a trifle . . . .

By the way only *very* early Victorians were 'arch'. Matt A. it is true wrote that hideous line about the 'archest chin': but Matt was 'primitive'.

Seriously, I can find no serious fault. Perhaps we don't see quite sides enough of St John — a scene in which he *actually* made himself fascinating to some other woman suggests itself: though I won't swear that it would be in full keeping. Of Taverner I ought not to say much — if there is anything of me in him why I'm very much obliged to you. And as for his 'liking *her* very much' — why that only shows what a sensible man he was. I compliment you (& Incognita Egyptiaca of course) very much on Elizabeth's feelings *after* the suffragette débâcle[?]. It is the kind of thing commonly attempted nowadays & nearly always spoilt. You haven't exaggerated in the least. The review as burlesque is a happy thought. But I laughed most at the St Kevin's purgatory with the modernists. And the home-coming with the disappointments is admirable & the passage where Elizabeth 'proposes' to Anne & in fact all to the end, especially that. What are you going to do with it? No publisher ever consults me about novels — worse luck!

I wonder if Elizabeth ever wrote a love-letter? I wonder if I have any idea what it would be like? I wonder — but that's enough wondering —

This is not a good letter — not worthy of Tav. But although you know I always maintain that criticism and love-making are not incompatible but rather complementary they cannot be done at *exactly* the same time. The same is the case with eating & drinking as we learnt in our nurseries. I ought to have typewritten the criticism & hand-written the other. But you'll forgive, *Two* Elizabeths *and* one Egyptian Incognita may slightly giddify even the very strong man.

I do want to see it in print.

Three days later he added: 'I shall quote Ben about it to everybody. "By God, 'tis good; & if you like't you may!"'

If Saintsbury had recognized at once the Gregorian note in the fictitious St John, it need hardly be said that Gregory Smith required no introduction to his mirrored self. The image goaded the Buddha into unwonted animation: to kick St John and to slap Elizabeth were, he declared, the two emotions strongest in him. He was philosopher enough to accept the portrait and asked only for one change: 'Gregory insisted, as far as his infinite leisure can insist, on our altering the title,' Helen wrote to Dr Taylor. '*Discipline* is too heavy: too like the early nineteenth century. I offered him *Discipline: a Comedy*, which he brooded over, and finally suggested *A Comedy of Discipline*. It remains — and went in its new clothes to Blackwood yesterday, with a letter of introduction from Gregory. He is a dear.' Helen had feared losing his constant presence and help, but events were to prove her fears groundless. Upon Saintsbury's retirement in 1915, Gregory Smith had suffered the humiliation of rejection when the Chair of Rhetoric and English Literature in the University of Edinburgh, for which he was the leading candidate, was given — possibly for political reasons — to Herbert Grierson. Gregory decided to stay where he was, and at Belfast he remained to the end. 'You see, Grierson, who got Edinburgh, left Aberdeen,' Helen explained in her Indian weekly letter, 'and for Gregory to humble himself to step into Grierson's shoes———. If it had been another Scottish University he might have been tempted. But Grierson's chair — not if he were out at elbows. I confess I'd feel a little like that myself, and Gregory is about ten times prouder than I am. I rather admire him for not letting the loss of Edinburgh go deep.'

Yet it was one of life's little ironies that it was precisely over chairs
and University appointments that for the next three years Helen was
to engage in stern combat with an anti-feminist, call him Edward St
John or Gregory Smith as you will. On 21 June 1916, she wrote to Dr
Taylor:

> This is a dead secret, for the appointment has not been quite ratified yet —
> but unless the anti-feminism of Queen's is too strong, Maude, *my* Maude,
> is to have the Chair of History for a year — or until the end of the war.
> Professor Powicke, her old chief, is doing war work in the Economics
> Department in London, and he wants her to fill his place. There's just a
> chance that the Academic Council will cut up rough about it, but I don't
> think so. There are a few men like Gregory who are dead against the
> appointment of women, but there is another thesis equally dear — at least
> to Gregory — which will counteract that: namely, that any professor shall
> be allowed to do as he likes.

No opposition was raised against Maude's appointment, and in the
autumn of that year she duly ascended Professor Powicke's rostrum,
looking bewitchingly demure and beautiful in her academic robes,
and enthralling her students as they had never been enthralled; they
hadn't the heart to misbehave.

The war was taking its toll of the University staff and students, and
conscription was looming on the horizon. Gregory Smith was in
despair: his only son, chafing against all restriction, was off to
Sandhurst in October 1916, wild to be in the trenches within three
months. It seemed also as if he were about to lose his assistant, and in
that event? Women were acting as stop-gaps throughout the whole of
Europe. A mere assistantship was not exactly vaulting ambition, but
on many levels it would have been a godsend to Helen just then.
Feeling exactly like Elizabeth in her novel, she decided to broach the
subject at her next meeting with Edward St John. He was evasive, and
in December she reported to Dr Taylor:

> Did I ever tell you that I had it out with Gregory about the assistantship at
> Queen's? I know now that I will never get it unless there is no available
> man. It's the old old prejudice, reinforced by Oxford and twenty years of
> academic discipline. I believe I *did* tell you, but it must have been one of the
> letters that were drowned. I can in a way understand it. Asking him to
> appoint a woman to the staff of a men's university is like asking R. I.
> Martin to appoint a Sinn Feiner. Either would smash the traditions of a
> lifetime. I'm glad we had it out, for I was a little haunted by the fear that it
> might be a personal matter: that he was afraid I would be too upsetting a
> colleague. But he said definitely that, only for his 'prejudice', he would
> much prefer me.

At this point her thoughts travelled to Maude Clarke with whom she had just spent an evening in rooms overlooking the river: 'We sat on a rug and watched a very leisurely sunset and ate strawberries and salted almonds, and I talked an immeasurable lot of nonsense. I was "splairgin'": do you remember that beautiful word in Stevenson's *Weir of Hermiston*: "there's nae room for splairgin' under the four quarters of John Calvin?"' All of a sudden the suppressed longing for freedom to achieve all that Maude had done breaks through: Helen's very protest is itself an affirmation.

> I don't worry about Oxford — really. Only now and then there's a twinge. 'So long as men do their duty, though it be greatly in a misapprehension' . . . . But do you know, I think there's one great instance of a man doing his 'duty' to his — and the world's — eternal loss. Milton's twenty years' service of the Parliament hardened and embittered and defiled him: plunged him into incredible scurrility of controversy. *Paradise Lost* is wonderful, but never in its humanity. And there is nothing gracious, nothing in the finest sense 'religious' in his vision of God.

If Helen's hope of treading Milton's olive-grove of Academe was growing steadily dim, her hope of achieving novelist-status was in total eclipse. No one was more keenly disappointed than Saintsbury who, like Taverner over Elizabeth St John, was quick to sense the heroine's dejection after every lost battle. On 10 January 1917 he wrote: 'I am afraid that my first opinion — that the publishers would funk the suffragettery — was true. They are the timidest of all tradesmen: & there is just now a most absurd tendency to regard all that business as dead & buried. "It's a gruesome thing is premature interment!" as Kingsley says.' With deadening monotony, the novel went the rounds, collecting rejection slips from one publisher after another. Saintsbury's gracious fooling was a gift rarer than gold, for he would never allow his 'Incomparabilis' to be swallowed up in sadness so long as he could swear: 'By the blessed cushions of the divan at Samarcand, by the two chairs in Gregory's dining room that once closed to each other, by our Seventies in the Calendar of Elysium, if you do not make yourself a place in literature, it will be a pity — not perhaps for you, but for the others.'

All the same, her literary stature was not the thought uppermost in his mind: it was the quality of her human living. In his appreciation of the novel, he had asked: 'I wonder if Elizabeth ever wrote a love-letter?' There is concern behind the banter, for he later repeated the question: 'I wonder (don't think me impertinent) whether you ever have been, are, or will be *really* in love?' This question exercised other minds besides his just then. When George died, Helen was twenty-six, said to be the dangerous age beyond which women become steadily less marriageable. She spoke of herself as one who had lived 'long hermit-crab years' and was 'almost convent-bred'. The literary collaboration that produced *Discipline* certainly made one thing amusingly clear: Babblative and Scribblative were no Puritan prudes on the prowl but, in Milton's phrase, the lips of neither had ever glowed 'celestial rosy red, love's proper hue'. E. L. Woodward's memoir of Maude Clarke published in 1937, two years after her death, opens with a striking analysis of the contemplative life of the scholar and the life of a professed religious. He closes with the observation: 'I think that by temperament and by natural gifts she belonged to the type of woman who ruled a medieval abbey.' One immediately remembers of course Helen Waddell's strange transition into Heloise, abbess of the Paraclete, lecturing to her nuns on Abelard's *Introductio ad Theologiam* all night, and with full awareness and no sense of change, finding herself a patient in the Institut Pasteur in Paris, and the date June 1924, when daybreak came. To the potential Benedictines, Maude and Helen, could be added Meta Fleming. After a brilliant academic career she embarked on a missionary life in India, where she was to die in a Bombay hospital on Christmas Day 1916 at the age of twenty-seven, in the presence of Dr Taylor kneeling grief-stricken beside her. It resembles a scene out of the Early Church — it might be John Chrysostom or Gregory of Nyssa with Olympias or Macrina. Three years previously, Helen had written to Meg: 'Meta Fleming and some of the outgoing missionaries are to be solemnly addressed and benedictioned last thing on Thursday night. Mustn't it feel strange to stand on the Assembly Hall platform and be committed to your long service — a wee bit like taking the veil. She has signed to marry no man for seven years.'

G. K. Chesterton said of Ireland that the quality which caused it in the past to be called the Land of the Saints might still give it a claim to be called the Land of Virgins, and he quoted the Irish priest who told him, 'There is in our people a fear of the passions which is older even than Christianity.' A more important gift than physical purity, according to Chesterton, was the clearness of intellect characteristic of the Irish character and the Irish attitude of mind, the lucidity and logic that Bernard Shaw compressed into five words: 'An Irishman has two eyes.' With one, he appreciates the sublime, with the other, he winks at the unreality of the dream. In all this it is not difficult to recognize all three young Irishwomen with their intellectual brilliance and — not least of their gifts — the laughter and gaiety that each had bought at a price. This may help to explain why Helen Waddell could be so startlingly direct and audacious precisely because she was so shamelessly innocent, because she could truly walk the woods like Diana,

chaste as an icicle curdied by the frost,

a challenge to many an Anglo-Saxon attitude.

Who but an Irishwoman could pillory in fiction Rhadamanthus, son of Zeus, the just and wise judge, proceed to bait him in real life with a display of antique silver buckles, and send her cry of triumph over oceans and continents to a Doctor of Divinity in Ahmadabad?

I saw St John's original today, and to my unbridled glee actually raised him from his chair to look at my beautiful new shoes. Can you imagine the Buddha in a massive chair entrenched behind a still more massive desk, and myself with an air of being settled for the afternoon in the only comfortable armchair in the University, and interrupting a long discussion as to whether or not I was to be allowed an exceedingly valuable edition of Greene's prose works for August, to tell him about my new shoes? They are blunt little shoes with large old silver buckles and ridiculous heels: and I was really in a mournful confession of extravagance when Gregory grasped the arms of his chair and raised himself deliberately to survey them over his desk. It was like making Rhadamanthus flirt. If I'd been a cat I'd have purred in sheer triumph. There is no joy like teasing the Buddha into animation.

It ended in my getting the Greene. After a final scene in which Mr Salmon was called in to protest that Greene would lose his back — his valuable quarto back — if he were read at all, I told them they were behaving like custodians instead of librarians, and Gregory turned upon Mr Salmon. 'Behold, she rails upon us like a fish-wife!' I'm afraid we all three shouted at that point, and I knew Greene was mine.

She sounds so deliciously young and she looked it, as a letter of 1916 to Dr Taylor proves. Duty had driven her to a dreary At Home:

I had on my youngest blouse, with a turn-down lacy collar, an Early Victorian muslin affair, and a floppy Panama: and I sat at the other end of the room from a very stately headmistress-y lady, Miss Rentoul, who was talking to Mother. One is sharp-eared where oneself is concerned, and I knew Miss Rentoul was saying smooth things about the *Lyrics* to Mother: then came 'And where is she now?' Mother looked across the room — 'Helen' — I rose up to be introduced. Miss Rentoul stared. 'You don't mean to say' — then remembered her manners and laughed a little. 'I beg your pardon, my dear, but I thought you were a schoolgirl and that "Helen Waddell" was an older sister.' Which is very comforting at seven and twenty!

A couple of years later, the headmistress-y lady was to meet a Helen Waddell who would prove anything but a schoolgirl, yet her deceptively youthful appearance went hand in hand with an almost incredible modesty. In spite of Gregory Smith's encouragement and Saintsbury's near-adoration, in June 1916, she could rebut with an ice-cold douche of level-headed uncommon sense, the high praise of his niece expressed to Dr Taylor by her father's eldest brother, a Presbyterian minister in New Zealand:

> Uncle Rutherford's remarks in no way affected me. To begin with, he is irrationally fond of me: he suddenly discovered me in rather a lonely old age and told me that it was like a butterfly opening its wings in the middle of a dusty road. Now even a very common little butterfly shows to great advantage there. What he calls 'ease' is only feminine facility in letter-writing. It's all nonsense about 'genius'. It's a word used more lightly in Uncle Rutherford's day than it is now. I know of course that I have 'ability' up to a certain point. But so many other people write exceedingly well nowadays. There's nothing like a 'University education' for showing you all the other little hills quite as high as your own. A girl in my own year, Miss Fisher, had a gift for 'versing' far daintier than mine. Academically, Maude has a far better mind: and when she once begins to *write* half the good things she *says*, I'll behave like Sir Walter Scott with Byron, only that my *Waverley* is already written. And somehow the whole thing is so paltry. It seems to me — I feel it more the older I grow — that living is so much bigger than writing. If I go on it will sound like Ecclesiastes.

Towards the end of the same letter she sets right a misquotation in Dr Taylor's letter:

> It must have been my own fault, but Saintsbury's quotation is wrong. It's not 'You have the mark of the Maker on your forehead. Be grateful for this, young woman,' but 'You know you have the mark of the Maker on your forehead — "Be grateful for this young woman." Which I am yours and I trust, His truly, G.S.' It's an absurd and — for the young woman — very delightful rendering of the mark of Cain. You know it is Saintsbury's theory that a young girl (and he thinks I am *really* young) is like radium, 'radiates delight without losing anything thereby'. I fancy Saintsbury would agree with me that the gift of *Life* that Geo had and that Peggy has still, is a far greater thing than brains.

Precisely because she never thrust her own ideas or learning upon the attention of others, but unobtrusively gave with reckless generosity, she was frequently treated in cavalier fashion by those whose minds, in Johnson's phrase, were as narrow as the neck of a vinegar cruet. Towards the end of 1916 it was evident that Meta Fleming was dying of incurable cancer. When news of her death reached Helen, 'I am content,' she wrote to Dr Taylor. 'Somehow I think she would have had it as it is. She had it in her so richly to enjoy. I wanted love and marriage and children for her, and because of the insanity in her people she always tried to put that thought from her. And now in place of emptiness —— I *did* love her, but it was not the intimacy that sometimes makes me afraid when I think of losing Maude. Meta's is a loss in love; but Maude's would be a loss in life. And the "loss in love" isn't lost.'

In February 1917 Helen sent seven quarto sheets of typescript *In Memory of Meta Fleming* to the Christian Union, the society which owed so much to Meta's idealism and power of organization. Like all Helen Waddell's deeply-felt writing, the memoir is pretty-well perfect in form and expression, sketching outward events with constant flashes of insight that reveal its subject's very soul.

> . . . 'Think of me with happy things,' she dictated before she died, 'things like rivers and birds.' They were her things. . . . It is a question if any one at Queen's was so greatly loved; it was a charm equally operant on women and men, so frank a charm that there was no more of jealousy in it than of a flower. I do not know if they will be able to reproduce a snapshot of her that gives her very self. It was the summer of her twenty-second year: herself on a low wall outside a little sunk cottage, gazing down a sunny road: behind her a shadow of trees. It was one of the rare moments when an attitude, a droop of the head, has something of the eternity of the symbol. That is how some of us will always see her, her head a little bent, that little wistful air of waiting, half-humorous, wholly tender: and some of us, daringly pre-Raphaelite, would see her in even such sun-flecked shadow, waiting in the ways of Paradise. . . .
>
> 'To what purpose is this waste?' Some said it when she went to India: more will say it now. Yet the years in India were her richest and her happiest,
>
> > For life, with all it yields of joy and woe,
> > And hope and fear . . .
> > Is just our chance o' the prize of learning love,
>
> and she learned it there to the full. And the end is not yet. Too much of the glory and honour of the nations, too much of the youth of the world, has gone down to death of late for us to think of it as final any more. One comes back to the wisdom of the Middle Ages — *Mors janua vitae*, Death the gate of Life. We believed in the life everlasting: but into the life everlasting we have come to read the life eternal, life infinite in its breadth and length and depth and height. For to know the will of God was not Paul's ultimate asking. It began 'with the knowledge of His will'; it ended 'with all the fulness of God'.

Helen's weekly letter to India told of its reception by the members of the Christian Union:

I sent it to Miss Sinclair (and dear, do you mind if I swear a little? I have never met her, but there is a peculiar rigid quality in her letters, in her very writing, that rubs my fur very much erect). She has read the *In Memoriam* with interest, and admired its 'poetic form'. She thinks 'its main appeal will be to students': and 'perhaps someone might contribute a few pages for the wider clientèle of the Girls' Auxiliary and plain Ulster people'.

Frankly, I am bristling with indignation. I shall sit down under her suggestion meekly, but I shan't act upon it. I know that I could read that *In Memoriam* to — to our charwoman and be surer of her sympathy. I don't believe the G.A. and the plain Ulster people want to be told about Meta's 'sterling character and devoted life'. You want something to grip people's imagination and melt their hearts — and if Meta under the lilacs in Symie's garden doesn't do that — but then, I *saw* Meta there. I suppose Miss Sinclair was put off by things like 'pre-Raphaelite'. They *are* above the ordinary G.A. member — but does that matter? It is a beautiful word, and they may some day fill it in. Do I sound awfully cross? I'm not really, but small neat judgements like Miss Sinclair's infuriate me so much more than Broad-sword criticism.

Maude Clarke spoke the dismissive word of Helen's writing on Meta for parish magazines, when she informed Helen that it was worse than the jewel of gold in the swine's snout, for the swine made the gold look tawdry. Shortly afterwards, Helen's generosity again met with rebuff from 'Presbyterian true blue' when she contributed the opening chapter to a biography of Dr Isabel Mitchell, daughter of the Reverend D. K. Mitchell of Crumlin Road Presbyterian Church, Belfast. Ten years older than Helen, she had responded to the crying need for women doctors in China, graduated from the University of Glasgow, and gone out as a medical missionary to Manchuria, where she died at the age of thirty-seven. Her mother was anxious to publish a memorial quasi-biography composed largely of tributes from those who had known Isabel. Both in style and content, Chapter I 'The High Calling' could have come from no pen but Helen's: its assured analysis of religious vocation anticipates by almost twenty years her Introduction to *The Desert Fathers* which many consider to be her finest piece of work. The chapter opens:

> The wind bloweth where it listeth, and thou hearest the sound thereof, but canst not tell whence it cometh nor whither it goeth. It is the accepted metaphor, in a book of great metaphors, for the way of the Holy Ghost. Yet Christ applied it differently. 'So', He said, 'is every one that is born of the Spirit.' It is as though something of the mystery, some depth of the eternity from which their life drew 'an ampler ether, a diviner air' should be about those born, not of the will of the flesh, nor of the will of man, but of God. Abraham the Hebrew, the Man from Beyond the River, had it

above all the saints of the older faith: St John, above all the disciples of our Lord: St Francis of Assisi, beyond all men since. It is an untranslatable grace; it leaves small record. Simply one knows that there are pages in St John's gospel where the air is never still; fragments of our Lord's discourses flung like boulders where the great winds have passed: stray sentences in unexpected places that bring with them

'Murmurs and scents of the infinite sea';

and lives of one's own knowing to which men brought their sick — tarnished hope and impotent desire — that at the least, the shadow passing by might fall on them and they be healed.

Like Helen's obituary of Meta Fleming, some might read with interest and admire the poetic form as did Miss Sinclair, but what of the Girls' Auxiliary and plain Ulster people? The writer was not left long in doubt. Feeling as if she had come out of a submarine after the effort of producing ten sheets of perfect prose, Helen sent the draft of the first chapter to Mrs Mitchell, half-expecting an immediate and enthusiastic letter of gratitude. Four days passed, and then a 'terribly embarrassed editor appeared, and with much circumlocution and infinite apology explained Mrs Mitchell's views. . . . The first paragraph and the last struck her as rhetorical flourishes, very fine writing no doubt, but an unnecessary "swagger" and quite unsuited to the understanding of the Girls' Auxiliary and the girls in Crumlin Road.'

Worse was to come. Helen was still grieving over the loss of her brother George, and one can sense the poignant sorrow that underlay her description of Isabel Mitchell's preparation for her missionary work:

There was another element in her preparation. 'Also the word of the Lord came unto me saying, Son of Man, behold I take away from thee the desire of thine eyes with a stroke: yet neither shalt thou mourn nor weep. So I spoke unto the people in the morning and at even my wife died.' They were the two youngest, Isabel, and the brother born on her fifth birthday. There is motherhood in that relationship always, even where the brother is older: the woman who has cared for a brother is not childless. He taught her that: and then taught her the sharpness of death. He, as well as she, was determined to be a medical missionary: she coached him in the vacations, in the intimacy of work that is an even better thing than the intimacy of play. In the summer of 1902 they had planned to work together: the boy was eighteen then. He had gone with his father for a cycling tour in the Derry hills, and the two were expected home on September 3rd. The evening before, his sister had gone out to the rocks to watch the sunset, and stayed there a long time alone. The glory of it broke that night in a storm of wind and rain. Word came the next day that the boy had spent the night in a country manse, and had gone out in the early morning to bathe, when the river came down in spate. They found his body three days after.

Mrs Mitchell considered the motherhood idea highly indelicate and demanded its excision. Helen's reaction was simply to agree to remove anything that offended, and to allow Isabel's mother to use whatever she wished of the rest, but without appending her name, since she could not admit responsibility for anything so formless and mutilated. Determined to show kindness to Helen (whom she had not even thanked for her trouble), Mrs Mitchell sent along a Miss McKerrow, Isabel's friend, to go through the chapter page by page, pointing out the sentences that had caused Mrs Mitchell sleepless nights. 'If I would be good enough to undertake it again,' Helen reported to Dr Taylor, 'Miss McKerrow would give me constant advice and suggestion in the writing. (My dear, remember to my undying honour that I took that with an unmoved countenance, and not even a very little devil of a twinkle.)' It ended in Miss McKerrow jumping at the suggestion that she should write the opening chapter herself. 'I behaved exactly like Pet Marjorie's turkey, when she saw her entire brood eaten by a sow:
> Yet she was more than usual calm
> She did not give a single damn.
'Don't think I'm really hurt,' Helen's letter concludes. 'I do think Mrs Mitchell is "ignorant" as they say in Co. Down, and I think she might have sent me a message of thanks. But that's a trifle. Miss McKerrow asked if she might use any of my stuff without quotation marks, and I gave it to her with my blessing. So that ends it.' Small wonder that 'the working-class' and the Girls' Auxiliary were rapidly becoming a scarecrow to Helen, she being the crow. Anyone who has attempted to compose liturgical prayers will know the immense difficulty of the task, and throughout these weeks Helen had also been wrestling with the production of a book of prayers for the G.A. The strange rhythm of giving of her best and having it declined with thanks because it was too good was to mark Helen's life. At the height of the Mitchell contest, Helen's weekly letter to India reported:

In the thick of it came a letter from Muriel Hamilton: the prayers were beautiful, but — did I think I could make them simpler, as they were partly for working girls? I groaned: and fell to them on Sunday. I did not change the prayer beginning 'Thy eternity dost ever besiege our life'. That was the only difficult sentence in it: and even that I left, as I told her, because by all means possible I wanted to hammer into the brain of your working class girl some idea of eternity, if it were only the beauty of the word. For to get any conception of infinity is like taking the stone off the mouth of a well.

Five weeks later, Dr Taylor learned the sequel: 'I had a very apologetic letter last week from Muriel Hamilton preparatory to a meeting of committee, to warn me that she was afraid all of my prayers but one — the organization prayer — would be chucked, as too difficult. I sent them *carte blanche* and my blessing and (never say I am not of a seraphic temper) a new short prayer for Bible Circles.'

Frequently frustrated and subject to moods of deep dejection, Helen often likened herself to the improvident Irish monks whom St Bede the Venerable styled 'grasshoppers' because they went a-wandering just before harvest-time, and returned to enjoy the fruit of others' labour. 'Listen Dada Sahib,' she admonished. 'What for did you send me twenty-five guineas instead of twenty? You're encouraging me in improvidence, and the morals of a grasshopper. You're making me believe that there'll never be a winter. No more there is for grasshoppers. I think the end of the summer is the end of them too — I've always remembered from my early youth two lines of Byron —

"He is an evening reveller, who makes
His life an infancy, and sings his fill."'

Yet if she was guiltily dependent upon Dr Taylor's bounty, it was not because of sloth. These years, outwardly so barren and aimless, prove on analysis to have been amazingly productive. In addition to her research into the origins of drama, she was contributing weekly articles to *Daybreak*, a flimsy children's magazine; conducting a Bible circle; giving catechetical instruction to a Japanese Buddhist; submitting original essays and stories — four on Ballygowan House, a lengthy study of Lady Mary Wortley Montagu, and a number of Eastern fables — reviewing for the *Manchester Guardian, The Nation*, the *Fortnightly Review, Blackwood* and *Asia* — among them, reviews of Herbert A. Giles's *Chinese Biographical Dictionary*, Arthur Waley's *A Hundred and Seventy Chinese Poems*, Ernest Bramah's *Kai Lung's Golden Hours* — and working over years to supply Edward Arnold with a series of unsigned stories, accepted on condition that the publisher was free to change or adapt to the mentality, not this time of the working class, but of seven-year-olds. 'Most people could do it with their left hand,' Gregory Smith stormed, 'you with your left foot!' Along with several others, her finest story, *The Princess Splendour*, was shoved into a cupboard and forgotten. Twenty years later, by that time a famous writer, Helen asked that the rejected material be forwarded to Constable, her publisher. There, it met with exactly the same fate.

Everything Helen wrote, even fairy-tales for small children, was an expression of her own philosophy, personality, and experience. She did nothing by halves; at times she could work with lightning rapidity when a blinding flash of intuition made time stand still. One of her most brilliant sallies, *Aut Proprium Aut Diabolus*, written in the spirit of the famous *Epistolae Obscurorum Virorum* (published in 1515 probably by a friend of Martin Luther), occupied her 'a very few hours', and sent Gregory Smith into a state of ecstasy. 'Do you see the drift?' she asked Dr Taylor. 'It will be a "rag" from start to finish: Bride Property as the sole legitimate spouse of Holy Church, inasmuch as Property and Heresy dare not go together. I am quoting Rabelais and the *Epistolae Obscurorum Virorum* and the Instructions of Bishop Williams in 1622 — all in a glorious welter of nonsense. But there's just enough satire to ballast it. That is why you are getting only a little letter.' Ordinarily however her work progressed slowly, simply because it was so profound. From girlhood she was engaged on one quest: to reach out to the eternal that lies behind and beyond the flux of phenomena enveloping man's temporal life. This is strikingly illustrated in the story of *The Uttermost Isles*, a title borrowed from Saintsbury. Brought out in America by Gertrude Emerson, assistant-editor of *Asia*, a magazine on the Far East, it was Helen's first introduction to a country and people who were to become very dear to her. At the high point of the narrative, the speaker becomes the little eight-year-old girl who, with bare toes, used to climb up the knobbly bark of the maple tree in the Tokyo garden and there, perched high among young green leaves beneath an azure sky, think white celestial thoughts about the *Letter to Hebrews*. Transfusing the Buddhist legend with her own deep Christian faith, she deliberately flings St Paul's 'mortality swallowed up in life' against the darkness. Her letter to Dr Taylor summarizes it:

I have been working at a sort of dream-article on *The Uttermost Isles*: the Japanese variant of the Orpheus and Eurydice legend and, with it, its descendant after I suppose two thousand years, the story of *The Peony Lantern*: how a samurai's dead love returned to him on the seventh night of the seventh moon, which is the Feast of the Dead, and brought him to death himself. It is a Buddhist legend, and one sees the fear of love, because it binds a man's soul so close to the illusion that is the world. With love, there comes a darkness, and what was vain and transitory and a passing show stands still, and eternity flows past like a river of stars. And nothing will shake the darkness, or give the man's spirit the eyes of discernment again:

There is no lantern can lighten
The dusk of the Way of Love.

I've been thinking of the most bitter-sweet of all dreams, the restoring of the dead. 'Women received their dead raised to life again, and others were tortured, not accepting deliverance that they might obtain a better resurrection.' I learned all *Hebrews* by heart when I was little, and I always pondered over that antithesis (for I took it for actual antithesis), thinking how great faith it took to refuse the intimate sure sweetness of return to this world. And I'm thinking how St Paul fought that absorption with things seen, the craving that it might be possible for flesh and blood to inherit the kingdom of God. And his way of fighting is to overwhelm flesh and blood with the intolerable glory of the spirit — sublimation by the heat of its fire: 'mortality swallowed up in life'. Over against him is the Buddhist in the same warfare, but his weapons are carnal. It is as though they took one sentence of St Paul's, 'neither doth corruption inherit incorruption.' Spirit must brand the flesh that it may live. You'll see the inwardness of this disjointed paragraph when *The Uttermost Isles* actually reaches you. The root of both the legends I'm working at is the depredation of death, its 'revelation of the body of our humiliation.'

Almost twenty years later in her Introduction to *The Desert Fathers*, her mind was wrestling with the same problem of human passion entangling the life of the spirit. With a characteristic flash of insight, she moves from a Greek philosopher of the fifth century B.C. through the Christian monks of the Egyptian desert of the fourth century A.D. to a Victorian novelist of the nineteenth century: '"Our mind is hampered and called back from the contemplation of God, because we are led into captivity to the passions of the flesh." The actual words were spoken by the abbot Theonas, but they echo sentence after sentence from Socrates in the *Phaedo*. "Spirit must brand the flesh that it may live", said George Meredith, who was no Puritan.'

Helen's first appearance on the American scene, with the publication of *The Uttermost Isles*, was made by seeming chance. An article of hers on Chinese Poetry in *The Nation* caught Gertrude Emerson's eye: she found it 'one of those rarely-informing and imaginative sketches which inspire and delight', and petitioned for something similar for her own publication. G. W. Massingham, the distinguished editor of *The Nation*, had reacted to the article in much the same way: instead of sending its author the expected rejection slip, he wrote to acclaim her 'very brilliant and carefully studied' essay; he was using it as the leader in the next issue, and asked for more work. So it came about that all unwittingly he handed Elizabeth a brick to hurl through Dr Edward St John's study window and bring the Buddha to his feet: he sent her, to review for *The Nation*, the recently published *Scottish Literature: Character & Influence* by G. Gregory Smith. The review is a masterpiece of creative criticism as well as a glittering display of erudition.

Allusions in the opening paragraph to Scaliger, opponent of Erasmus; to Gabriel Harvey, Edmund Spenser's ill-starred friend of Pembroke Hall; to Pantagruel, Rabelais' all-thirsty one, all witness to the wide range of her Renaissance study, but the skilful exploration of little-known works of Scottish literature is amazing. The review opens:

> Every critic, if he is to come to good, must sojourn for a while in the country of Quintessence. This is why Pantagruel heard the name of Scaliger spoken there, 'moody as a mule and stout as a Scottish laird', no less than Aristophanes the Quintessential. . . . Some, on the other hand, stay there altogether and become lean, admitting nothing to their mouths but Categories, Abstractions, and Second Intentions; these are the pedants, the Gabriel Harveys of criticism, though even Gabriel came very near being touched by the bouquet of white roses when he wrote to Edmund Spenser. But the elect *passent oultre*, to arrive at the great simplicity of the Word of the Holy Bottle. Mr Gregory Smith in his latest book has once or twice come near it, though he is still of those *qui tenoient de la Quinte*. Quintessence, at his departure, has retained him among her Abstractors: his 'Scottish Literature' is not a history of Scottish literature; it is the distillation of a long enjoyment:
>   'He that distilled this liquor distilled it smiling.'

As always, the review was sent at once to India. In his acknowledge-ment, Dr Taylor expressed puzzlement over many of the abstruse references and — not for the first time — hinted at disapproval of her Renaissance reading. Her next letter tried to reassure her Father in God:

> I am immensely pleased that you liked that review — 'swagger' as it undoubtedly was. Did I tell you that Gregory flung the gauntlet by assuring me, when he heard I was to do it, that I had *one* qualification — I knew nothing about the subject. It gave me peculiar delight to make him eat his words. Dear, I *don't* know so much about it. It just happened that I knew a little about those two people, Wariston and Melville and Drummond of Hawthornden, Ben Jonson's friend. And I knew some of the old faerie stuff from grubbing for material for the book of Scottish fairy tales. The ballads I knew in part, and grew to know better in the three weeks' reading that went to that review.
>   For the 'fragile four o'clocks of the Celtic twilight' — do you know the flowers they call 'Twilight Ladies'? Ghostly white flowers that only open in dark? It's the minor poets of the 'Irish Renaissance' that I was thinking of, and even the greater 'ghostly' people like W. B. Yeats, whose 'Celtic Twilight' is one of his most famous books. It was fantastic to call the Ballads 'the great re-entrant angle': it is because they became famous in the eighteenth century, and it is like a sudden door opened into the 'Before Time'. Most of them are medieval, in sentiment at any rate. As for Balkis,

it is the traditional name of the Queen of Sheba — in French tradition and I
believe in Mohammedan. 'Miss Griselda' is the irreproachable maiden
sister of the Antiquary, Thomas of Erceldoune, also called Thomas the
Rhymer, the half-legendary father of Scottish poets: he was taken by the
Queen of Elfinland and held by her for seven years. You'll find the ballad
in the 'Oxford Book of English Poetry'. Of Jehan de Moulec I know no
more than Melville tells us: but that Melville is the famous ambassador to
Elizabeth from Mary Queen of Scots, and is sometime going to make an
article. Did I not tell you his immortal differentiation between the two
Queens — 'The Queen of England may be the whiter, but our queen is
very lufesome.' 'Cantups' are cantrips, fantastic performances; 'splairgers'
— I'd need to summon old Hermiston to deal with that great word. It
means, I think, a sort of dilettante shuffling attitude to life and work
generally, swinging at a loose end, splashing aimlessly — in fact,
'splairgin'; 'glunch' is an inarticulate sulky scowl, a dreadfully expressive
word.

Now dear — about the opening paragraph. You know, we agree in the
main about Rabelais. But the country of Quintessence is on the whole such
a clean bit of writing, of sheer fantastic and very gentle satire — besides
being for years my summary, to Gregory's self, of Gregory's great fault in
style — that I used it quite frankly. Have not you yourself used the word
'Gargantuan'? And 'Pantagruelian' is almost a commonplace for the
greater humour, the humour of a kindly intellectual giant. As for the
'Word of the Holy Bottle' — one can't get over the comedy of that single
word, at the end of so vast compassing sea and land. It's the simplicity of it
that I commended. And I was thinking of the critics who say their great
things with the same economy of words. Like a glorious phrase of
Swinburne's for Chapman's translation of Homer — 'the stride of a giant
for the echo of the footfall of a god'; or Saintsbury's summary of
Bellafront, Dekker's Magdalene — 'Imogen gone astray', or Shakespeare's *Venus and Adonis* — young — but with the youth of Shakespeare.

Helen was quoting Saintsbury far too often for Dr Taylor's
comfort. Her early letters had been so filled with enthusiastic
appreciation that Dr Taylor had at once set himself the task of
digesting a little of Saintsbury's enormous output.

'I am very well content that you have discovered Saintsbury,' she
wrote in July 1916, 'and I can't tell you how pleased that you like him.
I think you must be feeling for him what I did before I met him —
sheer gratitude. He was a revelation in criticism, and rather like a
galvanic battery. But I was afraid you might be a little repelled: things
like the very Elizabethan descent upon the Evangelicals, for instance.
That "unsavoury phrase" as you justly describe it . . . I am almost
sure it is Rabelais. I think it's himself who says very delightfully of
Hazlitt that "when the wind is in the east with him" there's nothing for

his admirers but to do as Charles Lamb did in the literal east wind, "go to bed till it's over". Only — with Saintsbury — it is usually better fun to stay up: and it doesn't last long. He *is* good to play with: but it isn't only his seventeenth-century love-making: it's the immense kindness of the man behind it: his "humanity".

'Did I tell you that his presentation copy of *The Augustans* came to me with the solemn assurance that some of it was written for me? I didn't challenge it for a long time, and then came a legal document of items — the pages on Swift, especially the footnotes on the Duchess of Queensbury and the Polite Conversation; parts of the Thralia; touches in the Prior: and a passage in the poetry of Gray.'

Strong in a fearful innocence that knew not the doctrine of ill-doing nor dreamed that any did, Helen repeated to her father-in-God a fair amount of that delectable seventeenth-century love-making. She quoted Saintsbury's *Envoi* to his presentation copy of *French Lyrics*:

'Go, Book, to Her in whom do meet
All wealth of wit and witchery.
And when thou comest to her feet
Say, "Lady, I have brought to Thee
What once was worthless: but behold!
Since thou didst deign to ask for me
It were more precious far than gold.'

'Isn't it pretty?' she asked. 'And hasn't he caught the old manner?' Possibly she did not take into sufficient account the fact that behind the learned Minister of God's word was a man just as human as Saintsbury, and even saints are not immune from lurking green-eyed monsters. So while Dr Taylor warmly praised Helen's study of the Bible in her stories for *Daybreak*, his approbation of both Gregory Smith and Saintsbury was often slightly chilly. He made no secret of the fact that he did not care overmuch for their all-too-catholic tastes: he feared contamination, and expressed dismay at Helen's reading of Rabelais and the Restoration dramatists — but were they the real objects of his attack? His attack is no longer extant: her defence is as pertinent today as it was on 21 April 1918, when she wrote:

Dear,
I am the more bold to write this letter because I am in small risk of being accused by you of a leaning to 'the Fleshly School'. You've written an admirable letter on Rabelais: and I read it with a funny mixture of feelings. For though you meant to fling the gauntlet to Saintsbury you really flung it to me. You see, Saintsbury's Rabelais is the only Rabelais who exists for

me: I see him as he sees him. But I also know your Rabelais, for — I have been there myself.

It was years ago that I first tried to read Rabelais: and the first few pages — I never got beyond them — left me rent between sea-sickness and a bewildered astonishment that men could still be found to read such stuff. How Saintsbury, and Gregory, and Swinburne, and a great multitude besides, could speak of him with actual affection, even a sort of humorous veneration, I retched at the extraordinary digestion of the masculine mind, and still more extraordinary palate. Thereafter came slow years in which, unconsciously, I was getting Rabelais' background: a long series of plays, written most of them by churchmen, in which Rabelais was pretty well rivalled: controversial plays, purely religious, written by the Reformers, which for foulness and irreverence it would be hard to beat. My dear, no one who hasn't read them knows what cesspools the Reformation stirred — and emptied — on its opponents' heads. How religion survived that abominable atmosphere is another of the miracles — the Spirit of God moving upon the face of the waters that were very dark and very foul. You speak of Rabelais' profanity: the fifteenth and early sixteenth century were, I think, the profanest I know. When I first read our own Heywood, I wrote pages of fierce denunciation: the man seemed to be a perfect son of Belial, with as much regard for chastity as for religion: it took three readings widely spaced before I began to see. He was a loyal Catholic, one of the few who went into exile for his faith: a passionate lover of the Church, not as she was — that accounts for a lot of his, and Rabelais' ribaldry — but the Platonic idea of the Church, as the interpreter of God; and of a very sturdy morality, pitiful of the poor, and of the broken-spirited, with gleams even of the finest thinking on love — crude, like a March sky, but with something already of the blue infinity of love's heaven. The conciseness of the language, the sheer satirical power was so great that it took me in: it creates a twilight that it's hard to see distinctly in, but one gets used to it, and in that getting used to it lies all the secret of the 'historical' attitude to literature. It doesn't mean — though of course it is easy to say it for oneself, my saying it is no evidence — that you've lost your delicacy. I 'resent' things in modern writing just as fiercely as ever: my brother declared the other day that it was impossible to tell me an ugly story: but upon my honour, Saintsbury is right in saying that Rabelais is *for the expert*, time deodorised. I once said to Gregory that your first sensation — your *only* sensation — on first reading Rabelais is sickness at his filth, just as your first sensation in bathing is the astonishing coldness of the sea. Once well in, and it is the last thing you think of. Gregory meditated, and then said, 'It's a singularly perfect metaphor.'

I do not expect you to understand it, I don't think you could without the technical preparation, but Rabelais affects me as Shakespeare does — with the same sense of all but omnipotent humanity. But, dear, do read again those chapters wherein Panurge reasons of the estate of the Debtor and the Creditor, deeming it the only state of grace. It's the thing called humour, coming upon you like the waves of the sea. I send you to that because I know it left me almost transported with admiration of that transcendent mischievous gravity. But the little things: 'Tell me, I pray you, are any so wise as the Devils are?' — 'Nay, save by God's especial grace.' 'The testimony of the little fishes, which is of great importance with regard to the construction of —— old boots.' But you need the full paragraph there to get the sheer absurd delight of the anticlimax.

He *is* profane, but there again you need the background: the Schoolmen had made Holy Writ ridiculous, and do remember that it's *not* Holy Writ he's mocking: it's the fool's use of it that he is mimicking. I wonder have you read the *Letters of the Obscure Men?* You need them, to appreciate Rabelais. The historical attitude to literature is a little like one's behaviour in the dissecting room. The first sensation is a pretty strong disgust. One gets used to it there: heaven help the progress of anatomy if we didn't; but your nose remains quite as sensitive in other places where that smell need not be. And I disagree (hear her impudence) with Sir Walter about Rabelais' effect on religion. He was of the school of Sir Thomas More, of Erasmus, and you know I have some sympathy with them. I'd like some day to do an article on Sir Thomas More: his conviction that the Vine was the Holy Catholic Church, and that pruning was all it needed: his dread of the Reformers who would cut it to the roots and burn it. I am *convinced* that Rabelais 'did well believe in God'. But one needn't worry. Think of the awful stuff you are supposed to bed at the feet of roses. Mind — I suppose this is a woman's last word — don't think that Rabelais doesn't disgust me still. He does, heaps of times. But there is always the 'Passons vultre'.

Behind this defence of Rabelais, Helen's voice can be heard warmly championing a dearly-loved friend. To read George Saintsbury's letters to Helen Waddell from 1915 to 1920 the 'most letterwritingest' years of their association — is to form some idea of the preparation he so generously gave her for her future work. Nor must it be forgotten that on both sides the letters were absolutely free from any taint of writing for publication. A few unfortunate readers do not enjoy the style of Helen's published works; as Saintsbury said of Elia, perhaps it is a matter of personal constitution or, like colour-blindness, a thing to regret not condemn. But the letters of these two? 'I wonder if you have my feeling about burning letters?' Helen asked. 'I hate to tear them up for the waste paper basket: but burning always reminds me of Cleopatra's "I am fire and air: my base elements I give to baser earth." It's a sort of sublimation.' Her biographer can only render thanks that many of the letters were left for the moth rather than the fire to consume. They are so real, so human, so many-sided, abounding in acute literary perception, narrative excellence, and the power of making the smallest thing totally interesting. It is impossible to pigeon-hole the correspondence, and to make a selection is to grieve over what is omitted. Of the forty categories of letters classified by Proclus, a neo-Platonist, Saintsbury remarks: 'Of these, "love-letters" is the most important, and "mixed" the *canniest*, for it practically lets in everything', and 'mixed' is perhaps the canniest slot for the Saintsbury-Waddell letters; for what he has said of Swift's, might be said with equal truth of his own — 'the refreshment which he offers varies unceasingly from the lightest froth of pure nonsense, through beverages middle and stronger, to the most drastic restoratives — the very strychnine and capsicum of irony.' As for the most important category, the reader must understand, as the two eighteenth-century performers at either end of the speaking-tube undoubtedly did, 'the great, the beneficent, the much abused art of flirtation in all its branches'.

On 11 April 1916 Helen wrote to G.S.:

I don't think you have any idea — though your students in Edinburgh may have let you know something of it — of the magnitude of your gifts to the likes of me. They're like the blessing to Joseph, 'precious things brought forth by the sun, and precious things brought forth by the moon.' Just at the moment it's Carew.

'When thou, poor excommunicate', and 'Give me more love or more disdain' drugged me. The first verse of it has more of the actual lotos in it than any quatrain I know. I had to *rouse* myself to read the rest.

For the rest that were new to me, and already elect, there is Campion's 'Kind are her answers', which has a very opposite effect. I know she danced to it when he sent it to her. 'Beauty clear and fair' is like sapphires (I do not love the stone but the name always suggests the thing it was meant to be). And all Sir John Suckling's are 'little blisses'. I am not quite sure why I like 'Fain would I change that note'; it is as though it reminded me of some better thing, another of the 'fallings from us, vanishings'. The first verse of 'Tell me no more how fair she is' need be nothing but itself: one will never come nearer 'the story of that distant bliss'. Then there are lines innumerable: the last line of William Browne's 'Where no joy dies till love hath gotten more', and Rochester's 'And lose my everlasting rest'.

But the discovery that surprised me most was Dryden. He is very gracious. Tell me, who was the first to find the metre of 'Farewell, ungrateful traitor' (such an opening for such a close!). I believe it's my favourite of the more complicated measures. I knew it first in the 'drear-nighted December', and then in Swinburne's 'Red strays of ruined springs'. But I would burn candles to the first begetter.

Lord love you for giving me
       'To all you ladies now at land
       We men at sea invite.'

It is going, edited, to *one* man at sea.

And when they are all said and sung, one comes back to Donne. I had not realized how 'different' he was till I came on him here. But you have said it all in the last sentence of your preface, and I had better not begin on him. As this, in spite of appearances is *not* a thesis, and you and I are no longer, thank heaven, in the 'unnatural relations of examiner and examined' over which the Egyptian was chuckling this afternoon. It *is* a good piece of writing on Mrs Thrale. You know a very great deal about us, Excellency.

Yours,
Helen.

P.S. And so you think it is not in me to love you 'one whole day'? But after all, Excellency, is it not better done — concisely?

P.P.S. And what do I think of 'Greedy Lover'?

I think nothing, my lord.

Three days later, he acknowledged her letter:

. . . I am more sure than ever that you and I were at some time united in a star (probably Poe's El Aaraaf). You are the very first person whom I have ever got to *feel* with me about Carew and Dryden. Of course, as you say & I say, they shrivel beside Donne — but who doesn't? I did not think anybody — even you — could have put what 'Ask me no more' makes one feel in heart & backbone & so finally. But I have known people — even outside the usual books & people who were not shocked by the *Raptere* &c — refuse to consider him anything but a pretty conceited trifler. 'Cold' they call him — well, I believe you *can* burn your fingers on a wheel-tire frozen to about 70° below zero.

So in a less degree with Dryden's songs. I can't get my friend the Poet Laureate to acquiesce in my liking D. at all! As for 'Farewell, ungrateful traitor' I don't know any direct original. My old friend Beljame almost the first Frenchman really to understand English literature told me that most of these songs were taken from French tunes, if not exactly from French words. I was however never able to trace this.

Talking of French — you have my *French Lyrics* I think? If not you must let me as a 'greedy lover' give you that too. But I think you have it.

He had already given her the book, so he sent her three labels from which to make a choice: they rose from professorial remoteness to warm friendship. Her letter is not extant, but its contents can be gleaned from his reply:

I stand you in the corner! If I did it would be with your face towards me that I might see you better against the two walls. (But the ordinary punishment way would be a little amusing, especially if you had a low dress on, for I could watch your shoulders twitching, as you pretended to cry & were really laughing.) Besides you know it is a principle of mine that everybody should hate what he does hate & love what he does love.

You can't think, or perhaps you can, how it pleases *me* to have pleased *you*. I feel as if I were a youthful Homeric hero & you a maiden in a chiton — boiling me in a beautiful tripod of warm water, & then anointing me with the sweetest oil, & clothing me with white & purple, & feeding me with goat & pig & the best of wine &c &c. (you know the programme though you don't profess to know Greek).

But do you know (I think you do) that I *hoped* you would put all three labels in? It was just like your witching ways to do so.

Yes, when you and I are not in Samarcand, Camelot & Joyous Gard (& Carbonek) are the places for us. But one cannot be always in any of them: & it is not ill to visit Bath & Tunbridge Wells & Streatham now & again. The charm of the others is made more poignant.

Farewell for the present — you have put a garland on my grizzling head.

To mention a Greek chiton to Helen was bound to evoke a response. Far from robing her figure in a long woollen tunic cut on classical lines, she told him, she would wear her new dress of primrose silk fluted with frills when they next meet. 'Prima Rosa,' he flashed back, 'think of me sometimes in this new gown . . . I adore frills: their actuality is delightful & their associations more so. I think I heard once in the more scandalous Antediluvian society that Eve invented the frill as a study of the serpent in motion. . . . Perhaps Lilith started that story.' Even in the realm of fashion he was at least her equal, for he goes on in a later letter:

It is agreed that the black mantilla is the most becoming of all head-dresses to those who can wear it; also that the damsels of the Land of Ire can wear it better than most; also — but the third proposition is so self-evident that it would be an insult to write it in full. As for the dress an idea occurred to me which some folk would call commonplace but you won't I think. I figured yourself to myself as an angel all complete . . . with half outstretched wings &c *only* instead of that interesting *chiton* (a very nice thing in itself) which is the usual angelic uniform, you had the heliotrope dress & the Samarcand shoes & the wing sleeves in*side* the main wing-sweep so that the feathers made a sort of shrine for you. You were bare-headed of course — the mantilla wouldn't 'go' here. The picture was very refreshing to the joints & marrow.

By the way of the wing-sleeves did I ever tell you a story of my bulldog Cherub — the most lovable creature, not a cat or a girl — that ever existed? It was in 1890 — the year after you were so infinitely gracious as to be born — people wore their sleeves with a slight difference — at any rate they left the whole inner arm bare to above the elbow-hollow. My left-hand neighbour at dinner had a dress — apricot chiefly — made thus & for the moment she had her right arm dropped by the side of the chair so that her fingers nearly touched the ground. Whereat the dog who had been lying between us, stealthily raised himself up & then with one sudden stroke licked her hand & arm right up to the cup. The arm was very white & thin & the tongue very broad & pink. You can imagine how a half scream (for she didn't even know he was there) passed into a whole laugh. She is dead now.

In her letter of 11 April, Helen had thanked Saintsbury for a couplet to be sent post-haste to 'one man at sea'. This was Dr Billy Lynd, her constant dancing partner at Queen's weekly hops during their undergraduate days, whose proposals of marriage had been as regularly refused as proffered. Towards the end of 1917 he was home on leave, told Helen of the young woman he had met on the *Caronia*, and confessed that he was about to make her his wife. This piquant analysis of the situation was at once despatched to 'the Saint' on 25 October 1917:

This is written in a certain dejection. Just that an old 'friend and lover' of mine is weary at last, and going to be married next leave. I met him yesterday, very resplendent in blue and gold, and we were exceedingly glad to see each other, and went and had tea together. And then he confessed. I didn't tease him. I only said that I was glad he had really fallen in love at last.

You will have guessed that it is the Man at Sea. And I'm not blaming him. I'm just dog-in-the mangerish. He was such nice hay, not to eat, nor even to make your abode in, but just to stir round. And then he was so nearly my first. It's just a wail for youth, this letter. I keep remembering things, things like the look on his face when he would see me in the middle of a crowd, and come cleaving through it to demand seven dances. Curious, no matter how young and inexperienced and diffident you are, that look flings you to the crest of the wave, and you defy him as nonchalantly as if you were Cleopatra — not in her salad days neither, instead of all but convent-bred. I suppose it is true that there is something in the youngest of us that does not belong to us at all. I have felt it in myself. Have you seen Masefield's things on Roses, the old roses

　　　'Women that made summer in men's hearts
　　　　　Before . . .'

I forget how it ends: something banal about the Sphinx. But he has another line somewhere that is yours —

　　　　　'Eternal April wandering alone.'

And here, O Master of Casuists, is a question to debate before Quintessence. I was speaking of this with a kind of rueful laughter to one who is wise in these things, and she holds that it is better — even for one's self — to lose one's old lovers: better, for one's self, that they should despair of you and go away: for that if you have any tenderness for them at all — and it is hard not to — the thought of them is a sort of 'retainer': that subconsciously you judge the new men by them, and say 'The old were better', because of that glamour of youth. Better to go free. It is a good question.

Helen.

'"Something in the youngest of us that does not belong to us at all"? O Mignonne,' he replied, 'is there *anything* in us, young or old, that we can say "belongs to us"? The atoms float & clash & sever. But this is too lyrical.' Lyrical it may be: it is also a poignant insight into the heart of a man whose immense scholarship never quenched his deep humanity.

The year 1918 was one of refusals of more than the five suitors for her hand. Her uncle Hugh had wished to bequeath to Helen beautiful old Ballygowan House, standing in the heart of green elms and shadowy beeches against the Mourne Mountains, the house that was sole witness of the twelve-year-old's crisis of faith. She refused the legacy on the grounds that a doctor cousin stood nearer in the line and was more in need of it than she — an act she later regretted when, in a fit of pique, her uncle made quite other dispositions of the property, which then became a centre of acrid family dispute.

In the same year Miss Rentoul begged Helen to accept the headship of her private school for girls of wealth and social standing, possessed of no specific intellectual ambition. The offer was accompanied by a £700 per annum 'bribe'. 'It does tempt me,' Helen told Dr Taylor, 'it's like evolving the new heaven and the new earth. I'd take Hopefield House, which now lies desolate, with beds of iris growing deep in long grass, and set my heart on a school the very best of its type in Ireland.' G. D. Coates, her bank-manager and admirer, supported Gregory Smith in urging her to accept. With her imagination conjuring up all the alluring possibilities, Helen happened to stroll into Queen's library. No sooner had she crossed the threshold, felt the palpable silence, inhaled the dust and scent of leather and old books, met the bent figure of grizzly little Mr Salmon the librarian, than she knew with unshakable conviction that writing, not education, was her life. On 18 August she wrote to India:

> Did I tell you of Gregory's encounter with me on the telephone, à propos of Miss Rentoul's last offer — the one that assured me a profit of £700 a year? It startled him, for after all a chair at Queen's is only £600. '£700, you say?' 'Yes.' 'Well . . . £700 is not to be sneezed at . . . these days.' A long pause. 'But it in no way alters anything I said to you. What are you doing about it?' 'I've posted a letter refusing, on my way here.' 'You've — *what?*' Then came a burst of laughter at the other end, and something like a Bravo! And when he was sober again — 'I like the way you ask my advice. But I think you did wisely. Only — out of fifteen thousand people in Belfast,

there's only the fifteen thousand and first who'll think that you aren't a fool.'

From Bath, not Belfast, Saintsbury *alias* Taverner, considered Helen Jane Waddell *alias* Elizabeth St John anything but a fool, but he remonstrated with her, all the same:

O my dear, my dear!
Aren't you falling 'Into a fatal fashion of *refusing*' (an odd variant of a line of Wyatt or Surrey's which came straight into my head as I read your letter)? You refuse legacies; you refuse valuable appointments; *and* you refuse — . It is true that you would hardly have been Helen *or* Jane if you hadn't done the first: and probably you might have hated the headmistress-ship though you might also have given it a trial. As for the third refusal it is not easy for me to speak. Don't think me capable for a moment of thinking you likely to play the Siren. But you can't help being *magnetic* & we who are magnetisable must fly to you. I am sorry for *him*: for any one who has sense enough to *want* you must be horribly sensitive to not having you. And you know my unselfish & crossgrained notion that you *ought* to marry. 'The greatest happiness of the greatest number' is chatter. But if any one can add to the intenser happiness of the world I think they ought to do it. Only women and poets can — & I don't think many women could do it like you.

His letter of a week later corroborated his first findings, and added a comment on Helen's recently published story, *The Uttermost Isles*, which illumines the passion and meditation he brought to bear on that simple act of reading an ancient fable:

When Asquith married Margot Tennant whom I knew slightly & who *then* was 'vurry attractive' I sent her a message that 'I hoped it wouldn't lead to the Extinction of the Dodo' (you know Benson was supposed to have meant her). *She* was delighted but he (whom I did *not* then know) when he heard it gnashed his teeth & said 'D——n him.' I tell you this ancient legend for a comparison which you will have outgalloped my pen in reaching. If £700 or £7000 or £70000 &c &c a year involved the diminishing or damaging of Helen in any way let it be cast into the dustbins of Eternity rather than be touched by her.
I have read the 'Isles' twice & only wait till I am alone to read them again & again. They made me feel as if . . . I were in a room darkened with Venetian blinds & full of the mixed scent of live and dying roses. And somebody's head was on my shoulder — & ever now & then a blaze of summer lightning slipped through the flaps of the blind & I saw Somebody's face. This is truth.

How much of Saintsbury's Noncumsensediddledense, to use Southey's Lingo-Grande, was sheer absurdity, how much a mask for sheer heroism? Sometimes the grumbling in his letters grows to a mighty rumbling: He has a vile throat; a wife too ill to be left alone; many bills but few coos; the wheels of work drive heavily and he has to sell capital in order to pay income-tax; he has been thrown down by a motor, badly shaken but not broken, for 'luckily the thing took me as a cowcatcher taketh the trespassing cow, and toppled me on its bonnet, to which I clung'; the obtaining of tea and meat and bread and bacon is a daily weariness; miseries all summed up in the story of the clerk who sang to the most primitive of Gregorian psalm-tones: 'Many dogs have come abow-wow-wowt me.' Helen listened, laughed, sympathized and healed. 'Balm of Gilead is nothing to Balm of Helen. *How* do you manage to write so that something spreads itself like balm between the skin & the flesh of the soul, & trickles through its veins, & changes the marrow of its bones? For the soul *has* all these things you know, just like the body.' But the image of George Saintsbury, distinguished critic, historian, professor of Rhetoric and Literature, queuing up for hours to obtain two ounces of butter and a quarter-pound of tea, and cumbered with serving, distraught trying to find food his invalid wife could eat, proved too much for Helen. From childhood nothing had distressed her more than the thought of the hungry. The year 1918 was a year of increasingly stringent rationing in England, whereas Ireland still enjoyed a comparative plenty. Taking her courage in her hands, Helen dropped the elaborate play-acting and turned housewife. Rather shyly, she wrote on 1 March:

Excellency,
I took my nephews to the pantomime in the holidays: and Harlequin asked Columbine 'Do you love me?' and Columbine said 'Yes.' 'Then' said Harlequin with passion, 'tell me where I can get a pound of butter.' I thought of you, a little ruefully . . . and it was only yesterday that it occurred to me that 'smoked Limerick' might be as clearly a conveyance of one's tenderness as any. Do not be very cross with me, Excellency. They tell me that there is no more pig — the best of God's creatures for one meal anyhow — in the length and breadth of England, and it keeps me awake at night thinking what you can be having for breakfast. For there is only one breakfast for me. You once said I did not know the curious pleasure it would be to you to give me things to eat. Perhaps I do.
And you can spend the next six weeks devising the things you will have for me when I come to you at Samarcand in April. Myself, you perceive, confines myself with much propriety to breakfast.
Helen.
I wish to talk to you, Excellency. For I have just finished this moment reading *Manon Lescaut* — the last few pages in a sort of hot anguish.

I have just left it to them to send off in great triumph: for they vow that after this we will only be able to buy in pounds, and I feel as if I had cheated somebody.

Shortly after the delivery of the gift, Rudyard Kipling called on Saintsbury. As always during those hungry days of 1918 the talk turned to food, and Saintsbury told him of Helen's presentation of a whole ham. 'She must be an absolute angel!' replied Kipling with deep feeling.

In 1931 Helen Waddell was to publish the Abbé Prévost's *Manon Lescaut*, translated from the original text of 1731 into perfect eighteenth-century English prose, with an Introduction of 32 pages by George Saintsbury, and follow it up two years later with a play, *The Abbé Prévost*. It was on Saintsbury's and Gregory Smith's advice that she steeped herself during 1918 in the English and French prose writers and dramatists of the eighteenth century. Saintsbury had been the first to notice a falling-off in her style: 'But somehow, Mignonne, there has been a touch lately as if you were not happy. What is it?' He got the answer in three words: 'I can't write!' Gregory had warned her that she was wasting time on work that she could do with her left foot, and he was right. Her muscles had grown soft; she was suffering from paralysis of execution, so that a growing 'encrustation' of manner, as Gregory Smith called it, came between her mind and the page and produced a kind of sham-Gothic. Saintsbury at once reassured her: 'That terror of "I can't write" is — take my septuagenarian assurance — inseparable from those who *can* write. It is only some person who has nothing to say that can always say it. On all others there comes the "fallow" — the time when one must go into a temporary unblessed Nirvana — and can only escape misery by doing something else. . . . Therefore *sursum corda*, Mignonne chérie.' Gregory prescribed a diet of Swift, Congreve, and Anatole France. Its results were immediately apparent when Helen Jane was transformed into Millimant, the witty and coquettish heroine of Congreve's *The Way of the World*, after receiving from Saintsbury a gift that may well have been an expression of thanks for the solid 9 lbs of the best of God's creatures:

> Wednesday night.
>
> Excellency,
>
> This is the minute before the packet is opened, just to caress you. But Eve is barefoot, and dreadfully impatient.
>
> 10 minutes thereafter.
>
> She has it on black velvet, strapped sandal-fashion under the eiderdown: so that by virtue of one foot she is no more Eve but Cleopatra. You *don't know* how it glitters.

But to her mind it looks nicest on — do you remember the black and green brocade shoes with very high heels that I wore that night in Samarcand — the night I lost the opal thing under the apple-trees? They have been worn very little since. They were waiting for these. Now they are Millimant's shoes. I know they were Millimant's buckles. And may it please you, how did you get them if you were not Mirabell? But at any rate he has returned them. And on second thoughts if, as you say, I am Millimant, it's a question better not raised.

So she distracts him to a new question: is the buckle to stay where it is all night, or to be kissed and put under my pillow with its fellow?

Yours
Helen

But Excellency, how did you know? Years ago I told Miss Anne that the one thing I coveted was old paste buckles. But that I wouldn't buy them for myself, because it's the kind of thing only the right person should give you. Do all things come if one waits?

If I had not said 'if' before, I would have said it after that last paragraph. I am saying it now.

Like Saintsbury himself, she had certainly 'caught the old manner', but of a sudden all this 'brief, bright and beatific' nonsense was brought to an end with the signing of the Armistice and the return of the survivors from the war fronts. Slowly life resumed a more normal pattern, and high on the programme of reconstruction was a project to increase the professorial staff at Queen's to meet the throngs of students. Saintsbury had to slip back into the role of Taverner and watch Elizabeth again bait Edward St John — with what success? Helen reported to Dr Taylor:

I saw Gregory one day last week, and we discussed University reconstruction. There are one or two new lectureships to be created, and he has filed an application for a lectureship in English literature, in addition to the chair and the assistantship. It's at best a castle in Spain, for the authorities mayn't encourage a lectureship in a school already well staffed: but I'm not concerned about that. I want to know if — in that improbable event — Gregory's old prejudice will yield at last. Last night I took the obvious way out, and wrote very baldly to ask him what his attitude would be. There's no use pretending that it wouldn't be a job after my own heart.

In the event, Gregory Smith was not put to the test, for the Science faculty had a prior claim, and the government grant would not cover any extra appointment to the School of English. The whole complexion of things was altered, however, when it became evident in 1919 that the post of assistant-lecturer was likely to fall vacant. On 26 August Helen wrote to Dr Taylor:

I've just written a note to Gregory to tell him that I want to see him when the Library opens next week, with a suggestion that it's on business: he knows that Mr Poston, his present assistant, has applied for Reading and Newcastle, so he may have an inkling of what that business will be. Oh dear, I wish he may this time be reasonable. The more I think of it, the more I want it. Apart from everything else, the delight of working up the English school; for Poston though a good soul and a clever was mortally dull.

Maude warned me not to set my heart on it: that with a man so difficult as Gregory and so curiously obstinate, to have refused once makes it almost inevitable that he will refuse again. But I can't help hoping.

A week later:

Dear Dada Sahib,

It's over and done, the interview with Gregory that I so much dreaded. And the end is peace. If I still want it this time six months, I am to come and talk to him again: and *nous verrons*, which means that Gregory will do whatever I want. I know it's done with immense reluctance, and at the cost of a really horrible uprooting of prejudice but, bless his eminence, he'll do it, and with not too bad a grace. So now, my father, will you put all worry for the creature's future out of your head? In another year I should be earning something under £200 a year. And I feel as if a millstone were *gone* from round my neck, and drowned in the depth of the sea, and as if I were going to write half a dozen things at once: while, when this was pending, my wits seemed paralysed.

I'm so glad, so glad. It isn't only the satisfaction of feeling you've some definite end: it's the relief of knowing the affair safely over, and my liking for Gregory unshaken. For I knew the chances were even that he would be a little deaf. I was desperately afraid of quarrelling with him, not an open quarrel: just that one would leave him with a secret grudge. . . . Dear, *aren't* you pleased? And there'll be the long vacation — four months of it, in summer, for one's own work. Besides, once the back of the lecturing is broken, it shouldn't be very exacting. I'm brewing an article on Milton as Scholar. It ought to be fun to do. Ah, but you've been good to me all these years.

The author of *Discipline* should have known better than to build castles in Spain. One feels that just then her name should have been Perrette as she tripped along, milkpail on head, planning to exchange the milk for 100 eggs, the eggs for a brood of chicks, the chicks for a pig, the pig for a cow and calf—

> Quel esprit ne bat la campagne?
> Qui ne fait châteaux en Espagne?
> Picrochole, Pyrrhus, la laitière, enfin tous,
> Autant les sages que les fous.

The assistantship at Queen's came to nothing, and in the summer of that year Maude Clarke was appointed History Tutor at Somerville. Returning to the narrow house in Cedar Avenue and the sole companionship of a querulous stepmother after a day's celebration with Maude, Helen found relief in abandoning all idea of sleep and easing her hurt in a letter to Saintsbury:

It bids fair to be a white night
       'wishing myself . . . like him more rich in hope'
— do you know, I think that line hurt more to write than any of the others. So I am not going to try to go to sleep. You and I may resist the devil together.

    Did you ever in your life choose: and find the road that you turned your back on crossing your own road at intervals of years, so that every now and then you come face to face with a phantom self that might have been you? Only a glorified you. It was after one of those nights that you wrote me
       'If there were dreams to sell.'
Tomorrow will hardly be so fortunate; so I'm forestalling it.

    The immediate cause of this night's grouse is that Miss Anne is going to be History Tutor at Somerville. We have had a drunken day on the head of it; this is the reaction. I came back to find my invalid a little sorry for herself — I think I can leave you to finish. You can be bounded in a nutshell and count yourself king of infinite space if—— it's not your bad dreams that do for you: it's your good ones, when you wake.

    It's not the job; it's the place. It's the look on Miss Anne's face when she says 'It was worth two years of *this*, to be going back.' I didn't know when I refused Oxford ages ago that it was going to hurt like this. It's something like
       'Thyself thou gavest, thine own worth then not knowing.'
Only it's not so much one's own worth, as the worth of — life — that you don't know.

    Excellency, what for did the Almighty give women brains? But bless Him, if He hadn't, I wouldn't at this minute be writing to Professor Saintsbury.

    I am now refreshed. I really believe what rankles as much as Somerville is a four-guinea hat that she got in Regent Street. . . . You see, Fate can get at a woman in so many ways. Good night.

In spite of the spilt milk and the farewell to calf, cow, pig, and clutch of eggs, Perrette could have given Helen there and then in the face of seeming failure a strong reassurance of faith in the workings of the Providence that shapes our end: 'Dieu fait bien ce qu'il fait!' As her own life unfolded, Helen was to discover this truth for herself, so that when she found Meg grieving one day over an interruption in her son

Sydney's plans to take his degree in engineering at Queen's, Helen was able to put fresh heart into her sister by speaking out of her own experience: 'I know it seems as if it were just a stupid disaster,' she conceded, 'but it will mean a far better thing. My darling, will you quit beating your head on walls? "There's a divinity . . . " Oh, the things I've raged over — like Gregory's assistantship — are the things I thank God for now. And apart from everything else, I'd likely have been married to him by this time, and God help me if I had!'

CHAPTER VI

MAY 31ST, 1919, her thirtieth birthday, brought Helen the gift of a Brussels lace handkerchief to carry on her wedding day, with this greeting from George Saintsbury:

> A ta trentième
> O ma Lointaine
> Princesse,
> Moi, je t'adore
> Bien plus encore
> Sans cesse.

The neatness of the pastiche is undeniable, its content delectable, and yet a niggling little devil of a doubt rears an ugly head to ask: Are wit and wisdom to go on being exercised at the expense of life? Was there a basic truth in Maude Clarke's youthful swipe at her friend's 'fundamental unreality'? Like her own Princess Splendour is Helen returning to her home in the moon, leaving behind hopeless lovers ending their days in grief and faithfulness? Is she stepping out of actuality into a dream? The question is worth considering. She spoke of herself as 'me that could have loved terribly, and was born to have a house and children and a man.' Why didn't she? In 1919 — 'the worst and best year I've ever had' — Brice Clarke, newly demobilized with an M.C. to his credit, was expressing his love in words that sounded like 'broken bits of Donne, and the *Laus Veneris*, and *The Last Ride Together*'. William Sinclair Lynd, widowed within a year of marriage, looked to her for at least strong friendship; A. Okey Belfour, restored to his lectureship in English Language at Queen's after four years in Germany, was ready to cloak his love under the guise of good companion for the privilege of taking her to the opera; George Duffield Coates, her bank manager, a widower bereft of an only son, almost persuaded her to dwindle into a wife. To Dr Taylor she wrote:

> I might let myself begin to think of him but — I don't see how I could marry and look after Mother. I couldn't bear to leave her, and yet I'm terribly afraid of the 'ménage à trois' . . . I'll take each day as it comes.

There's no use crossing the bridge: I always knew this difficulty was waiting for me sometime. But up till now I had never seen the man who could ever bring it near. I don't know yet whether this one will even do that. It's possible that knowing him better may leave me with an immense affection for him, and an absolute conviction that he isn't meant for me. It brought that with other men. Gregory, for instance, I had a great admiration for; it's almost inevitable between master and scholar: and I used to wonder whether, if he had fallen in love with me, the sheer astonishment of capturing the Buddha wouldn't have made me fall in love with him. But even when I was liking him most, there was something in me that never gave in, that criticised, and held aloof. As someone said of Gregory, 'It's a great nature, with a kink in it: a great mind — warped.' I almost love the man: he's such a mixture of keen scholarship and childishness, intolerable egoism and unexpected gentleness: St John of the novel intensified.

A few weeks later, a walk with G. D. Coates along the river bank under a rainy sunset settled her mind. Her weekly letter to India reported:

Suddenly something seemed to die in me, and I had nothing left but the dull flat conviction that whatever happened it would never be *him*. One thing I am glad of, that I would never let him take me to his house. For it was *my* house — very old, with a huge garden and low-ceiled rooms: the gladness is not because the house would have tempted me, but I don't want to have it haunted for him. I can imagine few worse tortures than to watch your fire and remember the small Persian cat who was once impudent to you and sat on your hearthrug all one blessed afternoon — and isn't ever going to sit there again. I think he still means to see a good deal of me. I wish he would, for I think I could give him a lot of pleasure. You see he isn't young: somehow I think I was a sort of second spring to him. I know that if I were a man I'd choose it, rather than go away into the outer darkness until you're indifferent. For this way we can always dream,

'Et j'aime la lointaine
Princesse.'

I'm slowly adjusting myself to the realising that I shan't marry for years. I've been nearer it this last winter than I ever was before — partly I think because I was so unhappy and physically so dulled. Anyhow that's over, and I feel that I've gone out on the ebb, farther away than ever. I will not 'come this way again' for five years anyhow. That's the curious conviction that's upon me. Remains the necessity for filling five years. And somehow the 'domestic cat' in me has been so much in demand that my brain is a little rusty. The old joy in writing is gone, the old belief in my own power too. If only I am given peace to grow absorbed again it may come. It's hard at best for the housekeeper to be a scholar, but add this perpetual harassing. In brief, I'm hoping for kinetic energy: the potential is just at the moment very low. Saintsbury says I am lost for a complete change. I suppose he has noticed the faltering of my letters. But that mayn't be for a long time.

This Cupid without wings, love settling into friendship, formed the groundwork, so to speak, of Helen's life; but a passage from the letter just quoted throws a significant light on the principle that determined her decision:

I was talking to Maude about this curious question of love: wondering if it were only God himself that one loved, or should love, with the 'mind' as well as the heart and soul and strength. By the way, wasn't it an amazing conception, that, and did ever anything so encompass the power and possibilities of love? Heart and soul and strength, I can imagine caring for a man with those: but somehow one's mind — it's so impersonal and free a thing, that I could imagine it perpetually 'unmarried'.

The conviction of 'vocation' had always haunted her and was growing steadily stronger: to the end of her life she would quote with anguish from the Milton she both loved and hated the self-accusation

'that one talent which is death to hide,
Lodged with me useless.'

Her mind must remain perpetually unmarried in order to be ready for the work that time would reveal. Yet her whole outlook makes it abundantly clear that she never despised or underestimated family life — far from it.

I will be very honest with you [she told Dr Taylor], I think that to be married to someone you care for is the greatest thing that can happen to you; and just because of that, to marry anybody else seems such a pitiful thing. It means you have lost so much. There mightn't be any tragedy, not even much suffering. But — my Ruskin sentence again — 'I do not wonder at what men suffer, but I wonder often at what they lose.' I saw somewhere — it was quite an indifferent novel — a discussion between two women, both single: and one says defiantly that a single woman has many a time more happiness. 'Happiness?' says the other. 'What does a woman want with happiness? It's things and people to care for.' It came home to me those days just after George died: for the first time I felt I would like to marry and have children — it would be something to go on living for, for somehow George was like a son to me, he was so guileless and helpless and so gay. And I remembered Sydney and Jack and Mollie and Charlie, and as it says in *Acts* I thanked God and took courage. Those children are going to matter to me awfully. I feel a wee bit like the steward making friends with those who should hereafter receive him into everlasting habitations. I want the liking of things so young as they are. And so far, I have it. Jack and I seem to know each other without translation. It's such a perverse mortal: you sometimes think him an unlicked cub of a schoolboy, and suddenly when you're walking with him you find your hand surreptitiously kissed. Sydney is to get a *Boy's Own Paper* from me — the huge bound volume: he reminded his mother of it with his small boots in the air, turning somersaults. They arrived one day last week and stayed *hours*, while they talked about swimming. 'Aunt Helen, what made the first man swim?' To which Aunt Helen gravely replied, 'The first time, he tumbled in,' which they thought exquisitely humorous. Finally they went away waving their caps all the way down the street, and left the freshness behind them of new-hatched chickens. They're like that, such round bright eyes and eager voices and the same trick of scratching at every experience.

At this point it is tempting to quote another of the rare letters happily preserved from Meg to Helen. Throughout the trying circumstances of this 'lost decade', Kilmacrew and the children became a peaceful focus and vital centre, radiating calm and sanity. In their limpid simplicity and absence of any literary form, Meg's letters are a nice foil to her brilliant sister's: she wrote, according to Helen, as if she were doing needlework in the Japanese manner, but she shares Helen's vision of the reality of common things, and can write beautifully and profitably about truths which come home to everybody. Towards the end of 1918 after the epidemic of influenza, she assures Helen:

Sydney is all right again, eating and running about just as much as ever. They are having a great time with a Scouts' camp under the trees up the avenue — an old tablecloth and some meal bags make a fine tent — and a gypsy fire: they boil potatoes and make potato bread, and forage for sticks. Sydney is captain, and we don't call them anything now but Scout 1, 2, 3, 4. Last night No. 2 (Jack) was to sleep outside. You know what No. 2 is like for pertinacity, so for the sake of peace he was allowed, and departed with an old blanket and a waterproof rug trailing in a box behind him round the bend at 10 p.m. We waited until he would be safely in bed in the tent and walked quietly up to find Scout No. 2 sitting on an upturned box pensively surveying the fire, and a great quietness all around. It was a quaint picture — the big trees and the little tent and the solitary figure beside its fire, its hands on its knees in contemplation. It turned in and we left it; but somehow I felt loth to depart, and after I had my hair brushed, I slipped up. It wasn't sleeping. 'I could sleep,' he said, 'only the owls make such a noise up there!' So after some persuasion the valiant scout arose and came down to his feather bed.

For good measure she adds a vignette of her small daughter that cries out for Edward Ardizzone's crayon:

Mary is growing so, her legs hang out of the puce dress like fuchsia stamens, and it has short sleeves, so her woolly ones droop dejectedly out of them, but she is a brave wee soul. Next week I'll spring clean. It will be a relief to bump and thump reasonable things like furniture and beds — they are comforting that way, and get a nice fresh smell in the sun. If it were not for some wee birds I should nearly have gone under, but they have such a liquid warble, makes me think of you and me barefoot in some impossible soft and sheltered place, with sunlight on the moss and through green leaves. Some day — but here comes the family. Sydney whistling 'a wee doch-an-doris'* so goo'bye— .

It was the three elder of Meg's five children, Sydney, Jack and Mary Martin, who were the begetters of *Stories from Holy Writ*, a book published only in 1949, prefaced by this Note:

These stories were written during the six years between 1914 and 1920, for a small missionary magazine called *Daybreak*. The earlier stories had already been told to two small nephews and smaller niece whose names, to their great embarrassment, appeared in the first number: Jack, I remember, was found scoring his name out with a furious stubby pencil. These were the children who discovered Pharaoh's palace in the white-painted beehive, and for whom the huge umbrella that covered the pony-trap was Abraham's tent at Hebron. The background was an old white-washed house in County Down, its three foot thickness of wall sunk in ivy and in apple orchards, but with the silence of the bog behind it, where at night one could sometimes hear the drumming of the snipe.

The pertinacious little bulldog Scout No. 2 who could pass from starry contemplation of heaven's immensity at 10 p.m. to ear-splitting shouts of Sulyman-ben-David to test his lung power at 6 o'clock next morning, could no longer object to the use of his proper name: Jack, Coeur de Lion, was buried in a soldier's grave in Rhodesia in 1941. But to forestall the reproaches of the living, the other two became Stephen and Sarah. To those who know and love the book, the three children will remain for ever seven, five and three-and-a-half years old. The house of course is Kilmacrew, but few children can have been blessed with a teacher of such Coleridgean fancy and imagination. In a field behind the house, Sydney called for Aunt Helen to tell the story of Ali Baba and the Forty Thieves but, as it was Sunday, he had to make do with Moses in the Bulrushes. By way of preparation, however, this absolutely demanded splairgin' for if, according to Stevenson's *Weir of Hermiston*, 'there's nae room for splairgin' under the four quarters of John Calvin', there was room and enough under the trees of Kilmacrew:

*Gaelic: a stirrup-cup or a last drink at night; 'a drink of the door'.

We lay quite flat — you would wonder how different things look when your eyes are very close to the ground. It is too wet to lie on the grass now, but try it on the carpet the next time somebody is telling you a story, and you will see all sorts of houses and bridges and caves underneath the chairs. There was a stream through the grass where we were lying, a very little one, with rushes. But looking at it this way it was very big, and the rushes were higher than our heads, which is just what bulrushes should be. 'Now,' I said, 'this is the land of Egypt, and it's very sunny and very hot, and that's the river Nile. Where's the house where Moses' father and mother lived?' Jack found it. It was a big stone near the river, so that Moses' mother would not have very far to carry the water. 'And where's the big white palace where Pharaoh lived?' 'There!' shrieked Stephen. It was the wooden house where the bees live, but it was painted white, and it glistened like white marble in the sun, and the big brown and yellow bees walking up and down were Pharaoh's fat sentries.

Was Helen rehearsing this Bible lesson with Jane McNeill when a young man from Belfast, almost ten years her junior, recently demobilized from the Somerset Light Infantry, now up at Oxford and soon to be known far and wide as C. S. Lewis, was shown into the drawing-room? On 16 February 1921 C.S.L. wrote to his father: 'I met a friend of the said Tchainie's the other night at the Carlyles, a girl called Helen Waddell whom you may have heard of. When last I saw her she was lying face downward on the floor of Mrs McNeill's drawing-room, saying rather good things in a quaint Belfast drawl.' A letter from Helen to Dr Taylor gives a pen-sketch of Jane McNeill, the friend to whom C. S. Lewis was to dedicate *That Hideous Strength*:

I've just remembered that you asked me once who 'Jane' was. Do you remember the girl I used to coach, the daughter of the old headmaster of Campbell? Jane is very fat; outsiders think her a very nice ordinary good-natured girl, jollier perhaps than most — 'but isn't it a pity she's so fat? She'd be quite nice-looking if only . . . ' By dint of much knowing, I've begun to fathom Jane: a curious, very appreciative, very sensitive mind, not ill stocked, and an extraordinary *mélange* of out-of-the-way stuffs in it: and almost the biggest heart I know. She is one of the few people who only want to *give*. She knows that I care infinitely more for Maude than for her, and she is quite content if I just let her be good to me. That week at Portrush she and her mother fairly encompassed me with a sort of feather-bed of luxury — 'material, of course.' Jane says with a twinkle, 'Helen will get no conversation!' She was brought up in a set that is mortally afraid of being 'clever' and giving itself away. Jane read passionately and concealed the fact very successfully. Her great friends were the Ewarts (Sir William you probably know — the new linen regime), fine young women, shrewd and mannered and intelligent: nobody talked about books, or what was in them. (And very few people in

Belfast do: that's why some people find the Carnmoney Rectory a spring whose waters fail not. It's the only house I know where one really *talks* at meals.) Consequently my walk and conversation was of the nature of a high explosive to Jane: it was really like watching a fish discovering itself again in the sea.

Jane and her mother were to prove faithful friends, and as the days grew to months and the months to years during which the caterpillar and locust devoured and destroyed Helen's youth, others came forward with practical help and understanding. Chief among them must be reckoned Mrs McMillan, the 'daily', without whose motherly compassion Helen might never have survived. Out of her own meagre pocket, Helen paid her 25/– a week, no small sum in those days, but nothing could have repaid the devotion given to the girl by one who shared the burden of all-day and often all-night duty. A letter to Dr Taylor, probably written in 1917 (the first page is missing), admits that in describing her relationship with her step-mother, the writer is not being perfectly frank: 'I haven't told you everything even yet. But I don't know that I ever will be able to, unless I see you. Some things can't be written. Some day when it's all over, I might be able to tell you, and then I think you will forgive me for what must seem to you my harsh judgement. And I'm a pig for writing like this. Oh dear — if God judged us like that!'

The truth was that Martha Waddell's doctor had prescribed one tablespoon of whiskey as a nightcap to stimulate her heart and induce sleep. Before very long, Helen was finding empty bottles stuffed behind books and chests of drawers — the Rechabite whose fierce tirades against intemperance had sent her adolescent charges dashing out of the house in a frenzy, had herself succumbed and was a secret addict. Alone, Helen coped with the constant vigilance, the constant secret revulsion: not even to her spiritual father could she bring herself to admit the thing that made life almost intolerable. Finally at breaking-point, Helen confided in Dr Taylor and in Meg. Meg had been puzzled by the change in Helen, by her sorrowful dim preoccupation as if her soul had slipped away, she told her, and was standing by itself in a twilight place unless she was thoroughly roused and brought to herself. Then there was a crisis and Meg was providentially present. Martha Waddell procured raw spirit: 'It seemed almost like watching demon possession,' Helen wrote. 'It was the first time Peggy had seen what I had to stand, and it took her only last night to make up her mind. Next morning when Mother was quiet, ominously quiet, she went in and told her that she was taking me with her, that she wouldn't see my health and even my reason sacrificed any longer. Then I gave Mother my ultimatum: either she gave it up absolutely or I left the house, not to come back. It was a sharp fight, but we won. Dr McDowell shakes his head and says the craving is only in ambush, that the storm will break again. But I refuse to think about it. Only, dear, think very mercifully of me if my letters and myself seem unsatisfactory at times. For my brain *is* spent. I suppose, if it had gone on, it would have been nervous breakdown — for me who was, as Peggy says, the easiest-going girl she knew, and the most "placid" child!'

In the event, victory was short-lived and Dr McDowell a true prophet. A bad break followed by the peace of exhaustion provided the background to Helen's letter of only a fortnight later. On 30 December 1919 she wrote:

> This ought to be a cheerfuller letter than the last one, for I've had three peaceful nights. I moved downstairs to the room behind the drawing room: I can still hear Mother's bell, which rings almost outside the door, but I can't hear every movement the way I did. The thing had become a sort of nightmare to me — the perpetual tapping on the wall or, worse still, the door opening with herself coming in. Now it's so blessedly still. The first night I went down there, I lay thinking of Christina Rossetti's
>
> > 'Stillness that is almost Paradise,
> > Darkness more clear than noonday holdeth her,
> > Silence more tunable than any song.'
>
> Last week I was at my wits' end. It ended in her telling me I might go. And for a minute I thought with a mild gleam of catching up Maude and Brice at Oxford, and going on to the Pyrenees. But one can't shed one's responsibilities that way, especially after shouldering them for thirty years. I have written nothing but the stuff for *Woman's Work* and for *Daybreak* for weeks. What the end of it all will be, God knows. How one small person can swallow up hours and hours and days in trifles like 'That rug is too heavy. Could you pull it down a little? Not so much as that. Now tuck it in at the other side. That brings the jar too near my foot. That's better.'
>
> It's the first winter I've seen myself looking actually *old*. For one thing I've grown thin, developed an oval instead of a round for a chin. There — I'll not growl any more. I get dangerously sorry for myself sometimes, which is the greatest evil that can befall any one. I sicken — physically — at the nursing. I said I wouldn't growl, and in three lines I'm hard at it again. But my days are so full of things I want to forget. If one loved, it would be easy. But I don't love. Sometimes I hate. I've lived so long beside someone utterly self-absorbed. And her thoughts of people are so — well, when she wants her own way, she talks to me about changing her will. I saw it in her years and years ago, and would not let myself see it, but it is naked now. Dear, don't worry about me — my mind *is* diseased just now, and it's dangerous for me to write letters. I *don't* hate her. There's times she is

lovable and gentle even yet, but the weariness and sameness of things, and her perpetual exactions make me bilious sometimes. It's pretty hard to be patient with someone who has slept soundly for hours, and promptly comes in search of you a few minutes after waking — and you asleep half an hour after being awake most of the night before. Three nights ago she roused poor Mrs McMillan at half past two, made her put on her clothes, and come to her room. When she was falling asleep again, the poor old soul said she thought she might go back to bed herself and was told she was there to attend on her, and she might go if she didn't. Go — as if she wouldn't go ten times a day if it weren't for her soft heart. Two people in this avenue alone would thank heaven fasting if she'd go and housekeep for them: it would be an easy life and she knows it — and won't leave me.

In desperation I thought of getting a night nurse, but the doctor is all against it. He says she is perfectly able to look after herself. Dear, just put this letter down to very bad reaction after a long strain — that, and an abominable cold — result of nightly wanderings in dressing-gown. I could scold myself, for I'm whining worse than I did last year. The only excuse I have is that there *was* last year, and that there is something unnerving in repetition — like the Hindu shrinking from the round of births.

I had a letter from Brice this morning from Biarritz: expects to be home for the beginning of term on Jan. 18th, and trysts me for the Cellini concert on February 5th. Also Mr Belfour wants me for the Beecham Symphony concert on the 16th, so there'll be more Paradise after the Purgatorial stairs. But oh dear! Purgatory seems to make me worse. Maybe it wouldn't *be* Purgatory if you felt you were growing in grace.

The only faint store of comfort to which I can cling is that the people in the parable who nursed the sick and so forth didn't feel virtuous about it, and that God seems to take it as a favour to Himself even though you didn't think of it that way. It's a gracious thing, that about the cup of cold water, but the 'for My sake' sets it very high in the scale of spiritual achievement. And this seems to me far more gracious — to set the Great Seal on things done just for 'decency' because the people were sick and hungry.

I do hope this is the last black letter you will get from me. I'm glad it isn't the last day of the year — I'll have all tomorrow to repent of my cantankerousness in. Indeed the little book needn't tell me 'There remaineth very much land to be possessed.' Sometimes it seems to me that whole bran new tribes much wusser than the good old Hittites have sprung up out of nowhere and gone all over the place. I've just remembered the parable of the 'seven other spirits worse than himself' with a horrible chill. Life is a terrible thing too.

It's a wonderful parable — is there anything in psychic experience that Christ has not touched? After all, it's a relief after banging one's head against the bars to collapse like a bad child and submit. Do you remember that admirable irony — 'God *also* is wise'? I shan't tear up the letter that went before this. It's a bad road to come by, but it has left me nearer the condition for entering the kingdom of heaven than I've been for weeks.

I'm all in pieces, and maybe they'll come together in a decenter creature than the one that tore itself to bits.

I shan't write any more. But the old year bids fine to go out quietly now, and the best some of us can hope for is 'effacing rain'.

My love to you
Your
Helen.

This letter speaks of dew in the desert, an interval of relief when music opened the gates of Paradise for a spell of hours. The truth was that Helen's very physical appearance was betraying the strain that underlay her brilliant sallies and elaborate games: she lost her youthful contours, her hair was threaded with grey, there were shadows about her eyes. Friendly neighbours multiplied during 1919, among them Helen Beatty, a Presbyterian with many clerical connections and for that reason accepted by Martha Waddell as a worthy companion. Taking advantage of the privilege, Helen Beatty insisted on freeing the other Helen for a few evenings per week, and so gave her the opportunity — which Brice Clarke, George Coates and Okey Belfour were quick to seize — of sampling some of Belfast's musical delights. It seems amazing today, but in a world as yet unacquainted with radio and recorder, Helen was starved of music until she was thirty years old. In an early letter to Dr Taylor, there is a solitary reference full of Miltonic resonances to the great organ at Duncairn, 'and it came to me, listening, "The worlds were framed by the word of God", and I knew why. Sound is creative. One's life and oneself is solid, planté la: and that strange voice — for an organ is the voice of God, just as the violin is the voice of men — dissolves you, has you molten for the potter's hand.' But an orgy of opera-going through the winter of 1919 was a heavensent gift to counterbalance that dreadful year. So rarely did Helen display her narrative power, that perhaps a lengthy quotation is justified:

There were times this last fortnight [she wrote to Dr Taylor in December], that I turned into something like sheer fury at this new form of discipline. The Beatties used to have a puppy that went out when life was too hard, and bit the wall. I bit mine for a day or two. And through it all were the dream-nights when Mr Belfour came and took me to the opera — *Il Trovatore* and *Tannhäuser*, and for three hours one forgot. I think I have never had any pleasure so intense as last night's *Tannhäuser*. I'm glad glad glad that I had a Puritan upbringing, and that the theatre was barred to me for so long. It meant seeing Tannhäuser when one was thirty — 'with the senses exercised to discern good and evil'. I wonder if you have ever seen it? You know the story. How Tannhäuser, lover of the Princess Elizabeth, was taken by Venus in the Wartzberg mountains and held prisoner in the Venusberg for years. The first act shows the heart of the mountain, and Venus lying on her tigerskins, Tannhäuser sunk at her feet, and in the far cave beyond them a dance of fauns and nymphs, to the maddest shivering pagan music. He breaks free, though with a promise to return: and dawn finds him in the valley, at the foot of an old battered crucifix, dazed. Then very far off, one hears the Pilgrims' Chorus: it swells louder, and slowly the pilgrims, footsore and travel-stained come by. It's like a cry *De profundis*, but as tender as the *Miserere*. It brings him to his knees before the Cross. There his old friends find him. He tells them he has been wandering in a strange and far land — hears that there is to be a contest of song for the hand of the Princess Elizabeth, and comes to his world and his own again.

The next act is the hall of song — a glorious song of welcome from Elizabeth, a magnificent spectacle of knights and ladies making the grand entry (such management of medieval court trains my eye never beheld), and last the singing of the contestants. One by one they sing the praise of Love — and the demon enters into Tannhäuser, and he rises to sing the old wild music of the Venusberg in praise of Queen Desire. There is a great cry, and a wild flash of swords: the women fly the court, all but Elizabeth: she comes to shield him like an angel of God. She stands between him and the swords, pleads with the knights by the mercy of God: bids Tannhäuser go on pilgrimage to assoil him, and seek for pardon at Rome. She names the name of Christ, and every sword is held high by the blade, the hilt making the sign of the Cross above Tannhäuser. Kneeling in their midst, he kisses the hem of her robe, and she goes out. But the music — and the savage tension as Tannhäuser's madness rises higher and higher till the waves break over him — and then Elizabeth's singing — .

The last act is twilight in the valley: Elizabeth in the white robe of the novice kneeling before the Cross, praying for Tannhäuser's soul: Wolfram, his friend, beside her. They are awaiting the coming of the pilgrims from Rome — and Tannhäuser. Once again one hears the Pilgrims' Chorus — they pass over — Elizabeth scans each face, but he is not there, and with one last ecstasy of singing she goes away. She was beautiful in the hall of song, but only a beautiful *cantatrice*, and a tender woman. Here, in the twilight and the unearthly whiteness of the robes, she is indeed the angel of God. Wolfram waits on, watching a single star. Very faint and broken the Pilgrims' Chorus comes again. Tannhäuser, worn out and accursed, stumbles through the valley — Wolfram holds him, questions him. The Pope's answer had been that he who had shared the pleasures of hell might share the pains of it: when his staff broke into flower and leaf, then might Tannhäuser hope for the mercy of God. Even as he tells it, the old courage comes back. Hell will not deny him: and Venus is still fair. Suddenly on the sobbing despairing music there breaks the mad lilt of the Bacchic dance — one must have felt it to realize its sheer insanity of joyousness just then — but things like that are genius. The cave opens and Venus stands in the rosy light, with her arms outstretched, singing as tenderly as Elizabeth herself, and under it and through it the wild lilting chorus of the underworld. Tannhäuser darts forward but Wolfram holds him. The men sway and wrestle, surging against each other in a frenzy, and suddenly comes the Pilgrims' Chorus again. Behind Tannhäuser comes the bier of Elizabeth, dead. He turns and sees her: the light on the hillside turns grey and the Venus music dies. There is a cry from him on his knees: 'St Elizabeth, pray for me!' and he falls dead beside the bier. Enter the Pope's ambassador, with the staff in flower and leaf outstretched — too late. They lay it on the dead man's face, the Pilgrims' Chorus rises to its great swell of pain, and the darkness comes down.

I'm glad I went with Mr Belfour and nobody else. Some men would have spoiled it. He is taking Meg and me together to see *Figaro* on Wednesday. Mr Coates takes me to *Cavalleria Rusticana* and *Pagliacci* on Thursday night, and we have dinner with each man before it. So did you ever see a funnier mixture than my life in town? Cinderella feeling as if she were habited in cloth of stars night after night.

In *My Mind to Me*, Walter de la Mare has observed that a mere twilight expedition to the nearest pillar-box may fill the knapsack of a certain kind of mind with far more valuable treasure than an expedition to a far country: 'It is not distance that counts, or hope, or even longing; but the mind's looking-glass, which not only reflects but transmutes all that it receives.' Nothing could better summarize Helen Waddell's process of assimilation: she never forgot an experience, so it is no matter for surprise when she tells Dr Taylor:

I am in the kitchen watching a porridge pot. Such a homely smell as it has, and such a fat generous way of boiling. All the Scot in me rises when I'm over a porridge pot. You know, it takes a good cook to make good porridge: but it's such a simple thing that you can nearly imagine Eve doing it first. You feel no ancestry when you bake a cake: that is sophisticated. And all this is nonsense. Meantime I have *Daybreak* written, which was an oppression to me all last week. Nehemiah should by rights have ended this month, for in the last paragraph I had the wall built and finished. But I want one last chapter: the state of mind in which the last entry in the journal was made. I think myself it's 'These all died in faith, not having received the promises'. The chapter in *Hebrews*, certain verses in it rather, and the Pilgrims' Chorus from Tannhäuser go together. 'Remember me, O my God, and spare me according to the greatness of thy mercy.'

From there, one turns to the final section of *The Building of the Wall*: was Helen writing it for children, or was it her own life she had in mind? Twelve years have passed since Nehemiah finished the wall he had set his hand to build, and the King of Babylon has once again allowed him to return to his homeland as Governor of Jerusalem. He finds the great chamber of the Temple empty of offerings, furnished instead with the trappings of a foreign prince, the Sabbath profaned, the priesthood and covenant defiled. Was it for this he had built the city of God?

> The light was all but gone: Nehemiah went over to the window, and saw the last slow fires of the sunset burn on the battlements of cloud. . . . Slowly the bitterness ebbed from him. He stood silent before the vastness of the purposes of God. He had done what he could: he had built the wall of Jerusalem; but the kingdom of God is within. '*Remember me, O my God, and spare me according to the greatness of thy mercy. Remember me, O my God.*'
>
> So with his broken purposes, his yearning for a new heaven and a new earth wherein dwelleth righteousness, Nehemiah was joined unto the goodly fellowship, the fellowship for whom were written the two great Pilgrim Choruses of the world. '*These all died in faith, not having received the promises, but having seen them afar off.*' For he looked for a city which hath foundations, whose builder and maker is God.

The Vice-Chancellor at Queen's once told H.W. with delight that she had an amazing knowledge of divinity. It is true that no matter what her field of study, she approached it infinitely fresher, so she argued, if she had first broken her brain upon some theology. This is precisely what gives her writing its vigour, power and personality: unconsciously she brings her spiritual perception, her faith and her humanity to bear upon and interpret the matter in hand so that they become the drapery of thought which is weighty yet simple and intelligible. She was possessed of a kind of interior sanctity that saw truth as a living thing expressed, not only in revelation, but in the myriad relationships of facts, circumstances, and the realities of nature to one another. As she matured, this intuitive vision became ever more manifest in her style — not to be confused with manner, still less with mannerism — but it was there from the beginning. As became her father's daughter, she took her scriptural expositions for children and the 'working girls' of Belfast extremely seriously: a simple talk on a Thursday night or a short article in *Daybreak* might well represent the meditation of a whole week. Indeed, to treat adequately of Helen's 'amazing knowledge of divinity' would fill a volume. Here, only random samples may suggest how she could seize on likenesses and images in things and people as diverse, for instance, as Cleopatra and St Paul: one hopes that neither Miss Sinclair nor Miss McKerrow was present at the Girls' Auxiliary meeting to spoil with upraised eyebrows her rendering of *Antony and Cleopatra*. To her highly-appreciative Father in God in Ahmadabad, she wrote:

> I am tremendously keen about this circle of mine, and I'm half inclined to do very little but talk round St Paul — Tarsus, the harbour having once

borne Cleopatra's fleet. I harked back to *Antony and Cleopatra* and found that gorgeous description of Cleopatra sailing down the Cydnus, do you remember —

> The barge she sat in, like a burnished throne,
> Burned on the water; the poop was beaten gold,
> Purple the sails . . .

Well, it was to meet Mark Antony at Tarsus, about forty years before Paul was born. And Antony's subjugation is the great metaphor for the subjugation of Rome by the East — by the Greek civilization too for Cleopatra was pure Greek, as well as 'gypsy'. It's *only* a metaphor, but it is a perfect jumping-off place for an impression of the *ensemble* that Paul was born into.

Only a few of her articles in *Daybreak* — and she contributed them for years — found their way into her published *Stories from Holy Writ* (Constable 1949). The immense thought that went into every one of them may be inferred from this letter of 1918:

I have been working all day at the Baptism of Cornelius. I was almost sure there was going to be no illumination this time. At least, that the illumination was so obvious, a sort of all-over transparency. What first redeemed it from that rather flat light was something in the accent of Peter's question — that was yet no question, a kind of awe. 'Can any man forbid water that these should not be baptized, which have received the Holy Ghost as well as we?' It echoed something else to me that I could not fix, and at last I found it:

> Then felt I like some watcher of the skies,
> When a new planet swims into his ken;
> Or like stout Cortez, when with eagle eyes
> He stared at the Pacific — and all his men
> Looked at each other with a wild surmise —
> Silent, upon a peak in Darien.

I think they had thought of their new faith as the Jordan, in whose waters men might be healed. And now Peter saw it when it met the sea. For a little while the tide is broken and discoloured with the old sediment, and the rush of the river keeps its current visible a little way: but around it and beyond it — 'the multitudinous seas incarnadine.'

'What was I that I should withstand God?'

I have never more respected the greatness of that early Church: instead of the supremacy which Messiah was to have brought them, an equality that they had never before given. And yet, they glorified God, because that to the Gentiles also was granted repentance unto life.

And Joppa, where Peter saw the vision and the sea, reminded me of that other missionary — the unwilling one — who left Joppa for Tarshish. I looked up George Adam Smith,* and got an amazing illumination on Jewish prejudice, and the Greater who brooded over it. Do you remember —'With magnificent reserve he has not gone further; but only told unto the prejudiced faces of his people that out there, beyond the Covenant, in the great world crying in darkness, there live, not beings created for ignorance and hostility to God, elect for destruction, but men with conscience and hearts, able to turn at His word and to hope in His mercy. God has vindicated His love to the jealousy of those who thought that it was theirs alone. And we are left with this grand vague vision of the immeasurable city, with its multitude of innocent children and cattle, and God's compassion brooding over all.'

Helen Waddell the mediaevalist has her joys but is incomplete without the Helen rooted by nature and heredity in the Bible, whose profound knowledge leads to interpretations that even the undevout are likely to relish. For that reason, it is almost impossible to resist quotation, especially when an odd sheet such as the following turns up among scattered papers. This commentary on St Paul's shipwreck on the way to Rome (*Acts* XXVII) seems to have been set down in response to one of her Bible circle:

Unless you give your mind to being kind to everybody, you will often be cruel to somebody. The most conspicuous thing in the chapter is the extraordinary charm of St Paul.

One thinks of him too much as rabbinical theologian, and keen debater, and strict disciplinarian. You have to admit his passionate friendships — *cf.* Phil. about Epaphroditus (Phil. II, 22) — 'Indeed, he was nigh sick unto death: but God had mercy on him, and not on him only but on me also, lest I should have sorrow upon sorrow.' And for his tact, read the last chapter of the same epistle, 10–18. He is thanking them that they have been caring for his wants *again*: lest they think he is reproaching them by that 'again', he says he knew all along it was only lack of opportunity . . .

But in this chapter, it's Paul, the unofficial Paul, not with converts or churches or assemblies, but among absolute strangers: Paul in a new set. And before all is done, they're listening to the little man like a kinder sort of Buddha. It's your old priest in *Kim* with Luke as his 'chela', making absolute conquest of the young lieutenant who is bringing him to London for trial, with a gang of seditious prisoners, and a Lascar crew.

There was excuse enough for Paul to sit tight, and not take much interest in things. But he's in the very thick of them before they're many days afloat. They even let him give his advice quite near the beginning. And he got to care for them awfully. You can see that he was praying for every man of them by the answer, 'God hath *given* thee all them that sail with thee.'

*George Adam Smith (1856–1942) Scottish preacher and Semitic scholar. His *Historical Geography of the Holy Land* (1894) proved invaluable to General Allenby in the Palestine campaign of 1917.

Hear the nice old voice of him: 'Wherefore I pray you to take some meat, for this is for your health.' It's that sentence of Dowth's: 'Let the small coin of your courtesies have the stamp of the King's Mint. Let your familiar speech have the savour of the King's garden.'

Whether he won Julius or not, it does not say. He certainly won his heart. Even in the crash at the end, he is willing to risk his military reputation by the escape of the prisoners — a Roman soldier answered for his prisoners with his life — rather than have Paul killed. Cf. martial law in Ireland. When a man was left in charge of two soldiers near Clones — and they were told, if a rescue were attempted, to *shoot* the prisoner, rather than let him escape. It's not a special Irish grievance, it's just military law . . . '

'Hear the nice old voice of him' — to the end of her life, Helen never lost her Irish idiom. In a delightful letter acknowledging a bundle of *Daybreak* held up by wartime delays, Dr Taylor expressed his keen enjoyment of their contents:

A. B. Davidson's Biography has the story that there was an Irish student whom he frequently called up to read in class the passage set for the day because, so the others said, he liked to hear the Hebrew read with 'a sweet Cork accent'. Now it seems to me you are importing into the talk of these old-time Hebrew worthies an occasional Irish element, and the blend is charming. Here's a question that would, I fancy, floor most candidates for the B.D.

Render the following sentences into correct dialectic Hebrew:
    a) You mind where the big fight was.
    b) They do be saying that the men of Ammon are gathering.
    c) The sound of the keening struck on his ear.
    d) 'It was like this,' began Saul desperately.

When so minded, Helen could go a good deal further than that, as when she describes an old Irish vagabond: 'Full of big words he was, but he used them where they belonged. His stomach, he said himself, had a copper bottom; and the liquor he had put into it during his eighty years would float a battleship.' So much for the Irishman, cheerful, free and exhilarating. But what of 'the Irish question'? After all, in considering whether Helen was a young woman unable to bear very much reality, one must remember that in addition to the First World War she lived through the Easter Rising of 1916 and, living in Belfast, could never escape meeting 'Murder on the way — He had a mask like Castlereagh.' If it were asked: 'How Irish was Helen Waddell?' the answer should be 'To the very marrow of her bones.' For that reason, she and Dr Taylor arrived at opposite conclusions from a view of the same facts. Because of their mutual trust, they were perfectly honest with each other: he never imposed his judgements with any show of authority, she met his objections with reasoned and fearless argument even when the misunderstanding caused pain. To be honest, Shakespeare says, is to be one in a thousand, and the faculty of discernment is part, a very great part, of honesty. Why then did two such honest friends differ? Possibly, not because the facts were beyond the focus of the mind's eye, but because they were too much within it. That is certainly true of Helen.

Before entering upon her correspondence on Irish affairs as seen against her family background, one must bear in mind the total reversal of Presbyterian attitudes during the latter half of the nineteenth century from being Republican-Liberal to ardent Orange-Tory. The founders of the United Irishmen who planned the Rebellion of 1798 were Calvinists who, as friends, fought shoulder to shoulder with their Roman Catholic neighbours against the British Army and the Orange Yeomanry. After the rising, thirty Presbyterian ministers were convicted of taking part, three were hanged — Helen tells the history of one of the three — five fled to America, seven went to prison. Yet by 1857, only two generations later, under the influence of such parson-politicians as Henry Cooke, the 'Black Man' of College Square, Belfast, and his disciple, 'Roaring Hugh Hanna', their grandchildren were at the throats of Catholics in Belfast riots, Home Rule was identified with the Catholic faith, and both were held in abhorrence. To quote the Reverend S. E. Long in a paper read in 1983 to the Orange Lodge at Dundrum, 'the parson-politicians were easily recognized. They were always men of exceptional ability, tenacity, enthusiasm and courage, and were remarkably competent communicators who knew the thinking, the emotions and the fears of ordinary people. They have often been rightist in politics, fundamentalist in theology, capitalist in economics, puritan in ethics, and lacking tolerance in community relationships.' At the end of the twentieth century, they are still 'easily recognized'.

An undated letter to Meg in which Helen refers to her own brother's part in the Irish literary renaissance associated with W. B. Yeats, throws light on her mode of thinking:

> The real spiritual strength of the Irish Renaissance was that they wanted Irish literature once again to drink the nature of the soil. Where I think they were wrong — but this was only the extremists among them — was in the assertion that the Irish spirit could only fitly express itself in *Irish*, for one cannot turn back the sundial ten degrees, and for you and me to pretend that Irish is the natural language of our minds is absurd. Irish is not our native language. We are originally alien stock. *But* 300 years of Irish climate and Irish land has so profoundly modified us that we are no longer Scottish. We haven't a trace of it in looks even, and our language is

English with the Irish idiom. So was Synge's, so was Yeats', so is Sambo's when he abandons dialect and writes a piece of prose.

From the many references scattered throughout her correspondence, it is possible to build up a fairly accurate account of that 'alien stock'. The original 'Grandfather William' of the family fought for the Covenant at Bothwell Brig in 1679, escaped seizure by befuddling Claverhouses's dragoons, leaving them dead drunk while he sent all his horses scattering, and with his sons hastily took ship for Ireland. There, one of those sons as a marriage dowry speedily acquired no fewer than eight townlands in County Down near Newry, a mile or so away from the house where Patrick, father of the Brontës, was born. It was from there that Helen's grandfather was called to be minister in Glenarm, one of the Antrim glens. His wife, Margaret, was a sister of Captain Mayne Reid whose works, so Baden Powell affirmed, gave him the inspiration for the Boy Scout movement.

Literary antecedents mattered little to Helen. The figure she loved to recall — did she see in his integrity a prototype of her own father? — was an older kinsman, James Porter, hanged as a rebel on 2 July 1798 before his own manse door, at Greyabbey in County Down. He was a passionate lover of liberty, equality, and fraternity. Far from wishing, like a good Covenanter, to extirpate popery, he believed that his Catholic neighbours should have a vote and be allowed to live in peace. To that end he composed ironic pamphlets and *ça ira* ballads, sang the 'Marseillaise' along the country roads, spared neither the government nor the Marquis of Londonderry and, as a result, was forced into hiding in the Mourne Mountains where he was finally arrested and sentenced to be hanged, drawn and quartered for high treason, a sentence mercifully commuted to hanging on the green knoll before his own manse. Dumb in her agony his wife, mother of their eight young children, met the grim procession. He looked at her, smiling. 'So, dearest,' he said, 'I am to sleep at home tonight.' Helen loved this family legend of savagery, tenderness and pain, that flowered at the gallows' foot into high poetry. The exquisite and melancholy Latin prose of the sixth century Irish Columbanus, that she would one day translate, summed the whole thing up: 'O Life, a road to life art thou, not Life. And there is no man makes his dwelling in the road, but walks there: and those who fare along the road have their dwelling in the fatherland.'

Against the background of this patriarchal tree, the figure of the woman who 'broke her heart' over Ireland, as she put it, is sharply etched in her strength and pathos. As a member of the Protestant ascendancy, she had grown up painfully aware of the inequalities and injustices that surrounded her: 'social conditions that we take for granted; the iniquity of them is none the less.' A letter to George Taylor specifies a few of the iniquities, and is so characteristic of Helen's way of looking at things, it must be quoted as it stands:

I have just finished making notes on the Conversion of St Paul. Do you notice our Lord's characteristic method of challenging? '*Why* persecutest thou Me?' I am relating it with that great parable of identification — 'Inasmuch as ye did it not . . . ye did it not to Me.' Paul thought he was combating a heresy: he found it was a Person. We're all too abstract.

On Friday — it is not really off the point — I went to a lecture by Professor Henry on *Wages*. He has the Latin Chair at Queen's, is Secretary to the Academic Council, and beside that Chairman of one or two Trade Boards. It was rather horrible: the more for his dispassionate, half-sardonic manner. Some years ago Belfast denied with indignation that there was sweating in her borders: a Trade Board was set up, and it is proved to the hilt: 25% of the women in the embroidered linen industry get threepence an hour; 75% twopence, or less — about half of these a penny an hour. He gave particulars of two cases, out of many — one involving four children. Their mother had a penny an hour to keep the life in them and herself; something under five shillings a week.

It was at the end of his lecture that there came a gleam of hope. The Trade Board have appointed a minimum wage of 3d per hour, but they know that wage is not being given. There have been prosecutions for infringement, but so far it has been impossible to get a conviction. 'What is wanted in Belfast is a public opinion that will make a man ashamed of offering that wage, as much ashamed as if he had been detected in open sin.' At present, he says, and says bitterly, there is no public feeling in the matter. One dismisses the wages question as tending to Socialism and labour unrest.

You leave a lecture like that feeling rather like a chained dog but, as Maude said, fortunately not like a muzzled one. Words are wanted, and very badly wanted. 'Heaven and Hell are in the power of the tongue.' I have talked to everybody I have met since, and if I can see how to do it, I'll try to write something for the papers here. They'll probably not accept it: for they are tied hand and foot in the fear of offending the linen lords. And I'll talk to my people on Tuesday. I didn't see at first how I was going to bring it in — unless by violence. Which shows the fault of all our thinking, for what is the persecution of His poor but the persecution of Himself?

Do you know, I think what is wrong with Belfast is a too easy evangelicalism. For these men of whom Professor Henry spoke were 'good' men according to their lights: they were appalled at discovering a whist club among their workers, and at a strike being organized on Sunday. Doesn't it remind you of 'passing over judgement and mercy and the love of God'? They've never realized the terrible exaction of religion: or rather, they only realize its prohibitions in the way of things like dancing and the theatre and cards. It seems to me they have narrowed all religion to the saving of one's miserable soul, as Drummond said, 'the safety of Hermit-crabs.' Dear, don't think I'm too bitter, but I'd *rather* have a frank 'publican' grinding the faces of the poor, than these unconscious pharisees. It does less despite to religion.

At Queen's, Helen could not avoid being caught up in the turmoil of the times. In her final year, Asquith introduced his Home Rule Bill which sent Belfast ringing with the popular cry of 'No surrender!' Under Sir Edward Carson's direction, Belfast, Down, Antrim and Derry opposed with such force that Ireland was on the brink of Civil War when World War I broke out. There followed the tragedy of the 1916 Rebellion. Roger Casement went to Germany to solicit help, was arrested on his return to Ireland on 21 April 1916; a few days later, on Easter Monday, leaders marched at the head of 1,000 Irish Volunteers, proclaimed a Republic in Dublin which lasted just one week against British troops and artillery; Patrick Pearse and his colleagues were forced to surrender, and their speedy execution led to the defeat of Redmond's Constitutional party at Westminster in the General Election of 1918, the setting up of the Sinn Fein league, and the organization of the IRA. An ingrained habit of viewing the flux of time *sub specie aeternitatis* made Helen try to steer a middle course, but she felt black about Ireland, as she put it. Until 1916, Gregory Smith teased her mercilessly about her passionate love of her country, but in that year he stopped completely. To Dr Taylor, Helen wrote:

I suppose it is because God sees every side at once that He lets any of us go on living. Sometimes I envy you, envy you terribly, because you have no doubts in politics. For myself, there is no Irish party that I could give allegiance to. The one theory on which I have *almost* conviction is that Sir Edward Carson is the most sinister figure that ever influenced Irish affairs. I know the old kindly tolerance, and I saw it stiffen — under his hand — into obstinacy and hate. He cried havoc and let slip the dogs of war, and he practically created Sinn Fein. Curious, read a letter of General Lake's, the commanding officer in '98, denouncing Belfast to the Government: 'I am convinced that every act of sedition in Ireland has its origin in that town.' It's topsy-turvy, but it's true! But let's escape. The whole question smothers me. Anyhow, all politics deject me unutterably, perhaps because my heart is invariably with the losing side. You know, the father of me before me was a passionate Home Ruler, and he was also a fierce opponent of the policy in Africa that led to the Boer War, so that my earliest political sensation — I being about ten — was an overwhelming fear that we'd be beaten, and give the enemy cause to blaspheme, and a nasty little quavering fear that if we won, it would be by *force majeure*. It's like watching someone you like quarrelling with someone you don't like, and yet knowing that they're in the wrong.

The matter might have ended there but for the unforeseen action of Helen's elder brother Sam—or Sambo, as she affectionately called him. As a founder of the Ulster Theatre, he had produced Helen's first play, *The Spoiled Buddha*, at the Grand Opera House, Belfast, in February 1915. Towards the end of 1918, when the War was drawing to a close and paper restrictions likely to be removed, he gave the play to a reader at The Talbot Press, Dublin. As a result, the Press applied to Helen for permission to publish it. Dublin, of course, was suspect: could anything good come out of Dublin? On the other hand, the ultra-Conservative Gregory Smith agreed that the Press had done excellent work, advised Helen to let them have it, advice she followed once she had established that one of the directors was not only a devout Presbyterian but also a member of her cousin Harry's congregation—and all seemed satisfactory. Publication was planned for the autumn of 1919, to capture the Christmas market. The first printed copies reached Helen in July and were distributed to her close friends, of whom Dr Taylor was chief. The back cover bore a list of The Talbot Press booklets: it led off with the ill-starred name of Roger Casement. Helen was taken aback and scowled at the announcement of his Poems: Dr Taylor was appalled, and wrote at once to say so. 'The late troubles in Belfast' have a way of altering their tense with terrifying suddenness, and Helen's analysis of the situation in her reply to his strictures is as pertinent today as it was yesterday. Her letter is undated.

> Your letter has just come in. You *are* dear to write so frankly: and I'll be frank too.
>
> Listen: when the American colonies declared their independence, after not one hundredth part of the oppression this country received, was it treason? No. But it would to this day be treason, if it had failed.
>
> If there had been no Great War: if two hundred years from now Alsace-Lorraine had risen against German rule, would it have been treason?
>
> If three hundred years from now, Belgium, overrun by a triumphant Germany had rebelled, would it have been treason? If, her language gone, half her country settled by Germans from across the Rhine (many of whom, however, became imbued with the Belgian spirit), but nevertheless governed equitably enough according to Teutonic ideals, she had continued to conspire, to keep alive the Belgian nationality, the hate of the conqueror, the passion for her own individuality, would it have been the malignant outworking of the spirit of evil, or the unconquerable, unquenchable 'seed of fire' which makes a man love his own country and his own children as he cannot love the alien?
>
> The cases, you will say, are not parallel. They never are, quite. But they are going in the same direction.
>
> One *can* be a Home Ruler, and loyal to the greater issue as well. Witness

the Redmonds and Professor J. M. Kettle, and hundreds of less-known Irishmen.

I'm sorry I hurt you by telling you that about my father. But you know, it was his passion for lost causes, for 'the under dog', that makes me love him.

Dear, how *can* you possibly feel as we felt, he and I? You are English: you are of the governing nation. I see the same incapacity in Gregory.

You liken the cleavage to that between Cavalier and Roundhead. The issue there was 'government by consent of the governed': and the 'rebels' won. Only for that, they would be traitors still. It is the same issue still.

Ireland, given a Home Rule parliament when the electorate of the three kingdoms decreed it, would have given its blood like water. Sinn Fein had no love for Germany, except as a means to an end. Dear, *have* you forgotten the Ulster papers before the war? But then you didn't read them, of course, in India. The half-veiled references to German aid, that became frank outrage in wilder oratory. Do you not know that Ulster armed itself with German rifles?

What Sir Edward Carson did was to break down the hold that constitutional government had at last won in Ireland. He proved that a threat of physical force could paralyse 'government by the will of the majority'. English papers actually commented on the contrast between the red fury of Ulster and the apathy of the rest of Ireland, as proof that Ulster was much more in earnest *against*, than the rest of Ireland *for*.

Do you know that speeches on behalf of the Ulster position, collected in book form, are now suppressed as anarchic in tendency in Ireland? And by some of the very men who made them?

Ulster never feared religious persecution for itself: it used the case of the Protestants in the South and West as its strongest arguments. It must protect them, who could not protect themselves. It was offered partition: in five minutes the scattered remnant was thrown overboard, to make what terms it could, while Ulster grasped at a chance of setting up a sort of city-state. That action made the Ulster Covenant so much waste paper.

Another thing: you speak of Parnell's morals: 'these be thy gods, O Israel.' There is a monument in London to a greater than Parnell, greater even in sin, for his was a double adultery. Parnell had no wife, and Nelson had. And I do not think it likely that Parnell would have left the name of the woman in his will, to 'the care of a grateful nation', as Nelson left the name of Lady Hamilton. For this reason — that Parnell was dealing with a nation whose attitude to the marriage bond is infinitely more exacting than the English. Curiously, Gregory was talking of it the other day. 'Parnell would never have made shipwreck' he said, 'if his supporters had not been in the main Irish Catholics. And adultery is a thing they will not bear.'

But, dear, it only vexes you and vexes me. Put it this way: I'd be insane to discuss 'Home Rule for India' with my knowledge. I can only wish that Tagore had not had to renounce his title as a protest against the flogging in public of educated men. That I was sorry to hear: but I recognize that a Government in a terrible situation acts terribly, and does things it might not in cooler blood. Anyhow, I have no knowledge. I only know that my faith in the fairness of British administration is very great.

But here I know a little: and more than that, I feel.

> My father and mother were Irish,
> And I am Irish too.
> I bought a wee fiddle for ninepence,
> And it is Irish too.

All the same, I have no hatred for England: I've an immense liking for it: and for certain Englishmen, a great deal more than liking. I don't call them tyrants, and I don't call the Easter 'rebels' either martyrs or traitors.

I suppose I'm a hopeless trimmer. Just as my head was with the Roundheads, and my heart distinctly Royalist.

Does it matter? Saintsbury and Gregory, two of my best friends, are Tories *in excelsis*: Saintsbury's Toryism is almost a joy to me, it's so complete. I am quite convinced that he is a Jacobite in fact.

Dear — the men who died for the Pretender — were they 'traitors'? And upon my honour, scores of the men who died in Easter week died 'for a dream's sake'. And yet, to you, with your traditions, I see that they *must* be traitors. So be it.

I come back and back to the catalogue of the Twelve Apostles. 'He chose . . . Simon the Zealot' (as who should say, a man who had been 'out' in Easter week) ' . . . Matthew the Publican.'

And by tradition, it was Matthew who had denied his birthright who wrote the Gospel for the Jews.

But I see that mine is an attitude you can't well understand. But remember the tradition among us, that one of us was hanged for treason in '98, and that the Governor of the Jail where he was hanged was a kinsman of his own.

My dear love to you. And remember, dear heart, before you worry over me too much, that we're nearly all Radicals in youth!

The letter of the following week added a kind of postscript that dismissed the subject. Dr Taylor had sent stamps to distribute to Sydney, Jack, Mary and Charlie, all avid collectors:

I wish I could see them oftener [Helen wrote]. Especially Jack. Meg says he is the most difficult of the lot, like a 'square box' sometimes. He has one of those naturally rebellious minds that have no respect for authority *as* authority. He likes me: I think because I take him half-sardonically, the way he takes things himself. And he knows I understand him. He has a sort of humorous appreciation with passion under it, that makes him very *simpatico*. And it's funny to realize how my long acquaintance with Gregory Smith helps me to understand Jack, but I don't want another Gregory. I want more humanity and less egotism. And Jack might be a terrible egotist. He has a splendid brain, and an almost merciless gift of perception. And I do not want him to despise too much.

I have been thinking a good deal about Sinn Fein. Mourning too. For it is strong in Ireland, and there is just so much virtue in it that coercing it is like coercing Jack. You've won — but the spirit is unconquered yet. It seems to me that its great weakness is the weakness of all fanaticism — hating the devil more than you love God. In this case, hating England more than they love Ireland. There's that, and there's the other weakness in the very title — 'ourselves alone'. Except a corn of wheat fall into the ground and die . . . Even in the lowest, the animal sense, it's love that is creative, and hate that destroys. And even the Divine hate of evil works itself out in three, at the most four generations, and its love of goodness is a spring of life to the thousandth.

As for that hate of England, it is a strange thing to me, because I had the immense good fortune to play with a little American girl in Tokio, and the defensive spirit is strong in me yet. Also there was the sense of belonging to the most popular nation in the East. One felt that very strongly in Japan. But some things illuminate it; one is the knowledge of the hereditary instinct — and England's bill in Ireland is heavy. And the other is coming up against the final expression of the English governing spirit in this same Gregory Smith. He's a Balliol man, 'where they all come from'; he's typical of scores of the men about Dublin Castle. And he is no more fit to deal with the Irish temper than——. He can't help it, but at the back of his mind there's a sort of 'race contempt'. Long before Sinn Fein it was there. Do you remember Anne saying in 'Discipline' that a solitary inflection in St John's voice 'illuminated history'; that she understood the rebellious? That was autobiographical. A phrase of Gregory's has taught me more of the *hate* of the conquered race than all the history which I have (not) read. That is a reason why one race should not govern another. Nothing but the grace of God will keep you from belittling the qualities you haven't got. Just as I revenge myself on Gregory by remembering his massive stupidity. It goes along with an extraordinary quickness of perception — when he's awake: but when he's asleep, there's nothing left him but the stolidity of his race. He's a 'corrected' Scot, you know, and Balliol lies heavy on him.

But you're English, and so is Saintsbury. And you've more of the grace of God, I think, than anyone I know.

To her last letter Helen has added this postscript: 'Let's bury Irish politics in the Red Sea, half-way between us, though the Bay of Biscay would be most suitable.' Had she but known what lay in the near future, the River Jordan would have been a more appropriate choice than either. Harmony restored, like true Presbyterians, they resumed theological speculation on the Incarnation and Atonement, appealing on the way to a host of divines as familiar to Helen as to her preceptor: George Adam Smith, Alexander Maclaren, A. B. Davidson, Moberley, Fosdick and Perowne are names that frequently recur. Under such tutelage, it is fascinating to watch the mind that conceived the most moving chapters of *Peter Abelard* in the making. How many young women would relish letters that asked:

> I wonder if you happen to have read 'The Gospel of the Atonement', being the Hulsean Lectures delivered in 1898–99 by Archdeacon Wilson who, if I mistake not, was Senior Wrangler of his year? Speaking of the 'Forensic Theory' of Anselm, 'supported by Bernard, modified by Peter Lombard, and transcendentalized by the Mystics,' he reminds how Luther struggled 'not always successfully to escape from mere theories' and adds, 'It is well known that at one time Luther was disposed to make the parable of the Prodigal Son the centre of his theory of salvation.' Would that he had done so.

And how many young women could have met the argument with the fearless freedom and conviction of this reply:

> I'm inclined to say with St Francis, 'Brother Fire, beautiful above all creatures' — for I'm on the hearthrug before it. I've just finished 'The Gospel of the Atonement' — his theory, that the Incarnation is the identifying of Man and God, leaves me cold. 'This identification is the Atonement: there is no other.' (I wish people would stop using the word: it is so seldom used in the Writings themselves, and it always conveys the sense of expiation. I'd rather have St Paul's 'ministry of reconciliation').
>
> And I'd rather have St Paul's 'God was in Christ reconciling the world unto Himself' than this man's metaphysics — 'The indwelling of a Divine life in man, proved by Christ's life and death.' I don't think Christ lived and died to prove that God could be in man. I think he lived and died to show us what God was like. 'Show us the Father — and it sufficeth us' — God reconciling the world unto Himself, simply by showing Himself. It's the revelation of a Personality. The Incarnation to me is God saying to the world what Christ said in a narrower issue to Thomas: 'Handle me and see that it is I myself.'
>
> The whole 'problem of redemption' was how to make that Prodigal Son 'come to himself.' And so the father took upon him the form of a servant, and went into the far country, not to tell the Prodigal that he had a good deal of his father in him, and to show him how he would live if he would but realize that (I know I'm being horribly unfair to Dr Wilson): but a simpler thing — to show him what that father was like when you got to know him. It would be enough.
>
> After that, comes the desire to be 'partakers of the divine nature' — 'to be called Thy son.'
>
> More and more I am being haunted by that idea of God being handicapped in dealing with us, just as any father is, who respects the personality of his son. There are some splendid things in the book: the differentiation of Latin and Greek theology, and the 'necessity' of the suffering of Christ. Do you remember that glorious chapter in *Isaiah* —

'The Passion of God' (George Adam Smith's, I mean)? I think Archdeacon Wilson takes the 53rd of Isaiah a little carelessly.

No wonder Professor Henry had expressed amazement at Helen Waddell's knowledge of divinity. One more quotation must be made. Prominent among the Liberal agitators of the early twentieth century was Mrs Annie Besant (1847–1933), an ardent disciple of Madame Blavatsky and her Theosophical Society, who had become President of the Indian National Congress in 1917. Dr Taylor naturally viewed her activities with misgiving:

> Mrs Besant was recently in this city, just for twenty-four hours. Considering her age — she is now over seventy — she is a marvellously masterful woman, but I'm much afraid her power is exercised far more for evil than for good. You have, I trust, already received E. W. Thompson's pamphlet, 'The Christ of Theosophy and of the Bible and of Experience'. I am anxious to learn whether the Theosophic movement is at all catching on in Belfast, for I regard it as such an utter fraud and a distinctly dangerous one.

In her reply, Helen quotes from the paper she is preparing for her Bible Circle on the Forgiveness of Sin, her mind preoccupied as so often with the problem of suffering and what she terms 'the passion of God':

> I am glad you sent that pamphlet. I don't know how things are with the movement: Helen Beatty says she is afraid it has held a good many. I've been working again at my paper on the Forgiveness of Sins. I think one of the main points is the cheapness of theosophical thought of sin. They speak of it in terms of punishment: God in terms of penitence. It's partly our fault, our cheapness in theorising about the Atonement. This is a scrap of what I wrote today: 'We tolerate cheap thinking in ourselves about religion, as we tolerate it about nothing else. And in nothing has our thinking been so cheap as on this article of the Creed. How many of us translate "the forgiveness of sins" by "the remission of the consequences"? We deserved to be punished: Christ took our punishment: and so God lets us off. This is our travesty of the most poignant verses in Holy Writ. We have bridged the abyss of the passion of God with an easy metaphor: clutched at security: and over against that ignominy, this faith that refuses shelter, that chooses to pay to the uttermost farthing, has something fine about it: yet only comparatively fine. It opposes to a cheap thought of sin a thought only less cheap.
>
> 'For there is another attitude beside these: a faith that will pay to the uttermost farthing, and when the debt is cancelled feel there is something broken yet. David, his punishment ended, going down to the House of God to cry, "Cast me not utterly from Thy presence": the Prodigal, expiating in hunger and hardship and shame the sins of youth,

and on his lips the cry, "no more worthy to be called Thy son." In what coin of penalty will Peter pay, that he may face the Risen Christ, true man again?

> Ah God! Ah God! That it were possible
> To undo things done. To call back yesterday!

There is nothing in theosophy deep enough to call to that deep. Nothing in all the world but those unfathomable sentences: "As far as east is distant from the west, so far has He removed our transgressions from us." Unfathomable, because their soundings are in that Eternity to which our yesterdays and tomorrows are one.'

It's rough yet, the sentences hang loose, but I know you will like to see it in process of growing. I go on to a comparison of punishment and penitence in dissociating a man from his sin — personality is at the root of the matter, and the impersonal thought of the East has drugged sound thinking. Next comes the thought of the Passion as the Penitence of God: and last, salvation by the Indwelling of the Holy Ghost.

The best-worst year, 1919, seemed commonplace enough in its admixture of stern doctrinal analysis, frivolously romantic opera, and high heroic domestic duty, until death suddenly irrupted. On 26 October Helen reported that R. T. Martin, Meg's brother-in-law, had met with a motoring accident and was lying unconscious. Next day she added:

R. T. Martin died last night. He never recovered consciousness, only that for half an hour he caught his wife's hand and held it. I've just come back. Meg is there and is in sore grief. But it's 'Uncle Robert' that she'll miss most — for he was like a second father to the boys. Myself, I feel as if a bit of the wall that sheltered us was blown down. For there was nothing one asked him that he would not try to do, and if you wanted a job, he would move heaven and earth to get it for you. One railed at him sometimes, but the faults he had were on the surface. As Meg once said, 'He'd have been a dear if he hadn't tried to model himself on Dr Johnson, when he hadn't the figure for it.' But always very far down in him was the little boy who crept to the foot of the garden and cried behind the hedge because he had suddenly realized that his mother would some day die.

Time had thus resolved the conflict of 1900, when things 'ill done and done to others' harm' had been taken by the all-too legal doer as exercise of virtue, and Meg and Helen treated as pawns in a game; all had ended in reconciliation, magnanimity, and heartfelt gratitude. Meanwhile nothing seemed likely to interrupt the weekly flow of letters between Belfast and Ahmadabad except the pleasure, looming on the horizon, of once more meeting face to face. Dr Taylor announced that he was busy preparing a course of lectures on

'Comparative Religion and Christian Missions' which he had been appointed to deliver in the Assembly's College, Belfast, during the session 1921–22. But, as T. S. Eliot has warned:
> 'You shall not think "the past is finished"
> Or "the future is before us".
>   . . . the time of death is every moment.'

The year 1919 passed into 1920 without any forewarning. Letters could take some weeks — the postal strike of 1919 succeeded in disrupting mail even more effectively than German U-boats had done. On 7 February Dr Taylor wrote in his usual style, but complained that a review sent by Helen had arrived 'terribly torn and tattered'. He enclosed the plan of his forthcoming lectures in Belfast, asked her leave to use her paper on the forgiveness of sin, and then appended a telling criticism of her increasingly bejewelled prose style, heavy with literary allusion meant only for Gregory Smith and Saintsbury's delectation: 'At the first reading of your Review (on Lafcadio Hearn), I felt in some degree tantalised; for the cryptic element seemed dominant, an overspreading haze, delicious, even if mysterious, in its vague suggestiveness, which yet made for lack of definition. The thought, veiled in words themselves radiant, was strangely elusive. . . . There is such a rich treasure *underlying* all you write, that I could wish you would be pleased to lift it to the surface-level, "that he may run that readeth".' He finally begged her to lay in a stock of strong envelopes that would stand the toss and tumble of the 6,000 miles to India, and revealed that each of his own envelopes had cost him rather more than fourpence apiece. A fortnight later, he was dead. Helen did not give her sorrow words: her profoundest griefs she passed over in silence. His last letters to her must have been delivered long after his death, which took place on 21 February 1920 at Stevenson College, Ahmadabad, of which he was Founder and Principal. His obituary simply stated that, after being taken suddenly ill, 'with no reserve of strength he fell gently asleep in the city and land of his love.' Her reaction can only be guessed when she received his letter, begun on Monday, 16 February, in ink, and completed in pencil on Friday, the eve of his death:

> Helen dear,
>   It is a distress to me to be writing you so short a letter as this must be. But you will forgive me, won't you, for here I am in bed, down with the flu, or something like it. The doctor says I must take a rest-cure, and he wishes me to stay in bed for some days.
>   There is one matter I must mention. Mr Coates has written me a very kind business letter. He approves of my selling out my 3½% Government

paper, and transferring the amount realised to Ireland. The bank-agent
here also approves. So I have given him instructions to sell off the whole of
my scrip, and send the proceeds to the Northern Banking Co. But this
brings with it the need of my making a new Will. I have accordingly done
so, and on Saturday I took it to the Sub-Registrar's court for registration.
It's a shorter will than the last. I am leaving you a legacy of £800, and on
Mary's death all I have is to be yours, my darling precious daughter. I hope
to send you a certified copy of the will, but it won't be ready for some three
weeks yet.

Now I must stop. The doctor would scold me, did he know I was
writing at all. I am just tired, so awfully tired, but the strength is going to
come back to me. My old body is getting frail, but myself I am well, quite
well. How could it be otherwise, for sweet Christ is with me, very near.
[The rest is in pencil]
Friday: Dear, I'm better: sleeping fairly & the pneumonia symptoms are
gone but the malaria still present, & the temperature variable. The doctor
doesn't let me sit up & I fancy I ought to obey. Daughter dear, don't fret:
all, all is well. My dear dear love to you, now and ever.
                    Your ever fondly loving
                              Father.

Never was the spoken word of direct communication heard more
clearly than in the exchange of weekly letters between George
Pritchard Taylor and Helen Waddell: in the presence of the other, each
forgot the separation of 6,000 miles, forgot that the pen was a mere
substitute for the voice; they spoke because their hearts were full, and
they couldn't help it. When, at sixty-five, speaking of himself as one
who had reached extreme old age, Dr Taylor departed, he left no
successor. Perhaps Alcuin's poem of longing for an absent friend that
Helen herself would one day translate, expresses the grief she never
put into words at the time:

> Too wide the earth, mine eyes no more behold thee,
>   Love weeps for absent love: my friend is gone.
> Rare, rare in men the love that can unite them:
>   Cry to the world: thy heart is still alone.

Whereas she had shared all her friends with him, with no one else
did she share the man who had taken her own father's place. He had
left her financially independent for the first time in her life, but
deprived now of his counsel and strength in her daily struggle to
control her wayward invalid. A letter to Dr Taylor of 8 February 1920
opens: 'It's clear and cold, and a blackbird — more likely a thrush — is
singing in the trees behind us: the very first Sunday of spring. And
there's the Valley of Achor for a door of hope. After a frightfully bad

break last week, my patient is in her right mind again.' She had never revealed to Saintsbury the true state of affairs, and now, seated on the little leaded roof above the drawing-room window reached by stepping through the window of her stepmother's bedroom, she apologized for her long silence:

> I'm writing by a window very high up in a world that is unread and wet. Not my own window — it knows me no more, except as a haggard Eve who comes to it every morning about dawn and then dives gratefully into quiet waves of sleep. You don't get written to these days, because I have ceased to exist. Except for stray hours when an exhilaration like the exhilaration of drugs comes on me, and I feel as omnipotent as the gods. It passes, and I am again unslept and stupid and subdued to that I work in. My patient is practically well again — and will not believe it. I suppose it is nerves. Anyhow it is difficult. And I a most ungracious Gracieuse.

The Prologue to Helen's play *The Spoiled Buddha* is spoken by a Buddhist Priest: 'The play is about the Buddha, in the days before he became a god: and about Binzuru, who was his favourite disciple, and who might have become even as the Buddha, only that he saw a woman passing by, and desired her beauty, and so fell from grace. . . .'

When published in 1919, few critics saw its implications — it appeared to be merely flippant. To this, Helen replied:

> I don't know whether any of the reviewers will see that it's more than a skit. I know that it's daring to make the bronze image move and speak: but it's part of the preposterousness of the conception that these images are indeed the Buddha and Binzuru and Daruma, flesh and blood transmuted into rigidity by the impassive years. The thought at the back of the play is that the way of *ascesis* attracts either the finest natures or the weeds — narrow ill-minded people like Daruma, or great rich natures like the Buddha's. Binzuru has his possibilities, but the way is too high for him: his rich humanity is not high enough for perseverance in the way. And the life in the outer court though it has made him a kindly god has coarsened him. Withal, it is *life*, 'the passionate and the humorous life of men' that comes before the Buddha at the last: he all but yields to it, having found the emptiness of Nirvana: but tradition is too strong. I *think* it is tradition. For the Buddha by this time knows that one finds the Infinite here also.

It has already been pointed out that everything H. W. wrote was autobiographical, and the play is no exception. The theme gives a subtle answer to the enigma of her early life, her own *ascesis*: 'In a curious way,' she wrote, 'it sums up a lot of my thinking in ten at least of my nine and twenty years, the struggle between negation and enrichment.' Paradoxically she came to realize that this bitter decade of negation was a period of tremendous enrichment: it gave her time to think, time to read, and above all it gave her that insight into the human heart and condition that was to recreate the poetry of the Middle Ages with a freshness hitherto unknown. And as so often in life, it was death that resolved the struggle. On Thursday, 2 July 1920, she wrote to Saintsbury from Kilmacrew:

> It's wet, and the candle is blowing at the open window and there's a corncrake out in the dark. And I've felt human again for the first time. My mother died last Friday in her sleep. I found her, in the chair.
>
> I suppose it's the reaction after the long years. But I came down here dead. Not that I was grieving — except that bitter remorse for all the unkind things you ever did or said. Just I didn't care what became of me. I was free at last — and there was nothing on earth that I wanted to do.
>
> I don't much yet. But it's an old house, and they're all young, and they like me awfully. And Peggy and I wandered the lanes for hours, and it was raining a little, and you know the smell of wet honeysuckle.
>
> Lay this earth upon thy heart
> And thy sickness shall depart.
>
> Write to me here. After a while I'm going to Scotland, but only for a few days or so.
>
> I don't know what I'll do. I'd hoped for Gregory's assistantship, but that's gone. I want work like that. It feels as if I'd never write again. But that's maybe because I'm so tired. If only I cared about anything — except the kids here. They've just paid me a nocturnal visit — Jack last.
>
> 'What colour are your eyes, Aunt Helen?'
>
> 'Tell me yourself. Look.'
>
> '. . . Grey . . . and brown . . . you know, like thatch when moss grows on it — greeny-like.'
>
> Do you know, Excellency? For if Jack is right, it has your touch of gold.'

Martha Waddell died on 25 June 1920, aged seventy-five. Glad to be rid at last of the narrow house animated with the soul of a porwiggle, Helen at first let it to an Army man, but after nine months disposed of the furniture and put the property up for sale. On 3 April 1921, on a leaf roughly torn from a student exercise book, she wrote to Professor Saintsbury from 19 Cedar Avenue:

> I'm sitting on the last chair before the van men take it from me; the only cheerful thing in the house is the fire. And, in a fashion, myself.
>
> For I was not happy in this house, Excellency, except that I wrote to you from it. And also there is something in St James — 'Behold, we count them happy which endure.'
>
> And now I've got almost every one of the things I beat against the bars for. And I am so happy that — being a Northerner, I am afraid.

CHAPTER VII

———————————

HELEN WAS THIRTY-ONE, her hair streaked with white, her old
academic qualifications seemingly so very old when, urged by Maude
Clarke, she went up to Oxford in the autumn of 1920 and rented two
rooms up six flights of stairs in Keble Road. Her financial resources
were meagre but sufficient to meet the £3.10s. per week asked for the
rooms, plus fire, light, breakfast and dinner. The owners were
'reduced Dublin, with miniatures about the house, and a sort of nice
old unobtrusive religion'; but the blue distempered room with its
claret carpet, sofa in faded green enriched with a blanket in purple,
yellow, blue and red, the black American-cloth armchair beside the
gas stove, and the casement shrouded windows looking over to Keble
College induced a feeling of sick leaden desolation. 'It's a quarter to
eight; I'm to go round to see Maude at half-past, she being solitary in
Somerville,' she wrote to Meg on arrival. 'Monday I'll begin reading
at the Bodleian. Once I've begun to work I'll not feel like a lost dog.
You see, I have to live up to Maude. This was her planning, and
Oxford is the place of her heart, and I don't like to grouse or be
anything but cheerful. I'll no say I'm happy for that would be a lee, but
I'll feel better when I get unpacked, and some fresh stuff on the
cushions. You know things like that matter to me maybe more than
they should, but the gas ring and the little kettle are a great joy. Thank
heaven I've gas, for there is a coal famine in Oxford.'

At first she read without any supervision or immediate goal beyond
a vague hope that her research into the secular origins of drama, begun
so long ago at Queen's, would resolve itself into a publishable book
and perhaps collect a fellowship on the way. But she suddenly realized
that she was starving in the land of plenty, and before the year was out
was writing to Meg:

> I've made an awfully big decision — to work for the B.Litt. after all. It was
> sinking in on me as I worked that nobody would ever see what I was
> doing, that the chances of publication were so vague, and that I might
> waste this year and not be any further forward. I've become a member of
> Somerville, living out. You have to join one of the Colleges or a 'Society
> for Home Students' for the B.Litt. and they were awfully decent at

Somerville about having me. Miss Penrose the head said the worst of my living out was that they wouldn't get the 'value' of me in College. But it has made a tremendous difference in my feeling about the place, not such a sparrow on the housetops now, you see, when I do go to look for a job. I have all Somerville to back me — and Somerville is good to its own. Miss Lorimer — the one like Miss Matier — shoved it for all she was worth. It just means, as far as work goes, that I submit as a thesis what I'm doing now.

Poor little Maude has had a temporary collapse with overwork, and lies like a street-Arab with smudges under her eyes. You know how pathetic it looks in bed. She had eight people to coach today . . . as Maude says, 'Eight hungry sheep look up and are not fed.'

I'm happy here now. But it *was* bad at first. Not Oxford's fault. It was the first time I'd been really alone since . . . and you know how one is haunted. And also you know what it's like when you don't like yourself, and there's nobody to back you up by believing that you're nicer than you know you really are. That is over and done. I've swallowed all my gnats and camels. And I think I'm middling popular. And oh, I was nearly forgetting. Paul Henry has *given* me his last picture, 'Early Morning in Connemara'. You know the Donegal light? It's a lough with mountains round it, painted looking down from a great height, in dim blue and silver, with one soft cloud floating in the sky with light on it. Isn't he a darling? It was his last day — and he had asked me for tea with a very jolly crew and then brought me home — to tell me that he wanted me to have it. 'I'd rather far you had it than sell it to somebody who wouldn't like it the way you do.' And the poor old son only sold *one* picture in Oxford. However he's going up to London, and is sure to have better luck there. Here they are all for etchings of the Old Masters and the approved. But — my picture was £50. Can you believe it's really mine? Wait till you see it.

I'm writing this early before I go to Bodley. I'm enclosing the subject I've submitted to the Council. Let the Boss [i.e. Meg's husband, J.D.] see it.

The Council raised objections, as two letters to Saintsbury make clear:

I've transferred from the B.Litt. to the Ph.D. It's an untried degree but they say the tendency will be to lower the standard of the older. I wish they'd let me choose the gown. I'd have it orange and black. Last night I heard a glorious thing — Brahms — that made me nearly drunk. And after it a chaconne of Bach that sobered me: but in the middle of it I suddenly saw my first chapter which has been lying about my mind in unrelated boulders and chunks. And suddenly it was a Roman road. And then came a thing of Mozart in the mood of the *Magic Flute* that set me dancing on my Roman road, and I'm in that humour yet. So that the news that the new Somerville Fellowship won't be open to graduates of alien universities has in no way dejected me.

A month later during the Christmas vacation spent at Kilmacrew, she told G.S. of her tussle over the subject of her research:

They fell foul of my subject for the 'Fuff-Dee' (which is now my pet name and very suitable in the present state of my hair), and had to be reasoned with — which I did, singly, and in my own person, with the happiest results. But, at the moment, the Ph.D. is less than nothing. I'm afraid it's true, as Peggy says, that I am more of a domestic animal than a scholar. And I have a new jumper thing that I wear for dinner, which is called 'The Feast of Lanterns' and incites to riot. It's Liberty gold and burnt red and green-lanterned. Next time you come to Oxford, you shall see the Feast of Lanterns. It has brown feather stuff round the neck and sleeves. And Father O'Keefe, the scholastic philosophy man, says it has confirmed his intention to leave the Roman for the Greek Church. But I urged him to remain, assuring him that the great charm for me is that he is inaccessible. I most heartily agree with you about the Ph.D. I haven't much use for doctorates unless they are *honoris causa*.

Helen in Oxford was certainly the Helen Helenizing in Helenity, herself and nothing else, as Saintsbury once put it. In January 1921 she was admitted formally to Somerville, was a member of the Senior Common Room and sat at High Table. Before long, exactly as at Queen's, she was in the centre of the social life of the College. She had resumed the friendship with Cathleen Nesbitt, cut short so brutally by her stepmother ten years earlier, and on 14 February was writing to Meg:

Life is very pleasant. I was twice at *Antony and Cleopatra*. Cathleen was wonderful, not quite enough mystery to be absolute — it would take Maude for that — but according to the same Maude, one of the greatest actresses she has seen. Antony, God help him, has fallen wildly in love with her, and it was almost pathetic last night, for there was more than acting in his frenzy. Poor Cleopatra fairly reeled after one of his kisses.

The Senior Common Room at Somerville is nothing like the ordeal I feared, and Miss Penrose is a dear. She has Sam's quality and has a wide smile that endears her to me very much. My young friend in Bodley amuses me so much that I have begun to be firm, for it is very distracting. I told Miss Lorimer a tale he had brought me from the Patrologia, and she eyed me — 'You don't mean to tell me you've subdued Mr Lobell?' 'No' says I meekly — 'Just he is very useful.' 'What would I not give!' says Miss L. 'He's the most arrogant young man in Oxford.' It seems he was Craven scholar in 1909 and now lectures on paleography — which is the deciphering of manuscripts. These he pores over in his own little study in

Duke Humphrey. But it would surprise you — his ingenuity in finding objects which might be of use to my work. And all with the air of the untamed bull bowing his unfamiliar neck to the yoke.

Little by little Oxford was casting its spell over her. Her health improved, and with it her zest for work: 'It's the difference in my brain,' she told Meg — 'as if I had learned *how* to work, not in frenzied nibbles here and there, but a kind of horse, foot and artillery, and not an inch of ground left unquartered.' Her purse was made slightly less inadequate by fees for coaching, reviewing, and marking examination papers. Yet circumspect and determinedly cheerful though her letters to Meg were, they betray a certain unease and feeling of isolation. Once she refers to 'Maude's extreme caution'. The truth was that with her inborn hatred of silly gossip, Maude was deliberately avoiding the inseparable companion of her girlhood. She seemed too busily engaged with tutorials to be able to set aside any time for the claims of friendship. Helen was puzzled and hurt. It would have been kinder had Maude explained that while many in Oxford were afraid of God, many were far more afraid of Mrs Grundy — not for Maude to re-echo Bernard Shaw's 'What will *they* say? Let them say!'

One member of the S.C.R. of Somerville apparently sensed the situation, and with unobtrusive kindness came to the rescue. Like Helen, a daughter of the manse, Hilda Lorimer, a Scot from Edinburgh, was classics tutor at Somerville. Writing in 1984, Peter Levi has dubbed her 'that noble old dragon who presided for years over the antiquarian scrap-heap which used to be called Homeric archaeology'. One can only reply that it was just as well an infant dragon was about, to welcome Irish exiles stranded on the banks of the Isis — to judge from her treatment of both Enid Starkie and Helen Waddell. Not only did she share Helen's otherwise solitary meals in her lodgings, but she showed a lively interest and concern in her projects, and early in 1921 suggested they spend Easter together in Italy. Helen totted up her resources and gladly agreed. Easter Day fell on 27 March. As Helen dated none of her letters, it is difficult to time their route with exactitude, but her letters convey the excitement of this first taste of Europe. The two travellers reached Paris from Oxford on 21 March, and that same evening boarded the train for Milan. To Meg, Helen wrote a few days later:

We left Paris about eight on Monday evening and were in the train until eleven on Tuesday night — and no breakfast on Tuesday morning — and two *orful* hours in the douane at Medan [*sic*] where you are penned like sheep waiting to have your baggage passed by customs. But it was worth it

to go to sleep in Milan, and all the next day travel through the great gentle
Lombardy plain, with the Alps like quiet ghosts on the horizon, and near
hand oxen ploughing in the fields, and little canals with willows, and on
the nearer hills monasteries, walled, with their belt of cypresses — and
suddenly Lake Garda, like a vision of the Inland Sea. Miss Lorimer is a
dear, the kindest creature to travel with, and enjoying it almost fearfully —
her first great pleasure since the war.

Experientia does it, as Mrs Micawber's papa used to say, and
although Miss Lorimer was dear and kind (the 'Miss' was never
dropped in all the years Helen spoke of her), compared with Meg as
travelling companion, she was as a farthing candle to the sun. On 23
March they arrived to find Venice throned on her hundred isles bathed
in moonlight. Here they stayed for a fortnight. Next day Helen
despatched her usual diary-letter to Meg:

If you were here it would make it real. Just now it cannot be really me. It's
about half-past five and the sun has gone behind the funny rough-tiled
roofs opposite and I could throw a bun into the green water of the Grand
Canal. This street ends in the Canal, and is a sort of stand for gondolas.
They come in and out all day long through little slim trees stuck in the
water to make stalls for them, like horses, and they are slender and black
and romantic; but if one is poor one goes in a dreadful little fat steamer that
roars up and down the Grand Canal. Last night we came in from Milan by
moonlight about seven and were determined to bust, and arrive in a
gondola, but a little voluble man sent by the *padrona* to meet us, insisted on
the steamer, which finally threw us off at a landing-stage very far off: after
which we were panted through innumerable dark lanes and across tiny
canal bridges. Finally arrived in Piazza Santa Maria Zoberigo, panted
afresh up innumerable stairs to the Pensione which is the top flat of an
enormous house, and fell with joy into two awfully comfortable rooms,
with low broad windows and armchairs and a view of the Grand Canal
aforesaid, and a marble palace which must be about fifteenth century if not
older.
    There's the strangest smell, half eastern, a mixture of seaweed — for the
sea-tides run through Venice — and warmth, and pleasant things being
fried in quite agreeable oil. I'll never cease mourning that you are not here.
Venice *is* eastern, and St Mark's positively barbaric. Anything less like our
sombre western cathedrals you cannot imagine. At its best it glows like a
sea-shell, marble tinted pale pink and yellow and veined with blue, endless
domes and sculptures of angels perching winged, and climbing up to our
Lord on the topmost pinnacle — those against the sky looking as if a breath
of wind would blow them away, and lower down a blaze of mosaics,
pictures of the Ascension, another bringing of St Mark's body from
Alexandria to Venice — blue and crimson, but above all gold. . . . This

morning by the most incredible luck we strolled into the Cathedral in time for the Holy Thursday washing of the Apostles' Feet — and beheld the Archbishop of Venice, gold mitre and all, kneeling in turn before twelve old beggar men with a copper basin and attended by his clergy with silver jugs and towels, and washing every one. He really washed them: I saw him scrub, and at the end, he being corpulent and elderly, he was red in the face and had to be helped up and down. He had previously exhausted himself by preaching a terrific and sonorous Italian sermon, which I could with pleasure have shortened, as I was balancing on a very small and rickety chair to see above the heads of the crowd. Had also the joy of seeing a procession of the Host, headed by a crucifix of our Lord draped in purple — every crucifix is shrouded now until Easter Day — and four huge candles the size of broom handles. The Host itself was carried with immense reverence by the Cardinal-Archbishop — six bishops pacing before him, and himself under a magnificent gold canopy held by four men. When he reached the altar where the Host was to be laid, and where the canopy could not follow him, an attendant priest helped out with the most preposterous gold umbrella, and held it over the Archbishop and Host till it reached its destination. It surely is the Eastern idea of sovereignty. But it was for the Host, and not for the Archbishop, for he was allowed to walk away without either umbrella or canopy.

In describing Catholic ceremonial and worship, Helen never puts a foot wrong. Yet the two women from Oxford who, of all their generation, worked to prove that the classical grind above all other disciplines gave human beings a common meeting-place of the mind, made not a single allusion, showed not the slightest desire to turn their steps, even for a day's excursion, to Rome, golden Rome, *Roma immortalis*. There are echoes indeed of *The Wandering Scholars* evident throughout Helen's letters from Italy, but it was St Francis of Assisi rather than Virgil or SS Peter and Paul who held her mind captive. She longed to hire a gondola and drift across the marshes of the lagoon to the tiny cypress-covered island graced with a single monastery, San Francesco del Deserto, where St Francis had once lived. Since her tentative suggestion took no root in Hilda Lorimer's mind, she did not pursue it but vowed to return one day with Meg. Scorning guide books, they would simply gaze their fill at the mother-of-pearl waters, the old stained marble, the tenderness, the light, and the strangeness of that enchanted land. On the Wednesday of Easter week, the two holiday-makers took the little steamboat from Venice to Burano and then bartered with a gondolier to take them across the stretch of water to Torcello, to the little landing-stage nestling beneath the walls of the tenth-century church, inlaid with incomparable mosaics, its single campanile rising majestically above the white-thorn blossom. 'They built it,' Helen writes to Meg in the unmistakable voice of *The Wandering Scholars*, 'the people who fled from the Lombardy plain when the Lombards surged down from the Alps and sacked their cities; it's the old Roman civilization taking its last stand in the marshes of the lagoons where the Goths wouldn't follow them.' With a gesture typical of his Incomparabilis, Helen gathered a posy to send to George Saintsbury in Bath, which she did immediately:

> Venice
> 30 March 1921
>
> Thursday morning. This letter is a little drunk, but it was written in the middle of the night.
>
> > 'Because all words, though culled with choicest art,
> > Failing to give the bitter of the sweet,
> > Wither beneath the palate.'
>
> Take these flowers. They will be withered too when they come to you: but just now the violet is surely enough, and the other — it is samphire? — is salt with the sea. I could find nothing in Venice to send you. But today I gathered these on the island of Torcello — *Venice antica*, as the gondoliers called it — where the streets are little grassy paths with lagoons on either side, and for houses there were peach trees in blossom, and only the cathedral left with a pavement like the body of heaven at sunset. It was a day like the colour of your moonstone, and the doors of the church were wide open, and the faith of it — the faith that knew the taking of the manhood into God. I found the violets beside the wall, and the samphire at the edge of one of the little paths close to the sea edge, and beside it a blackthorn in blossom. I do not think I will ever see the like of Torcello again. Torcello is a new dream that it had not entered into my heart to conceive. I know now that I have been in one of the 'hazy lands that float beneath the rising sun's new rim.' And these are the grasses of it, that you may take seisin.
>
> > Your
> > Helen

Who, upon reading such a letter, would ever connect *Venice antica* with the modern megalopolis of New York? Yet, her experience hand in hand with insight, that is precisely what H. W. was to do fourteen years later. In 1935 she was on her way to receive an honorary doctorate from Columbia University. As the S.S. *Berengaria* approached harbour, New York City rose above the airless damp mist like an island of ancient churches with high bell-towers, the skyscrapers endlessly repeating the campanile of Torcello's Santa Fosca. She has expressed her vision in her arresting poem, *New York City*, a powerful blend of biblical, classical and mediaeval allusion, historical watchword, and contemporary slogan. It opens:

> *The presence that so strangely rose beside the waters.*
> Torcello with its single campanile
> Above blackthorn and salt lagoon
> Multiplied in the mist . . .
> *The Berengaria will dock at six.*

The two Oxonians left Venice for Ravenna about 7 April, and from there to Rimini and Mantua, spending one night in each before settling for a few days in Verona. The reader of Helen's letters to Meg is tempted to wonder whether occasionally Japan rather than Italy was uppermost in her thought. This is the more curious, since those who later considered themselves her close friends knew nothing about her life there, beyond the fact that it was her birthplace. To Helen, Japan was a secret Symie's Garden set thick with lily and red rose, wherein she and Meg alone had the right to wander. 'Just before we left Venice,' she wrote on 8 April to Meg, 'the wisteria had begun to come out, and it was queer to see it again after such years — made me suddenly hanker for Tokio.' And for Billy, to whom she had sent her little Japanese haiku?

> 'Being tired
> Ah the time I fall into the inn.
> — The wisteria flowers!'

The hotel at Verona offered her 'a most blessed and peaceful room; it has a balcony right over the river, a beautiful swift clear river down from the Alps, and brawling on the pebbles just like the stream at Karuizawa' — where two children in pith helmets, she and Billy, would play to all eternity? But it was perhaps a prophetic instinct that led her, while at Mantua, to Virgil's birthplace. 'They don't know the exact spot,' she told Meg, 'but they've made a little green enclosure at a crossroad with lilac and bay trees and a few pines, and in the middle a thin kindly statue of Virgil himself, very high on his column, and below it the lines from Dante about his "ombra gentile", his gentle Shade. I liked that. Did you know that he was a small farmer's son?'

But no place in Europe beckoned so powerfully to Helen Waddell as did the city that was the goal and climax of this Easter holiday. 'What was it the Irishman wrote the other day?', Peter Abelard would ask himself in the opening pages of Helen's novel. '"In those days when youth in me was happy and life was swift in doing, and I wandering through the divers cities of sweet France for the love I had of learning . . ."' From her student days at Queen's, H.W. had dreamt of Paris and Abelard and

'Helowys,
That was abbesse not far from Parys' —

and now at last she was standing under the roof and cloisters of Notre Dame. Here were experience and intuition and prophecy in plenty. Eternity flowed about the four days in Time that she spent there. Meg received her first impressions:

> Paris! Henry James talks about its light at night: 'a twinkling grin set on the face of pleasure', and that's Paris all day long. I never was in a city so gay and friendly and kindly, and for all I've seen of it no wickedness but a kind of innocent naughtiness. *Rianté* is the word for it, especially now that it's April, and warm sun in between the showers. Today we climbed the tower of Notre Dame, and the sun showered itself over Paris, and the wind blew, a kind of gay rollicking wind, and the old tower hummed with it; a happy *bourdon* with a big tree, and beside us the old *Penseur* gargoyle sat with his chin in his hands and his wise gargoyle face in a sort of sardonic grin, wide for all Paris below him.

Helen returned to Oxford on 22 April. Here, stern concentration was soon threatened by a whirl of social activity. Had Meg's analysis been correct? Was Helen 'more of a domestic animal than a scholar'? One of the tasks immediately facing her was to organize an Oxford Committee to raise money for Somerville. On 17 May she wrote to Meg:

> I think I told you Cathleen Nesbitt was going to give a matinée for Somerville — she came down for one night and saw all the people, and has departed to try to get hold of an all-star matinée, Irene Vanbrugh and Mrs Pat Campbell and Cyril Maude. She's not only getting the people, but she is getting wealthy persons with cars to run them down. It's something to be a popular actress. You would love her. There's something in her, inside, reflective and patient and sad: it makes her awfully understanding and she has not a shred of affectation. There's one thing, it does you no harm in Somerville to be the origin of Miss Nesbitt's interest in the place, as you may imagine.

But if the olive groves of Academe were open to an actress, it did not take long for Oxford dons to recognize that the actress's friend was possessed of a solid intellectual power and brilliance that few of their clever men could equal. In the Michaelmas Term of 1921, Helen was appointed to a lectureship under the Cassell Trust Fund by the

Council of St Hilda's Hall. At midday on successive Saturdays she gave a course of eight lectures on 'The Mime in the Middle Ages'. Although it was possibly the worst time of the day, the lecture hall became so crowded that the entrance was besieged by students unable to get in for what they considered the best lectures ever heard in Oxford. The soil from which the work sprang had been tilled and sown those many years ago under Gregory Smith at Queen's: this was merely the harvesting. By some happy accident, her first lecture, a typescript of nearly 24 pages, has escaped Helen's final holocaust and, but for two opening sheets, is extant in its entirety. It repays analysis.

Not for nothing had small Helen sat at her father's feet in Uyeno Park listening to his oratory. Those who later heard her speak in public testify to her Irish clarity of diction and organ-like resonance of tone. Her voice was a musical instrument on which she could convey every variety of human emotion, and at chanting pitch she could reach the furthest end of a large lecture hall. The text, studded with her own original translations, looks backward to her days at Queen's and forward to the publications that were to bring her fame. If at first the audience feared a sleep-inducing talk on the barbarian frolics of Goths, Lombards and Franks, they must soon have been jolted out of their torpor by her arresting and provocative assertions:

> French, Italian and Spanish are provincial dialects, not of Gothic, the language of the conquerors, but of Latin, the language of the conquered . . . Roman language and Roman Law, Roman Christianity and Roman paganism, these, however brokenly, survived.
>
> What of that which was admittedly the master-passion of the Roman people, that had steeped their senses till they were indifferent even to the Gothic swords, their passion for the stage? Did the Roman theatre survive? The shows of the theatre and the circus were a gift from rulers to people, as much as our own police protection. Besides the State subsidy, the games were the necessary complement of taking office: the speech of thanks delivered by the new member to his constituents. One overhears the dinner-table conversation at the table of Trimalchio, wealthy *parvenu* in the provinces, like your war-profiteer in Surrey.

The theatre as a Roman institution disappeared because of the utter bankruptcy of the public purse, and the actor vanishes from the official records 'as completely as the crossing-sweeper from the pages of *Punch*'. Helen has now got into her stride:

> Consider the probable effect on our own stage if every theatrical company in the kingdom suddenly went bankrupt, like Beecham Grand Opera in 1919. . . . The music hall would fare best, resolving into their component

parts; so too the one-act sketch with no scenery and perhaps only two dramatis personae. But were there the equivalents of these things in Rome?

Nothing, I suppose, will cure us of our conviction that the Roman people were different from us: and nothing so confirms us in our Pharisaism as their recorded passion for the circus and the gladiatorial shows. As for their passion for the circus, it was a mixture of our own immense affection for the Zoo and our national passion for racing. The chariot race in Rome was simply the equivalent of the Derby and Newmarket, Ascot and Goodwood: and when Nero insisted on driving his own chariot, he scandalised Rome exactly as Edward VII would have scandalised England if he had insisted on being his own jockey.

The distant past springs to life under her touch. She deals with Greek classical tragedy in terms of the Nō drama of contemporary Japan (she had just reviewed Arthur Waley's *The Nō Plays of Japan*), and then leads a generation who had seen Pavlova and the Russian Ballet to an understanding of the supremacy of the pantomimes on the Roman stage. The list of mimes from Pomponius and Laberius that she reads aloud is anything but highbrow: 'When the Pig was sick'; 'Pantaloon is dead and gone'; 'The Washerwoman'; 'The Punch Twins'; 'Punch gets an Agency'; 'The French Polisher'; 'My Father's Uncle'; 'Old Clo''. Whereas the long robe of tragedy and the saffron of comedy passed from the theatre, the patchwork of the mime in Harlequin's many-coloured coat and in Pierrot's spots and patches still holds the stage, and 'acts on every flimsy seaside platform the comedy as old as its foreground of the sea.' The survival of Harlequin, Columbine, Punchinello and the Fool brought her lecture on the Mime to a close but, before her final bow, Helen swung off to *I Pagliacci*, to be performed in Oxford the following week. 'Remember while you watch it,' she told her audience, 'the most sophisticated, diamond-cut, technically flawless of all operas, that it is the immemorial setting for the immemorial tragi-comedy, the woman and the lover, the husband and the fool; that

> "The voice you hear this passing night was heard
> In ancient days of Emperor and clown."'

Her lectures were received enthusiastically. 'If you want to get shaken up from your very foundations, and a rattling good time as well, come to a lecture at twelve on Saturdays, a Miss Waddell' — this tribute from a graduate submitting a doctoral thesis summed up the general acclaim, and resulted in a shower of compliments and requests for more: would she speak to the French School on the jongleurs; translate Geoffrey Rudel, the twelfth-century troubadour, for the Clarendon Press; lecture on Chaucer's *Troylus and Cryseyde*? Had the

University of Oxford then 'accepted' her? Years before, when Maude Clarke first went up to Oxford, Helen had begged Dr Taylor not to envisage a similar future for herself: 'It's not the scholarship,' she told him, 'it's the tradition and the method of work that are so incommunicable and distinctive.' In 1921 C. S. Lewis was expressing his despair over repeated failures, after a five-year residence, to break into the circle of the academics. 'People talk about the Oxford manner and the Oxford life and the Oxford God knows what else,' he wrote to his brother. 'The real Oxford is a close corporation of jolly, untidy, lazy, good-for-nothing, humorous old men, who have been electing their own successors ever since the world began and who intend to go on with it.' Where precisely was C.S.L. during H.W.'s lectures? In a letter to his father, already quoted and dated 16 February 1921, he said he had met Helen 'the other night at the Carlyles' — a reference presumably to an Oxford clergyman, the Reverend Alexander Carlyle. He had already made her acquaintance at the McNeills in Belfast. Yet voluminous letter-writers as both were, apart from this single reference, neither ever mentions the other. One can only draw the obvious conclusion. All the same, Helen would have agreed with him that the fortress was unassuming but impregnable and, to the Irish temperament, Oxford proved a 'provokingly intangible stone wall'. C.S.L. would have battered it down; Helen possibly might have leapt over it but she did not try: she faced facts and decided to go. The demanding work of coaching for hours, setting and marking examination papers, and preparing lectures consumed not only time but energy, and left her with little remuneration and no opportunity whatever to pursue her own research. The dry collegiate atmosphere of pure scholarship was too rarefied for deep breaths of sheer enjoyment of life and people essential to Helen. In June 1922, after spending five of the eight statutory terms at Somerville, she decided to take a big risk, go up to London, look for congenial work, read at the British Museum and thus, if Oxford would agree, submit her thesis for the doctorate as an outsider. Apologizing for her failure to obtain the Fuff-Dee, 'I'm horribly afraid', she told Saintsbury, 'that artists and journalists are more my sort than academic people.'

She was to spend the rest of her life in London. Leaving Oxford in June amid the lamentations of many, she went straight up to town and rented the top floor — her eyrie, she called it — of a three-storey house in St Edmund's Terrace. Here she could pass swiftly over the canal and into Regent's Park. Before settling in for good, she decided to enjoy the summer at Kilmacrew with Meg and the children, a step that almost brought her plans to nothing. On the eve of returning to take possession of 9 St Edmund's Terrace, N.W.8, she wrote to Saintsbury in her customary eighteenth-century manner:

> Tomorrow she goes to London — to be in the flat in time for dinner. It is not possible that he could have a note there to receive me — carry me over the threshold but please, Excellency, *soon*.
>
> This summer, I know it rained everywhere, but it didn't in the Mourne Mountains; we thought the weather wonderful, but do not say so publicly, because the world looks very much astonished, and would conclude that we must have been in love. One of us was. . . . There was a bungalow under the mountain for sale, and for a little while the balances swung even that 9 St Edmund's Terrace would never see her.
>
> But she is still — even in that issue would be
>
> Your Helen
>
> partly because he never calls me Helen unless in public, but always Brownie which means that half of me is lost on him. And I believe that is the reason why I'm not choosing chintz for the windowseats in the bungalow at this minute.

Her love of London was akin to Thomas More's or Samuel Johnson's or Charles Lamb's — all three were after her own heart. She nowhere specifies who the suitor of the summer of 1922 had been, but in spite of her renewed zest for work and appreciation of London's delights, she was haunted by her refusal to marry. To Meg, she wrote:

> Life is good. These London dusks, with the lamps lit and the big red sun going down in the smoke — and yet on Saturday night, an odd thing happened. I was coming home from shopping, just in that dusk, with the streets at their liveliest — and — ah, you know the excitement of a crowd, and the way innumerable voices and a kid crying and the booming of taxis all blend into a sort of Wagner chorus. And suddenly for a moment I was at the back of the Mournes, at the door of a wee earth house, looking over the slopes of heather and the wet bog, in the same twilight, with the sun just down. But ah, the quiet of it. And I was watching for my man coming home, and there was nobody but the two of us in the world. Maybe it *did* happen — about two thousand years ago.
>
> I feel as if those two years in Oxford were a bad dream. . . . And I found myself writing to Maude last week with the same old chaffing assurance. Does one get back everything, as soon as one can do without it?

News of her intellectual brilliance had spread far beyond Oxford, and no sooner had she settled in London than she was offered a lectureship for a year at Bedford College with the possibility of a permanency. She found her young students 'as soft as a litter of puppies, the same yapping, twinkling sheer interest, and their round eyes get awfully excited.' In that same year of 1922–23, she gave a course of public lectures on 'The Stage to the Closing of the Theatre in 1642'. Hopes of a permanent post at Bedford fell through when the English lecturer returned after a sabbatical year in America. Helen's future was as uncertain as ever. Marriage would have solved the problem once and for all, yet she refused as always to consider it. She crossed over to Kilmacrew for Christmas 1922, wrote out Browning's 'Two in the Campagna', handed it to 'the Mourne man', and added another rejection to the growing list:

> No. I yearn upward, touch you close,
>   Then stand away. I kiss your cheek,
> Catch your soul's warmth — I pluck the rose
>   And love it more than tongue can speak —
> Then the good minute goes. . . .
>
> Just when I seemed about to learn!
>   Where is the thread now? Off again!
> The old trick! Only I discern —
>   Infinite passion, and the pain
> Of finite hearts that yearn.

Then she sat down and wrote to Saintsbury:

> I've broken with the Mourne Mountains man, definitely. At least, I'm still to see him very occasionally. But it's final this time. Write to me. I know it wasn't the real thing — I could forget so easily in London and be so happy, but for a long time I pretended to myself and 'played at houses'. Now it's as if I had blown out the candles. And daylight is very cold before the sun rises.
> Wonder if it ever will? But what I was doing was keeping the blinds down and the candles all burning. And one misses the sunrise if you do that too long. Are you exasperated with me, or do you understand?

Back in London, she applied for vacant lectureships advertised for both Westfield and King's Colleges. That she failed to obtain her object is not surprising, to judge from the interview with the Council of King's College, London. According to the report sent to Meg, it was held under the chairmanship of Professor T. Barker, 'lean and gaunt and grim, like a big plunging dog,' and Canon Barnes of Westminster, thin and middle-aged with gentle smiling eyes. It went something like this:

> King's: Are you prepared to become warden of the hostel as well as
>   Tutor?

H.W.:   No. Wouldn't it eat up one's whole life, tutor and general adviser all day at King's, warden for 53 girls all night? At Bedford there are only 90, and Miss Tuke has a Bursar and Resident Tutor and two resident staff as well as matron.

K.:   . . . Yes, it would eat you up. Would you be content with the very elementary lecturing involved in the post?

H.:   I would not. (Sudden strangled chuckle from Dr Barker.)

K.:   Does this post really attract you?

H.:   No, except that I like girls, and would be ready to try it.

Dr Barker: Well, no matter how this appointment goes, I think we are all agreed that we want you at King's in some capacity. We'd be honoured to have you as lecturer, if opportunity comes.

It was an odd ten minutes of sheer naked truth, as Helen remarked to Meg. It must have been a refreshing ten minutes for the Committee. It left the future as uncertain as ever. To help her finances, Helen was applying to various publishers for work as reader, but nothing was forthcoming. On 29 May, two days before her thirty-fourth birthday, Helen told Meg of the letter she had just received from her old headmistress, Anna Matier, offering her the headship of Victoria College, and of the reaction of Dr Spurgeon of Bedford College:

£400 a year, and rooms at Drumglas, the new house. I can't bring myself to do it, something in me has gone dead to it. It's only the thought of not being the usual 'Irish absentee' that goads me. I've spoken to my blessed Spurgeon and Miss Tuke, and they both say it is almost 'criminal' to go and bury myself alive in administration. Miss Tuke says — 'Child, give yourself another ten years. It would be cruel.' And the Professor said with a sudden roar of wrath, 'You seem to have a passion for self-immolation, but I think once might have been enough for you.' I'd do it if I were sure it was my duty, but I can't see it . . . I'd love to be near you, but somehow I think I'd see little more of you in the end than I do now, and with less comfort to the heart.

Less than three weeks later, like Alice in Wonderland standing in the long low hall with many doors, all of them locked, Helen was suddenly presented with the golden key that fitted into the hidden door opening into the landscape of her dreams:

Lady Margaret Hall
Oxford   June 16th 1923

Dear Miss Waddell,

I have much pleasure in informing you that the Council elected you today to the Susette Taylor Fellowship. We had a wide field & some strong candidates, but we were clear that no other candidate was likely to do such distinguished work. We feel we are fortunate in having secured your election & we hope to hear that you are willing to accept the Fellowship.

A hope was expressed at our Education Committee that you would change one word . . . i.e. that the 'literary *influence* of the Wandering Scholars' should become 'the literary *importance* of the Wandering Scholars'. We did not think that as we were presenting the sentence as a title you would object?

I hope that you will visit us some time soon; I feel that we should all like to give a hearty send-off to our first Fellow. Meanwhile will you be so kind as to let us know how you would like to be described in the papers? We will insert a brief notice as soon as we hear from you.

Yours sincerely,

L. Grier

This letter from Lynda Grier, Principal of Lady Margaret Hall, was to give Helen the opportunity to put her latest theory to the test and was, in fact, to change the whole course of her life. Before assuming its final form, the title of her studies would undergo several more changes, but already she had begun to challenge the accepted theory of the purely liturgical origin of the mime against the setting of the Mass and yearly festivals. Was there not, she asked, a distinctive independent tradition? She had come across Du Méril's text of the *Carmina Burana*, and would never forget her shock of delight when, in the Benedictbeuern Nativity Play, she met a Joseph 'with a prolix beard' fleeing from Herod with Mary and the Child, being greeted by a procession of the King of Egypt and his court with a pagan paean:

> And so the feast of Venus,
> Wherever Love holds sway,
> By mortal and immortal
> Is kept a holiday.

Most of the material for further study was in manuscript in the Bibliothèque Nationale. Secure financially on £200 for each of the next two years, like many an Irish wandering scholar before and since, to Paris she went.

On arrival, she took up residence at the Anglo-American Club in the rue de Chevreuse. Here she was nearly demented by the noise: the shrieking smelling dizzy buses outside, and inside the strident voices, the incessant singing, the student parties, all of which served to throw into relief her own inner loneliness. To Meg she wrote:

I'm in bed, because it is the only warm place. The radiator is like a tombstone, and their old boiler which burst a month ago isn't mended yet. But am going to Room 27 on Thursday for good, I hope, which is in the

main building and hot all day and all night, also cubby hole to serve as
scullery and wash-house — but all of Club very friendly — too friendly.
My only comfort is that a full day's work at the Bibliothèque Nationale
leaves you like a mat at night, so that you really can't do much but sit
around.

I'm happier about my French. Did I tell you that I'd found a rather
wonderful Russian girl who knows mediaeval Latin and scholastic
philosophy, and I go and talk three hours a week? . . . The Sorbonne
opened last week, and I'm going to a lecture of Faral's once a week.
Mercifully I no longer feel as if water were roaring in my ears when I'm
addressed in rapid French — I'm even screwing up courage to send him
Miss Pope's letter of introduction at once, instead of waiting till after
Christmas. It is on my own subject, mediaeval Latin.

I feel quite hollow inside, because I know all these people and go skating
round all the time on nice polished floors, and never see anybody who
knew me before — and nothing matters in life but getting the book
written. But it's a satisfaction that I'm in honour bound to L.M.H. to do
that book. 'It may be that you are not in that place which God would once
have had you choose. Serve Him where you are.'

Maude Clarke would have been well content with that concluding
paragraph, as the following letter to Saintsbury suggests. It must have
been written as soon as Helen got into her stride:

> 4 Rue de Chevreuse,
> Paris.
> October 24th 1923

Yesterday was your birthday, and I forgot it . . . I am a reed to pierce the
hand of him that trusts in me, but I am *so* sorry afterwards.

I think I wrote you a very dim letter last time. Odd things have
happened inside me since. I suddenly discovered that I *like* being by
myself. And when people wrote asking if I wanted introductions, I said
no. Not till after Christmas. I can't manage work and people together. The
Egyptian once said that I never did anything decent unless I had been
driven to get my excitement out of the work instead of people. And this,
like many but not all of the Egyptian's sayings, is true. My present content
is partly because Paris all by itself is a good shadow-show; and chiefly
because of the Scholars Vagantes. Just now I am doing an amazing thing —
reading nothing but the things they read. I found to my disgrace that I had
taken Virgil for granted ever since I was sixteen. It was a revelation to
come back to him, with some living in-between. And I know now why
Alcuin cried over Dido, and Odo saw the brood of serpents in the
porcelain vase.

Also I came upon the *Copa*. For a foolish moment I hoped it was his.
Anyhow I've translated it. May I send it to you when it's finished? It's so
contemporary: perhaps nearer to the very end of the nineteenth century —

but younger than anything I know of them. But there are scores of things I want to talk about. Yesterday, after a morning of the *De Arte Amandi* I came out into the Avenue de l'Opéra — and suddenly I realized why we speak of the 'Latin' nations. There was no transition. And I thought with a sudden hankering of Great Russell St or Piccadilly itself for that matter. It may be your 'accepted hells beneath'; but they *are* beneath. And if we accept them, and go down into them, at least we call them hell, or else 'the heaven that leads men to this hell'. It's very good, after a long morning's saunter past French print shops, to come back to the Sonnets. I don't think I need tell you at this time of day that I am not a Puritan. And I *like* Donne's 'Full nakedness! all joys are due to thee.' I am inconsistent. Perhaps it's because this art is so aware that it just took off its clothes a minute ago.

The reader familiar with *The Wandering Scholars* will recognize at once the craftswoman at her toil: she is well under way.

To say that Helen was at last free to pursue her studies in solitude and silence would not be true — she was besieged by no fewer than three suitors; also there was Enid Starkie; and there was Dr Albert Vaudremer who, with his family, was to become a lifelong friend. The conclusion of a letter to Meg, after days spent in nothing but dining, wining, driving in the Bois, and making circular tours by moonlight to Montmartre, Versailles, and St Germain, leading to a final dismissal at the Gare du Nord, sums up her customary reaction to impassioned ex-future husbands: 'I came home and slunk into bed, throat, cough, and all the rest of it. But oh, the peace! Surely this will be the end!' As for Enid Starkie — 'the little girl without a sense of humour', according to Evelyn Waugh — she was in no sense a friend of the calibre of Meta Fleming or Maude Clarke. She showed kindness and affection to Helen in Paris in 1924, amply rewarded and repaid in the 1930s by Helen in London, but it would require more than a moment's suspension of disbelief to associate Helen with the fabled Fellow of Somerville, future creator of a Quartier Saint-Gilles in Oxford, presiding over her gold and peony-pink 'opium-den' in Chinese trouser suit, chrysanthemum in flaming auburn locks. Eight years Helen's junior, Dublin-born of a cultured Catholic family whose faith she later repudiated, Enid had gone up to Oxford from Alexandra College in 1916, and in 1920 along with Dorothy Sayers was among Somerville's first graduates. From 1921 to 1924 she was studying for a doctorate at the Sorbonne, so that she and Helen were naturally thrown together for a year. Through the kind offices of Hilda Lorimer, both were warmly befriended by Dr Albert Vaudremer, whom Miss Lorimer had met on board ship during World War I — he on his way to the army hospital in Salonika, she to work for six months at the Scottish Women's Hospital. After the war, he devoted most of his time to the Institut Pasteur in the rue de Vaugirard: Enid Starkie was to pay high tribute to his scholarship, medical skill, and the Christian charity which placed that skill at the service of the poor, but she never experienced it directly, as Helen did.

The trouble began after a luncheon given at the Vaudremers' house in Auteuil, probably to celebrate Helen's thirty-fifth birthday two days later, for on 1 June Helen wrote to Meg:

> It was a lunch at the Vaudremers, and then they took me to walk in the Bois de Boulogne which is the Hyde Park of Paris. And it was a fête — Ascension Day — and all Paris was driving or walking, but chiefly driving. And we seemed to go for miles down huge avenues of trees, with a nightmare of cars moving-moving-moving, like the spokes of a wheel. Then Nichole said she would bring me to the nearest station for home. It meant one more hour of the same thing, and then a plunge into a Metro (same as London tube) also crammed. I had to stand and after about five minutes I knew I was going . . . and crawled out . . . and then got home. You know how we never believe we are really ill. Never Paris again for me. I'm going to London next year. Life isn't worth living at this rate. Europe is all right for a holiday — but oh, give me the North.

In spite of the fever that persisted for days, robbed her of sleep, and made her feel as if she were just out of a laundry tub, she was at her post on Monday morning in the Bibliothèque Nationale, ploughing through volume after volume of mediaeval source material and resolutely ignoring headaches and burning throat. By four o'clock on Saturday afternoon she found she could not go on. The throat weakness inherited from her father was taking its toll, and she was in a state of collapse bordering on delirium. Her finances were low, and it was possibly common sense that drove her to Auteuil where Dr Vaudremer, after asking a few questions, whisked her at once into the Institut Pasteur for professional treatment under his own eye. At first, sleepless, in considerable pain, with an ulcerated tooth adding to her miseries, Helen lay like a log unable to read or write: she almost lost heart. 'I saw myself here for ever,' she told Meg.

> Dr Vaudremer came over (I think my blessed little Breton nurse secretly sent for him) and looked down at me like a Chinese mask, awful worried, and wouldn't smile. But they got something different to make me sleep, and oh, the ecstasy of it. Such kindly sleep, with dreams about making the fire at Kilmacrew together to warm milk. They still give it to me at night, but I think I can soon do without it. And I'm having food like a Christian — actually biscuits with stewed fruit at lunch today, and on Saturday you might as well have offered me ground glass. . . . I don't think I'll go till

they put me out. Nobody is allowed to see me, because this is an isolation hospital, even though I'm not infectious. But they come and look at me from the window, and bring books and flowers no end.

It was Enid Starkie's visits to Helen at this time that sealed their incipient friendship. Helen never forgot a kindness and years later she wrote to Enid, recalling gifts of roses received, and money given: it is not difficult to see how money simply melted in Helen's hands:

> You didn't need to talk to me in Paris. Always from the first moment I saw you I respected you, and divined something in you almost fierce — not your shyness, which is also fierce but your power and your spirit. And I also thought of you as a terribly shy little animal — not a hare, but something like a little white ermine, with eyes blazing at you out of the dark, and I used to feel that if I lifted my hand suddenly or spoke too quickly it would be out of the door and tearing down the passage before I could stop it. That Sunday I'd heard — from the Vaudremers I suppose — about the mumps quarantine. I can't remember now if I knew you were hard up . . . if I hadn't I don't suppose I'd have had so much with me, but that part didn't stick in my head because it is so simple. You see, you and I were friends. All I remember saying to you is that it made it all right when neither of us were rich, which is really the way I feel about money. I like going shares but I do hate largesse. Lord knows you gave it back to me pressed down — the times I used to be lonesome in the Pasteur, and then the little figure in the white coat would come to the window with a bunch of yellow roses, that you'd probably spent a dinner on. But it was all utterly simple, my dear, just I cared for you and knew you were ill.

All the same, Helen did have a niggling fear that she would be presented, after weeks of intensive care, with a bill that she could not meet, but the fear was dispelled as a cheerful letter to Meg proves:

> I have tons of things to tell you. I was overjoyed yesterday to hear that this place is absolutely free. It's the great experimental hospital of the Pasteur Institute. I'd no idea whatever but that it was maybe one of the most expensive in Paris, and was quailing. All one may do — for the nuns have *no* private property, being nuns — is to give the Mother Superior something to make a fête for the small children of this very poor *quartier*. It's not that it's so richly endowed: but when you get skilled labour given for nothing but the love of God, like these Sisters of St Joseph — it does reduce expenses . . .
>
> The endless things there are to tell you — one of the funniest, the way French doctors 'listen-in'. Stethoscopes must be démodés: they use their plain ears. Large redheaded young man arrives, spreads a clean hanky on your chest, you wondering a little anxiously what's going to happen, suddenly pounces and rolls his head on you like an affectionate collie dog.

It was very alarming the first time it happened, but thank heaven I kept my face. He then says fiercely 'Respirez' and you respire, and he rolls his head from place to place — and then begins afresh on your back.

Pause to look in handmirror. I've never seen anything like the look of me yesterday, skin like brown leather, bloodshot eyes, perpetual scowl because the bed faces the light — can't have it any other way, and for T.B. purposes they use all the sun and light available. They let down a big blind for me now outside, and I live like a happy fish that swims darkling.

Now that it's over, I don't think I'd cut it out. I think pain is good for people now and then. Not that my own midge bite was anything to talk about. It was just nasty, and I lay and thought of people in *real* pain, like childbirth and cancer. It leaves you dumb.

As soon as she felt more like herself, she obviously called for the tools of her trade, and with uncertain pen on the opening page of what is now a very tattered exercise book, she set down her Belfast Presbyterian reactions to a Parisian Catholic environment in a hospital staffed by nuns:

The Sisters outside my window sound like swallows under the eaves. It is their one hour in the day, this, and another after lunch. They pull wooden benches across the gravel with a scraping sound, and sit in a bunch round the Mère Supérieure and sew and talk. They seem to find a good deal to laugh at, and someone gets teased and a protesting cry of 'Ma Mère' rises, and is lost in a shrillness of many voices. Ma Mère has clapped her hands, and the voices drop silent. There is the noise of the garden seats being dragged back again, and the silent shuffling of the large heelless slippers across the gravel. Now they go to bed at half-past eight, all but the night-sister. And I sit up in bed, having said 'Bon Soir' to my night-sister an hour ago, and think what W. B. Yeats calls 'Protestant thoughts'.

Not so very Protestant either. It seems unthinkable this life, with no exit beyond the great gate, and all Paris outside. Audible outside too, for the crying of the taxis ceases neither day nor night. And for all *expansion de coeur* an hour in the courtyard round Madame la Mère. Sister Laure who is a Breton is going into the country next week for a month to rest. What will she do? 'I will gather marguerites in the fields, and I shall make Sister Godric walk, walk, walk, and she will come back thin as Mees, and red in the face. Voilà' — and Soeur Laure lifted a bunch of yellow roses — 'Voilà the complexion of Soeur Godric' and, lifting a lusty bowl of pinks, 'Voilà Mees.' 'It is a lie, ma soeur. I have now the air of an old boot.' 'Not now, ma petite Mees. But last week, Mees was très souffrante. But not like l'Anglaise là bas. Mee-ow!' said Soeur Godric, rubbing her stomach. 'J'ai du douleur, du douleur! Mee-ow . . . toute la nuit.' 'But that was because I couldn't speak. If my throat hadn't shut up, I would have said Mee-ow too.' 'Non, non, ma petite Mees. The Irlandaises are better than the Anglaises.' To that it is clearly impossible to reply.

Dr Vaudremer says it is the principle of obedience, since obedience is the beginning of peace. There is, of course, in vocation the *fond mystique*, but for the pavement of life, l'obéissance, once accepted, gives that something of *solide* which the heart craves. Isn't it in the Brothers Karamazov that the Inquisitor condemns Christ to death, because He gave men the torture of choice, the worst torture of the human brain?

Towards the end of June 1924, Helen's physical torture of pain and sleepless nights was over, and the Institut Pasteur had become a pleasant backwater where she could happily relax and sleep. All the same, the fact that she had now spent almost a year in Paris, and had as yet put nothing whatever on paper, was obviously haunting her and may very well have precipitated her breakdown, for she wrote to Meg: 'Odd, but just as I fell ill I was reading again *Samson Agonistes* — look at it, if ever you've time, towards the last, I think: one lovely utterly ordinary line about "God his friend again", and I felt that it said for me what had been coming slowly for weeks — the queer *farouche* feeling of the man who buried his talent all gone.' Alas, not gone for ever and aye. The grim terror that had held her in its grip, since girlhood, of possessing one talent lodged with her useless, would renew its attack with increasing and relentless force. For the moment however, sleepless nights added to an already weakened body evidently sharpened her paranormal sense of the past for, in the same letter to Meg, she casually mentions that one night she had found herself 'Héloïse grown old and abbess, and hearing a complaint from her nuns that "elle parle toujours la théologie d'Abélard".' Her well-known novel, *Peter Abelard*, published in 1933, the fruit of twenty years' imaginative pondering — she had determined in 1913 to write a book on him one day — was seven years in the writing but, judging from her own account of her experience in the Institut Pasteur, she had herself lived an important part of it before ever she put pen to paper. In 1955, when she made her last B.B.C. broadcast, she referred to her mediaeval studies in Paris in 1924 which brought her up repeatedly against the baffling tragedy of Abelard's life:

. . . Here was a man who followed after truth and served the soul of understanding in things, broken by hammerstroke after hammerstroke of the judgement of God. It was a long time before I saw that the reconciliation of his tragedy is the reconciliation of *Lear*: the breaking and transfiguring of a great egotism into something like sainthood: as though Lucifer should die a St John.

Should she write a biography of Abelard or a novel? That was her problem. It was solved in her room in the Institut Pasteur when

I passed, fully awake and not I think delirious, into some strange state of being. For suddenly I was Heloise, not as I had ever imagined her, but an old woman, abbess of the Paraclete, with Abelard twenty years dead: and I was sitting in a great chair lecturing to my nuns on his *Introductio ad Theologiam*. It was near the end of the lecture, and I pronounced the benediction, and sat watching them go out, two by two. And one of them, the youngest and prettiest of my nuns for whom I felt some indulgence, glanced at me sideways as she went out, and I heard her whisper to the older sister beside her, 'Elle parle toujours Abélard'.

It stabbed me. And even when the first hurt of it was past, the realization that what was once a glory in men's minds had become an old woman's wearisome iteration, I began wondering if it were indeed true: if after all these years I was lecturing on this theology for the sake of now and then naming his name. And from that, I began to remember that his theology had been condemned as heresy: and — for by this time Abelard had done his work upon me and had brought me to some sense of God — I began to wonder if I had perilled the souls in my charge by teaching them heretical doctrine for the sake of gratifying this ancient lust. And from that there stirred in me again the old dread for Abelard's own soul. But I remembered that Peter the Venerable had absolved him on his deathbed and had sent me the copy of the absolution, signed with his seal: and I rose and went to the ark where the charters of the convent were kept, and took from it the parchment of the absolution: and I sat there hour after hour, fingering the rough edges of the great seal of Cluny in my hands, and finding some dim comfort in it. Then the morning came, and with no sense of transition I was myself, but with full awareness of the other who I had been all the night before: and when the Mother Superior came to see me during the morning, I laughed and said, 'Ma Mère, I too was an Abbess all last night.'

She now knew for certain that her book would be a novel, but she seems to have planned a trilogy. She concluded her broadcast with the statement: 'I have still to write the second part of the story as Heloise saw it, who survived him so many years: this second part is to be called *Heloise*.' But her letters also refer to a projected sequel to *Peter Abelard* under the title of *Death of a Heretic*, and that presumably would have formed the second of the series. The books that Helen projected and never wrote were legion.

All the same, she had to be busy with her pen, even in hospital. A letter simply dated 'Monday' begins with a cheerful 'Och darlin', the Lord hath delivered us out of all our afflictions, so we'll cheer up and take notice. I'm leaving on Thursday . . . and I don't know what I'll feel like out of bed. My conscience has been a lot easier since I began to translate — and as usual the stuff is so much better than I'd dreamed.' She then enclosed for Meg a rough draft of the first of her 28 lyrics

translated from the thirteenth-century MS of Benedictbeuern — better
known as the *Carmina Burana* — which she was to publish in 1929:

> O Sorrow, that art still Love's company,
>   Whose griefs abide with me,
>   And have no remedy.
>
> Sorrow doth drive me. How else might it be?
>   I go to exile from my darling one.
>   There is none like her, none.
> Had Paris seen her, Helen were alone.
>
> O valley, still be gay,
> Valley with roses climbing all the way,
> Valley, the fairest that is in the hills.
>   Among all valleys, one.
> Soft on thee shines the sun,
> Softly the moon. The birds
> Sing there: the nightingale
> Her sweetest dost sing
> For thou, most sweet and fair,
> Givest thy solace to the sorrowing.

I may be able to link up the rhymes better. But isn't it rather a lovely thing?
I'd like to have a lot more done for criticism when I come home. These roses
make me think of Ballygowan, and Aunt Minnie. God rest her — she left a
green memory.

After bidding farewell to the Institut Pasteur, Helen followed the
dictates of common sense and made a bee-line for Kilmacrew. There
during the summer of 1924 she recovered her health. One morning a
postcard from Enid Starkie told her that there was no need to return to
the Anglo-American Club; Enid had made all arrangements for Helen
to take possession of the tiny flat in No. 1 rue de Passy which she herself
had occupied. E. S. had completed her study of Émile Verhaeren for her
doctorate (a work to be crowned in 1929 by the Académie Française),
was returning to England, and would put in three years in Reading as
assistant-lecturer in French before settling down in Oxford for the next
forty years. In late September Helen parted once again from her family,
crushed down the 'grief without a pang, void dark and drear' that
always seized her when left alone, travelled Newhaven–Dieppe
second-class, suddenly saw the Normandy plain in a wonderful sunset,
and like St Paul thanked God and took courage. Next day, as always,
Meg was sent the chronicle of events:

> I'm settled in: collected all my goods from the Club, where everyone was so
> agreeable that my conscience smote me, but fled from it with secret

thanksgiving. The wee room is as bare as a barn, there isn't even a rug on the polished wooden floor, and the only armchair is thin and bony. The bed is a divan, and awfully comfortable, I've slept sound, even the first night. . . . I've a nice wee restaurant across the road, where the food is really delicious. It is much frequented by house painters in white coats and they look perplexed at the creature in elegant furs who sits in their midst, but the cheapness — today for lunch I had roast goose and green peas, fried potatoes and cream cheese for about 1/3. Last night the same, only it was beef and carrots instead. So I'm in great hope of repairing my shattered income.

From 9.30 a.m. until 6 p.m. daily, she worked without interruption in the MS room of the Nationale — 'only about twenty people, old priests in soutanes and shovel hats, and people copying Arabic MSS at your elbow, and me with a magnifying glass borrowed from Felix,* transcribing things like "Letter from a Knight to a Bishop that he command his son-in-law to return to his wife", and you learn that he sent his wife back to her father, and himself is likely living with some disreputable Thaïs. Letter from the Bishop. The letter from the Son-in-Law — It was his poverty. He would rather have his wife in her father's house and himself suffer alone, since suffering must be. "God who knows all things knows if I ever went to another woman's breast. But day by day I put my hands to unwonted labour, and some day when better fortune laughs upon me, I shall ask for my dear wife again." I'm awfully happy. Somehow — you know those breathing spaces when nothing happens to rack your heart or even give great exaltation — like green grass beside a broad road, neither up hill nor down. No sudden glories like the Atlantic that day at Greencastle, but no heartache.'

The new room cost 10s. a week; the owners of the house, Monsieur and Madame Favre often invited her to their meals, while their little son Jean-Jacques who at seven years of age was deep in the enjoyment of de Musset and Baudelaire, careered about on a scooter posting and delivering Helen's letters, and was her willing slave — although he couldn't quite decide whether he loved her more than Felix, her friend: 'Mees Waddell, elle est la douceur, et Mees Rowe, elle est la joie!' Her letters lose the feeling of strain, she faces the fact that she may have to stay in Paris beyond Christmas, and at long last she recovers her creative power:

I never thought I'd live to see myself so content in Paris. Today I went with the Vaudremers to Versailles — if you can imagine all the things you liked at Hampton Court made infinite — great solemn rows of trees and quiet

*A fellow-student at the American University Women's Club.

walled ways, and figures of gods, and the Grand Trianon like the Sleeping Beauty's palace. I ached for you [she wrote to Meg] for it was one of those enchanted days when there's only a step between you and a revelation — you know, like Twelfth Night in Wadham Garden.

The Vaudremers have told me of a tiny flat that I could get very cheap, with a little kitchen and a sitting room and a bedroom. I'm awfully tempted, for somehow I think I'll be longer in Paris than I meant. There's a queer stimulus in it for me now. Dear, you were right. It was that awful club that drained me. I never knew anything like the goodness of the Vaudremers. I believe they'd have me for dinner every night in the week. I said tonight that it seemed to me I inhabited this house: to which Monsieur replied: 'It is not *we* who complain!'

Thus far she had been held in the grip of a paralysis that seizes upon most writers, a blockage that prevents the hand from committing a single sentence to paper. Suddenly she was able to report to Meg that the life-blood had begun to flow: 'I got a wee bit written the other day — just a paragraph or so, but it has broken the ice, and broken the fear. For it was good stuff, with a thing about the imitation of Virgil's verse in the early years. I was thinking of the emptiness of it — the form of his hexameter, but the soul gone, and yet it has its value still. And then I likened it to a shell — blue-veined, intricate, empty: but put it in your ear, and it still has the voice of the sea. Also I see more how the poetry and the prose are going to be divided.'

Just when she had achieved some small measure of stability, she had to strike tent once more. In a letter merely dated 'Friday', she tells her sister: 'Alas, Madame has just heard from Monsieur that he has found a house in Bordeaux, and they leave Paris in about a month. I've grown so used to being emptied from bottle to bottle that I'm nearly past caring. I can always go to the little Hôtel Réal where Felix has a room, but it's much dearer. I'm slogging at the MSS because I can't get them anywhere else, supposing I do go back to London, but I'm counting on being through by Christmas, and I feel I've courage enough for anything.'

Her next letter, headed 'Thursday', is sent from the Hôtel Réal, rue Bellini. It informs Meg that they must give up attempting to live like other people: the contents of the letter are quite sufficient to show why:

Today has been dreadful — my déménagement from the Rue de Passy here. Passy was on the fifth floor, and no lift, and no hotel porter, just heavily-tipped taxi man and me. I am now a little feeble. There were five huge armfuls of books tied with string which came undone when the dear taxi man carried them (never with me) and flip-flopped melancholy-like down to the next floor. Luckily he thought it was funny — and we grinned at each other each time. Then there were two suitcases also filled with books: and a reading lamp lent by Enid Starkie: and two hat boxes filled with anything but hats — the hats came on my head by relays — and my green trunk. But it was worth it all. I'm so high and it's so quiet, and Paris seems very far below; even the taxi man gazed out of the window and said 'Mais vous êtes bien ici'. It's very tiny, with a red-tiled floor and a sloping roof, but a glorious window, and it has a big wardrobe filled with shelves, and a curtain wardrobe and a writing table, and a mirror, full length in the wardrobe, and a really enormous bed.

I wish you were here, to tell you about the work — it's getting better and better. I've often wondered if there was anything behind the paganism of the *Carmina*: how the Middle Ages could write anything so completely unconscious of morals and the whole system of Christian thinking — with Venus really in the apple orchard, and Bacchus in the tavern. But two days ago I began to read Bernard Sylvestris, who was one of the most popular masters in the XII century in France — nobody reads him, though in his own day they called him the greatest of the Platonists. He is a poet-philosopher, like Shelley, and the rush and sweep of his imagination takes your breath. He's describing Nature in search of Urania — the two together are to create man. Urania is the goddess-soul of the universe, but Nature can find her nowhere, and there's an amazing paragraph in prose of how Nature went seeking her — through parallels and magnitudes and the circuits of the planets and the orbits of the spheres. 'From splendour to nullity she sought her, from heaven to the kingdom of Dis; from eternity to those misshapen bodies that lie in the House of the Crab, that purer essences have denied to habitation and abandoned, shuddering.' It's ghastly, but the power of it. And last of all, it's the intellectual counterpart, this, of the *Carmina*. And I can trace an almost immediate connection between him and the most famous of my poets, a kind of early Rabelais at Orleans. He once complained to the Pope in a very good hexameter about other men plagiarising him.

'I, the Arch-poet, write for all poets.'
and the Pope capped it with another, just as good,
'Aye, and you drink for them too'.
I think I'll leave about the 19th or 20th. I'm due to speak in London on Jan. 10th at the L.M.H. thing. Och! I do feel triumphant.

That letter is the germ of the greater part of Chapter V of *The Wandering Scholars*, a discussion of Humanism in the first half of the twelfth century. As a sample of H.W.'s creative writing, it is illuminating to compare the seed with the final fruit: her own spiritual travail in childhood, her rejection of Milton, her discovery of St Augustine, her poetic response to Creation, her instinct for analogy and mutual relationship have all gone into the moving exquisite prose of the last page. Only part of it can be quoted here:

The poet in Bernard, as in Shakespeare himself, has his moments of rebellion against the muddy vesture of decay, of lament for the 'poor soul, the centre of my sinful earth', for 'the gross body's treason'. One of his most splendid tirades is the vision of the spirits wailing at the house of Cancer the Crab: 'From splendour to darkness, from Heaven to the Kingdom of Dis, from eternity to the bodies by the House of the Crab are these spirits doomed to descend, and pure in their simple essence, they shudder at the dull and blind habitations which they see prepared.' But when he comes to the making of man in that place of green woods and falling streams, he holds, plainly and determinedly, the dignity of his creation. He has his discrimination among the senses: in his glory of sight he is in the tradition that begins with Augustine's 'O queen light, sovereign of the senses,' and ends with Milton's invocation. Of generation itself, plainly and fearlessly, the Greek ideal of moderation, of discretion. . . . The spirit is richer for its limitations; this is the prison that makes men free. His Adam is the Summer of Chartres Cathedral, naked, fearless, and unbowed. He saw him as Michael Angelo did, wistful, beautiful, potent for evil or for good, already prescient of the travail that God hath given to the sons of men that they may be exercised in it. . . . And if the world of Bernard Sylvestris is a dewdrop too crystalline for philosophy or experience, it is for that moment of vision that poets are born.

Helen bade farewell to Paris and was back in London a few days before Christmas 1924: she had decided that the last six months of the Fellowship could be spent at least as fruitfully at the British Museum. She was able to rent a flat in the same house as formerly — the next ten years, the most productive of her life, were to be spent in two terraces at right angles to each other, forming a kind of square bite out of the south-west corner of Primrose Hill. Two days after arrival, she sat down after her usual fashion to tell Meg all about it:

> 9, St Edmund's Terrace.
> Monday.

My darling,

I can hardly believe it's me — it doesn't seem quite right that anyone should be in such peace. It's a cold wet night, and it comes driving against my windows, just like cottage windows, broad and low. And I've a low ceiling with beams, and a little warm fire — gas, it's true — but after the last few days of *awful* cold in Paris when you perched miserably on a radiator, I'll never turn up my nose at gas again. I've told nobody I'm back, though I'll begin stirring tomorrow. I'm so elegant, for I've my own oak table and my own silver, and napkins and teacloths. And I have four saucepans and two frying pans and a kettle and a carpet-sweeper and an O-Cedar mop (all provided by the management) and a small dinner service and four tumblers and a dustpan and an imposing bucket with a lid that says in noble letters GARBAGE, which the management empties every day, for eggshells and tealeaves and all the squalors which one once wrapped in newspaper and dropped unwillingly into wastepaper baskets.

But I don't regret Paris — I couldn't have got this flat sooner. And I've proved that I can't live in Paris, but that I really do like it, quite different from last year's dread. And now that I've my little house I'm going to be a smug old maid, and I'll have birds on the wee balcony outside for crumbs. It's all ridiculous, but you have to have wandered for about 18 months in clubs and hotels, and lived and slept and washed and cooked in one room to feel like this — it's like your belt being too tight and suddenly loosened, only the belt is round your head. Felix came here the first night and could hardly bear to go away, especially when we had bacon and egg and toast for breakfast — my own bacon, our frying pan, our kitchen. *Must* shut up. I've asked for a berth for Saturday . . .

The Christmas spent at Kilmacrew was as hilarious as usual, but it also brought Helen face to face with a deep personal crisis. The 'Mourne Mountains man' as she called him renewed his suit and she wavered. Her considered choice, to reject all thought of marriage and return to London alone, left her weary and dispirited. 'It is a queer world,' she wrote to Meg on her return. 'There's G.D.C. and Russell and Stanley — all wasted. And me that could have loved terribly and was born to have a house and children and a man, solitary up four flights of stairs, writing a book.' Years later, she sent one of her poems to Gladys Bendit, a writer better known under her pen-name of John Presland, with this undated covering letter:

Here it is. I *think* it was written in January of 1925. I'd come home to Ireland from Paris, very sleepless and weary, with a mass of material without form or cohesion; and I'd been at Kilmacrew for three weeks at Christmastime, and dragged myself away from it to an attic flat in St Edmund's Terrace, with a gaunt raven of a landlady, and my unpacked box of MSS and books — and no courage to deal with them. And finally I went to bed, defeated and doubting, and as I lay in the dark it seemed as if I heard a voice speaking, and it was saying this fragment of verse, and in the morning I remembered & wrote it down.

And that day or the day after, I wrote the first few paragraphs of *The Wandering Scholars*:

The Mournes

I shall not go to heaven when I die.
But if they let me be
I think I'll take a road I used to know
That goes by Slieve-na-garagh and the sea.
And all day breasting me the wind will blow,

And I'll hear nothing but the peewit's cry
And the sea talking in the caves below.
I think it will be winter when I die
(For no one from the North could die in spring)
And all the heather will be dead and grey,
And the bog-cotton will have blown away,
And there will be no yellow on the whin.
But I shall smell the peat,
And when it's almost dark I'll set my feet
Where a white track goes glimmering to the hills,
And see, far up, a light
— Would you think Heaven could be so small a thing
As a lit window on the hills at night? —
And come in stumbling from the gloom,
Half-blind, into a firelit room.
Turn, and see you,
And there abide.

If it were true,
And if I thought that they would let me be,
I almost wish it were tonight I died.

The decision Helen made that Christmastide was irrevocable. She returned in January 1925 to her semi-paradise in St Edmund's Terrace to resume work. Like all earthly gardens of Eden, it harboured the serpent which she variously calls her gaunt raven, the dragon, or more often Medusa, the Gorgon whose gaze froze man into stone. Longing for Kilmacrew resulted in Meg's receiving a rather bilious post-Christmas letter:

It's all very still — walked across from Chalk Farm in the faint muffled brightness that is London light, and let myself in with latchkey to hall in some confusion and violent odour of paint, but no sign of dragon. Good crossing but slept badly. My mind keeps running on the other side. Chuck and Tote and Mary in bed are so much more real than the abominable smell of paint. I have tracked it down to the newly-painted bath. It looks so white I feel that visitors will be requested to wash themselves before entering it. . . . When I've posted this I'll come back and get a hot water bottle and sleep. But you know I am a family man, and it is difficult at once to become a bachelor. And London is so odd, its old quiet background of grey houses and trees, and a girl walking bareheaded in a flame-coloured dress and heel-less flame-coloured long leather shoes, like Turkish ones, and smoking a cigarette in a holder, and behind her an old charwoman with large pathetic black boots — also heelless, and walking almost the same flat-foot way. And London so old and tolerant of them both.

P.S. Hurroo! The Dragon has gone away for change of air till Monday.
Feel better already. Left last Saturday . . .

All the same, it was with deep satisfaction that Helen exchanged Paris
for London. 'Och, there's no place like London,' she exclaimed about
this time, 'the kindliness of it, and the big grey solid houses, and large
bobbies, and the generous old B.M. that lets you go in and out
unchallenged, even if you leave with an armful of books. The *Nationale*
makes you show everything, and then gives you a permit. But I was
right to come to the B.M. — I'm getting just the stuff I want.'

The Susette Taylor Fellowship expired in June 1925 and the modest
income along with it. Helen hoped by then to have completed all her
research, thought to spend possibly a whole year integrating the
material into a publishable book, and while doing so to find some
congenial work that would bring in a regular sum and tide her over her
difficulties. She was already booked to give lectures in Oxford where
she paid a flying visit on her way back from Kilmacrew after Christmas:
'I went to Oxford—Maude so glad to see me. Spent the night in College
and saw everybody. It was very pleasant, and had a terrific conversation
with Miss Pope—the only one who knows anything about my subject,
which left me like a fish gasping. But she confirmed some of my
doubtful feelers, and scratched her own dear little head — you know it
has a face like a nut, or the small kind of animal what would eat nuts,
very bright-eyed and awful unworldly . . .'

She has enclosed 'just to impress you, the History lecture list. I'm on
the English list as well, and I think Mediaeval French', and adds that she
intends to spend every Sunday tramping for miles about the countryside, even though it is 'not a bit like Ireland, very like Gray's Elegy
country, gentle valleys and a soft bloom on all the distances, a brown
purple, not our unearthly blue'.

In January 1925, the month of Helen's visit to Oxford, the fourteenth
number of *The Heritage*, published on behalf of the four Women's
Colleges, all badly in need of funds, carried a four-column Foreword
Scholares Vagantes by Helen Waddell, Susette Taylor Fellow at Lady
Margaret Hall. This is the first time the title has been used *tout court*.
Only a vagabond or goliard of Paris or Orleans in the twelfth century
could have rivalled such comic scholarly beggary. She begins by
admitting that the mediaeval church never much approved of
wandering, and then embarks as a wandering Irish scholar herself on an
apologia pro vita sua:

> Most of the great scholars were peripatetics sometime. Columbanus, half-
> Druid, half saint, taught Greek metres from his eagle's perch at Bobbio, and

St Peter himself met Coelchu on the road and carried his books for him. . . . Adelard of Bath came back from seven years' wandering in Asia Minor and Egypt and Arabia to write a book on natural history, and dedicate it to the Bishop of Syracuse. When Buoncompagna fell out with the University of Bologna, he wrote a letter as from a scholar returned from conversation with Arabs and Satraps and the study of Uranath who maketh even the deaf asp to hear by his enchantments, and Catarath who distinguishes on the Astrolabe of Solomon, and Zinzaniath who interprets the barking of dogs; and then prepared, on a certain day in July, in the Piazza of St Ambrose, when the sun should be at its full heat, to turn an ass into a lion and thence into a winged fowl, in presence of the whole university. 'Yet in very truth in the end the ass shall remain.' On the appointed day the entire University, doctors and scholars, assembled in the Piazza and on the very rooftops, and waited agape for the ass and the lion and the winged fowl. The heat was terrific, and at the end of several hours it dawned upon the University that the ass indeed remained.

With a characteristic light deft touch, she closes her financial appeal on a serious note. She is asking a harassed, overtaxed but not ungenerous world for money, and ends by quoting a thirteenth-century Oxford student who concludes his recital of ill-fortune with 'a sudden straightening of the suppliant back, a lightning flash of vision of his right to the thing he asks: "Sine Cere et Bacone frigescit Apollo" — without Ceres and Bacchus Apollo grows cold. He was a bold scholar, with that spelling, to identify himself with the god; yet from Villon to Verlaine, Wyatt to Housman, the Universities have justified his claim.' One should very much like to know how much her appeal netted.

Meanwhile, time was flying, never to return, and she had just six months to complete the work that had actually occupied her mind for some fifteen years. She admitted to Meg that her ever-present thought was, 'You'll possibly get finished in time', alternating with 'Tomorrow you will get a great deal done and will not be too tired'. The twelfth-century street song that she quotes in Chapter VI of *The Wandering Scholars* had a deep personal application before ever she used it as the opening of *Peter Abelard*:

> 'Temps s'en va,
> Et rien n'ai fait;
> Temps s'en vien,
> Et ne fais rien.'

Maude Clarke who had resumed the old affectionate and frank relationship with Helen, sat and listened, as she had done in time past

at Larne on the Antrim coast when they concocted the novel
Discipline. There was no one whose appreciation of her work Helen so
much coveted, and to her delight Maude loved what she heard. 'I was
afraid she'd think all my ideas too popular and pretty,' Helen told
Meg, 'instead of which she said she had grown sick of facts without an
idea to make them luminous.' But few knew Helen as did Maude: to
praise she promptly added dispraise. 'But Helen,' she said, 'will you
ever finish it? You never finish anything!' The experienced tutor of
Somerville probably deliberately goaded her procrastinating friend,
whose motto so far would seem to have been

> 'Time goes by,
> And naught do I.'

The naught was only in seeming, for Helen had mapped out the
whole plan of her book, and several important chapters were already
on paper. It was just as well. Suddenly desperate at the thought of a
possible two years ahead in real financial straits, on her way to the
British Museum one day she walked into Constable's business
premises in Orange Street, and asked if they were in need of a reader.
She was shown into the office of the chairman, Otto Kyllmann. 'I
think he'll have something for me to do next term, after Easter,' she
wrote to Meg. 'I told him how things were, and the gap before I could
get another job. He asked me whether I had anything in my mind to
write — so I told him about the MSS in the B.M. He looked awfully
interested, said they sounded very promising, and finally, "Now go
home and finish your book, and I'll talk to you when you bring it to
me." So I came home stepping delicately.'

Almost afraid to hope, she sent him the chapters of her book that
were relatively completed. Within days, she received a letter asking
her to call in person on whatever day suited her. At this meeting, he
made no bones about it: he wanted to publish. What she would have
described as a drunken letter was at once despatched to Meg. It is
simply dated 'Wednesday':

> I nearly wired, but thought it was maybe foolish. Constable was utterly
> benevolent: he wants the book — wants a *big* book — has given me carte
> blanche to say anything I want — appendices and all the rest of it, and is
> already talking about a simultaneous American edition, and getting it
> reviewed by Edmund Gosse. He says it is madness for me to attempt it by
> July, let him have it in October, to come out in the New Year — that you
> get far more attention in the early spring for a book of this kind. I think he's
> right . . .

He's elderly, Constable's director, very sardonic and engaging, and delightful manners. We got on — well, you know, I *do* get on with that type. And he likes my kind of joke. And he *does* want my book. I mentioned the Oxford University Press quite frankly as a possibility, and he began — it was very clever and very delicate, but I could see it — adroitly dissuading me from them.

I can't believe it's me. To have a publisher taking for granted that I'll be worth 'the full page column in The Sunday Times', as he said casually. Well, the agony and sweat begin again tomorrow, but I have had my day. The solid ground is at last under my feet. And it makes all the difference in the world to have a certainty before me. Of course we didn't discuss terms — contracts will come later. But I'm safe — and he was so *awfully* kind about not overworking.

H.W. was not blind to her own creative power and originality of thought and style, but to have her work put out as a major publication by the very house that had issued her *Lyrics from the Chinese* over a dozen years earlier was good fortune almost past belief: it also raised problems. How would Oxford react? The Susette Taylor Fellowship had been granted her to prepare and submit a study for the degree of D.Phil. Any alteration of title called for official permission, yet the old title no longer applied. Whereas the Committee of Lady Margaret Hall had fixed it as 'The Literary Importance of the Wandering Scholars', the subject matter had sprung to life under Helen's hands and taken its own shape. Her interest, at first dramatic, had been deflected from what the scholars did to who they were. The whole field of enquiry had been narrowed; she had been captivated by the songs of these jongleurs of the clerical ranks. The only title that summarized the contents of the book in its present state would be simply *The Wandering Scholars: an Introduction to the Mediaeval Latin Lyric*. Texts, translations and appendices would follow in a second volume. She must inform and consult the University.

At this point, she acted on Otto Kyllmann's advice to take her time. Her old Belfast friends, the widow and daughter of the sometime headmaster of Campbell College, were ready to descend and seize on her as their guest for a long-planned motoring holiday via Folkestone to Touraine and the country of the Loire — an expedition that was to lend immediacy to her subsequent appreciation of her hero Alcuin, and of Hildebert of Lavardin. A breathless letter to Meg, merely headed 'Tuesday morning' might well be labelled with her own phrase, 'It's so like me':

I ought to be up and doing, for the McNeills arrive today and I have (a) to meet them at the 12.15 Euston; (b) if possible to escape and lunch with

Leonard and a writing man called Harrison; (c) visit Dodo in the nursing home; (d) copy out the report for Miss D.; (e) pack; (f) write a letter officially demanding the change of subject for the doctorate, with full statement of case. Instead I wish, though it is only 9.45, to go to bed and stay there. Nuffin wrong with me except that yesterday was a very exciting day in the B.M. for the book, which always takes me in the legs, and when I came home I at last got an idea for the report, and wrote it, which takes me even more vitally. This morning I am quite dead. Also yesterday I had a long interview with my supervisor, Percy Simpson. He is afraid they won't accept the new subject without two years' residence, which I won't hear of, though he regrets it awfully. But I'm to try anyhow. He was awfully nice about it, funny little redheaded fat man, and thoroughly impressed by Constable's eagerness, which he says gives an almost unheard-of opportunity, and advised me to rub it well in. But also that though he knows they'd be as nice as could be, it's the dangerous precedent — 'we have not often to deal with work so secure as yours' — and his idea is that once publication is settled, I can rather whistle for the degree — it won't matter then at all.

It's so like me to crowd everything into the last two days, but a good deal of it I couldn't help. And anyhow I've been concentrating on the British Museum — stuff that involves 3rd and 4th chapters. I wonder even if I could now write them down at Folkestone. It's the Irish scholars on the Continent in the ninth century. I wish I had you to tell you about them, and how they've come alive to me, starting with a Sedulius Scottus (Scot means Irish in the Middle Ages) and Sedulius is Latin for Sheil! He came to be schoolmaster at Liège, and wrote verses, and a Greek text of St Paul's epistles with a Latin translation — but the names in the margin of the MS are Dubthach and Fergus and Comgan — and his own. And these same names occur in a Latin MS of Priscian now in the monastery of St Gall (founded by an Irishman in the sixth century — the most famous centre of learning in Europe). They don't know when it was written, maybe by Sedulius's fellow-monks before they came to Europe, but the marginal notes are 'A hot Easter Sunday'. 'It's getting dark'. 'I'm cold'. 'Would you rather I went?' (which means a conversation in the scriptorium just like schoolboys). 'Cairbre and I both come from Inchmadoc', and this that struck at my heart, all by itself, 'Nendrum on Mahee'. You remember. Think of it, Peggy, somebody maybe in Liège or St Gall, suddenly remembering the peat. Then in odd corners of the MS there are poems in Irish.

> 'Bitter is the wind tonight: it tosses the ocean's white hair.
> I fear not the coursing of the clear sea by the fierce heroes from
>   the Lochlann' (the Norsemen).

another: 'A hedge of trees is round me, and a blackbird sings,
             Above my ruled book I hear him.
             There's the cuckoo.
             I write well under the greenwood.'

and another: 'Pangur Ban, my cat, and I,
          We have fun together.
          He for mice and I for words
          Sit and watch together.'
   Do you wonder it took me in the legs? And I got on the track of it almost
guiltily, thinking it's Irish sentiment in wasting your time — and now it
has made a whole rather dull century come alive. . . . Will write from
Folkestone. Address till the 20th Garden House Hotel, Folkestone. It's
going to be lovely after all — five days in a private car, all round Touraine.

The itinerary begun and ended in Folkestone, took in Boulogne,
Paris, Tours and Chartres. Helen's letters to Meg contain delightful
sketches of her septuagenarian companion: 'When we are 70 I only
hope we'll be like that,' Helen writes, and goes on to compare Mrs
McNeill darting about with the cry 'But sure, I like to *see* things', to a
large interested fowl. But Helen herself was seeing things. As she
stood under the grey stone lacework arches of Canterbury Cathedral
looking into the peaceful grass-covered garth, she was building up the
décor for her study of John of Salisbury, archdeacon and faithful
henchman of Thomas the Archbishop, 'Phoebus Apollo turned
fasting friar', as they traversed those cloisters and walked side by side
through the chapter house door to face four ranting and truculent
butchers. Thirty years before, John, little more than a boy, had stood
in Paris greedily drinking in every word that fell from the lips of Peter
Abelard before that great voice was abruptly silenced, and it was again
in John of Salisbury's company that Helen stood in Chartres Cathedral
— 'that gracious miracle of living stone' she called it — where, as its
bishop, the last in a long succession of saints and scholars, John at last
came in the phrase of Petronius 'to the harbour of a stilled desire'. Not
for the first time, Helen cried out to Meg: 'I'll never be happy till you
and I go to Chartres together.'
   At Tours, where Alcuin, another of Helen's heroes (whom
nothing could make a spectacular saint, and nothing make less than
an English gentleman, as she put it), ended his days, 'We went to
High Mass in the Cathedral, and Mrs NcNeill knelt and bowed to
the altar like a good Papist. I do love her more, every day. When I
talk to her about the Middle Ages, she listens as if I were the Ancient
Mariner. I was describing Chartres, where so many of my great
bishops lived, and since then it's always: "Now tell me more about
Ivo. Helen, it's good company you keep in your work. I'd like to
have the Fathers all round me like that" — a percipient remark that
pleased Helen mightily.'
   Unpromising as it had seemed at first, it was this fortnight's holiday

with the McNeills that illuminated for Helen the mediaeval France of the twelfth and thirteenth centuries, and provided her with the setting for *Peter Abelard*. Modern Paris had made no appeal to her, and she revolted against the France of Boileau, Racine and Corneille, and the balustrades and sham classic stuff at Versailles, but driving from Paris and Orleans to Tours brought a real revelation:

> I know at last why people love France. . . . I'd looked out of the windows several times between Paris and Orleans, some flat country, uniform and green. And suddenly I looked, and saw the Loire — a great gentle expanse of water, with shallows and sand and green islets of grass, and on the further bank trees and steep-tiled houses and a grey château on the hill. It was as faded and gentle as an old colour print — an aquatint, and after that, you felt you had come to an older country, not Vogue and Montmartre and the Champs Elysées. Even the hotel is like an old country house with shining polished wooden floors and faint pleasant colours in the curtains and the rugs, and shallow wooden stairs, and the most wonderful cooking. Tours itself is just an old country town with a cathedral, and some old houses and wee streets that you could really shake hands across — the street of the Halberd, of the Four Winds, of the Cherry Trees, and every here and there a green gleam of the river.

They approached Chenonceaux, where Mary Queen of Scots spent her honeymoon, in a downpour of rain. 'And suddenly it cleared and the sun came out very gentle, and the trees stood with their feet in grassy shining water, and we came down a long avenue of trees to Chenonceaux. The Loire flows all round it. It's all green and glancing like being under water, shallow enough for the sun to shine in it.'

When, nearly a decade later, Helen described the green meadow that gave Beaupréau its name, where the aged hermit Hervé, solitary in his earthen hut amid the elders and immemorial oaks, had offered a night's lodging to Abelard, she was writing of things her own eyes had seen:

> Abelard stooped to pass under the lintel, and stepped out into the early light. There had been heavy rain in the night — it had been a wet spring; he had noted coming through the Loire country how many pools caught the sky in the forest, and even in the open fields. Here, a corner of the meadow was under water; he crossed over to it, thinking to bathe his hands and face, and hesitated, unwilling to break the surface of that shallow world. Each small green blade stood up, distinct and delicate in this strange medium of another element; he saw the faint pink of the daisy buds tight closed: and farther away the white stems of the long grass gleamed in deeper but still translucent stretches of quiet water.

Mrs McNeill's compassion received its hoped-for reward: Helen returned to work rested and invigorated — nothing now mattered but the book. 'All my notes seem so poor and meagre and dull,' she told Meg, 'and then a fresh morning comes, and I'm swimming before I know.' She was able to work at astonishing speed: 'The tenth century is finished. I got through it last night. Today the eleventh. At this rate I'll have three weeks to do all the technical references and appendices with real care,' she reported to her sister. Oxford had proved itself magnanimous; Miss Grier, Principal of Lady Margaret Hall, had booked her for six lectures, and offered her free accommodation whenever she wanted it. 'Miss Lorimer was here for dinner last week, and made me read her what I'd written. She thinks the book will make my name.' Best of all, Maude Clarke had taken to slipping away from Somerville to make St Edmund's Terrace her pied-à-terre: 'Maude is here for a week, and awful happy. She is out most evenings, and most of the day at the B.M. . . . M. is awfully taken with the book. I read her bits. She is just revising her own,* and we do some of it together. It's more like our old holidays than we've had for half a dozen years. The Dragon is back again and I walk once more on eggshells.'

Sick with apprehension, Helen caught the 8.40 train to Oxford to give the first of her six lectures, all duly reported to Kilmacrew:

L.M.H. *awfully* kind to me, but miserable about the lecture. 'Why did they put you on first day of term? *Nobody* goes anywhere first day. And Professor Gordon is on at the same time, and the whole English school is bound to go there. And worst of all, Mr Gretton is lecturing on Aristotle — just at the last minute, and we've had to send our History students there.' I'd faced the worst when I saw Gordon was lecturing, and was prepared for — three! And they took me down in a taxi, and we went, me very bleak and weak at the knees, through stone corridors to lecture room 9 as posted in the hall. Crowds passed us, and I muttered to Miss Jamison 'Damn them, who are *they* going to?' Dear, they were coming to *me*. No. 9 reached, Jimmie says, 'There are people at the door, evidently the first lecture isn't out yet, and they're waiting to get in.' 12.5 came — Doors open, and crowd comes out like bees out of hive, and stream past us. Jimmie plunges for porter at the door: comes back bursting with elation. 'There's been standing room only since five minutes to twelve, and they're moving you to the North School.'

She had actually drawn a bigger crowd than the Astronomer Royal had done the previous term: 'L.M.H. burst with pride and joy, and Miss Pope came back to lunch and glowed, for though no longer Somerville, she feels they own me. But oh, I am almost dead. I came

*The Medieval City State, 1926.

back very limp to find a charming note from Constable asking me to lunch today. And there's the interview on Friday. After this week I'll begin to live again, but at the moment it's like shooting rapids, or rather catching trains all the time.'

She was still anxiously applying for work that would bring her in a decent salary, and had been short-listed for the post of Head of Department at Westfield College: the interview was fixed as she said for Friday, and she had been given to understand that the advertisement was a mere formality—the post was hers. At the same time, Maude was applying for the Bedford Chair of History. When the Westfield result was made public, Helen's cry of 'A man has got it' was uttered by the small child who had listened wonderingly to her Japanese nurse's scornful 'Girls? What are Girls for?' and by the brilliant young graduate set aside by Gregory Smith at Queen's simply because she was a woman. All her hopes of London appointments were dashed, but Helen had a great gift of forgetting — it arose largely, of course, from her settled belief in the Providence that shapes the end not only of man but even of woman. 'I've never had a cruel disappointment yet that didn't mean some far better thing — like Gregory's assistantship. I'd never have seen any place but Belfast if I'd got that,' was her philosophical reflection. And then she quotes the Anglo-Saxon Deor: 'Such a lot of one's life is a patient waiting till "this also will pass".'

At lunch with Otto Kyllmann, she was offered two minor jobs — to give expert advice on mediaeval subjects, and make suggestions. 'I came home on air. No terms mentioned, but I feel I'm pretty safe in their hands. The only bitter drop is that he wants to bring out the book just *after* Easter, not before it. Tons of reasons. But somehow I've been so often disappointed that I'm dull to it now.' There was now no Dr Taylor to give her strength and comfort; perhaps by way of compensation she had taken to the Congregational Church at Buckingham Gate, which she found 'like old good days "even with the multitude that kept the solemn holy days" . . . very like our service, more it than the English Presbyterians, who treat the Psalms as hymns, cut out the pretty bits and sing them.' To go and hear Dr Hutton's sermons became a regular cure for fits of despondency.

She had met Constable's deadline and sent in the completed script of *The Wandering Scholars* by the middle of 1926: waiting month after month for publication was tiresome and depressing, until she dropped her literary persona and became her father's daughter. As always she shared her thoughts with Meg:

I'm glad I went to Dr Hutton tonight. It was on 'We know not whither

Thou goest. I am the Way.' He began about Christ's promise of a spiritual presence: 'How much of our thinking is really about material things? Man after man in the street but the mind behind the face is working over again that quarrel with a friend yesterday, that broken home, that undeserved failure. Speak to him and he'll answer with cheerfulness and gusto — the heroic human convention that hides a troubled spirit. But we live with ghosts . . . Christ never answered a question — He knew no answer is of any use to us except what we find for ourselves. But I once worked under a great mathematical genius. He never lectured, but we could bring him any problem we had, and he would put down his pen and look at us. "Sir, I can't see how . . ." "But don't you see?" And nine times out of ten, we saw. There was something about that naked intellect that quickened one's own beyond recognition. That is Christ's way: "Jesus steadfastly set his face to go to Jerusalem" and after that — I have my moods, all of us have them, when I ask uncomfortable questions about life, especially my own life, and am grieved and indignant at my unmerited misfortunes. It cures me if I have to go and see someone in St Thomas's or Bart's.'

Oh Peggy, it's true. And all the way to church I'd been fighting down that dull despondency — partly because I'd been looking at the flaming Christmas book lists and wishing that the *Scholars* had been there: thinking that it would come out unnoticed at Easter, and likely too late for a decent job, and I'd go on in the wilderness till I was too old to be anything but a hack. All because of eight wasted years of doing my duty as I saw it. Oh, you can fill it all in.

But tonight has shut me up, I hope for life. 'Never ask questions about Absolutes. The absolute becomes relative when it touches you.' It has linked up in my head with that picture in Ben Hur, the Cross swaying and stumbling above the heads of the crowd. Not that anything we've done is worth anything. But that shuts your mouth.

In amusing contrast, and yet just as integrally a part of Helen, is the letter she sent after spending that Christmas at Kilmacrew. She returned as she always did, homesick 'even for the funny smell of the henhouses and the morass outside', and the bare trees and wet underfoot, and Meg with her buckets and white pullets. She then adds: 'Darling, could you bear to pack my waterproof — the yellow one, and nailbrush, any time — no hurry at all. Don't bother with toothbrush or wash-cloth, because bought same. Might send bathing cap, which is in workbasket in big bedroom. No sign of Medusa. But the sinking of heart with which I mounted the stairs is enough. P.S. Could Mollie post Jack's essay — I think it's on washstand in her room.' A later postscript bids her long-suffering sister: 'Don't look for bathing cap — I've found it here — I used it as a sponge bag.' With her happy haphazard ways, one may doubt whether Helen of the tender heart, the meteoric spirit, and the spacious intellect, would ever have dwindled even by degrees into a dutiful wife — for her, probably any marriage would have been unsuitable. Yet it was part of the rhythm of her life that in spite of her choice of single blessedness, she was dogged by constant domestic trials and trivialities. Her next letter to Kilmacrew explains that she would have written sooner but Medusa 'took out again', demanded compensation for an imaginary flaw in the carpet, refused to admit Helen's friends, and was so thoroughly obnoxious that Helen wrote her a brief but merciless letter in which she gave her notice on the grounds of her 'gratuitous and deliberate offensiveness'. 'Temper', she remarked in her letter to Meg, 'is a kind of self-indulgence like drink, one form of excitement, though it would never appeal to me. Much as I love this wee flat, she is poisonous.'

As a result, Helen exchanged St Edmund's Terrace for No. 3 Ormonde Terrace, a stone's throw away: here for the next six years, until town planners and a demolition squad moved in, she was enabled to concentrate on the masterpieces that made her name known far and wide. 'I'm happier than I've been for ages. I'm living like a rabbit, taking little runs across Primrose Hill,' she told Meg. A couple of minutes' walk took her over the canal and into Regent's Park, a path across the hill led to a village-like shopping centre, and another to St Mark's on Primrose Hill. 'I'll never be a Catholic,' she remarked to Meg, 'but I'd never get my work done if I didn't now and then dive into that strange divine sea.' This, in spite of the 'sanctified stupidity stamped on the priest's face' by over 1,000 years of candles, incense, processions, and a liturgy celebrated in the immemorial Latin tongue.

To prove indeed that the immemorial Latin tongue of the classical poets was the soil in which the Christian faith and Western civilization took root and flourished was the very essence and purpose of *The Wandering Scholars*, published by Constable in April 1927, in a small edition because it would have so little appeal. As Helen later wrote: 'That the book was read by men in factories, and that it reached a very much wider public than the one it was written for, delighted and amazed both myself and my publishers. The smallness of that public may be deduced by its being published first at a guinea.' To 'factories' she might also have added 'prisons', for when a copy of the book was taken down from a prison library shelf, it transformed the life of at least one reader, condemned to penal servitude. Before 1927 was out, there had been three editions. All the leading newspapers and literary journals gave it pride of place, none could praise it too highly. George Saintsbury's in the *Observer* was, of course, the weightiest. From her student days at Queen's, he had watched this brain-child of Helen's grow. He pointed out that her study of 'that most curious, interesting and subterraneously important influence of Latin on the formation of the great mediaeval literature of Europe' possessed rare qualities not only of style and learning but also of arrangement. 'To have the whole province of Latin mediaeval literature mapped out at once exactly and delightfully will probably be not the least enjoyable novelty to those who already know most about it'.

The acclaim was astonishing. Bumpus, the London bookseller, asked for an autographed copy for the Royal Library at Windsor. 'Is it George or Mary is going to read it?' a bemused and amused Helen asked Meg. 'It's werry funny and werry queer. I feel like Rip Van Winkle coming back to his own house.' A chorus of applause in America, England and France rose from scholars of such distinction as C. H. Haskins, F. M. Powicke, and Ferdinand Lot. Henri Bremond, the formidable and distinguished historian of French Literature wrote: 'Your book has been a sheer delight to me. You will find me *très vaniteux*, but reading it I said to myself at almost every page, "Mais est-ce bien elle, n'est-ce plutôt moi qui ai écrit ce livre?" Apart from the marvellous translations, there is a note très français and — bear with me — Bremondicum? God knows that I adore English scholarship, but here there is a je ne sais quoi beyond it, that enchants me.' Eileen Power, Julian Huxley, Walter de la Mare, Dean Inge — the list could be prolonged almost indefinitely — showed equal enthusiasm. The Royal Society of Literature elected her to a Fellowship and awarded her — the first woman to be so honoured — the A. C. Benson Foundation silver medal.

Helen's own reaction to this conquest of the London drawing-rooms with their ovations and banquets in her honour was expressed in a laconic note to Meg: 'I suppose if it had come years ago, it might have turned my head, but now it all seems just in the day's work, and I'd as soon go and have supper with wee Miss Covernton.' She quotes to her sister the sobering apostrophe of their fellow-countryman, the Irish St Columbanus, founder of some of the greatest strongholds of learning in mediaeval Europe: 'A road to life art thou, not Life. And there is no man makes his dwelling in the road, but walks there: and those who fare along the road have their dwelling in the fatherland. So thou art that naught, O mortal life, naught but a road, a fleeting ghost, an emptiness, a cloud uncertain and frail, a shadow and a dream.' Self-revealing was her after-dinner speech to a group of distinguished scholars assembled to do her honour. Sir Frederick Pollock, sometime Professor of Jurisprudence at Oxford, lame, fierce, very dry and rather a terror, made the percipient remark that the author of *The Wandering Scholars* showed not only knowledge — knowledge did not take you far in the Middle Ages — but so uncanny an understanding that he was tempted to believe in pre-existence. He then offered a toast to 'the great champion of mediaeval letters'. Helen got to her feet, observed that she felt like the Elephant's Child in the *Just So Stories*, a little warm and very much astonished, and after a short witty preamble veered round to John of Salisbury's theocracy, and concluded with John Scotus Erigena's prayer for light 'that will turn to darkness the false light of the philosopher and will lighten *the darkness of those that know.*' It was a daring prayer to make before such an audience, and humble as all great men are, they received it first in eloquent silence and then with rapturous approval. J. W. Mackail refused to move a vote of thanks: 'We won't thank her for her speech,' he said. 'We shall take it home with us.'

What precisely was it that took the world at large by storm? The truth is that there had never been a book like it. Helen had blazed a completely new trail. Until she revealed its power and beauty, mediaeval Latin had been the monopoly of the philologist with his interest centred upon vocabulary and syntax, and the historian searching Church Councils and Acts of Monastic Visitations to prove that the 'Dark Ages' (the title is significant) were nothing more than a conglomeration of sterility, superstition, vagabondage, wars and rebellions. Into this arid desert the author stepped with a large retinue of saints and scholars, of men and women abounding in vitality and intellectual activity, creatures of flesh and blood who laughed and loved, prayed and cursed, sinned and repented, suffered and died. In the light of later research, it is all too easy to belittle her achievement. It has to be remembered that she accomplished her task single-handed. She had no tutor, no *apparatus criticus*. When *The Wandering Scholars* issued from the press, such standard works as C. H. Haskins' *Twelfth Century Renaissance*, F. J. E. Raby's *Christian Latin Poetry*, S. Gaselee's *Oxford Book of Medieval Latin Verse*, P. S. Allen's *Romanesque Lyric*, or E. K. Rand's *Founders of the Middle Ages* had not yet been published. The massive series of the *Monumenta Germaniae Historica*, and the Hilka-Schumann edition of the *Carmina Burana* which now adorn a solid wall of the gallery in the Duke Humphrey Library, were by no means complete. To Helen's mind there was only one solution: if she was to make an adequate study of mediaeval poetry, she must know something of its roots, and in order to trace its past she must plough through the 217 volumes of Migne's *Patrologia Latina*,* the repository of the poetry and prose of all Latin ecclesiastical writers from apostolic

*The Hildebert and Marbod volume runs to 1832 columns; Peter Abelard to no fewer than 1896.

times to Pope Innocent III (1160–1216). The natural reaction of anyone acquainted with that dreadful microscopic type set in close double columns 9¼ by 2 inches on cheap discoloured paper is to shudder — small wonder that Helen landed up in the Institut Pasteur. Caterpillar-like, she wormed her way through one tome after another, all 217, and for good measure added the *Poetae Latini Carolini Aevi* and Mansi's *Concilia*. This wide browsing in the literature of the Christian past from Juvencus and Prudentius to Peter Abelard and the *Carmina Burana* is the key to *The Wandering Scholars* and their accompanying lyrics.

Even so, none of this really answers the question — what precisely was it that appealed so powerfully to twentieth-century readers? The style of *The Wandering Scholars* is dense, packed with allusion and association of widely-separated ideas (as when she speaks casually and perfectly naturally of the tutor to the Emperor Gracian, Decimus Magnus Ausonius, in terms of the Chinese poet Po Chu-i), full of analogies, of twists and turns that make demands upon the reader. All this is the art of the thing, it makes the reading thoroughly exciting. David Jones opens his Preface to the *Anathemata* with a quotation from Nennius's Prologue to the *Historia Brittonum*: 'I have made a heap of all that I could find.' Nothing could better sum up Helen Waddell's long years of preparation in the libraries of Queen's, the Bodleian, the Bibliothèque Nationale, and the British Museum. To this heap, she gave form, made a shape out of the very things that had shaped her. Journalists and reviewers did their best to analyse the book, and old Sir Frederick Pollock came near to revealing the secret of her power when he pointed out that, in her, knowledge was so wedded to understanding that the past sprang to life in the present; she had to wait half a century for the perfect accolade.

Fittingly enough, it was bestowed in the Chapel of Lady Margaret Hall on 25 June 1978 by the Very Reverend Michael Stancliffe, Dean of Winchester, in the sermon he preached during his celebration of the Holy Eucharist, to mark the Centenary Gaudy. In a moving and practical address, he faced up to the agonizing problems of contemporary society, especially acute in such a traditional stronghold as Oxford. What to retain, what to jettison? 'Remember the lady who stopped to look back with regret at the passing of the good old days and dear old Sodom,' he warned his hearers, 'and so became a geological specimen of monumental proportions.' He then turned to a profound exposition of possible forms of 'remembrance', and focussed attention on Christ's words of institution of the Eucharist, 'Do this in remembrance (*anamnesis*) of me' — a word that denotes not merely a historical event over and done with, but a re-call and re-presentation that makes history present, and here and now operative. Through Christ and in Christ every Eucharist is a recalling of others — of Elizabeth Wordsworth and all connected with the founding of Lady Margaret Hall — 'And out of it all, out of this 2,000-year-old ritual act of memorial, who knows what life-enhancing power will be released to inspire and strengthen us? Who knows what miracle will come of it?' Dean Stancliffe then concluded his sermon with a passage which will be quoted in full, for Helen Waddell never obtained a D.Phil. from Oxford University, but in the interchange between Lady Margaret Hall and herself — a financial grant on the one hand, and on the other lustre and renown for the College who gave it — who would deny that Helen's was the greater gift?

> 'The scholar's lyric of the 12th century seems as new a miracle as the first crocus: but its earth is the leafdrift of centuries of forgotten scholarship.' That powerful image was conceived, that sentence of haunting beauty was written by a girl whom this College, to its undying credit, elected to the Susette Taylor Travelling Fellowship in 1923, and so enabled her to create the book which has itself seemed to many as new a miracle as the first crocus recalled by its opening lines — *The Wandering Scholars*, which Helen Waddell followed with *Medieval Latin Lyrics*, *Peter Abelard*, *The Desert Fathers*, and posthumously, only two years ago, *More Latin Lyrics*. I never met her, I know little of her life; but present company excepted . . . no member of this College has given me so much; and only David Jones has taught me more about the meaning of anamnesis and how what is past can be recalled to work life-enhancing miracles in the present. And I end with a paragraph of Helen Waddell's (almost her last) to sum up what I have tried to say about the meaning of commemoration.
>
> 'Medieval Latin poetry, read in these days, has something of the quality of the eleventh chapter of the Epistle to the Hebrews: "These all died in faith, not having received the promises . . . that they without us should not be made perfect." If there is melancholy in the realization that the wisdom and kindness of mankind has profited the world so little, it is that we are still in Newton's square box of a universe; that Boethius' definition of eternity, "the possession of all time, past, present, and to come, in full plenitude, in one single moment, here and now" is seldom hazarded in our experience. Yet by these things men live, and in them is the life of our spirit.'

CHAPTER VIII

R. L. Stevenson, progenitor of the spiritual ideals of Helen Waddell's youth, cut for her hard and clear lines of a philosophy of life that went with their common inheritance of Presbyterian dogma. Quotations from his works abound in her early letters, a favourite being, 'To travel hopefully is a better thing than to arrive, and the true success is to labour.' The unexpected triumph of *The Wandering Scholars* liberated Helen's creative power — her mind became a river in spate. The immediate task, however, was clear. Originally, the prose scaffolding had been planned solely to support the verse, but the book had taken on a life of its own that forced the author to discard her initial design and publish it as a study in its own right. It was incomplete without its companion volume of translated mediaeval lyrics. She needed freedom to concentrate, but she also needed money. 'True success is to labour' — so when Otto Kyllmann offered her a permanency on Constable's staff on the very day of publication of *The Wandering Scholars*, she gratefully accepted: 'He said — och it sounds so vain, but you know — that he devised this scheme because they want to keep me to themselves, and also because he thinks I have genius. "I think I know it when I see it. I saw it when George Bernard Shaw brought me *Man and Superman* first" — and wants to give me a chance to work unharried by money.' It was a questionable boon. Solitary in the Trappist silence of her flat in Ormonde Terrace, Helen could trample through the work, cutting like a mowing machine, as she put it. Whenever she wished she could trek across Primrose Hill and dive into St Mark's where, as she told Meg,

This time I came up with a translation of Abelard:

> How mighty are the Sabbaths,
> How mighty and how deep
> That the high courts of heaven
> To everlasting keep.

> What peace unto the weary,
> What pride unto the strong,
> When God in whom be all things
> Shall be all things to men.

Jerusalem is that city
Whereof the yoke is peace,
A peace that is surpassing
And utter blessedness.

There finds the dreamer waking
Truth beyond dreaming far,
Nor is the heart's possession
Less than the heart's desire.

To sit in Constable's office day after day at the Chairman's beck and call was a different proposition altogether: how much time or energy was it going to leave her? A letter to Meg sketches her routine:

Things very prosperous here. I'm pegging away at the Lyrics, and some of them will be lovely — one haunted me for days after I finished, it's the old familiar spring song:
> 'Time's in prison
> Spring's arisen.'

Then a complaint of some secret love that is poisoning his days, and then a last cry
> 'O gracious Cyprian
> Have pity now.
> Have I not borne enough?
> Lay down thy bow.
> Yea, thou hast conquered, lay
> Thy weapons down.
> Thou hast been Beauty. Thou hast been Desire.
> Be Love alone.'

The minor jobs continue — a long correspondence with a woman about a rather crying blunder which she is defending, but has no evidence against my serried ranks, and I am so sorry for her because she is ill, so am trying to let her down lightly. It's really merciful, to save her from the reviewers later on. Then writing a biographical note to Hornby, which his daughter will sign, her own being too amateur. And spending half a day correcting the name of one obscure Japanese village. It meant an eight foot map, and an assistant to the British Museum coming to speak to me found me under it as under a tent, almost on hands and knees. It wasn't worth it of course — but I got it — and once you begin saying things aren't worth it, you're a lost soul. Do not quote this to me next time I protest against a visit to the hens at midnight.

This letter, written a whole decade before Europe was in turmoil, ends on a strangely prophetic note. Helen tells her sister of an evening spent with Otto Kyllmann and Theodore Dreiser, the American author: 'A great big sad man. He wants O.K. to go to America just to talk. You see, we're drifting apart pretty much, America and Europe, and it might be dangerous; and on the other side we are a little like the Romans — Ausonius' crowd — watching the Goths.'

Excitement over the *Scholars* showed little signs of abating and, as O.K. had foreseen, Helen was besieged by publishers wanting a book from her. Peter Davies, J. M. Barrie's adopted son, asked whether there were any chance of securing her translation of Latin or mediaeval writings likely to lend themselves to finely-printed expensive editions *de luxe*, adding that he had read *The Wandering Scholars* with the keenest enjoyment, finding it a rare and delightful combination of learning and liveliness that opened up in an entrancing way a whole field of unknown, though dimly surmised literature. 'Dear Peter, poor Peter,' Otto Kyllmann murmured smilingly, as he adjusted his eyeglasses, tortoiseshell at the end of a long black ribbon, to read Peter's letter. 'I told you so. They'll all be after you.'

Beneath the banter, Kyllmann was deadly serious: he knew his publishing world and was aware of the danger of an offer that would banish Helen's financial worries for good and all. On the first anniversary of the publication of *The Scholars*, Helen was hard at work in the British Museum, drawing up a complete table of dates for her mediaeval lyrics, now almost ready for publication. As there was no Encyclopaedia of the Middle Ages, she frequently had to go right back to her sources to find them. Her task was interrupted by the appearance of Otto Kyllmann, who asked if he might collect her and go home with her to tea. To Meg, Helen wrote:

> Mercifully the flat was presentable, with roses and tulips and wide-open green windows. And I gave him tea and he fell to questioning me. 'We don't want you to go off into some other job. We want to secure the output of this brilliant young scholar for ourselves.' So finally it was worked out —retaining fee of £350. I to advise and suggest and do their stray jobs, and interview people for them now and then, and do my own writing. And on the woeful question of holidays — well, he said, probably you could go on doing our work even in Ireland. It won't be freelancing altogether, and I may have to shut myself up now and then, but I needn't tell you what peace is on my soul. In my own little raft still, but I'm being given a tow. It will be a funny job. I think I'll have to get in a telephone and this awful grind of ha'pennies will be over at last. And when Bun comes to town we will go to the theatre in a taxi, and she shall have a new hat in the summer. I have made up my mind even in small things not to think ahead: you know our bad habit of half-doing the next job half-way through the present one, so that one powders the nose of the kettle instead of one's own.

Self-supporting at last, and with an assured future, Helen would not have been Helen had her newly-acquired horn of plenty merely contained a summer hat for the sister who was the anchor and shield of her life. From girlhood she had longed to take Meg to Chartres as sole companion, and with her to roam Paris and the Loire countryside associated with Abelard and Heloise. As early as 1913 in her striking Introduction to *Lyrics from the Chinese*, she had written of the magic ring of candlelight, the only illumination permitted in Babylon: 'This is the magic of the lyrics of the twelfth century in France, lit candles starring the dusk in Babylon; candles flare and gutter in the meaner streets, Villon's lyrics these; candles flame in its cathedral-darkness, Latin hymns of the Middle Ages, of Thomas of Celano and Bernard of Morlaix. For if Babylon has its Quartier Latin, it has also its Notre Dame. The Middle Ages are the Babylon of the religious heart.'

Naturally Meg was the first to receive a copy of the Chinese Lyrics; on its flyleaf Helen had inscribed the solemn promise already quoted:

> Here's in token of the day
> You and I will go away,
>   You and I alone.
> And on some soft summer night
> Through the dusk and candlelight
>   Enter Babylon.

She kept her word. As soon as she had delivered the proofs of *Medieval Latin Lyrics* into Otto Kyllmann's hands, she set out with Meg for La Douce France. Naturally no letters preserve the shared delight of that holiday together, but two short records remain to chart their itinerary. In 1938 Constable reissued the Chinese Lyrics in an eighth printing. Helen again presented to Meg a copy inscribed:

Carissimae et dulcissimae semper.
  March 30, 1938
  As you had the first, with its inscription, so you must have the last, with the same inscription, altered for a dream that came true.

> Here's in memory of the day
> You and I first went away.
>   You and I alone.
> And on one September night,
> In the dusk and candlelight
>   Entered Babylon.

Paris, Chartres, Le Pallet, Vannes, St Gildas
September 1928.

The only other evidence of a French tour with Meg is a sepia postcard reproduction of the almshouse and St Lawrence's bridge at Chalon-sur-Saône, covered with Helen's script. It reads:

> You cross the bridge on the other side of the Island, and go down a long road between poplars, and come to a shabby dusty village and a bare church, very gaunt and plain. And you go inside, and see the well where St Marcel was martyred under the Antonines, and suddenly your eye catches an inscription on a slab in the bare wall:
> *Hic primo jacuit Petrus Abelardus*
> I was looking for it here, but the sudden sight of it was as if I had come upon him dead, while I thought he still lived. And all my old anger at the ways of God and man with him broke over me —
> "Had he come all the way for this?"
> But —
>> 'The souls of the just are in the hands of God, and the torment of malice shall not touch them: in the sight of the unwise they seemed to die, but they are in peace.'

Inevitably one turns from this to the memorable scene towards the end of *Peter Abelard*, to Peter the outcast rejected by God, the branded Cain. Seated during Mass on a ledge in the stone porch of the tiny church near the river at Coincy, he listens to the hermit-priest Herluin reading the Gospel of the Beatitudes that are for broken men, followed by boys' pure voices singing the solemn Offertory chant: 'The souls of the just are in the hand of God, and the torment of malice shall not touch them: in the sight of the unwise they seemed to die, but they are in peace.' But the torment of malice *has* touched the listener; he is not cradled in the hand of God. He rises, goes out of the church and, with face upturned to the quiet sky, he wrestles with God, struggles against all the traditions, all the memories of faith and family:

> And standing there, braced against heaven, the wind that had blown upon him once and been forgotten, breathed upon him again. It came without observation, for the kingdom of God is within: a frail wisp of memory, voiceless as the drift of thistledown, inevitable as sunrise. 'Neither do I condemn thee: go and sin no more.'
> He saw the heavens opened: he saw no Son of Man. For a moment it seemed to him that all the vital forces in his body were withdrawing themselves, that the sight had left his eyes and the blood was ebbing from his heart: he felt the grey breath of dissolution, the falling asunder of body and soul. For a moment: then his spirit leapt towards heaven in naked adoration. Stripped of all human emotion, with no warmth of contrition, with no passion of devotion, but with every power of his mind, with every pulse of his body, he worshipped God.

All the characters in *Peter Abelard* save one — Gilles de Vannes —
had historical existence, but as Helen brought them out of the twelfth
into the focus of the twentieth century, she clothed them in familiar
flesh. It would be difficult to overestimate the creative interchange of
thought and experience as the two sisters — Helen *alias* Heloise, Meg
alias Denise, Abelard's sister — visited their holy places during this
first holiday together. Here is Abelard returning to Le Palais in
Brittany — otherwise known as Kilmacrew in County Down — the
home of Hugh the Stranger, his wife Denise, and their six children. He
had taken Heloise there to await the birth of her child, and catches
sight of the two women.

> Abelard had vaulted the orchard gate without waiting to open it. Smiling
> and mischievous, he came across the grass, then suddenly halted, his arms
> resting on a branch, his eyes fixed on them. Standing there as they did, side
> by side, with the budding apple-boughs above their heads, their faces
> turned to watch him, he felt suddenly remote, walled out from their
> mysterious ancient understanding. It was no altar-piece that he saw: it was
> an older thing than Mary the mother of Our Lord, and Anne the mother of
> Mary. It was Demeter and Persephone, with Pluto come to claim her, the
> six months ended.

In 1928, when the expedition to the Abelard country was in the
planning stage, it was not farmhouses but the most exclusive London
drawing-rooms that opened wide their doors to welcome 'the most
popular thing in London' as Helen was called. No acclamation was
more heartfelt in its praise of her achievement than Edward Hudson's,
editor of *Country Life*. It was at his beautiful house in Queen Anne's
Gate that Helen met a host of national and international celebrities,
foremost among the latter, the Portuguese Guilhermina Suggia the
famous cellist, and the two Hungarian violinists Jelly d'Aranyi and
Adila Fachiri, nieces of the great Joachim, friend of Brahms. In such a
setting, the orchestration of praise and admiration of Helen's work
rose to symphony proportions — it all left her unmoved. Was it her
upbringing in a Presbyterian ambience of simplicity and renunciation
that made her suspicious of flattery, or was it a deep Christian humility
that looked on life and especially on herself, with common sense, a
sense of proportion, and a blessed sense of humour? 'All terribly
swagger,' she wrote to Meg after dinner at the Hudsons, 'titles and
ex-ambassadors and the Dean of Windsor, in beautiful silver buckled
shoes, and an order dangling. Such a *mannered* crowd . . . met Mr
Basil Blackett, who was finance minister in India, is a scholar in
Byzantine Greek. Swedish Ambassador also there, and his wife. And

Lady Londonderry has asked Stephen Gwynne to bring her to lunch and have me . . . and I don't give a tuppenny damn: queer how indifferent you and I are, unless it's something like a day together, or shrimps by the fire.'

She then wrote to George Saintsbury, centre not only of gravity but also of sanity, to say that Edward Hudson, 'a trifle elderly, a bachelor of long standing, but it has such a good face,' had pressed her to tour Spain in his Rolls-Royce with himself and his goddaughter — 'But I want to do Abelard's country, in poverty, with my blessed sister. Here is a sentence from her last letter: "Must go and feed those dratted chickens — it's endless. There is the sound of a great sea outside, and the wind in spring excites me — there is such a lift in it, as if it were hurrying all life before it. I think it's partly because through its roar and rush you hear the birds sing and the wee ducks pipe, and the hens cluck. You never get that in winter."'

The pen-portraits in *Peter Abelard* are many and memorable — one thinks especially of Bernard of Clairvaux, Gilles de Vannes, Fulbert — but none is so exquisite in its sheer simplicity as that of Denise, Helen's 'blessed sister'. The figure in George Saintsbury's letter finds its counterpart in Book II, Chapter 4, of the novel. Heloise is making her way through the orchard at Le Palais with a handful of corn for a brooding hen nesting in a hollow tree:

> . . . She saw that someone was before her. Denise was kneeling beside the prisoner, lifting the grain and letting it fall again to tempt her, and making small crooning noises: and at last the hen replied, though querulously, lumbered with caution off her sitting of brown eggs and began to peck, grudgingly at first, then suddenly ravenous. Heloise, hidden among the apple-boughs, stood watching: she was never weary of watching Denise. It was her patience, not holy like the conscious patience of the saints, offering up all vexation as a mortification, but a kind of natural wisdom: like the verse in Isaiah 'and shall gently lead those that are with young'. She could be brisk enough with anything that could run about on two or four feet, but with Peter Astrolabe, or a blind puppy, or a beast that was near its time, she seemed never to grow weary. She stood up now, deep-breasted but still slender; 'crossed beauty' they called her in that country, for she had brown eyes set far apart under hair that was very fair; then stooping, the hen now safely absorbed, she caught up an egg from the nest and held it to her ear, listening for the first faint tapping within. . . . She looked down at the nest, the same humorous gentleness in her eyes as Heloise had seen, watching the youngsters busy with their bowls and spoons. 'Look at them, Heloise,' she said once, 'trying so hard to live.'

So much for the 'blessed sister', but what of the poverty? With *The Wandering Scholars* running into three editions, and its companion-volume *Medieval Latin Lyrics* already going out for review before publication early in 1929, was the poverty real or fictional? The decade following upon the Great War had seen a spate of Memoirs: Winston Churchill bought a country house and 80 acres of land in Kent on the proceeds of his; Lloyd George refused to disclose the fabulous sum he had reaped; Margot Asquith received £10,000 in advance for a trashy novel, and boasted of having earned £25,000 for a book of babbling gossip, dashed off in a few weeks, that sold 1,500 copies within six hours on publication day. Helen and she met at lunch with Ellis Roberts, literary editor of the *New Statesman*. 'Lady Oxford — you know, Asquith, nutcracker face, smouldering dark eyes, but such fun, a kind of reckless tongue, and a terrible egoist, but really almost irresistible. She is so alive and impish, but she drains you rather,' Helen informed Meg. 'De la Mare crept over to me after it, and sat beside me like a mouse, and said — "Can you do with this kind of talk. Really?" And we held hands spiritually, and said how nice it was to be slow and stupid.' It is amusing and ironical to turn from the swagger statesmen to the sober scholar's undated letter to Meg, obviously written after the appearance of *Medieval Latin Lyrics*:

I expect you'll have seen The Observer, but I'm sending it just on spec. I got it before breakfast, on the 8.40 at Lime Street, and sat for awhile half-afraid to open it for fear I'd be disappointed, and then took courage — after that, it felt like swimming at Bloody Bridge. Don't you like it? And hasn't he been clever to suggest the scholarship and yet make it popular? The opening sentence is from the refrain of the *Pervigilium Veneris* (written for the first of May) —

'Who hath not loved, tomorrow will love:
Who hath loved, tomorrow will love again.'

Maybe the Boss will already have spotted the thing in Friday's *Times*. That pleased me *awfully*, for The Times itself doesn't often review, unless rather important things.

Oh I needed sumfin to comfort me. Do you remember, the agreement had the usual clause about corrections in proof above a certain amount being charged to me? It's invariable in all agreements, but I had no idea what the printer's scale of charges might be. Saintsbury wrote to warn me — but at the last. Gregory I suppose took it for granted that I knew. And my corrections and additions in proof were terrific. I'm paying for it now — £35. And this, though Constable doubled their allowance in mercy.

The bill from the printers was the first thing I opened when I got in. I don't suppose it's excessive, though Kyllmann writes bitterly that by Trade Union Rules proof correction is time work, so the longer a compositor takes over corrections, the more money he makes, and there is no way of checking. Gregory once said every book he wrote cost him about £100, so perhaps I've come off cheap.

I'll sell some war loan, I think. Darling, don't be too dejected. It was like a bullet wound yesterday, and then I began to laugh, and have laughed ever since. The poor little £50 that seemed such a gold mine. Don't tell Edith & Co. for in ways, I feel such a fool. And honestly I don't regret it. The new stuff I put in, like that lyric of Abelard's, was worth anything to me.

With admirable delicacy, Otto Kyllmann found this the opportune moment to pay her salary, as an excited letter to Kilmacrew shows:

And my dear, Kyllmann gave me a cheque for £87.10 — the first quarter, and says they are counting as from January 1st this year, so that I get another at the end of June. O.K. treats me as if I were the Queen of Sheba. Queer, he feels about the book as I do. 'My dear, I don't care now what the reviews are. When I finished it, it seemed to me I saw the procession of the dead, and they blessed you. It's like a revelation of religion.' And then he laughed his funny short little laugh — 'There's nonsense from an old hide-bound publisher' . . . I've sent Jack £1 for his tennis racket, and I'm sending Mary a pair of really nice gloves.

No wonder Helen was always poor, for she begins by saying how lovely it is to be able to buy Meg a few things again, and sends her the first fruits of the windfall: 'I thought they were just your colours. It will have to be a lot shortened, but if the neck is too low, you can always show an edge of white above the little vest, but isn't it very new and elegant? And darling awful cheap — spun silk 29/11d.' For herself, nothing.

At Easter, she received the first royalties for the *Lyrics*: the work of many years' scholarship could not hope to rival Margot's political tittle-tattle:

Let us whiffle and sing. Oh darling, the cheque for the *Lyrics* and *Scholars* is coming, and O.K. says he has seen it, and it's £119. I'm nearly drunk. I never dreamt it would be anything like that, and I didn't know when it would come. Don't of course say it, because Marie's £70 will snipe most of it, and yesterday I was so blue, for having paid in my salary and paid last quarter's rent, I had £10.4.6 to do till Christmas. But now I feel the hell of a crow, and here is a little cheque to make you also sing.

I was wondering how a pattern like this would do for Mollie's dress. Poor Mollie, I had to flee without giving it anything, but I'll send it sompin at Trinity. Feel like ten crows.

Medieval Latin Lyrics was greeted by scholars and reviewers alike with the enthusiasm and discerning appreciation accorded two years earlier to its companion-volume, *The Wandering Scholars*, save for one dissentient voice that added pepper and piquancy to the bland diet of pure praise. 'It is advantageous to an author that his book should be attacked as well as praised,' Johnson observed to Boswell, during their tour of the Hebrides. 'Fame is a shuttlecock. If it be struck only at one end of the room, it will soon fall to the ground. To keep it up it must be struck at both ends.' So long as the battledores are evenly matched and obey the rules, it's 'a wery good game' as Sam Weller opined, but if the shuttlecock is replaced by a human being, then 'it gets too excitin' to be pleasant' — as Helen was to discover. She first suspected the identity of her formidable critic when she saw the review of her book in *The Times*, and wrote to Meg:

> I am frightfully pleased with *The Times* review. Don't get cross your wee self about his animadversions — 'exuberance' in style and 'translations rather weak': that doesn't matter, for it isn't a 'literary' man's review. What does is that he says I am 'a credit to English scholarship'.
>
> I never thought I'd live to see that day. You see, everybody else goes off the deep end about charm and ease and all the rest of it, but the scholarship they can't judge. This man conspicuously can (though I disagree with the findings *twice*), but he knows the whole literature of the subject, and in spite of that, see what he says.
>
> I think myself he is old G. G. Coulton of Cambridge, a mighty but rather dry old scholar, who is a very great medieval authority. And they don't like their subject taken with levity. About the translation — the *Saturday* says they are better than the originals, and the *Glasgow Herald* says the 'final graces of scholarship': so don't worry.

If the anonymous reviewer was George Gordon Coulton of St John's College, Cambridge, it was not long before he declared himself in the open. According to Blake,

> Cruelty has a human heart,
> And Jealousy a human face.

In that sense Coulton was human. Helen Waddell, an unknown woman, was trespassing on ground that was his by right of possession ever since his discovery in 1876 — years before she was even born — of the Archpoet's drinking-song. He was the English authority on Salimbene, Guibert de Nogent, indeed on all aspects of mediaeval life and people. Echo once again repeats the old Japanese nurse's question, 'Girls? What are girls?' G.G.C. was determined to wipe his female rival clean off the earth, and he would not rest until victory was his. Early in 1931 Helen wrote to Meg:

Did you see G. G. Coulton's whack at me in last week's *Observer*? — reviewing a new history of late Latin. Don't know why the old boy hates me so, unless that he was at the Middle Ages long before me, and also that he is an almost venomous Protestant and always running them down. . . . Maude says Coulton is no longer, she thinks, quite sane, that it's fanaticism gone mad. I expect Squire's praise of me three weeks ago was just the last straw to old Coulton's patience.

For once, Helen decided to defend herself publicly. G.G.C. had taken the trouble to repeat the jibes of an American mediaevalist, who had held up her work to ridicule after having lifted from it an entire paragraph without any acknowledgement in a book of his own — *The Romanesque Lyric* — published a whole year after *Medieval Latin Lyrics*. On 11 March 1931 Helen wrote to the Editor of the *Observer*:

Sir,
    I am a little puzzled by Dr Coulton's sudden foray against two books of mine in his review of Professor Wright's admirable *History of Late Latin Literature*, since neither of them comes into any specific comparison with the subject of his review, and the one book which does — Mr F. J. E. Raby's massive and documented *History of Christian Latin Poetry from the Fourth to the Fourteenth Century* — he does not even mention. That the name of W. P. Ker is also omitted is less surprising: for it is sometimes dangerous to evoke that great and magnanimous shade. Can it be that Dr Coulton was less anxious to survey the literature of the subject than to indulge that wider charity which, like Tertullian's, rejoices in a just damnation?
    One other omission may perhaps be supplied: the name of the critic whose bellow of wrath against my having 'jazzed the Middle Ages' Dr Coulton is happy to echo — 'barber-shop harmonics' was another phrase, if I remember aright, in one of the best and liveliest pieces of invective I ever read. Its author was that lovable and splenetic scholar, Professor P. S. Allen of Chicago, who lately dismissed the researches of his more distinguished fellow-medievalists, Wiener, Faral, and Winterfeld, as 'the running about of persons . . . who have published so pretentiously in the field of my effort.' Or, as Miss Betsy Trotwood would say, 'Janet! Donkeys!'
                                    Yours etc.,
                                    Helen Waddell

G.G.C. was neither appeased nor amused. Presumably working from his copy of *The Wandering Scholars* which he had spattered throughout with his own private code of symbols to mark inaccuracies in quotation or translation or, worse still, factual errors, he fired a warning shot before bringing up his heavy artillery. A letter from Helen to Meg sketches the course of the campaign:

. . . Last week tiresome old G. G. Coulton of Cambridge suddenly began writing to me out of the blue, challenging a single reference. I moderately replied, and he wrote apologising, but challenging four more things (one of them a genuine misprint), and apologising for troubling me, but it was all 'in the interests of exact scholarship'. I again replied temperately and gratefully and, 'in return' as I said, pointed out a howler in his own last book in which he mistook St Hugh of Cluny for a very inferior abbot, Hugh of Flavigny, and on that based an indictment of all monasteries in the eleventh century. I did not describe it as a howler, only stated the facts, with reference to original sources which Coulton had not used. I think it gave him the shock of his life. However, he controlled himself, thanked me politely, and with considerably more respect than before, explained naively that he had been having a controversy with a friend of his, a scholar of great eminence, as to whether my book had any value as a 'contribution to knowledge' apart from 'its exceptional literary excellence', and enclosed a 'charge sheet' in which he brought about a dozen charges against the book, and wound up with a few vicious sneers about window-dressing and so on. This, he said, he had sent on to my champion some time ago. Again I controlled my temper, which is warm as you know (for after all he is an old man, is fanatically Protestant, and a savage controversialist — 'the law of correspondence with Dr Coulton', said one Catholic scholar, 'is the survival of the rudest.') and replied as quietly as a summer day. 'I am on your side in this controversy with reservations. I am no scholar: but am a tolerably industrious and, I hope, tolerably honest student of the Middle Ages. The W.S. was a first book, written with all the passion and most of the faults of the amateur, except one: respect for evidence, and preference for primary authorities: it was further marred by the fact that I am, I think, the worst proof-reader in the world. I could supply you, from my marginal notes and corrections, with ammunition far more deadly than anything you have here.' I then handled his charges, broadly indicating the opinions of Haskins (the chief in America), Powicke (for England), and Ferdinand Lot (for France) on *The Wandering Scholars*, and bowed myself out. The result has been incredible: on the points at issue he will probably wrangle as long as he lives, but as to the book as a whole he has just collapsed and in such a decent letter — it must have cost him agony to write it. 'It is hard for an old man, and one nearing the end of his work, not to feel jealous . . . And I had been challenged to say the worst I knew, or thought I knew. . . . I had my back to the wall. It was my own reputation that was challenged.'

I could have wept when I read that letter. So I wrote him, almost affectionately, asking his forgiveness if in any way I had seemed impertinent to 'a man of his vast erudition'. So the end is peace. But it has really been rather dreadful, for he is a kind of Mussulman in a holy war, and I now feel as if the Timber Wolves were licking my hands. I think it was worth doing, for he was a deadly reviewer. 'Just hint a sneer and hesitate dislike' is his method, when he isn't downright savage. That's why you got no letter last week, for I had to spend days at the B.M. Just waste of time, and yet really it removes a kind of poison-spring — and in Cambridge of all places. I have no idea who my unknown champion was.

Whereas none of G.G.C.'s letters to Helen are extant, a single photocopy and some rough drafts of hers to him survive. From her letter of 24 March 1934, it is clear that he was still an adversary: he was intent on keeping records — after the fashion of police on the trail of a criminal? He must have sent her another 'list of charges' before the publication of a revised edition of *The Wandering Scholars*. She wrote:

Dear Dr Coulton,
   I am distressed, in spite of your most kind letter, to send you back a book so mauled and disfigured. I have tidied it as much as indiarubber will: but if I had thought of your keeping it as a record, I should not have trampled all over the pages with my own black ink — though it does but make it a more damning *pièce de conviction* even than before. But still, if you will allow me, I shall send you a copy of the new edition when it is ready, and one for M.X. I am returning the corrected proofs today — I still find that the same fate overtakes me in proof as in the beginning — the printer mistakes the *re* of the subjunctive★ for a plural *n*, and I fail to detect it time after time.
   Some of the differences between us in the comment of Innocent IV (161) are due to the edition. But I am especially grateful to you for correcting *tertium* to *tantum*. It was abbreviated in 1525, and I read it as 'once, thrice, or oftener'.
                              Yours sadly, but with real gratitude,
                                                  H.W.

The snort that issued from Helen's tough customer if he checked her reference to Innocent IV and found it on page 261 may best be left to the imagination. There is something about Helen amusingly like Teresa of Avila, a wrong ending or a missing letter — did they really matter? 'You mustn't give yourself the trouble of re-reading the letters you write me,' Teresa told Lorenzo, her brother. 'I never re-read mine. If a word here or there should have a letter missing, just put it in, and I shall do the same for you.' That was certainly not G.G.C.'s style: vocabulary, syntax, versification, prosody — these were the essential elements of study of the mediaeval lyric, and they demanded meticulous attention to detail. With that strange bitterness that marks so much of his writing (oddly enough, his studies of St Thomas More and St John Fisher are notable exceptions), Coulton's concern was

★Thus, for instance, *regnaret* would be misread as *regnant*.

with the cold logic and dialectic of historical movements; Helen's was
wholly with the men and women who made the history. Years later,
when correcting proofs of her W. P. Ker Lecture, Helen wrote to Meg:
'I was trying to verify a reference and realized I had no idea where the MSS
that supplied the raw material for the *Scholars* had gone. I fear they may
be in a box that I found half-rotted with damp in the corner under the
stairs where the cistern leaked — the ink has run and the paper decayed
in fringes. They'd have been inaccurate notes anyhow . . . when you
get a reference like Notes et Extraits XXIX.i.pp.257–296 and let me
loose on it you'd wonder what I can do.'

Helen may have suspected but did not know for certain that G.G.C.
remained an adversary. He never forgave her for trespassing on his
preserves. In an undated letter to Meg, probably written in 1932,
Helen asks that the information it contains should not be revealed to
anyone, even to Meg's husband:

> I had to tell you, though please don't mention it *even to J.D.* There's a
> chance I may get something from the British Academy. I don't quite know
> what it is, but I've just heard from J. W. Mackail. 'Professor Saintsbury
> and I wish to bring up your name for recognition by the British Academy.
> For this purpose it is necessary that the date of your birth should be stated.
> Will you let me know it?' The letter is marked 'Confidential' and I am not
> breathing a word of it to any one here except O.K. who is very discreet,
> because if it all comes to nothing, there is no need to say why. I've no
> notion what it is, an 'Honorable Mention' or what, but as it is a very august
> body any recognition from it is most pleasing. I've written to Mackail that
> I feel like the Dormouse when they tried to put it into the Teapot.

Nothing came of it, and Helen asked no questions, so she never
knew why. On the fly-leaf of G. G. Coulton's much-annotated copy
of *The Wandering Scholars* an entry by one of his Cambridge colleagues
records with evident satisfaction that Dr Mackail had proposed Helen
Waddell's election as a Fellow of the British Academy. 'G. G. Coulton
had to provide the counter-arguments, which he did most effectively.'

Unlike Oxford, Cambridge never took to Helen, nor she to
Cambridge. Sir Arthur Quiller-Couch proved an agreeable companion often enough in the London salons but they never became real
friends, and in 1945, at the end of the war, Sir Sydney Cockerell ran
across her for the first time. The famous Director of the Fitzwilliam
Museum at Cambridge, from 1908 to 1937, was an acknowledged
collector and connoisseur of the distinguished, and the encounter, one
might surmise, would be awarded his customary epithet of 'rapturous', but all that he entered in his diary was a laconic 'I found her

pleasant company but deliberate in her speech like an American and therefore inclined to be prosy.'

As Helen Waddell never strove after effect, she would probably have been amused. She hated strangers in bulk, as she put it, and her friendly exterior hid pure panic: for years she lived at the centre of a whirlwind of cocktail parties and dinners and receptions. Compliments and adulation were offered her in plenty. Like every human being she liked to be appreciated, but in the face of flattery she became the Helen Jane of Belfast who shocked or delighted nice English people out to make everything easy for everybody else. The letters of one correspondent, breathless with adoration, were simply left unanswered: 'I told her that I found adoration intolerable,' Helen wrote to Monica Blackett, 'that it's like atmospheric pressure on a vacuum.' As might be expected, her letters to Meg describing the social merry-go-round abound in unforgettable phrases and vivid pen-portraits. Early in 1930 she wrote:

> I am so vexed at the long delay — I took out yesterday's letter with me, was so late I had to rush to the restaurant, no stamp, and no time to buy it en route, and after lunch Stephen Gwynne took me straight on in the car to Lady Londonderry's, said he had promised to bring me there, and when that was over, I had missed the post. It was a wonderful lunch — James Stephens is little and stooped, and the kind of face you would cut out of the knot of a stick, slouches along like a wee leprechaun, with unseeing eyes. I have never heard such a beautiful voice in my life — and it's the first time I've felt I was talking to a poet. I can't tell you what we talked about, mostly the value of sound, and the vowels in poetry and so on, but it was breathless, like whirling at the tail of a great wind, and every now and then he'd stop and sing to me under his breath. You could but love that little man, talking about the delicate little hind legs of a young ass. Which is quite true. They are very delicate. Think of the ones on the Mournes. Darling, this is just to explain about no letter.

A few days later, without being aware of it, she was giving her sister a self-portrait:

> Feeble this morning, but only after dining out — the Swedish ambassador at Mr Hudson's. A dark, very intelligent man with a queer vivid speech, and a tremendous reader. I had a new frock — in the sales — rose and burnt orange chiffon, falling from the shoulders, and modestly say I looked my poor best. He interrupted me once to look at dear old Edward Hudson. 'What can we do with them — these Irish fairies?' And remarked at the end I was the second great surprise of his life — that when he met James Stephens he was expecting a giant and found a leprechaun, and with me was expecting a wrinkled scholar and found a fairy. He said a lovely thing

about the *Scholars*: 'It is music from beginning to end. You write as if you wrote music.' He has been translating James Stephens and Yeats into Swedish.

In her early forties, Helen still looked extraordinarily young. At a Press Club meeting, she was chatting to the chairman about her nephew Jack. 'Do you mean to say that anybody on earth calls you "Aunt" Helen?' he asked. 'Dozens,' was her reply. With an abstracted gaze, he murmured, 'Well, I suppose somebody may have called *Antony* uncle.'

All this time she was living in 3 Ormonde Terrace where she spent her six happiest and most productive years. Meg's daughter, Mollie, who came only second to her mother in Helen's love and concern, has sketched her aunt as she was at this period of her life:

In Ormonde Terrace Helen had two rooms on the first floor — large sitting room, high ceiling, beautiful proportions, two French windows opening on to a narrow balcony facing Primrose Hill, folding doors opening into her bedroom. At the bend of the stairs to the next floor a tiny shared bathroom. The money in a slot gas geyser H. always lit for her guests: unless handled with respectful knowledge it was liable to explode. I stayed there several times. A Jacobean settle turned into a very good spare bed. Mrs Beney, the housekeeper for the whole house, cleaned H's sitting room early, her bedroom later. She also brought up dinner. O.K. often dined there. My chief memory is of breakfasts cooked by Helen on a gas ring in the sitting room hearth — Helen on her knees turning heavenly smelling smoked bacon and French toast, a bottle of olives on the small gate-legged oak table in front of the fire, waiting to add the touch of final ecstasy. It was a lovely room, and the ideal life for Helen the scholar. Over the mantelpiece the oil painting Paul Henry gave her in Oxford: 'Early Morning in Connemara' — a lough with mountains in hazy blue and silver. On the opposite wall, what I think was Helen's dearest possession: a line of Chinese script (framed it must have measured about 3' x 15"). Her father had taught English to a Chinese noble, using the Bible as textbook. When he was returning to China, the student presented his teacher with this scroll which read: 'Your kindness has made me forget I was a stranger in a strange land.'

Einstein once observed that people who write or think should be given jobs in a lighthouse. Perhaps more realistically, in a youthful letter to Dr Taylor, Helen complained about having to entertain Mar's visitors, but concluded with the profound remark: 'It takes a long time before one realises that the interruptions are as much a part of life as the things they interrupt: and I suppose by the time we've quite realised it, we're ready for the last interruption, which is Death.' She was well-schooled in her own philosophy but, all the same, the speed at which she worked and her output during the six years spent in Ormonde Terrace were astonishing. True she was at last freed from financial and domestic worries, but in addition to her morning attendance at Constable's, she was giving lectures — notably the famous one on John of Salisbury in 1928 printed in Volume XIII of the English Association's *Essays and Studies* — writing reviews, seeing new editions of her *Scholars* and *Lyrics* through the press, answering critics, helping needy authors to find publishers, lunching and dining daily with poets, artists, politicians, and coping with the ideas and projects that bubbled up like a volcano in action, especially during hours spent at the British Museum. In 1930 while working there she discovered and wrote long Introductions to two books, *The Blecheley Diary of the Rev. William Cole 1765–67* and his Journal of *My Journey to Paris in the year 1765*, published by Constable in 1931; in the same year, *A Book of Medieval Latin for Schools*, a selection of Latin short stories and verse, which went through ten editions between 1931 and 1962; she wrote a three-act play *The Abbé Prevost* issued by Constable in 1931 concurrently with her translation into faultless eighteenth-century English of the 1731 *History of the Chevalier des Grieux and of Manon Lescaut*, to which George Saintsbury contributed an Introduction of thirty-two pages with unabated brilliance; 1933 harvested the fruit of almost thirty years' meditation and seven years' agonizing toil in the publication of *Peter Abelard* in May; this was followed in October 1934 with *Beasts and Saints*, illustrated with woodcuts by Robert Gibbings which ran to 14,000 copies in three months; and for good measure she threw in a translation of Marcel Aymé's *The Hollow Field*, for which she received fifty guineas. All this was accomplished amid demands that would have paralysed another. A letter to Meg rejoices at the thought of life as it goes serenely on at Kilmacrew, a life so remote from her own preoccupations:

I'm now gathering courage to
(1) Write a brief introduction to Charlotte Charke★ (funny 18th century autobiography I came on).
(2) Write to Thornton Wilder (He wrote *The Bridge of San Luis Rey*, I think the most beautiful prose I have ever read, and almost shatteringly poignant, only its own perfection produces a kind of peace) — to suggest that he write a life of Keats. He is oddly like Keats in himself.
(3) Write to Walter Starkie in Dublin to suggest a book on the influence of Spain on English literature.

★Actress and youngest daughter of Colley Cibber (1671–1757, poet-laureate and hero of Pope's *Dunciad*), scandalized her contemporaries by masquerading as a man.

(4) Report on a MS on Charles I and his first Parliament, a good one.
(5) Report on Alfred Percival Grave's MS of Irish Poems.
(6) Report on a new novel by the woman who wrote *Adam's Rest*.
(7) Write to Lowe about the Coleridge Notebook.

It's all so dreadful I think I shall continue to sit over the fire and do nuffin. May McKisack and her mother were here last night, and I've suggested to May that she do the Life and Letters of Sir Thomas More, and she is on her knees to me for the sheer beauty of it, her present work being Parliamentary Boroughs in the 14th century.

Her next letter shows with what unerring instinct she could seize on the possibilities of some seeming chance: in the Rev. William Cole she at once saw a true reflection of the Rev. John Dunwoodie Martin, 'the Boss':

I've been devilling hard at that review for the *Scottish Historical*, and then that d——d article for L.M.H., and had the great excitement of a new discovery in the MS room at the B.M. — an old diary kept by an antiquarian parson who was the intimate friend of Walpole's and knew Gray. Lots of it reminded me of the Boss, like — 'cutting the Clay Pit field today, five loads, not so heavy as last year. Will Tansley very drunk, and quarrelling with the other men all day. Jem Trumble cutting for us. Should have dined with the Chancellor of Lincoln, but would rather be in the hayfield. Drank tea with him instead.' There's also a 3 months' diary: visit to Paris with Horace Walpole. Went nearly drunk, and half-way through rang up O.K. and went to the office.

I'd never have come upon it, except out of sheer dogged cussedness. I was editing Charlotte Charke for press, and wanted to get the original of a short article on her by a Dublin man who went to see her when she was a sad old woman living among the refuse dumps at Clerkenwell in a wee thatched house (she had acted *Aurora* at Drury Lane in 1731, 25 years before): it was quoted in 1812, a few paragraphs, and I wanted the original so I set my teeth and raked through 40 volumes of the old *Monthly Magazine* to find it, page by page. I didn't, but I saw a reference to this old man's antiquarian MSS as having been left to the B.M. to be opened 20 years after his death. Thought they might be worth looking at, and did, and found *this*, along with about 18 volumes of antiquarian notes on monuments etc. Do you wonder I went up in the air? And O.K. was always saying, 'Charke isn't worth that grind. Leave it.' And I said 'I can't.'

It's now being copied by one of the assistants in the MS room at the B.M., a little old dry man with white hair and an anxious manner. I'd have loved to do it myself, but they said it would be waste of my time. But oh, so restful! He is so like the Boss. 'Mr Stanmer came to see me at ten, and nearly stunned me with talking.'

Throughout all these years, she had never ceased to work on her novel of Abelard: subconsciously it was always with her, but in the early 1930s her creative power was in abeyance owing to intense mental fatigue. That explains why she found refreshment in saunter-ing up blind alleys off the main road of her concentrated thought. At least her discoveries made for a good weekly letter to Meg:

> I've been reading a long MS diary of a governess 1786–90 (Jane Austen was then about eleven to fifteen), who was left in charge of three Anglo-Indian children and one little boy about six, who was undoubtedly Tote [Meg's youngest son, George] in a previous incarnation. I read O.K. about his going to the seaside — I hadn't said a word of the resemblance — and O.K. said 'That's *exactly* like George.' He went into the sea 'like an emperor' says his fond governess: he wanted his papa to buy him a commission in the cavalry (at the age of seven), but not to tell mama, because she would be frightened: he wrote a novel at the age of eight: he began Latin and insisted on teaching all the maids: and begged to buy a horse and cart for his ninth birthday, and when told he was too old for it, said 'But it is such a noble one.' I do want us to publish it, rather cheap.

She did not tell Meg about having had to write an apology to Sir Basil Blackett, after entertaining him to dinner in her flat, where the conversation had obviously been a drain on her compassion, for her letter to him ran:

> Forgive me being such a collapsible frog. Please, I don't do it often, and never before in public: it's when I've been doing too many things at once, and your head gets like a broken string that you've screwed too tight. Felt a pig for not even coming to put the light on, but couldn't trust myself not to faint on the stairs — which would have been a 'situation'. You were such a dear to vanish as you did. I crawled to bed, and am now on top of the world, but still cursing myself, for I wanted to hear the other half of your talk.
>
>   You know, Basil, you are lucky, far beyond most men. To be able to give all oneself away, and to someone who can use it all — it is the richest thing in life. Think for a moment what it would be like if you weren't sure you were loved. That is the real torture. And that is what happens to Heloise at the last. I shirk writing that, it will hurt so damnably.
>   Yours,
>   Helen.

The last paragraph of that letter is not a mere literary exercise: it goes deeper by far. What precisely did its writer mean by the torture of feeling unloved? As for herself, she was constantly being plagued with offers of marriage and the comfort of a loving family life and would have none of it. At this very time she was telling Meg the usual tale: 'I have a feeling that he is in a rather dangerous mood. However I am always so very friendly, and so slippery, that these things don't come

to a head. Nothing could be nicer or more regretful than the letters I
write, so sorry that I can't come and so on, and a smile that is childlike
and bland.' At intervals throughout her life she repeated with great
emphasis and in several different contexts a stray sentence from some
forgotten novel read in youth, enunciated by the second of two
women characters. The first maintained that marriage alone crowned
a woman with happiness. 'Happiness?' the other retorted. 'What does
a woman want with happiness? It's things and people to care for.'
Then what did Helen mean by 'love'?

From student days, she was resolved to make love the theme of the
book of her dreams. Her many letters and published works clearly
demonstrate that her thought developed much but changed little —
the same dominant ideas are encountered over and over again. As
early as 1918, when she simply seemed to be marking time, she had
written to Dr Taylor:

> At the moment the great BOOK is beginning to exert its old spell. It's the
> struggle dating from the Middle Ages, between love and the thing called
> love, which good old Fielding says is an appetite as gross as any of the
> others: the damning of all love by the Church, confounding the love which
> is of the imagination with the love which is of the senses only, in their ideal
> of virginity. 'No one will ever understand the earlier middle ages who sees
> in monasticism a different ideal from that of the Christian Church. It was
> the ideal of a layman's life that the religious sought to embody.' It's the
> eternal process by which men have made themselves gods — the idealising
> of a natural instinct: or rather, it's — in a sense not wholly profane — the
> Platonic word becoming flesh, 'mutability swallowed up of life'. I have a
> *motif* for the chapter on the attitude of the medieval church which is its
> great apology. It is Meredith's 'Spirit must brand the flesh that it may live'.

In 1936, her Introduction to *The Desert Fathers* simply worked out in
greater detail the implications of that last sentence:

> . . . the Fathers are the *athletae Dei*, the athletes of God. Human passion,
> the passion of anger as well as of lust, entangled the life of the spirit:
> therefore passion must be dug out by the roots. 'Our mind is hampered
> and called back from the contemplation of God, because we are led into
> captivity by the passions of the flesh.' The actual words were spoken by the
> abbot Theonas, but they echo sentence after sentence from Socrates in the
> *Phaedo*. 'Spirit must brand the flesh that it may live,' said George Meredith,
> who was no Puritan.

But what is the exact length to which this branding of the flesh may
legitimately go? Must a Christian ever repeat in his heart, like the
Desert Fathers: 'I alone and God are in this world'? Does the world as

such lie in wickedness? She had answered those questions quite definitively out of her own experience when she lived with her stepmother in Cedar Avenue. A letter to Dr Taylor of 6 April 1919, summarizes her preparation for the Bible class she was to give the Girls' Auxiliary on Luke 18:22.

> I got my illumination for Tuesday's class just the night before. It came in a flash before I slept. It was Christ's promise of 'treasure in heaven'. Take all his teaching on money, and that follows it — even the much-vexed parable about the Unjust Steward. It is to use it to win love, 'the everlasting habitations', for of all things that abide, Love only has eternity. That was what the ruler lacked: it wasn't renunciation that our Lord demanded — it was consecration. The thing condenses into a phrase: Christ does not ask us to 'give up': he asks us to *give away*.
>
> It's the parable of the Talents again. What you have you are not to renounce and bury: but you are to *use*. And the 'treasure in heaven' — it was a new world that Christ was calling him into — 'for he that loveth, dwelleth in God, and God in him.' That story is the meeting-ground —and battle-ground— of asceticism and Christianity. Before, I always saw it as a possible bulwark of the monastic ideal. But don't you love the other way of it?

To her way of thinking, there were no opposing standards of earth versus heaven: eternity and love were both vertical and horizontal. She had penetrated deeply into what is called 'the sacrament of the present moment.' Life with her stepmother had taught her that the daily humdrum round can be like swordgrass in one's hand, as the Buddha said, and yet 'with our neighbour is life and death.' There is a letter to Meg which deserves to be quoted in full, as it must have been written in the early months of 1932 when she was under great pressure on every side:

> I'm just scribbling this for meditation on your 'white unto harvest'. (a) Look them up in Alexander Maclaren: it's a wonderful standby. (b) It seems to me another instance of Our Lord's perpetual awareness of the value and significance of life — every minute of it. Harvest *looks* six weeks away, so now only mark time and wait: No, says He, get at it *now*. And it isn't only the harvest of souls, but God's work generally, in other words, the ordinary business of living and doing our job. God himself doesn't count only religious exercises as His peculiar property, but every decent action a man does cf. 'Lord, when saw we Thee hungry?' He does identify himself with every kind thing done.
>
> > And every virtue we possess
> > And every victory won,
> > And every thought of holiness,
> >   Are His alone.

This is of course a far cry from the original intention — the cure of souls —
and the verses are one of the great missionary phrases. But they do show
His trick of piercing below the outward appearance of things.

Again 'the harvest truly is plenteous, but the labourers are few.' For
some reason best known to Himself, He does not coerce human souls, but
works through men. It is as if the old Zoroastrian myth were true, that
Good and Evil fight for ever, and that Good *not* being omnipotent, it takes
all the decent men in the world to pull all their might on God's side. I have
always liked that explanation myself. And whatever the original truth may
be, it is certain that in dealing with men and perhaps, as my old Gilles de
Vannes says, 'out of respect for the creatures He has made', He limits his
omnipotence. There's a strange cry in one of the *Carmina Burana* things —
a Crusade song:

> 'Man, have pity on thy God.'

Darling, I doubt if you'll make head or tail out of this.

I am struggling with the little textbook, and cursing it ten times a day.
All the good stories are in such bad Latin. The first real try-over of Holst's
Wandering Scholars opera is on February 27th at St Paul's Girls' School.
GBS has read the play, but only spoke on the telephone — he was down in
the country and telephoning about something else, but interrupted himself
with 'About your young friend's play, it ought to do. A charming actress
for Lenki . . . She's got Prévost, but the difficulty will be to get an actor
good enough for the part. But I'll write you about it. That's the worst I can
say of it!' I am terribly bucked, for I was afraid he'd pooh-pooh it
altogether. But still keep it dark. I am hoping for his letter to O.K. but the
old man is terribly busy with the Shaw–Ellen Terry letters.

When Shaw did write to O.K. it was to turn the play down: he did
not think it would 'get across'. Helen was not unduly upset, even
though for two years or more she had fallen into a Slough of Despond
over her inability to rise to really creative work. The Abelard novel
was stuck fast until suddenly the sap began to flow once more, and she
dashed off a letter to tell Meg so:

The chapter finished and a new one planned. You don't know what it feels
like to find oneself swimming again and I have a kind of hunch that the
novel is going to make us a good deal of money. Of course I had high
hopes of the play, but then it depends on other things outside one's
control. Darling, you don't mind my writing like this? It's because I got
into a sort of despair. And then I began writing again, and finished in such
an exaltation that it's even given me confidence in life again, not only about
my being able to write, but other things. You know I really do think that
things work together for good to people who care even so little as we do
for God: the number of times I've vowed and denied it, and in a little while
eaten my words again. And this includes even our own foolish mistakes. I
most heartily hope it isn't true, but if it is, we'll 'accept' once again and

think about it as courageously as possible. You and I must never be afraid of anything, so long as we have each other. Fear is the shattering thing.

The chapter finished and a new one planned — but not according to the pattern designed from her very schooldays. Her main interest had always centred upon Peter Abelard, the arrogant undisputed Master of the Philosophical and Theological Schools of Paris, the intellectual nerve-centre of the Christian world, hailed by his students with hysterical rapture as the Socrates of Gaul and Plato of the West, yet forced at the Council of Soissons in 1121 to cast his writings into the fire, condemned as a heretic twenty years later at the Council of Sens — largely owing to the implacable hostility of Bernard of Clairvaux — and ending his days as a Cluniac monk at Chalon-sur-Saône, sheltered and revered by Peter the Venerable. For years Helen had got her teeth into the tough disquisitions on the *Unity and Trinity of the Godhead*, and Abelard's *Theologia christiana*, and his *Sic et non*. Why then the sudden shift in balance? In 1924, when she underwent the strange transformation in the Institut Pasteur and became the aged abbess of the Paraclete, with Abelard twenty years dead, her self-reproach had lain precisely in the fact that she was teaching her nuns the specific dogmas that had evoked ecclesiastical censure. The needle was still pointing to the pole, but the magnetic field was altered: from a study of heresy, Helen's *Peter Abelard* had grown into a love-story that expressed the absolute of human passion. The deliberate twist given in Chapter V to one of her favourite quotations provides a possible clue. Gilles de Vannes observes to the seventeen-year-old Heloise that men like to postpone delight because they live in their imagination as well as their senses, whereas women lack that wisdom as a rule, and are guided far more by their senses:

'I have sometimes thought,' he said at last, 'that this is the difference between loveliness and beauty. Wisdom, the knowledge of things past, the memory of the tree in Eden. Loveliness is an easy thing, an appletree in blossom, and most women have something of it, in their youth. But beauty — one or perhaps two in every generation . . . '
'And are they happy?'
Gilles sat up with a sudden violence almost as of anger. 'Happy? What do they want with happiness? They know ecstasy. Happiness? A dog asleep in the sun.' . . . There was no sound from her, and when he turned to her, his heart stood still at the look on her face. 'They know ecstasy,' but what was in the words to bring transfiguration? A moment later, and his duller ear had caught the sound of Abelard's foot on the stair.

Cras amet qui nunquam amavit: Tomorrow love will come to her who has never loved — the *Pervigilium Veneris* had come true. Helen Jane Waddell had fallen in love and, as a result, her story of Abelard and Heloise had taken luminous wing.

Otto Kyllmann, director and chairman of Constable & Co. was twenty years Helen's senior. His skull, close-cropped hair, bristly grey moustache, intense brown eyes (the excellent photograph he gave to Meg in 1934 is aptly labelled 'Scenting a spot of trouble'), all betrayed his German origins. A brilliant conversationalist, especially on his favourite topics of literature or politics, a connoisseur of people as well as of food and wines, cultured, courteous, and expensive in his tastes — he never walked if he could take a taxi — he was a publisher of the first rank. As he informed Helen early in their acquaintance, it was he who had spotted Bernard Shaw's genius as he now spotted hers. For him, 'publishing' meant only one thing: a good book issued under the imprint of Constable & Co., whose unpretentious premises in Orange Street he once gazed on from some distance, as he murmured, 'Bone of my bones, and flesh of my flesh.'

In *Orange Street & Brickhole Lane* (Rupert Hart-Davis, 1963), Ralph Arnold, his successor at Constable's, has drawn a pen-portrait of this 'old bull' of the herd, as he calls him, far from flattering and indignantly repudiated by Meg. Yet even so unsympathetic an observer concedes that although O.K., as he was invariably styled, could be 'difficult, inconsiderate, unpredictable and monumentally selfish, he was admired, liked and respected, partly because he was a "character", partly because he was a thorough-paced professional, and partly because he could be, all of a sudden, extraordinarily kind and rather endearing'. He goes on to describe the ritual luncheon every Wednesday, when the board of five directors assembled at the Ivy Restaurant. As they made their way along the insalubrious alleys said to be a short-cut, O.K. would constantly stop 'to inquire after the health and well-being of one of those bundles of rags and misery camped out in various dark corners. "My old dears" he called them. He was for ever getting derelicts of this kind into hospital, and going to pay them lengthy visits when they were there.'

From their first meeting in 1926 the attraction between Helen and O.K. had been mutual. The elderly sardonic and engaging publisher had done all the right things — appreciated her humour, admired her fur coat, courteously helped her into it, applauded her genius, given practical advice, and promised to promote her forthcoming book that he had adroitly secured for Constable's. He also offered her occasional work in the office to augment her finances, and asked her to aim at delivering the typescript of *The Wandering Scholars* by Eastertide. Having met his deadline, Helen rushed off as usual to Kilmacrew to enjoy the company of Meg and the children. She was standing in Mullan's bookshop in Belfast, when the sound of a man's voice in a room above the shop made her heart stand still. For a moment, she thought it was Otto Kyllmann's. 'You'd better watch out,' she told herself, 'you are falling in love with that man.' On her return to London the promised work at Constable's brought her into daily contact with him. Increasingly he became counsellor and friend, invited her frequently to lunch at his favourite restaurant in Soho, found excellent business reasons for calling on her, until the inevitable day dawned when they found themselves in each other's arms in her flat in Ormonde Terrace.

She was thirty-six, an age at which many a woman has known the joy of motherhood. She had always hankered after children of her own. Years before, with George and Billy in mind, she had observed in Dr Isabel Mitchell's obituary: 'The woman who has cared for a brother is not childless: there is motherhood in that relationship always, even where the brother is older.' Only the year before her meeting with O.K. she had bewailed her life of single blessedness after her refusal to marry the Mourne Mountains man: 'Me that could have loved terribly and was born to have a house and children and a man.' When Abelard and Heloise separated as man and wife for ever, there broke from her lips the cry that the poet Lucan puts into the mouth of Cornelia, wife of Pompey: 'O thalamis indigne meis' — O wedlock beyond my deserts. One day, Helen would tell her niece Mollie that the distillation of ecstasy in giving and receiving love, mingled with the agony of lifelong frustration and torture of self-denial, gave her the power to sink into Peter Abelard's soul, and share some of his and Heloise's crucifixion. Otto Kyllmann was not free to marry. Years later in a moment of rare self-revelation, Helen answered a question about her relationship with him, daringly put to her by Monica Stiff, a close friend; she reverted to that first embrace: 'I can see now the patch of sunlight in which we stood and the joy of it, but I *had* to draw back and say, "It can never go further than this; I can never take what belongs to someone else." So, Monica, I have never experienced physical "love".' Monica Stiff adds that their love, still and aware but not with the stillness of possession, seemed to her in 1936 as passionless as it was deep, but 'the situation must have involved much frustration and ambiguity.'*

*Monica Stiff: letter to the author.

Three things in that situation must be kept in mind. First of all, a woman's love in its essence is often an overwhelming tenderness, possibly part of the natural preparation for motherhood, a keen pleasure not untinged with pain. The joy and security that accompany it in the thought of loving and being loved may be quite secondary. In Helen, human tenderness amounted to a passion: it gave her the power to enter into — almost to be changed into — another person; and while the gift made her what she was, it may finally have unmade her. Secondly, as Professor Spurgeon once told her, she had a positive passion for self-immolation. Thirdly, as already observed, like Meta Fleming and Maude Clarke, she was possessed of that innate innocence and purity that seems peculiar to Irishwomen. It was George Saintsbury in his Introduction to *Manon Lescaut* who pointed out that although 'purity' is pretty close in spelling to the ugly sham virtue of a not over-clean-minded 'prudery', there is a world of difference between the two: Helen Waddell was no prude. Clearly everything in her thoroughly Christian upbringing and outlook militated against any illicit relationship, in spite of the fact that the loneliness of a still-handsome man, with two broken marriages behind him, living in drab lodgings yet making generous financial provision for an estranged wife, his sole human solace a sad pilgrimage to a daughter in a mental home, was more than sufficient to awaken her compassion to a dangerous degree. 'O.K. was here at the week-end,' she wrote to Meg from Ormonde Terrace, 'went to see Lorna, but came back not unhappy. The doctor says she just lives in a silent world of illusion of her own, but no longer an unhappy one, and that he thinks this will always be so. O.K. talked about her a great deal and I think has now accepted and given up the torture of hope. Odd to unite those two words together, but it is true.'

'Happiness? What does a woman want with happiness? It's things and people to care for.' Meg had once observed that all her life Helen needed to be needed. Otto Kyllmann needed her, and that was enough. Even so rigid a moralist as J.D., Meg's husband, never questioned the integrity of either: O.K. was accepted pretty well as part of the family, enveloped in all the warmth and affection and beauty of Kilmacrew. From this time, there is scarcely a letter of Helen's which does not mention him, and so it would continue to the end. Naturally there were those who resented and criticized, who refused to believe that so strange a companionship ran straight, but Helen simply refused to listen to the dinging of, 'What will Mrs Grundy zay? What will Mrs Grundy think?' Her own conscience was clear, and for the rest, 'What will they think? Let them think!' Long ago at Cedar Avenue, she had reviewed a book of Chinese poems entitled *Coloured Stars*, in which she wrote:

> There are two ways of love, east and west: that which discerns the person incarnate; that which concerns itself only with the flesh — and one may hear either of them sung divinely enough about the Tokyo streets. It was the East that gave us the symbol of ultimate ecstasy, alike of the spirit and the flesh,
> 'Far off, most secret and inviolate Rose'.
> And the pessimism of so much of its verse, like the *nequidquam* which is the tolling refrain of Lucretius on the passion of love, is but the affirmation of some better thing:
> 'What the world's lips are thirsting for
> Must be substantial somewhere.'

The passion of her own love was sublimated by its own heat: there was desire in it, but it was desire of the person. As for Otto Kyllmann,

> 'My lady is perfect, and transfigureth
> All sin and sorrow and death.'

From the very outset, with disarming charm, Helen shared O.K. with Meg. She was soon writing to her sister:

> I am waiting for O.K. to come and fetch me; I don't know where we'll go today, but I have so longed for you, and it seemed to be going with me everywhere yesterday. We went down to Savernake — it's in Wiltshire on the Downs, walked about 14 miles, thermos and sandwiches in little brown school bag. It was leagues and leagues of Downs as far as your eye could see, and you know the peace and full breath a wild countryside gives you. And it was hot, and the cowslips out everywhere, and bits of wood here and there, and we passed a farm with little familiar black houses and piping voices and O.K. at once began to talk of Meg. And in the evening came to the old forest hotel, kept by Mr Bain who is 80 and Mrs Bain who is 83, and had an enormous dinner, where again I *ached* for you, because there was a wonderful salmon, and cold lamb (it being Sunday), with beautiful salad, and a little of Burgundy. And it's as quiet as the hills. It was quite mellow with sunset when we left, and I could hardly bear to come away. It's a wonderful place even in winter, for they keep up huge fires — there was one burning even yesterday evening — and at another table a thin brown man talking to a deaf grey-haired lady — 'Twenty-five years ago when I went to Sumatra . . .'
> Wednesday
> Darling, I must get this off. I did want you so, it was just as if you were walking beside me. Back at work again and very fresh. O.K. moves in tomorrow (a flat in Newman Street). Tonight I'll be helping him get his books on to the shelves. It's a dear little flat, but you'll see it.

Helen immediately expressed the joyousness of that spring day on the Wiltshire Downs in a poem of six stanzas but, as always, the singing bird was haunted by a feeling of transience and fear of loss:

> The sun shone out on Martinsell
> And warmed the barrows of the dead.
> The Down was topaz at our feet,
> And the sky sapphire that was lead.
>
> And love that had been in our hearts
> Long-suffering and grave and dumb,
> Leapt to his stature, with a light
> Disdained the shining of the sun.
>
> The sun went in behind a cloud,
> The barrows of the dead were cold.
> More ancient they than their high trees,
> This stone beside them not more old.
>
> And is our passion brief as light?
> Shall nothing but the dead abide?
> Still in their barrows, and outlive
> The ecstasy they knew and died?
>
> Or is their passion in this place
> As present as their ancient peace,
> But only those that are their peers
> In love, can give that love release?
>
> The dead are dead: their ecstasy
> Eternity itself doth own.
> This moment of this day outlasts
> Even this imperishable stone.

'Back to work again and very fresh' — but no longer full time at Constable's. The royalties from her prodigious output of 1931 had enabled Helen to dispense with the annual salary of £350 and substitute work picked up at the office, done at home or at the British Museum, and remunerated according to the time spent and the expertise demanded. She was planning to spend Christmas at Kilmacrew, but hoped to complete the novel before setting out. She could no longer submit her work to Gregory Smith, and listen to his mellow Oxford voice appreciating both it and her. He had moved to London in 1930 to be near the theatres — and Ormonde Terrace; but 1932 closed that memorable chapter in Helen's life. A letter to Meg recounting various misfortunes concluded: 'Then Gregory died — they rang up to tell me, and you know how one grieves for the dead who were thwarted in their lives, and I was haunted by the pitiful patience of his eyes. Mercifully I'd gone very steadily to see him of late. Saintsbury, bless him, was furious about the poor notice in *The Times* and is writing one himself.'

Saintsbury, aged eighty-seven, passing his days at Bath 'in the Augustan twilight of the house of his last inhabiting', as Helen put it, 'a solitary indomitable figure with straggling grey hair and black skull-cap, gaunt as Merlin and islanded in a fast-encroaching sea of books' she never saw, in spite of her journeyings to the West Country within easy reach of Bath. They met only twice: in 1914 at Gregory Smith's table; of the second meeting there is no record. But old age had no power over that free truly catholic spirit, and their interchange of letters ceased only with his death. Meanwhile Maude Clarke was made free of Ormonde Terrace, and her keen interest and pertinent criticism of *Peter Abelard* kept Helen from having to be wheeled about in a go-cart as she neared the end of her labour. For some years Maude had suffered the loss of her religious faith: she recovered it possibly under Helen's tutelage as she reclined on a settee listening to the latest chapter. Helen as always had to share her gladness with Meg:

I'm busy revising Abelard. Maude was here for Monday night, and I think likes it almost as much as you do — especially the religion of it. But on that point she seems to me to have changed completely, though neither of us have said anything. It gives me confidence in life, if it can do that. . . .

Och, I'm so nearly out of the wood — the wood that has beset me for three years. Maude wants now my next book — 'Literature in England in the XII century' and then a great historical novel. It would be about a student under Abelard, if I ever did do it. Odd, Maude used to make me academic and critical — now it's the romantic creative half she brings out. I think because she enjoys it so. That too has come again. You always said I hadn't lost her. I sent Saintsbury the wee photo — 'More than ever *La Belle Dame* not *sans* but *de Merci.*' Don't you like that?

At last, with a triumphant cry of 'Och, darling, it's finished!' the novel *Peter Abelard* was sent in to Constable, and Helen sped to Kilmacrew. She returned to London early in 1933 to find the directors in a state of great excitement: if *that* was not a success, they'd better quit publishing and open a butcher's shop; the thing was a miracle and could happen only once in a generation: it was queer to have the heart torn out of your breast for two creatures a thousand years away. No praise touched her so deeply as Meg's; she had read it, she told Helen, 'with passion and amazement, borne on a tide that was beyond bar or delay'. Frequent letters kept Meg abreast of events:

> The excitement about the novel mounts. Jacket to be designed by the man who did the marvellous woodcuts for Shaw's *Black Girl*: I saw him yesterday, and he told me he would like best to illustrate the novel right through, and that he couldn't leave it down. He's going to do Abelard leaning against the window with the moonlight outside — do you remember the chapter where he is in a devil's mood, and Gilles watching him, with the arms outstretched along the crossbeams of the window, 'God have mercy, it's a crucified Apollyon'.

But bitter was intermingled with the sweet, for on 28 January, George Saintsbury died: on 1 February, Helen wrote to her sister:

> I suppose you know that dear Saintsbury is gone. I find myself thinking at every turn — 'I must tell him this.' I hadn't realised how absolutely he was part of my brain; but just because he was bone of my bone I believe it will make less difference to me, his being dead. We were so extraordinarily alike that his books are just his living voice, as if it were only a prolonged correspondence. But if only he could have seen the novel. I was hoping and hoping that he would live for that. I even caught myself thinking, 'I must write and tell him that it has spoiled half my pleasure, if he won't see it.' And now Galsworthy — do you remember you were reading *The Man of Property* at Greencastle, under the little sandy tree on the beach? There's only Shaw and Barrie of the old guard left. But George Moore, Saintsbury and Galsworthy within ten days of each other is a heavy reaping.

A letter at the same time to Enid Starkie concluded: 'There won't ever be another Saintsbury. I know it is better for him to be dead, even though he lived in most rich memory for the last few years. . . . All the same, if you've been as much enriched by a man's mind as I was, you can bear to let him go, for a part of him goes on living in your mind, continuing that endless *entretien*.'

Peter Abelard was published in May 1933, in time for Helen's forty-fourth birthday, and before the year was out it had been reprinted fifteen times. Helen was already at work on *Beasts and Saints*, hoping to have it ready for the Christmas market, but her mind was simmering with fresh ideas, dashed off in letters to Meg as they arose:

> I don't think it will matter now if I died — except for the people I'm fond of, and don't want ever to leave. And yet already I am beginning to see tremendous things in a possible sequel. You know what we saw on the steps of the Château of the Paraclete — the winding road, and Abelard coming back to her in that slow black procession, dead.

You and I once stood watching Geo go — the long long coffin, and the men who were his friends carrying him down the street. I think it is perhaps almost worse to watch one's dead come home. But that first memory was the root, I think, of the absolute agony I felt for one moment on those steps, that still September day, with the decent stout concierge beside us.

If I do the next novel, you and I will have to travel down to Cluny where he took refuge, where there is a tremendous abbey, and to Sens where he was condemned a heretic, where there is a marvellous cathedral — and this time we'll go to Père-la-Chaise [*sic*] in Paris, because it seems they have kept the actual tomb in which his body was first laid down at Chalon (which was a dependent house of Cluny: he'd been sent there to recover); and the effigy on it is believed to be Abelard. A keen thin aquiline face, very like Dante's. And maybe we'll do the pilgrimage up through France from Cluny, as Peter the Venerable did it, to bring his body home.

There can be little doubt that in 1933 Helen was resolved to make the Heloise–Abelard story a trilogy, possibly after the style of Sigrid Undset's *Kristin Lavransdatter*, a book given her by Baron Palmstierna, the Swedish ambassador — through him, the two women met and became friends. Letters assign three titles to the project: *Peter Abelard*; *Death of a Heretic*; *Heloise*. In 1932, she had informed Meg: 'I am to lunch with Basil Blackett and meet Mr Baldwin — by special request of same. S. B. says he has been wanting to meet me for years.' This was followed by: 'Just back from breakfast with Baldwin. A lovely quiet room and a little round table just for three — himself and the man who is secretary of the Pilgrim Trust, and runs a very luxurious private press, which he wants me to do a translation for. . . .' The secretary, Thomas Jones, C.H., LL.D., entered into his diary under the date 27 August 1933: 'I got her [Helen Waddell] to come down here for a week-end, and I've arranged that we shall do at the Greg-y-nog Press a new translation by her of the Letters of Heloise and Abelard.' To Meg, Helen wrote her version of one of the many books that were never written:

I was away for the week-end at the Greg-y-nog Press, which is partly run by Tom Jones, the dear little man I met at the breakfast with Baldwin: it's a most lovely house in Wales lapped in luxury, and exactly like something in the *Pilgrim's Progress*, including the two Davies sisters who own it, and who might be Mercy and Discretion. They are so good and so gentle and — God bless them — they would like to work out some scheme that would endow one to do no more hack work at all. Meantime I have promised to translate the letters of Heloise and Abelard for a superb Limited Edition (not to interfere with Constable later) — Japanese vellum and so on. I

haven't fixed my fee yet, but it will be a big one. And Abelard goes on
selling, and has begun in New Zealand.

The paean of praise that greeted the appearance of *Peter Abelard* —
the novel was soon translated into no fewer than ten languages — was
slightly marred by the discordant drums and fifes wafted from over
Boyne Water. Abelard's *Historia Calamitatum* taken out of the decent
obscurity of Latin and put into plain English was indelicate — that
most capital of all sins. It affronted the fierce refinement and rigid
righteousness of the clerical élite of Antrim and Donegal, some of
whom formed branches of Helen's own family tree. Helen retaliated
with amusement and great goodwill:

> I gave Emily one more biff — said Gilles was intended to represent the
> cynical clerical attitude to marriage, and did she also think he was
> expressing my view when he said that all love is transient? That it was what
> my friends thought my impossible idealism about love that had kept me
> from marrying ten times over. That the love between Heloise and Abelard
> was the absolute, but that thanks to the impossible celibacy convention
> they had put it to wrong uses: and if she thought the only two scenes in
> which passion was described — the breaking of the Holy Week fast, and
> the sacrilege in the refectory 'made what was wrong beautiful', I had
> written nonsense. And I asked her to send on this letter to Mabel. All the
> same, I liked old Emily's letter — it's so exactly Emily, but not
> cantankerous.
>
> It delighted me to reflect that Mabel's conversation used to leave you —
> a hardened 'married lady' with the 'unpleasant taste in the mouth' that
> *Abelard* seems to have given her. But none of it really ruffled me, and I
> enormously enjoy a little laying about me when people turn sancti-
> monious.

V. S. Pritchett's column of praise in the *New Statesman* of 27 May
expressed, in its operative sentence, the dead opposite of what the
author intended: 'Not the personal downfall of Abelard but the
collapse of reason before something primitive and irrational — this
view of Miss Waddell's is both superbly fitted to the irony of an age
struggling against the gods it has created, as to the private story of
Abelard.' At the top of the printed page, Helen has written:
'Extremely commendatory. But it is curious to see how Pritchett who
loathes Christianity has twisted the whole meaning of the book
completely round. Several people have commented on it with sheer
bewilderment, but explain it by his own obsession.'

Keen critical appraisal of *Peter Abelard* was to come from the pen of
two eminent Europeans who, like H.W. herself, knew no frontiers
other than those of the mind: Ida Friederike Görres, daughter of the

Austro-Hungarian ambassador in Tokyo and his Japanese wife; and Étienne Gilson, the distinguished French philosopher and historian of mediaeval thought, under whose impulse and guidance the Institute of Medieval Studies of Toronto produced the critical edition of the Abelard–Heloise letters, published between 1950 and 1954. Frau Görres, formidable Catholic intellectual, intensely loyal to the Church but just as intensely critical of its surface weaknesses, in a letter of the 1950s was inveighing against the 'ghastly boring style' of Catholic articles and lectures, all polished smoothly and so framed as to include all truth at one go. Only what is jagged and sharply pointed, she says, can really make an impression, and turns for illustration to *Peter Abelard*: 'The corpus of Catholic opinion mustn't be like a sack full of balls and glass marbles, all smoothly rounded — for these just roll away in all directions and get lost: it must rather consist of sharp-edged bits, which can be fitted together to form a mosaic. I realized this for the first time reading a criticism of my beloved Heloise and Abelard by Helen Waddell. The reviewer condemned the book as "not really Christian", since it is only concerned with sorrow, with no mention of "the meaning of Easter" — as though a novel, a literary work of art, must always be a compendium of every truth in the catechism. All the difference between false completeness and true wholeness.'*

It was this true wholeness that Gilson commended in the Introduction to his *Héloïse et Abélard*, a masterly examination of the philosophical and theological ideas motivating the actions of the two lovers: many will consider his verdict on Helen's work more authoritative than any other. Remarking that, curiously enough, the best studies have been English, he selects four lines from Pope's *Eloisa to Abelard* for special praise, pays George Moore's fluid and musical prose style in *Héloïse and Abélard* a dubious compliment by ignoring his treatment of the subject, and concludes: 'But above all we should not forget that vital, charming book, penetrating and infinitely more faithful to reality than George Moore's, the *Peter Abelard* of Helen Waddell, author of *The Wandering Scholars* so familiar to medievalists. Indeed, English literature has paid greater tribute to the memory of Heloise and Abelard than has our own.'† He goes on to commend the work of Charles Rémusat in the mid-nineteenth century, a work every scholar must consult for the purely historical facts, and quotes with warm approbation Rémusat's affirmation: 'We cannot assist at their strange and final transformation of love without a blending of consternation,

---

Broken Lights: Ida Friederike Görres (London, Burns & Oates, 1964).
†*Héloïse and Abélard*: Étienne Gilson (Chicago, Henry Regnery, 1951).

pity and respect.'

Let Helen herself have the last word on the book that had taken her twenty years or more to bring to birth. On 2 September 1936, she wrote to acknowledge a letter from Arundell Esdaile, of the British Museum:

Dear Mr Esdaile,

I wrote to you and tore it up, because I was so grateful to you for your letter that it was difficult to thank you for it without being either rigid or silly.

It was a terrible book to write, so that when people talk to me about it as if I had managed to do well with the delphiniums this year I open my mouth and shut it again. And I think with a twisted grin of Ben Jonson's 'That which was wrote with labour deserves to be read with such.'

I think Rémusat and R. L. Poole were Abelard's best understanders. That queer *Historia Calamitatum* is a twisted pathological piece of work, and queerest in the apparently cold-blooded selection and scheming at the beginning of the love-affair. Poole says somewhere that Abelard always 'rationalized' (look it up — *Illustrations of Medieval Thought*, 124–5): when I knew no more of him than the *Letters* I thought him a prig and a cad. But the more I have read of his other works, the more I read into that strange autobiography. Perhaps I read too much.

I have never thought it boasting, the story of their passion: but that trying to write coldly and hatefully of his, as he thought now, most grievous fault, the fire came about him again.

The keynote to the story I found in two words of his own, speaking of Fulbert: *summa traditio*. Remember that he used it, not of Fulbert's cruel betrayal of himself, but of his own betrayal of the old man, and that it is Fulbert's victim who speaks.

I believe that it was, as he says, for her own protection he sent her to Argenteuil: he himself says that Fulbert imputed the other motive — his wish to be rid of her. The final taking of the veil was, in the twelfth century, probably the best thing for her. It meant at least safety, and a 'career'.

I could not let Guibert commit suicide: for there there is the plain fact. That was a dreadful thing to write. I saw how to do it years before, when Suggia was playing. And I had not thought of Fulbert's madness till I was writing. He just went mad, as the book went on. And Gilles: I hardly know what went to the making of Gilles. Henry of Winchester's passion for buying antique sculpture; John of Salisbury's humanism; Peter Damian's denouncing of luxurious ecclesiastics; the same John's love of a good wine; my deep liking for George Saintsbury whom I first met at seventy. There is no Gilles in the story in the skeleton evidence.

There is another great revealing phrase, in a later letter to Heloise about their marriage, 'when I desired to bind thee, immeasurably beloved, to

Meg and her husband in 1943 with the portraits of their two sons
killed in the war

Helen and Meg in the garden at Kilmacrew in the late thirties

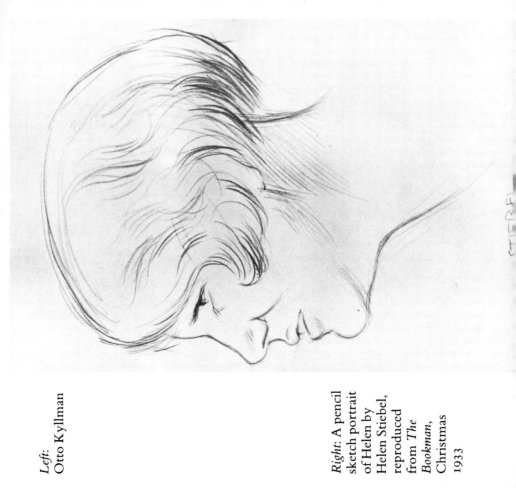

Right: A pencil sketch portrait of Helen by Helen Stiebel, reproduced from *The Bookman,* Christmas 1933

Left: Otto Kyllman

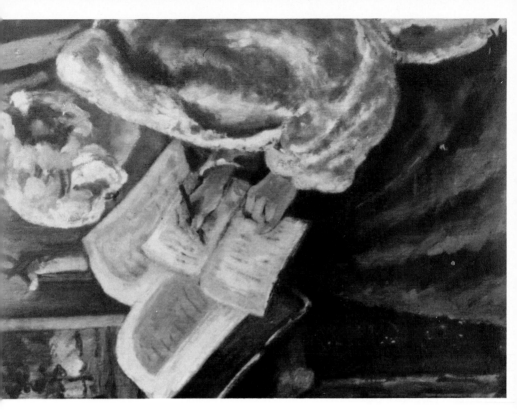

Left: Helen in the garden at 32 Primrose Hill Road, holding her cat, Wugs

Right: Portrait of Helen by Grace Henry, 1939, painted at the same time as that on the back of the jacket

Meg in 1968

Mollie as a young woman

Mollie and Meg in the garden at Kilmacrew House in 1965, the
year Helen died

myself for ever.' I am translating the Letters some day for the Greg-y-nog Press. Scott-Moncrieff hated Abelard, and the dislike made him astonishingly inaccurate: not deliberately so. Simply it blinded him to the Latin before his eyes. . . . I do not attempt to thank you for your letter.

Since the authenticity of the letters ascribed to Abelard and Heloise is still hotly debated,* a second letter from H.W. to A. Esdaile is pertinent to the discussion:

> The difficulties in the *Letters* are so overwhelming that I — this sounds paradoxical — am almost driven to believe in their genuineness. It was the clumsiest of all forgers — if they are forged — and it was at the same time a genius like Shakespeare's. . . . But I determined some time ago to suspend all explanations even to myself, until I had submitted the whole text to the most intimate test of all — and that in word for word translation, with the background firmly in my mind. I had the dream at first of editing a critical text, but I know now that I am congenitally incapable of that kind of exactness, grievous as it is to me to admit it: or rather *was*: for now I only wonder that I ever had the ignorant presumption to consider it . . .
>
> I think where most readers go wrong is in judging Abelard only by the letters, written at a singularly cruel moment in his life. That is another argument to me of their genuineness. They are psychologically so strange; so credible, if one goes deep enough, so preposterous, if one is superficial.
>
> I have not read George Moore's *Héloïse and Abélard*, and shall not until I have written the last years. I was angry when he wrote it, because I had meant to do a book on Abelard since I was an undergraduate: I was busy with the *Scholars* then, and felt sadly that I could never attempt it now, knowing that wizard prose. But my own conviction of those two, and of the *Lear* quality in Abelard's tragedy, grew: also from friends of mine who had read the book, I heard enough to convince me that I was not copying him, even unconsciously. So I shall buy myself a copy on the day that 'Death of a Heretic' is published, not till then.
>
> Some day when I am at the Museum, may I ask to see you? Talking is swifter than writing.

Set in the context of her own life, of which it is a paradigm, Helen Waddell's *Peter Abelard* unfolds like some majestic fugue in three voices. She has played on the theme with variations in several places, but never stated it more specifically than in the first chapter of *The Wandering Scholars* where she speaks of 'the pain of solitary hearts, the suffering divinity of human passion' which transmutes its anguish into ecstasy. Abelard and Heloise open the fugue with a deeply-moving melody in the tonic key, expressive in its beauty and pain of

*See *Women Writers of the Middle Ages* by Peter Dronke (Cambridge University Press, 1984).

lifelong sacrifice and separation; Otto Kyllmann and Helen Waddell answer in the dominant, as of two lovers who will never be husband and wife; Abelard's servant, Guibert the scullion, and Bele Alys the harlot, both of them historical characters, fix the counterpoint; Gilles de Vannes, Bernard of Clairvaux, and Abelard's sister Denise *alias* Helen's sister Meg, supply the interweaving episodes.

Helen rarely mentions music possibly because, as the Swedish ambassador once remarked, everything she wrote was music. That the craftswoman wrote with her ear comes out clearly in a series of letters tutoring Enid Starkie, who did not always appreciate the forceful criticism. Enid sent Helen her study of Baudelaire and the draft of an autobiographical novel, later to be published as straight narrative. Helen was making frantic efforts to complete her novel, *Peter Abelard*, yet she laid her own work aside to help and encourage the younger writer; after smartening up the punctuation, she sent the typescript of *Baudelaire* to Constable's, and then sat down to write to its author:

> Here is my final considered judgement. If I were reviewing it, I should enrich it a good deal with illustration and delete the criticism, but you asked me for no reservations.
>
> It will come up at the Board Meeting today. . .
>
> I've been thinking about your style. Swift, for instance, is a bald writer, but he makes up for it by a kind of balance — and you haven't yet mastered the English balance and the English rhythm: your adverbs and your subsidiary clauses are liable to go where a Frenchman would put them, which is usually the opposite end of the sentence to ours. Again, your trick when you're moved of having three or more sentences in one, with only commas between. 'He did not care . . . it was indifferent . . . he only wanted . . . ' is a kind of emotional piling-up which English prose is very shy of. It makes all the difference if you use a semicolon, takes away the effect of breathlessness, and makes it a considered and melancholy judgement. I put in a good many semicolons re-reading the MS. I knew you wouldn't mind. And one thing I did which I shuddered at doing, yet I was sure you'd let me if I could tell you. You had once used three adjectives, one of those too suggestive of the Hohenzollern *cliché*, and I think Anatole France's advice to beware of the adjective is the beginning of wisdom. It was about Baudelaire's indifference to women — 'his glorious strong shining armour'. I cut everything but 'glorious' which to me suggests the archangel and is superb. I did this because you were working in dry point and you must not dash into oils. I said in my report that the style was bald, often deliberately bald: but that its very plainness could be almost intolerably moving. I almost hope I'll have *Abelard* in rough draft by Christmas.

The sequel is best told in Helen's letter to Meg of 2 December 1932, written the day after she had completed *Abelard*:

. . . It's finished. I finished it last night. I felt more than ever writing the last pages, that this is not the end. But it's the end of one stage of the journey anyhow. I was rather excited and shaky, but not either sorry or glad. And then, as luck would have it, I crept downstairs at eleven after writing the last page, to look for letters, and found one from Maude — that Enid Starkie was knocked down by a bus in Oxford, and is in the Acland with concussion, and worrying frightfully about her *Baudelaire* which Constable's refused, and would I please send the MS on at once. And I had sent it registered a week ago. So I crept to bed and, as is the custom of our family, quite sure it was my fault somehow. And as she was frightfully cut up about Constable's not taking it and had even blamed me in a frantic letter for encouraging her to believe it was good, you can imagine how cheerful this rather deflated animal felt!

Not surprisingly, Helen soon discovered that the invalid was not half so badly injured as rumour had it, yet without a word of reproach, she dropped all she was about, to approach another publisher on Enid's behalf. On 2 February 1933 she wrote to Victor Gollancz, explaining that her own publisher had seriously considered the work but 'the conviction of one reader that the appeal was for a French rather than an English public turned the scale against it'. Her letter continued:

I think the book is remarkable . . . the thing that has remained with me is the figure of Baudelaire, a kind of discredited Don Quixote, with pitifully clean linen and shabby boots. And some scenes — the fly-blown trial for obscenity; Ancelle, the decent provincial lawyer as literary agent; the publishing adventure of Poulet Melassis; the lectures in Brussels to empty benches; the scanty funeral with wet umbrellas — are unforgettable.

Helen hailed Victor Gollancz's acceptance of the book with an accolade in her letter to Enid:

Oh my dear, it couldn't be better. For no matter what one may say about Gollancz's advertising, he is a *very* important publisher, and may end by being a very great publisher indeed: for he has tremendous intelligence and really cares for literature. It's all my eye about thanking me for it. It was your own book and the goodness of it that made its own way. The terms seem to me very good indeed — so good (for a book of serious scholarship) that it shows he is really keen, and really believes in it . . . I am so happy, for I believe Gollancz in addition to being frightfully good at his job is absolutely *decent*, and I feel you are in *very* good hands.

So at long last, as Helen wrote to Meg, the starved cat had got her saucer of cream. But a mere saucerful was simply an appetizer: what did Helen think of the novel that Enid had submitted to her judgement? The novel was frankly autobiographical, and self-revelation irked Helen, who felt she was the last person to give an unbiased opinion. Even those who considered themselves close friends never pierced Helen's extreme reticence. She never attempted to keep a diary — the very thought of it, she explained to Enid, brought on a nightmare of self-consciousness. She often wished she had never written in her own name; journalists were always foiled of copy and one took his revenge with a large caption: 'Shy authoress outdoes Greta Garbo'. Apologizing for her clumsiness, she warned Enid in advance: 'I come to a friend's autobiography with dread, and unless the thing is like a formal dance — like Harold Nicolson's stuff — I grow embarrassed, almost as if I were reading the wretchedness of my own youth.' Disregarding that friend's petulance, Helen advised her to re-write the book without thought of publication, simply under the impulsion of spiritual necessity: to this she added an analysis of the novel's shortcomings:

> My dear, I never wanted you to make it a pretty book. My only plea is for economy. Over-emphasis dulls and destroys. You are always inclined to explain too much. It wearies the unintelligent and irritates the quick-witted.
>
> I suppose it is because Shakespeare explains so little that he provokes such reams of controversy. And speaking of Shakespeare, the thing I was pleading for wasn't sophistication or cheerfulness: it was that instead of publishing your *Titus Andronicus* you should discipline yourself into the economy of *Othello*:
>
> > 'Strike the *second* beat
> > Upon the Muses' anvil.'
>
> You know there is hardly any beauty in this book of yours at all. I don't mean beauty of writing — I mean the apprehension of beauty in the girl's heart: no sense — or little — of transport in music, of that tremendous overshadowing. I think that is why it seems to me a little unreal, once the obsession of reading it is past. . . . But there, don't take anybody's advice. Write it your own way, and be damned to the rest.

Ultimately 'A Lady's Child' dropped the fictional form and published the story of her youth as unvarnished autobiography under the Faber imprint in 1941. When the publication of *Peter Abelard* in 1933 made the name Helen Waddell known far and wide, Enid assured her that she would not become a parasite, 'one of the people that hang round'. To this, Helen replied: 'Don't hurt me. Surely at this time of day you and I know where we are with each other. To the end of time you will be the little creature in the white coat that waved a bunch of roses at me through the windows of the Pasteur, and I the so grateful rather haggard creature mouthing wordless thanks from the bed. Don't ever think of me as a "Success". It doesn't do anything to one's inside. Except, I think, to make you hold rather more to the people who had liked you before you had written, and were still afraid you might never write.' If ever anyone discharged a debt of gratitude with Gospel measure, it was Helen Waddell.

Whether she repudiated it or not, her novel was 'un succès fou' and she herself a celebrity. In his *Recollections*,* William Rothenstein recalls an invitation to luncheon which he issued to A.E. (George Russell) during one of the latter's visits to London. Helen Waddell would be there also, he added. A.E. promptly refused: every hostess in London, he explained, offered Helen as an attraction so that he was tempted to believe in a bevy of young women made to Helen's image, and sent out from a bureau to make parties specially attractive: 'I am going to tax Helen with her substitutes,' he told Rothenstein, 'but I suppose she has to get time to live and write. I am not trying to get out of meeting Helen, but I fear she may be sick of meeting me. I lunch with her on Thursday. At least, she has promised to be at Lady Londonderry's. I met her at G. B. Shaw's, Lady Ottoline Morrell's and at other places where she (or a substitute Helen) was the attraction. And of course I like to meet her.' That the most dormouse of mortals, as she called herself, had become a hardened diner-out and was rather enjoying it is clear from the letters to Meg giving the low-down on high life, much after the fashion of the schoolgirl writing to her wee Waddly from her uncle's imposing manse on the Antrim Road:

. . . The Rothensteins took me to the old Ranee of Sarawak (English — I suppose the only province where the Rajah is an Englishman) — a magnificent old pillar of 82, like Trilby grown old, and devilish witty; bolt upright in a high chair, no cushions, and an old butler calling her Your Highness. She was just foolish about *Abelard*, and also very flattering about my personal appearance: an irresistible combination. But oh, she likes oriental heat. Lady Rothenstein (who is a darling, like Alice-in-Wonderland grown stout) retired half-way through, took off her corsets, and hid them inside her fur coat. She showed them to me with a wide smile in the car afterwards. My fatigue was excessive: then lunch, a large party at the Blacketts', tea at Lady Ottoline Morrell's who has a kind of salon: full of large teeth, dark huge eyes and thin, but somehow lovable. A.E. was there and we almost huddled together.

As he had informed Sir William Rothenstein, A.E. did meet Helen at Lady Londonderry's. Accompanied by O.K. — like an ambassador

Since Fifty: Men and Memories 1922–1938 by William Rothenstein, Faber, 1939.

in tails — Helen arrayed in her best frock and green and silver shawl
arrived at Londonderry House for 'a small party':

> The first person I saw on the stairs was Neville Chamberlain, then the
> Londonderrys themselves, she looking about twenty-two, and once inside
> O.K. said 'There's Baldwin' — and I said 'There's Ramsay'. And I
> introduced him to Baldwin, and he introduced me to Ramsay MacDonald,
> who looked exhausted and sad but extraordinarily distinguished, and told
> me he had given away three copies of *Medieval Latin Lyrics*, and I promised
> him the *Scholars*. And Baldwin came over and said 'When am I going to see
> you?' . . . and told O.K. he'd never forget a letter he had written him. . . .
> And then Ramsay told O.K. that the Centenary Edition of the Scott
> Letters which was absolutely ruining Constable's is going to be financed
> by a colossally wealthy friend of his, for the honour of Scotland. So we
> came away on top of the world, and altogether I felt excessively important.

For a mediaeval scholar, a woman at that, to find favour with the
British Cabinet was no mean achievement, but Helen was to rise to
even dizzier heights when the Baldwins invited her to a luncheon
party at 10 Downing Street, to present her to Queen Mary who
wanted to meet her. Looking 'quite nice' so she told Meg, in a moss-
green frock, green amber beads, grey gauntlet gloves, a little grey hat,
and silver fox fur, she faced a battery of cameras as she walked up the
red carpet and took her seat between J. M. Barrie and the Governor of
the Bank of England. During coffee, Mrs Baldwin led her to the
Queen's sofa, to explain how she was attracted to the Middle Ages,
and to listen to the Queen's delightful chuckle as she tried to decline
mensa, only to stick fast half-way. Yet characteristically as she left the
awe and majesty of royalty and statecraft behind her, it was to the little
farm in County Down that Helen's thoughts reverted: 'Tell Daddy
from me,' she wrote to Meg, 'that I feel about him and Magherally as I
do about Stanley Baldwin and the Cabinet — and told him so today —
"Wherever the MacGregor sits, will be the head of the table".'

Beneath the brilliant banter and Irish wit, one ear was always
attuned to Kilmacrew, the other listening to the still, sad music of
humanity, the 'giant agony of the world' to which her letters so often
refer. Meg was the sole recipient of these deeper thoughts:

> Maybe if all this had happened to me younger, it would have 'changed me
> chemically'. But now, one knows when one finds 'the body's rest, the
> quiet of the heart,' and though you get frightfully bucked and all fizzy
> when things like this happen, it never seems to touch the inside of you. It's
> still true
>
>> 'Still to my brother turns with ceaseless pain
>> And drags at each remove a lengthening chain.'

At least, it isn't pain, it's only an ache of tenderness. Lord, but Goldsmith could write. We never did him justice in our youth.

And again:

Things are coming real to me that I never thought about much — why *in middle age* Job lost everything, his sons and his money and his health — till he could have prayed for death. You go up a hill when you're young, and then there's a kind of pleasant tableland, with grass and water and cornfields, and think you will go on walking into the westering sun. And then you find a precipice and a valley of dry bones — and if one looks for Him, I suppose, God
> 'remembering, where forgetfulness is blind,
> For ever pitiful, for ever kind.'

Of all the eminent litterateurs who met and admired Helen in the 1930s, the one who most closely shared her vision was A.E., her fellow-countryman. He had recognized and read into the history of Abelard and Heloise the story of his own life: his analysis of sin reads strangely like Evelyn Waugh's *Brideshead Revisited*:

. . . I began it with some terror for when I read the letters some thirty-five or forty years ago I was more moved by that love story than by any other, for I had in myself then an anguish of struggle between so rich and glowing a love and my longing for a spiritual life . . . and I dreaded to have a resurrection of that old battle in my heart. But I read on because I am old and knew I could not feel as I once did. I think your tale is most moving and beautifully imagined and told, and with many profundities and illuminations and intensities, as when Heloise tells Abelard:
'What we must not do is to pretend it is not a sin, and sprinkle it with holy water, and cover it up with holy words until it rots us.'
To speak like this is to speak out of a passionate wisdom which foresees the pit into which it is falling. We do foresee like that even when we go on as Heloise goes on to her destiny of love and agony.
We do go on to our martyrdoms knowing all the while in the spiritual part of us that we are marching to our crucifixion and by our own will, and there is another part of us which clutches at gallant straws as Heloise does when on the same page she would have her lover belong to 'the community of noble souls' and for herself she says her passion has burnt up heaven and earth into a glory and 'I know they are wrong St Paul or St James or whoever it was, and yet I know, I feel in my heart they are right.' And in that contradiction of faiths you are speaking out of profundities for we have moments when our dual nature holds up torches to light heaven and our sins, and imagines that in some ineffable way it may be that they will be finally reconciled, and our hope is for a wisdom which will

> Teach how the crucifix can be
> Carven from the laurel tree
> And Sappho lay her burning brows
> On white Cecilia's lap of snows.

I have not found you speaking anything through your characters which is not true to our triune nature in which body, soul and spirit cry each their own cry, and go their own way, and have no pity for each other.

This tall thin mystic and poet, who united Blake's apocalyptic fire with Teilhard de Chardin's vision of the living earth and Fritz Schumacher's practical zeal — he depicted the Prince-Archangel Michael standing above a man planting cabbages in a wet field, and pedalled up and down Ireland on an old bicycle, welcome and loved equally in presbytery, vicarage or manse, preaching his gospel of agricultural reform — was the only contemporary, in Helen Waddell's estimation, who made credible the legends of the saints. It was therefore ironical that when she published her *Beasts and Saints* in 1934, he met it with protest as well as praise:

> I like the Hermit's Garden & the Penitent Wolf: the ending of the last is beautiful, 'the power of Christ, with whom every brute beast is wise, and every savage creature gentle.' Your preface is very good Helen Waddell, & the decorations many of them admirable, like St Cuthbert and the Otters which suggests an ecstasy of spirit in a madness of nature; and I enjoy his dragons whether rampant as on p. 12, or repentant as on p. 23.

So much for the praise, but on another sheet of paper he adds advice: 'Get on with Heloise [she had told him she was already at work on a sequel to *Peter Abelard*], and don't think so much about saints. They don't bear looking into. The Irish bards said the saints told lies. "We, the Fianna, never told lies" said Usheen to Patrick — "and goodbye & victory & blessings be on you", as the old Irish used to say.'

Apologizing for his 'petulance about the saints. They are too much with us in Ireland, and I forget that elsewhere some might deserve the name,' he embellished his letter with a sketch in coloured chalks of a lion couchant on crimson and blue sand in a blaze of golden glory under a cloudless sky, above the caption: 'Lion meditating in desert, after partaking of a saint. Notice God-given halo. A.E.'

It was a drawing after Helen's own heart, for when preparing *Beasts and Saints* she had become so immersed in the behaviour of small animals and birds that, on reading of one of General Booth's revival meetings in Manchester, she had taken the report quite seriously for a moment when it stated that as his train steamed out, a large crow remained on the platform singing lustily, 'God be with you till we meet again!' Coming to herself, she suddenly realized that 'crow' was a printer's error — he had dropped the final 'd'.

'Get on with Heloise!' The words were an urgent summons to return to the task which only Helen Waddell could accomplish. In the context of his other letters to her, A.E. was implying that her duty was to obey the unknown deity within her own self, whose trumpet call sounded louder than any hollow blast of praise from men's mouths. True, her charming legends of the mutual charities between saints and beasts translated from Latin sources were shot through with her own particular brand of wisdom and scholarship, but she was seeking escape, frittering away her time and gifts. She, the artist, capable of brooding on the past until it sprang into life, of living into another's very being so that she experienced the 'life within the spirit crucified', possessed a talent which was death to hide.

He had warned her. He was to warn her again even more forcefully before the year was out. But his warnings went unheeded.

CHAPTER IX

─────────

IT SHOULD HAVE been a Virgilian Eclogue, it was in fact a satire of Horace that perfectly articulated Helen's secret longing, once she felt that her future as a writer was assured:

> Hoc erat in votis: modus agri non ita magnus,
> Hortus ubi et tecto vicinus iugus aquae fons
> Et paulum silvae super his foret —

This was translated sixteen hundred years later by Jonathan Swift into a verse that exactly expressed Helen's hopes in the King's English — Jonathan Swift whom she so much admired, who must often have passed very close to Kilmacrew House, as he rode from Kilroot to Dublin along the 'Broad Road' over the bridge across the Bann, the river which has given to the almost mediaeval little town of Banbridge its name, and to Kilmacrew its local habitation and postal address:

> I often wished that I had clear,
> For life, six hundred pounds a year,
> A handsome house to lodge a friend;
> A river at my garden's end,
> A terrace walk, and half a rood
> Of land set out to plant a wood.

But it was not Kilmacrew that Helen coveted: that was her Valley of Heart's Ease and it belonged essentially to Meg. She had dreamed of inheriting Ballygowan, the romantic two-storeyed property, contemporary of the seventeenth-century Westminster Assembly of Divines. After family litigation, it had been put up for sale, as Helen sadly told Dr Taylor in her letter of January 1918: 'I used to dream by the hour what I would do to Ballygowan. Did I tell you that the man who has bought it is one Cunningham, a Liverpool stevedore? He was brought up in a little cottier house nearly in sight of the trees of it: a Catholic: and made his fortune at the Liverpool docks. Heigh-ho. It's a sair doon-come for the old house.' Here, were it not to antedate their meeting by ten years, Thalia, Muse of Comedy, should lead on stage 'the wickedest caricaturist' of the century, the friend whom Helen was to nickname Petronius Arbiter, *alias* Max Beerbohm; gazing upon her out of two wide-apart blue eyes with childlike innocence and sympathy, his murmur would faintly echo her moan: 'O the disgrace of it — the scandal, the incredible come-down.'

The truth is that Helen's shadow-land contained but one house in which she ruled as sole mistress: Number 25 Nakano-cho, Azabu, Tokyo. It stood impregnable in the centre of all her memories of the past or visions of the future, even though it no longer existed. As early as 1925, when occupying rooms in St Edmund's Terrace rented from the stony-faced Medusa, she wrote to Meg:

> Yesterday I wished for you because I saw the big empty house at the corner overlooking Primrose Hill was let. 'Keys at Number 6' . . . It was awful pleasant wandering in and out of great empty shuttered rooms with a bunch of keys and no caretaker to fuss me. And one I saw such possibilities in — on the ground floor, once the drawing room: one window to the front into the street, two at the side into a great old conservatory-verandah with little wooden stairs to the garden, and the only way to the garden is through this room. Not much of one, just a sloping bank up to a wall, with a funny little summer-house, and shabby shrubs, but the remoteness of it, and the old verandah where you could dump things, and in the room a big fireplace for a real fire. Also a tiny kitchen about the size of a chobo, with a little gas cooker. I don't know price or anything, but I sat awhile on the verandah steps and invented freely. You know how I love something a wee bit queer. The conservatory opens the whole way along, with doors and windows, so that it is almost open air, and one could sleep there in summer. For a minute it was like Japan.

'It was like Japan.' A visiting missionary had once remarked of Helen's mother that she possessed a heart large enough to hold not merely her own ten children but a whole presbytery besides. She must have bequeathed that heart to her babe for, as soon as Helen had a little money in her purse, she yearned for a house of her own, situated neither in Tokyo nor Belfast but in London where, like Samuel Johnson, she found all that life could afford. There the nephews and niece who, as children, had discovered Pharaoh's palace in the white beehive and Abraham's tent in an umbrella, should always find a warm hearth, a hospitable board, and a roof. It might well have remained the stuff that dreams are made of but for the unforeseen intervention of Helen's landlord. As the house in Ormonde Terrace was to be demolished and replaced by a block of modern flats, he gave his tenants notice to quit in the spring of 1934. Helen had no option but to find quarters elsewhere. She had been happy in Ormonde Terrace as never before: her little flat was ideal, for it provided an excellent housekeeper, Mrs Beney; gave her unbroken privacy for her scholarly work; and could supply no spare beds for would-be guests. For six years her literary output had been prodigious, she had won laughter and the love of friends, and had been accorded academic recognition. In May 1931, robed in scarlet with gold hood and black velvet cap, amid the pomp and splendour of a Cathedral that reminded her of Chartres, she had received from Durham University the degree of D.Litt.; in September 1932, she was made an Associate Member of the Irish Academy of Letters; in July 1934 her own University of Queen's, Belfast, conferred on her an honorary degree in the presence of Stanley Baldwin, saluting her with loud acclamation as Ulster's Darling, and the most distinguished woman of her generation. There was not a University or College that did not clamour for her to give lectures, and a reviewer in *Punch* applied to her in life the 'Nullum quod tetigit non ornavit' — he touched nothing that he did not adorn — that Samuel Johnson had taken from Fénélon on Cicero, and given as epitaph to Oliver Goldsmith. If ever fame seemed assured, it was hers.

Meg, who knew her as no one else did, saw in her sister two Helens: one of the head, the other of the heart. They were in frequent conflict but, in the immediate crisis of house-hunting, heart gave head no quarter. Helen refused to listen to reason. Her inner eye had always registered the demi-paradise of her childhood's home with map-like distinctness, and she now travelled the streets of North-West London until she found some seeming reflection of both Nakano-cho and Kilmacrew in No. 32 Primrose Hill Road; she decided on the spot that she must make it her own. Family and friends unanimously disapproved. A stern Maude Clarke prophesied that if she burdened herself with the upkeep of a large house with an ever-open door, she could bid farewell to scholarship: she would never again produce any 'truly great' work. Ignoring all appeals to common sense, Helen went straight ahead and, in the spring of 1934, purchased the house on a thirty-years' lease, accepting as part of the fixtures the two Quakers, Dorothy Matthews and Florence Surfleet, who occupied a self-contained flat on the top floor, ate neither milk nor eggs, taught English in their rooms to foreign students, and were to prove a handicap during the War — but not for anything would Helen have evicted 'the Little Ladies' as she called them. She also had plans to give a home to Rosamund Tweedy who, like herself, had been forced to leave No. 3 Ormonde Terrace.

In the early summer months her niece Mollie, newly graduated from Trinity College, Dublin, left Kilmacrew to help Helen settle in: she was to remain with her aunt and work in England for the next eight years. As soon as she recovered her wits and strength Helen wrote to Meg a letter that already strikes an ominous note:

> I have been so rushed and kind of sleepless and dazed, I have just let the days go by. The house is a dear, a little like Killy in its ring of quiet trees, and I am afraid the same queer power of absorbing: but indeed when one sleeps in a different room every night, thanks to painters and joiners still in, it does leave one a little woozy. Mollie an absolute darling, don't know what I would have done without her . . . .
>
> We only want one thing — Momma here — I am just dying to have you over to see it all. Builders and painters due for another month, I'm afraid. O.K.'s Mrs Reynolds comes and helps — awful happy that he is coming here, for she says he wasn't fit to live alone in that flat. The poor dear came for one night to sleep in a bare room on a makeshift bed — just Sunday night, on his way back from Savernake — and adored it so he asked to stay on, never slept so well for years. So he encamps upstairs with crumbs of furniture stolen from Rosamund and me, and is as gay as Wuffles. Brice Clarke here and full of advice about garden — and altogether we are having the time of our lives: only as I have been trying to do that Introduction in odd hours, I got a head like a hot oven, and have just finally given it up until next week. . . .
>
> I am taking darling garden room after all, with bathroom next door — couldn't sleep in large dining room on street for anything — it was like the Euston Hotel somehow, not too noisy but very public, so given it to the Beneys. Now I shall have French window from bedroom leading to rose arch into garden, like lady in picture book.
>
> But *wait* till you come.

So Otto Kyllmann had exchanged the 'dear little flat' in Newman Street for an even dearer one on the first floor of No. 32 Primrose Hill Road. Helen's letter to Basil Blackett of the previous year spoke of love as the richest thing in life. 'Think for a moment', she urged, 'what it would be like if you weren't sure you were loved. That is the real torture. And that is what happens to Heloise at the last.' Had it happened or would it happen to the Heloise who was herself? Even though it cannot be resolved, the doubt will not be silenced. No one acquainted with both ever questioned the deep bond between them, and if O.K. was as 'monumentally selfish' as Ralph Arnold made him out, then the gentle loyalty and even heroic self-sacrifice of his last years were to make ample amends. From the first, he had admired Helen's genius, and loved her personality — but so did countless others. Was he ever 'in love' with her as she undeniably was with him? True love discerns the whole person. Had he wanted nothing but her welfare even at the cost of his own happiness, could he have walked into her house so complacently, settled down for ever and aye, and thus subjected her not only to what she herself described as lifelong frustration and the torture of self-denial, but to the inevitable innuendoes of gossip, mistaken though it was? Johnson's advice to young Hester Thrale in 1784 is valid for all time: 'In matters of human judgement and prudential consideration, consider the public voice of general opinion as always worthy of great attention.' Even though Helen refused to attend to it, O.K. should have done so.

A.E., one of Helen's first guests, sipping coffee with her in the garden, met her raptures with a prophecy of doom: 'You'll never be able to work again. The roof will leak, the bath taps will drip. Nobody who works with their head should ever acquire property or possessions, they should live out of a suitcase. You watch, or you will become nothing but a handshake and a brilliant talker, like James Stephens — that was what ruined him.' Mollie, who lived in the house for years and had an unrivalled knowledge of its workings, has described it:

> It was an ill-planned Victorian monster, and hard to run: but with its big rooms, lovely curving staircase and wrought iron balusters, there was a graciousness about it and we all lived in great comfort. In the early years Helen and I colour-washed the garden walls a gay tangerine, and planted rambler roses all round. It was no use as a flower garden. The cold London clay and generations of cats had seen to that; but there were two almond trees, a soft green acacia, a tall pear, a purple-leaved plum, and two enormous crimson hawthorns at the foot of the garden. The neighbours' flowering trees also hung over the walls and, except in winter, other houses were barely visible. In spring there was a secret enchantment about it, with drifts of crocuses and daffodils under the dark of the hawthorns, and the almonds heading the succession of flowering trees.

Whatever its many disadvantages, the house never ceased to charm its owner, who loved the gentle spaciousness, quiet wide hall, and its friendly shabby peace. An undated letter to Stanley Baldwin opens: 'Sunday, at 9.15. I have just heard that the hump in the middle of Primrose Hill is an old grave mound, and that this was Barrow Hill on the oldest maps till the romantic sixteenth century called it Primrose Hill: but we still have a little slum called Barrow Hill Road. This pleases me foolishly.' Especially in her letters to Meg, beneath the rhapsodies there runs the recurrent ground bass of Ballygowan and Tokyo:

> I am so well again and the garden so like old Ballygowan. Oh darling, there was a sound like the wings of wild geese the other morning about sunrise, and I began thinking of you, and of the old Japanese lyric of exile:

'No messengers there are,
I shall have gone so far,
But when you hear the crane
Cry unto them my name
For they my heralds are—'
and I sent that cry to you.

She was to push her desires to the limit of wanting to reproduce in
Primrose Hill the sanitation of Nakano-cho: 'I am all for an outside
closet—what about that secluded corner beyond the tomato house—
Japan taught us its charms, I think. Do you remember Adela Fachiri
saying that when she was five, it was the only place where she could be
alone to think about God? This was in the middle of a large dinner party
and I think I was the only one not to be embarrassed, for it was so
profoundly natural.' The Hungarian violinist was in good company,
for the boy Augustine found it the ideal spot to sing psalms at the top of
his voice, much to the discomfiture of his mother Monica.

Meg, Clerk of the Works as always, had not yet seen the house, and
Helen's cries rang over the mountains and sea that divided the two until,
in August 1934, as soon as the place was fairly habitable, Meg arrived
for a holiday. It was not to be. She collapsed almost immediately with a
strained heart, was dangerously ill for a time, and had to remain under
Helen's care until May of the following year. In addition to nursing an
invalid, Helen had now to cope with endless domestic problems as well
as with requests for reviews, lectures, articles and the like. One of the
most important came from Edward K. Rand, Professor of Latin at
Harvard. His *Founders of the Middle Ages*, a seminal and influential study,
first issued by Harvard in 1928, naturally found a ready English
publisher in Constable where Helen's influence was paramount. The
two mediaevalists became firm friends. He now wondered why Helen
had refused to review F. J. E. Raby's two volume *Secular Latin Poetry*,
just issued by the Clarendon Press that had published the same author's
Christian Latin Poetry in 1927. In the Preface to *Allegory of Love* (1936),
C. S. Lewis would salute 'Mr Raby's great works' as a mine of easily and
pleasurably acquired knowledge of Latin poetry; later on in the book,
he would invite the reader to compare his account of Bernard Sylvestris
'with the equally favourable, but differently directed, account of Miss
Waddell, who touches nothing which she does not adorn'. If there are
seven types of ambiguity, that exemplifies one of them. Helen's reply to
E. K. Rand is dated 18 November 1934:

. . . I am terribly rushed and a little distraught—my only sister, Denise in
Abelard, is with me, in bed with a sudden and nasty heart, and likely to be

there for months; and it just happened when the good little Sussex woman who had looked after me for eight years had had to leave me and go to her own people. She — my sister — is really recovering, but it is a slow and very up and down convalescence.

About Raby: he is youngish — I suppose about 40–45: a very good Civil Servant, and a friend of Stephen Gaselee: thoroughly decent and pains-taking, and in himself, I think, gentle and generous. But of a dullness——. This is piggy of me, but with you, I do like a sense of humour and humanity in handling medieval stuff. I was asked to review it here, but it was again in the height of my domestic worries, and after hovering over the 2 volumes for some time, I felt I could not face it.

It will, I think, be a kind of Companion to Medieval Studies, and he was right to give the originals (I say this, even though I *like* my own translations): in fact, I believe he has sometimes used stuff that is very inaccessible: like the Spanish-Latin things which I could not myself get in the Brit. Mus.

Another reason why I didn't want to review him is that he has always been extremely kind in reviewing me: because he does himself like to be made to laugh, and he does really like my translations. But I never find his judgements illuminating, and I don't think he is a good critic, though he knows a great deal.

I had your two articles before me for delight, though yesterday's visitor Sir Basil Blackett carried them off with him. He has just published a glorious translation of Damian's *De Gloria Paradisi* which I send you.

A letter to Stanley Baldwin on 10 January 1935, speaks more cheerfully of Meg's progress. To comfort Helen, he had sent her the gift of a book which elicited a characteristic response:

This that you sent me almost broke my heart, at first for the courage, the terrible courage of the letters: and then for the transporting beauty of *The Halcyon*. Transport in the literal sense, for one's heart goes out of one's body. . . .

It came singularly home to me, even though the sister I told you of has only been on her back three months instead of seven years. . . . It was years and years ago that I thought of her as if touching her was touching an apple tree with the sun on it — that you feel the kindness of the earth. Only apple trees ought not to be sent to bed for months. Anyhow, she is getting better.

I am sending you prose for your verse — a play that my brother wrote after the troubles in Ireland. He was in the Irish Land Commission, so saw plenty of it. And the agony in Ireland after the agony in Europe suddenly made him write this — though he had done only comedy before.

Do you remember the speech you made about two years ago — the bomb that need be only the size of a walnut? I remembered it — reading this.

My love and duty,
H.W.

Perhaps owing to Meg's quiet but steadying influence, Helen settled down to really solid work again during the months of her sister's convalescence, and was soon immersed in translations from the literature of the early anchorites of the Egyptian desert: their doings and sayings were excellent invalid fare. In the early months of 1935, her play of 1933, *The Abbé Prévost*, again surfaced and despite Bernard Shaw's doubts was to be given a London production. On 29 April 1935, Helen wrote to Stanley Baldwin:

> My dear S.B.,
>
> Do you remember a small play of mine, *The Abbé Prévost*? It is at last finding a small lodging in the Arts Theatre, the first night the 19th of May, which is a Sunday, comes on, I think, about nine o'clock.
>
> You know that I would be happy if you were there, but I am not going to ask you to add one more to your fatigues. *But* I am going to keep two seats, on the bare chance. You know that I shall have no 'feelings' if you say right off that it's out of the question. Otherwise I shall keep on hoping.
>
> Columbia (this is still confidential) is giving me a D.Litt. on June 4th, and fetching me by the Berengaria and returning me by the Aquitania. Very expensive for them, but very agreeable for me. I sail on the 22nd, just three nights after the play comes on.
>
> Anyhow, whether you are there or not, burn a kind of candle for the Abbé.
>
> Yours always,
> Helen.

When the curtain of Drury Lane Theatre fell on the first perform-ance of Charles Lamb's play *Mr H——* in December 1806, the audience rose to a man and hissed — 'Damn 'em, how they hissed!' Helen's audience was kinder: for hisses, they returned kisses and prolonged applause. The *Observer* next day was as kind as could be, the *Daily Sketch* said that the emotional highlights got across the footlights very nicely, all hoped the play would reach a wider public — and so the funeral service was decently concluded. The *Abbé Prévost* was as dead as Mr H——. Undeceived but not unduly dispirited, Helen was preoccupied with Meg's recovery and her own imminent departure for New York. From a letter sent to Meg on her return to Kilmacrew, it would seem that the collapse in August 1934 had been psychosomatic in origin: Helen was having to deal with mental stress. She did it with her usual deep compassion and spiritual directness:

> I wish sometimes you would cut the moral 'austere man' aspect of God out of your mind, and accustom yourself to a more wayside God, a man that other men wanted to go along with, before they thought of their sins or repentance. Did you ever think that St John never said, 'He that is chaste

dwelleth in God, and God in him.' It was, 'He that loveth dwelleth in God.' A grievance is a kind of cancer of the heart. . . . Darling, I have so marvelled at you all these years, not only your courage, but your soundness and sweetness. Don't let the dark tide that is in us all, of littleness against man and God, come any higher, and don't constrict God's infinity of kindness by making bargains with him.

The ten months' treatment at 32 Primrose Hill Road sent Meg back to Ireland renewed in health and spirits so that Helen was able to leave for New York free from anxiety. A single short letter to Kilmacrew, written on hand-made grey stationery adorned with the letterhead, 'Cunard White Star   On Board *Berengaria*' shows the traveller revelling in the liner's luxury, the seeming miles of glass-walled deck, the old rose tapestries of a lounge covering acres of ground and, above all, the vastly-agreeable companionship of the Scot Muir of Powallen and Sir Henry Barraclough — quickly abbreviated to Barry — a man with 'J.D.'s slow malice and extreme detachment so that he is the most agreeable exercise I have met for a very long time'. Upon arrival in New York, feeling 'a very dead little dog' after a late night of festivity, she went straight to her hostess, Virginia Gildersleeve, Dean of Barnard College, and from there sent Meg her reactions:

The Dean is a darling, huge dark eyes put in with a smutty finger, half French, and very entertaining. She is giving a dinner party for me tonight but left me in great peace yesterday. . . . The sultry airless damp heat almost makes one's lungs labour in breathing. It fell on us coming up the river, a fog as well, so that New York rose like a Byzantine island (it's like Paris, the kernel of the whole city with the river meeting at the prow), and the incredible skyscrapers looked in the mist like campaniles: in fact my first impression of New York was an island of ancient churches with high bell towers: and the sun flecked through the mist, and you saw the queer roofs gleam like the greenish bronze that you see on Notre Dame. I can't but love the place, when you read inscriptions like 'the people of New York, by the grace of God free and independent' — and old Grant's mausoleum, round and squat, on a bluff above the river, with for sole inscription about the doorway, 'Let us have peace'. You can't but love them — even the Customs man who spied the *Patrologia*, flung his arms above his head and said: 'Shut them all up — *You'll* do no harm!'

My D.Litt. gown is exactly what they want: their own hood is white velvet lined with black and bordered with the same blue as I have on my vermilion and white: so as Virginia says, it was evidently predestined. The whole ceremony takes place in the open air, on the steps outside the old library, which once was King's College founded by George II. They can't get a building large enough to house the crowd. The procession comes out of the library down a long flight of stone steps and out on to a terrace made wider by a wooden stage — and there the Senate and the graduates sit, with old Murray Butler★ in front of a gold statue of Alma Mater. It is a far cry from Durham Cathedral, but it is terribly exciting.

Even in the United States of America,

> 'The best laid schemes o' mice an' men
> Gang aft a-gley.'

On 5 June Helen had to report:

Everything went wrong yesterday — the rain poured, no procession through the campus, 30,000 people turned away. 4,800 graduating infants crowded into very hot gymnasium: the senate and non-doctors led through the bowels of the earth, with miles of hot-water pipes (this on a wilting day), and shepherded up to a hastily improvised platform. There was only myself in scarlet, Murray Butler in grey and red (Oxford D.Litt.) everybody else in black with hoods barring the Archbishop, who was in purple — very stately — he asked to be introduced and said how he loved my books. I stood up and had a little speech made to me, and being the only woman the audience was very hearty, and the two marshals (who stand between the victims and hang the hood like a halter over their heads at the exact moment of reception) stood behind me. And when I got back to my seat through a general racket my cap fell off, after which the audience gathered me to its heart and yelled.

Three more days of sight-seeing, cocktail parties, theatre and dinners culminated in a kind of harlequinade, when 'Barry' and she agreed to act upon Swinburne's

> A little while, a little love
> The hour still holds for thee and me,
> Who have not drawn the veil to see
> If yet the heavens are lit above.

We set off, down down through Central Park in an amazing sunset, with all the western side of those lovely terrible Babylonish buildings one glory, and then to the Plaza, where Barry had not been since the war. And then had cocktails, and then down on to the Rainbow Roof of the Radio City Buildings, 80 storeys up and dinner somewhere in the sky above New York — all mist and light at our very feet. It was the kind of place where you dance in between the soup and and fish — so we dined and danced there till midnight, and then on to the Casino — the Folies Bergères straight from Paris (very wicked but extremely lovely in places) — and long intervals for dancing. And there we danced till three . . . And so miles back to the Deanery, and walk for a while under the moonlight there

★Nicholas Murray Butler, President of Columbia University.

in the Dean's garden, and a farewell worthy of Verona. (So like me, as Barry said next day, to bring the Romeo and Juliet madness upon a respectable Dean of Engineering in the garden of the Dean of a Women's College.) . . . As I pointed out to him earlier, there is a kind of curious delight in the 'without tomorrow, without yesterday' — and I recalled enough of my mathematics to remind him of those curves that meet only once and are called — can't you still see the gleam in Mr Harvey's eye? — 'osculating circles'.

With many a last goodbye and a feeling that all the bubbles in the champagne were suddenly gone, Helen boarded the *Aquitania* on 8 June and sailed at midnight for home. On the way she wrote to Meg: 'I've been writing a long queer poem on New York. I don't know if it is good or not. I must wait till the New York fever dies out before I can judge it. The Building I speak of at the last is Cornell Medical School and Hospital, about the most beautiful thing I've seen, barring the greater cathedrals.' The poem, issued by the Greg-y-nog Press in a limited edition of 350 copies with a woodcut engraving by Stefan Mrozewski on 5 December 1935, has always been a rarity. It opens with a visionary New York, seen in terms of the tiny island village of Torcello, *Venice antica*, where Helen gathered violets and samphire to send to George Saintsbury in 1921: as the *Berengaria* docked in 1935, the skyscrapers rose like the campanile of the twelfth-century church of Sta Fosca, and the ruined cathedral of Sta Maria Assunta with its ninth-century baptistry and Byzantine mosaics:

New York City
The presence that so strangely rose beside the waters.
   Torcello with its single campanile
Above black thorn and salt lagoon
Multiplied in the mist.
Island of stooping bell-towers, Holy Island,
Not Cuthbert's Lindisfarne,
Set in the grey Northumbrian sea
Where men so valiant and so great lights of the Church
   Lie and take their rest.
Not Lindisfarne, and yet a holy island
Prester John might have builded, if he had chosen
To take his kingdom west instead of east.
Byzantium with Christ an emperor.
Byzantium not any more a ghost.

The Berengaria *will dock at six.*

The whole poem is a fascinating blend of biblical reference, classical and mediaeval allusion, historical watchword and contemporary slogan, a map of Helen's mind as she surveyed the American scene.

Helen had left America with a deep love of both the country and its people, but she never returned. The English and History Faculty of Columbia invited her to go as visiting Professor, and the Medieval Academy was to honour her with election to a Fellowship, but she was already working on a study of the Desert Fathers, planned a book on John of Salisbury, and the figure of Heloise as a sequel to *Peter Abelard* was always floating in the background: lecturing absorbed time and energy that she could ill afford, and so she refused the tempting offers. By the time she reached Primrose Hill, cut the grass, put up a sweet-pea trellis, emptied a sack of soot and pounds of naphthaline over a plague of black slugs, dealt with a backlog of work at Constable's, wrote ninety letters, and despatched half a dozen MSS, she was ready to acknowledge that life had resumed its rural and domestic routine. Not long afterwards, Macmillan the publisher asked for details of her connection with America. 'It's odd', she wrote to Meg, 'how close that connection was when America was young. And for myself — the Americans who taught us at Torizake, and kind Mrs Large and Kate at Karuizawa, not to speak of our own kin, and the American University Women's Club in 16 rue de Chevreuse, and the Livingstone Lowes and E. K. Rand, and Murray Butler at Columbia, and my New York revels and Virginia Gildersleeve: and the fellowship of the Medieval Academy of America.'

In spite of the heat-wave that greeted Helen on her return from New York, she hoped to get through 'long, long swathes' of work, but as so often, her hopes were dashed. On 15 August, Basil Blackett driving to Heidelberg to give a lecture at the University collided with a train at a level crossing and was killed. In the same month, Helen wrote to Meg:

> I put off writing to you last week because I was a little distracted and sad. A.E. is very ill, and it is incurable. I went down to the nursing home at Bournemouth yesterday with O.K. He wasn't able to see O.K., and me only for about two minutes, but he had begged to see me. Very thin and waxen, and strangely young. The surgeon said that he told A.E. before he operated that it would be only temporary. A.E. never moved a muscle, or flickered: he discussed the whole thing as tranquilly as if it were the tilling of a field. . . . The surgeon was so shattered by the sheer saintliness that he had to make some excuse and leave him, or he'd have broken down.
>
> And darling, Maude is to die too. She doesn't know in how many months: but when she left Oxford at the end of the summer term she knew

it was for the last time. She wanted no one to know, because it was easier to pretend it was neuritis, and not have the goodbyes. Don't say anything about it, for probably she is not telling anybody at home except her father.

O let's be thankful for the people we have still left us, and for darlings like Mollie and the boys, and that we have each other. I'm working manfully at the Fathers, and very peaceful. The garden is dishevelled but lovely — all marigolds and stocks. The sweet-pea did no good at all, but the antirrhinums and the Canterbury bells flowered superbly. The trees just stand keeping on their feet round the garden, all in a trance of heat, and the marigolds and nasturtiums blaze.

Dearest, I couldn't write to you about A.E. and Maude at first. I told A.E. I would never be without him —

'Light in valley . . . the twilight air
That has made anchorites of kings.'

Before the month of August was out, A.E. was dead. Helen's undivided attention was then given to Maude whose loss would prove a loss in life as well as in love. She went up to Oxford as often as possible and, filled though her days were, found time to meet Enid Starkie's loud complaints of being refused admission to see Maude, with frequent letters of comfort: 'I know. Three times I have *resented* death, as you do for Maude. It's not that I think eternity isn't much catch, but this particular piece of it one can only have once, and not to have it in its entirety seems to be incomplete. Yet — "Ripeness is all" — and she goes out with incredible richness.'

Towards September, Maude's grief-stricken father, Canon Clarke, saw his only daughter return to spend her last days in her own home. Just as once the two collaborators, Elizabeth and 'the Egyptian', had sharpened one another's wits as they sat in Larne on the Antrim coast gazing over the Irish Sea, so now Helen sat by Maude's side in Coole Glebe as they looked across the Lough and beyond the delicate sea-coast of the Ards to what Catherine of Siena has called the 'Sea Pacific' of God's immensity and eternity. 'She is profoundly at peace,' Helen wrote to Enid. 'It is like the going out of the tide, with the gentleness of heaven on the sea. I do not know if you had gathered that even before her final operation God had become the ultimate reality, after years of agnosticism. So that Fate cannot harm her.' Maude Clarke died on 17 November 1935. Helen's deeply-felt and exquisite tribute in *The Times* of 25 November 1935, ends with a sentence which, she said, summed up her whole reaction to the death of the woman who was her dearest friend from girlhood: 'That she should die at her meridian, with a single sickle in the standing corn and all that vintage yet unharvested, is to make death eloquent of the life everlasting.'

Everlastingness, infinity, eternity — these concepts were woven inextricably into the pattern of H.W.'s thought and conduct. One recalls Mr Harvey's 'sinful little vagabond' so enthralled by the mystery and wonder of infinity revealed by her study of Pure Mathematics that she decided the subject should be made compulsory for any student proceeding to Divinity; or the undergraduate refusing to alter a prayer she had written for the Girls' Auxiliary: 'I did not change the prayer beginning, "Thy eternity dost ever besiege our life"; I wanted to hammer into the brain of your working class girl some idea of eternity, if it were only the beauty of the word. For to get any conception of infinity is like taking the stone off the mouth of a well.' Again, when Meta Fleming died, and the alabaster box full of sweet spices was poured out, Helen asked the question, 'To what purpose is this waste?' in order to answer it with the truth that she herself so clearly apprehended: 'The end is not yet. One comes back to the wisdom of the Middle Ages — *Mors janua vitae*, Death the gate of Life. We believed in the life everlasting: but into the like everlasting we have come to read the life eternal, life infinite in its breadth and length and depth and height.' She had already begun to envisage a book on the Middle — not Dark — Ages, 'clear and fine and high, like cliffs and sea in the sun. I think what I covet most in the Middle Ages,' she told Meg, 'is that absolute conviction that God was the King Eternal, Immortal, Invisible, and that the Judge of all the earth would do right.' It might be said that the text she has quoted from 1 Timothy 1:17 provided her with the motif of a substantial part of her future work. The opening pages of *The Wandering Scholars* plunge into the two mighty observers of mighty things, Augustine and Boethius, breaking their minds upon eternity, and the first page of the first chapter discusses 'the sense that besieges every gate and inlet . . . that leaves St Paul beating about for words of length and breadth and depth and height, stumbling on the threshold of the fourth dimension, the *tanto oltraggio*, the mighty outrage on the experience of the human mind of Dante's final ecstasy.'

This seed of a lifetime's contemplation of eternity had almost certainly been sown as early as 1897 in the mind of an eight-year-old Helen, cradled in the knobbly boughs of a maple tree through which she could see nothing but young green leaves etched against a blue sky. She had just learned the whole of Hebrews by heart, and there could sit and ponder over the strange refusal of sunlight and trees, and choice of torture, death and resurrection. As time went on, the seed flowered attractively in *The Wandering Scholars* with the companion lyrics, and *Peter Abelard*, but did not yield its ripe fruit until the

publication of *The Desert Fathers* in 1936. What had hitherto been no
more than dark hints and shrouded intimations of a 'discord in the pact
of things', that called for a reconciliation between life's immensities
and littlenesses, was brought out and unfolded and examined in the
uncluttered sands of the desert under a burning sun. In a sense
therefore she had been working on the book all her life, although she
herself traces its genesis to the year 1920:

> I first came to the *Vitae Patrum* sixteen years ago, not for its own sake, but
> in a plan I had of reading for myself, with a mind emptied, what the
> ordinary medieval student would have read, to find the kind of furniture
> his imagination lived among. It held me then, as now, with its strange
> timelessness. I began a translation of it, continued at intervals in the years
> since. . . . This selection, fragmentary and arbitrary, represents that part
> of the desert teaching most alien and most sovereign in a world that has
> fallen to the ancient anarchs of cruelty and pride.

Beasts and Saints had been a playful illustrative prelude, so to say, but
The Desert Fathers is in a category all by itself: some would claim that it
is Helen's greatest work. Graham Greene has observed that his most
penetrating critics are Marxists and Catholics. In 1936, Hilaire Belloc
and G. K. Chesterton (whom Helen had met in 1932) commended
The Desert Fathers in terms of the highest praise. 'When three qualities,
scholarship in a foreign language, especially in the language of
antiquity, prose style of the highest sort, and full commentary meet,
you get something quite by itself,' Belloc wrote. 'It is not once in fifty
years of a national literature that the combination is found.' Constable
inserted a large notice in *The Tablet* of 24 October quoting various
appraisals, and appending a piquant footnote in italic to say that the
work had been chosen by the Spiritual Book Associates of America
and would be issued with the Cardinal's imprimatur — the Cardinal
was unspecified. The review in the *Manchester Guardian* concluded:
'One naturally is hesitant about declaring boldly that the Introduction
is the most revealing piece of writing about the Desert Fathers for
many hundreds of years, but it is a judgement which time may very
probably endorse.'

One is driven to ask the same question about *The Desert Fathers* as
about *The Wandering Scholars* — what precisely makes it remarkable?
After all, the nine men she mentions in her Preface surpassed her in
learning; her skill as translator had worthy competitors; as a writer of
English prose she had rivals — even though Belloc, himself a master,
having first saluted her as an 'excellent writer' deliberately corrected
'excellent' to 'great'. To read Helen's thirty-page Introduction and her

commentary to each of the ten sections that comprise the book must be a deep spiritual experience for any Christian, and at least an aesthetic one for others. The thought and language are so perfectly wedded that the prose glows with an inward life all its own, and to those acquainted with the writer's own future, there are times when it becomes almost unbearably poignant and prophetic. It is as if Helen Waddell were unconsciously proclaiming: 'I have seen the truth and can speak the living words which are born of having seen it.'

A biography cannot embrace a detailed critical analysis but must content itself with one or two examples. The germ of many of the book's most striking passages lies in Helen's letters written to Meg while she was working on the text. Dealing for instance with the anchorite's delusion that solitude is peace, 'To be alone to the alone' — *solus ad solum* — she observes that this supreme temptation of the saint, the artist and the lover only makes articulate the sighing of the human heart in a clattering world. It may be profoundly true of the first encounter of the soul and God, but it is not true of the ultimate adoration that burns up all consciousness of the self:

> The truth is that solitude is the creative condition of genius, religious or secular, and the ultimate sterilising of it. No human soul can for long ignore 'the giant agony of the world' and live, except indeed the mollusc life, a barnacle upon eternity. No artist ever desired the soundless world more fervently than the younger Keats: it is as though he foresaw the baptism wherewith he was to be baptised, and shuddered from it. *Lear* haunted him: 'Do you not hear the sea?' The black moods in which 'Poetry, Ambition and Love' passed by him with averted face, when the creation of beauty seemed to him an impertinence in the face of anguish, and a poet's coronation an outrage in a world 'where women have cancers', these are barren for the craftsman, but the matrix of the supreme artist.

She concludes with a quotation from Keats's sonnet:
> 'The moving waters at their priestlike task
> Of pure ablution round earth's human shores,
where every word is an abyss of human experience.'

Shortly after Sir Basil Blackett's death, she wrote to Meg a species of meditation on Christian love, occasioned by the thought of Basil's widow, Beatrice, now left solitary: the very phrases Helen employs may be paralleled in the *Scholars* and *The Desert Fathers* — she is all of a piece:

> I made O.K. go away to Savernake, just to sleep and slump, and stayed here the way I'm used to do, and reflected how lucky beyond all women

we are to be so fond of each other. I thought of poor Beatrice alone in that Chinese puzzle of a flat, and reproached myself for ever grousing about her passion for companionship. And in short, for ever grousing about anything.

Because if one loves, one really isn't lonely: it is the unloving heart that is always cold, and has no fire to warm itself at. 'Beloved, let us love one another, for love is of God: and he that loveth is born of God, *and knoweth God.*' Don't tell me there are theological explanations of it — that the love must be 'in Christ'. He that loveth . . . knoweth God. Which means that it is when one's heart goes out to anything, it is, in that moment, close to God. And what if it were really true, that the power at the back of all this cruel universe were love. Love as we know it. It's no wonder Dante said, when he saw that vision of 'love that moves the sun and the stars', that it was *tanto oltraggio* — a kind of outrage on his being. For to come within the least whisper of it is to leave one gasping.

It is good to be alone like this, for when kindly talkative people are moving about, and Rosamund trampling upstairs, one stays in a carpeted room, with a ceiling and pictures and a ticking clock, and plays patience. But to know that I'll be alone till O.K. comes back from Savernake tomorrow evening, to know that gives one a kind of key to space.

Only I must not think of all the lonely women in the world, or one would never do a stroke of work again, but go round with a chirping voice in and out of all the boarding houses. Let's hope very few of them have our kind of imagination.

I begin to see what happened to Abelard, when he saw that the Holy Ghost was love, and that the whole world lay in it, moved by it, the love of God the Father and God the Son.

Darling, one writes it, and it is trite — the familiar commonplace that we've heard from our cradles. But if ever one comes within its breath, it is so terrible that one almost looks about for familiar little shelters of noises and buses to shut out the stars. 'There shall no man see Me and live.'

And so the Son of Man comes eating and drinking, it being the only way in which human beings can endure to apprehend God.

I think when I come to write the new Abelard, I shall have to send O.K. away for a lot of week-ends.

Monday

I stopped there, for I was getting tired. Reading this through, it seems trite and worn. It is no wonder the Fathers could never get into words their times of vision. But by the time it comes into *Abelard*, it may have found some way of getting down on paper.

St Antony, called the father of monks and prince of solitaries, declared, 'With our neighbour is life and death.' If then the love of God is best expressed in love of men for God's sake, what was the legacy of the Desert Fathers in their solitude? H.W. replies:

One intellectual concept they did give to Europe: eternity. Here again, they do not formulate it: they embody it. These men, by the very exaggeration of their lives, stamped infinity on the imagination of the West. They saw the life of the body as Paulinus saw it, a shadow at sunset. 'The spaces of our human life set over against eternity' — it is the undercurrent of all Antony's thought — 'are most brief and poor.'

> 'Think you the bargain's hard, to have exchanged
> The transient for the eternal, to have sold
> Earth to buy heaven?'

And paradoxical as it seems, their denial of the life of earth has been the incalculable enriching of it. . . . They thought to devaluate time by setting it over against eternity, and instead they have given it an unplumbed depth. It is as though they first conceived of eternity as everlastingness, the production to infinity of a straight line, and in time men came to know it vertical as well as horizontal, and to judge an experience by its quality rather than its duration. The sense of infinity is now in our blood: and even to those of us who see our life as a span long, beginning in the womb and ending in the coffin or a shovelful of grey ash, each moment of it has its eternal freight.

This is no mere theorizing, for she was writing to Meg about the same time:

I'm still so far behind with the Saints — this last spell of worry nearly finished me for work. It is an odd world these days, but we have each other and O.K. and dear dear Mollie — and small crowd about the fire. And the dark behind is not really dark. In fact I had a sudden revelation one quiet gentle autumn day in Primrose Hill of the eternity of every moment of time. The Desert Fathers did bring eternity into men's minds by their exaggeration of it, and contempt for the bus-stop of time. But the great thing is the conviction of eternity: and now we have the balance adjusted, and each moment is deeper than ever plummet sounded. It is this non-dimensional world that one is released into by music.

Helen's letter refers to a 'last spell of worry' that made concentration on her work almost impossible. The deaths of three friends within a year were, of course, devastating for a woman of her sensibility, but from the very outset Maude Clarke and A.E. were being proved true prophets, for the house she had chosen to live in would constitute her main trouble to the end. When writing to E. K. Rand, soon after taking possession of No. 32 Primrose Hill Road, she had bemoaned the loss of her housekeeper Mrs Beney. The letters of the latter part of the 1930s are peppered with tales of the exploits of the Widow Twanky, the Ancient Mariner, and 'our Aggie McLeod' —who all came and went, often with a considerable portion of the owner's property. Mollie has provided this first-hand account of daily life with her aunt:

The house was a terrible mistake, but any house would have been, for Helen let it absorb her. She loved her house, and buying the beef, and mending a fuse. She was very practical, adept with hammer and nail, and even electricity held no terrors. How often I came in, and Helen hearing the front door close would emerge from her sitting-room: 'Let's put the kettle on, and then you must see what I've been doing'; or the voice would come up from the kitchen — 'I've put the kettle on, come and look what I've done.' To my horror I would find that a book-case, which in the morning had been full of books in O.K.'s bedroom two floors up, was now full of books in the garden room, all humped down by Helen on her own. Like all houses, electric plugs were never in suitable places, so it might be a bedside lamp working the width of a room away from its plug. Helen would gleefully show me how she had got it there by lengthening the flex, threading it behind book-cases and under the carpet — enough to make an electrician shudder — but it worked, and nothing ever happened. I could go on indefinitely: Helen smothered in whitewash; Helen black as a crow; Helen making me walk the new path of stepping-stones to the bird bath.

Even when she had good help, she was incapable of closing her sitting-room door and getting on with her work. Being Helen, she always became heavily involved with them and would let herself in for hours of talk which left her flat and exhausted. Brian and Anita having measles, Helen would chase the mother home because it was going to kill granny — then revelling in the peace of an empty house would settle down for a morning's work. The laundry would come: Helen down the basement stairs to the side door. Back up, start again, side door bell ring — butcher's boy. Fresh start. Front door bell. The postman can get no reply from the top floor flat: would Helen mind taking this parcel in? By this time her day was irretrievably ruined. She couldn't work in bits and pieces — she had to become absorbed. A good day she could work right through to three or four o'clock oblivious of time or hunger. It was peace she always craved, and that the house denied her. Brian and Anita, still not fit for school, would come with their mother. Now, on top of the dentist's drill whine of the vacuum cleaner (hated more than almost anything), there would be the shrieks of the children chasing each other up and down stairs.

Helen began her day tired. She was a very bad sleeper; was usually down to the kitchen before 5 a.m. for a pot of tea, then back to bed to read, Wugs the cat (full name Hippo, St Augustine, Bishop of) on the bed beside her. She insisted on getting up to cook my breakfast, but waited to have her own with O.K. — that could be anywhere between 9 and 10, for O.K. rang his bell as he left his bed for his bath, and in theory half an hour from the time his bell rang, he would be at the breakfast table. With Helen's power of abstraction, the effort needed to gauge the right moment to put on the egg and make the toast, and her long hours of fasting, left her wearied out by the time O.K.'s taxi came. O.K. did become a rather tiresome old man, but to do him justice it was partly Helen's fault. She was too selfless, tried to anticipate his every want, and fussed him into becoming an old man long before he need have been.

Sundays in summer we quite often went to Lewes for a round of golf — lovely links right up on the downs. Sometimes, if I had a Saturday morning off we would go on Saturday and stay one night, or maybe it would be Hythe or Brighton for the night. Helen, though no great swimmer, loved the sea and had a passion for getting into it. Occasionally it would be Savernake for a lazy rest. Once, Charles and Hilda Morgan were there. After dinner Charles and Helen were arguing about the merits of Thomas Moore as a poet, Charles deriding, Helen defending. Helen quoted 'She is far from the land'. Charles scoffed that any fool could churn out that sort of stuff, and began:

'She sat on the edge of her old trestle bed' — now Helen, go on —
Helen: 'And threw all the bedclothes from off her,'
Charles: 'With her shoes on her feet and her hat on her head,'
Helen: 'She refused Mr Morgan's good offer.'

The speed of the volleys was breathtaking.

Helen usually shopped in England's Lane, only five minutes' walk away. It had the air of a village street with the regulars and shopkeepers all knowing each other. In fact the greengrocer knew Helen so well that when he was under threat of eviction for non-payment of rent it was Helen he turned to, and Helen who rescued him. Sometimes on Saturday afternoon Helen and I walked to Camden Town for the week-end shopping. The grand opera chorus effect of the street stalls, the crowds, the arguments, the haggling, the colour, appealed to us both. Also it gave us an excuse to walk back up Chalk Farm Road. It was a shabby road but very dear to Helen because of its second-hand shops. Flattening our noses on the grimy windows Helen's quick eye would spot a plate, or an Indian carpet which, with any luck, would do the garden room. In time lovely plates turned one wall of the kitchen, lined with shelves and cupboards underneath, into an outsize Welsh dresser. And the Indian carpet of soft blues and greens was perfect for the garden room. Very little worn, it was bought for a few pounds because of a jagged two-foot diameter ink stain. A judicious arrangement of furniture left that scarcely visible. Then there was the red-letter day when Helen's eye fell on the little oak chest. It was very grubby, had a split in the front and one side panel: but with Helen, it was love at first sight. To the shopkeeper it was a bit of almost worthless junk, and he asked 5/–. To Helen it was a chest that centuries ago must have held manuscripts in some old monastery. She paid the 5/–, grabbed a passing taxi, and joyfully bore it home. With its grubby face washed and well polished, the carving on front and sides was lovely. It was a sturdy little chest, and sat in front of one of the leaded glass windows of the big bay window in Helen's sitting-room. Helen's words: 'The great folio (*Vitae*

Patrum) lies on the oak chest in front of the side window, and small winds blow over the old 17th century pages: and I sit on a little stool before it, with my writing block on my knee.' From the time the chest came, that was always Helen working at home.

This is the Helen who never could be old with the beautifully-dressed thick bobbed hair fixed in Grace Henry's portrait, almost backview and faceless yet powerfully suggestive of elegance, concentration and scholarship, as she sits in loose fur wrap and flowing draperies before the vast tome of the 1628 folio of the Lives of the Fathers issued by the Plantin Press, against a background of Paul Henry's oil painting of an early morning in Connemara, and a statuette of the Madonna. The latter got her into trouble with one of her many dailies. Helen had been suffering from that 'laryngitis of exhaustion' diagnosed by Dr Vaudremer in Paris, but inherited from her father: this did not exempt her from having to engage necessary domestic help, and she tells Meg of her latest:

> Mollie has gone back to work again today, and though I am now in bed myself it is only the kind of temperature you get with fatigue. Our very nice new Mrs Moriarty (though Glasgow Scot), a sweet-faced silent woman, perhaps a little righteous like most Scots, is a vehement John Knox Presbyterian — had assumed that we were Catholic — I suppose Grace Henry's Madonna and the crucifix — said to me as I lay in my bed, à propos of her own disastrous 'mixed marriage': 'But you're a Catholic, aren't you?' I have seldom replied with more fervour, 'I'm the daughter and the granddaughter and great-granddaughter of Presbyterian ministers, and our ancestors fought at Bothwell Brig.' In fact I felt exactly like St Paul in face of the assembly: 'I am a Pharisee and the son of a Pharisee.' I think it did her good, though I had the 2nd Commandment recited to me about 'making no graven images.'
>
> It is so long since I sat down to the old desk and I'm afraid to say that I'll be free now — look at my dreams after the departure of Mrs McLeod.

Then there is the typical Helen touch: 'I asked her to give us a week's full time for 10/– more, beginning today, but as she had arranged to meet a daughter this afternoon I said it didn't matter, and indeed the peace of the house is great when they're away.' In other words, she simply got up and did the work herself.

However unco' guid and rigidly righteous the John Knox Presbyterian may have been, she speedily followed the Widow Twanky and our Aggie, and with her departure life resumed its customary rhythm of the backward-forward throw of two shuttles — scholarship and household. *The Desert Fathers* was published on 18 June

1936, and a week later Helen travelled North to receive an honorary Doctor of Laws degree from St Andrew's University. 'I'm frightfully pleased,' she told Meg, 'because they really are a medieval university. They've been there since 1120.' She stayed for two days with Sir James and Lady Irvine at The University House, 'an enchanted house, on site of old castle above a quiet lovely sea . . . Sir James ended in two days as Jim and his wife (a darling) as, I am sorry to say, Mabel.' She does not refer in any way to the actual ceremony but makes an ominous admission: 'I nearly died of fatigue at St Andrews — face about as grey as grey chiffon dress, would honestly have rouged if I'd had any. I did love the people, and I've got Bynin Amara at last and will faithfully swallow same, for St Andrews really scared me, not that I'd be ill, but cease to have any vitality in pleasure, live dim sub-aqueous existence in green pond.'

For years Helen had planned a full-scale study of John of Salisbury and had worked intermittently at a translation of his letters. This should have followed *The Desert Fathers* but, as events turned out, everything was abandoned: the charming, witty, learned, modest friend of the world-famed, the Helen Waddell who was the main attraction of the London salons, had maintained a steady output of scholarly work for a mere decade. Eleven years were to pass before anything original issued from her pen. England was to undergo trial by fire and Helen, like everyone else, was suddenly swept into the vortex of politics and war. The violent transition about to change the face of Europe was heralded in England by the abdication of King Edward VIII in December 1936. It evoked in Helen a passionate sympathy that expressed itself in a letter to Baldwin:

> I began many letters to you, and could not go on, for there was so much bitterness in my heart. Never against you — but against mankind — their cruelty, their fickleness, their smugness in the face of tragedy. Your own final speech was like a mountain.
>
> But the days before it and after it were poisoned to me by the slow distilled venom of the leaders in *The Times*. What blackness of heart was in Geoffrey Dawson, wounded vanity or secret spite, that made him pursue that haunted figure, that 'Love in Desolation masked', not *tigris ut aspera*, but with the malice of a cat. It was anguish to me to read them —like seeing a wounded man surrendering his sword and being struck by the victor in the face.
>
> Three people in that tragedy redeem it: the lad that is gone — the brother who succeeded him with such heartbroken chivalry — and you that were a father to them both.

On 28 May 1937, after the coronation of King George VI, Stanley

Baldwin retired from public life, with the reward of an Earldom and the Garter. Helen wrote to him a letter which sufficiently explains why she could so captivate others:

32 Primrose Hill Road,
N.W.3
May 28 1937

My dear S.B.

This brief note goes to you because I want one more time to address the envelope to the Rt. Hon. Stanley Baldwin. Not that I grudge the Earldom: it has a heavenly Sir Walter Scott Ivanhoe flavour about it: and it has the huge advantage of anchoring you in the House of Lords, away from 'the sea of hoarse noises and disputes': in short, it is your own magnificent resonant tub — the Tub you always threatened you might end in thumping.

But none of these things move either you or me. It is the old medieval distinction between the substance and the accidents: and the substance remains S.B. and I his obliged if not very humble servant,

H.W.

Neville Chamberlain assumed the Premiership and during the two years' pause that followed, England's peril became clear while Germany was given ample time to strengthen for war and Hitler to gain control of Austria and Czechoslovakia. Then came Munich. Self-avowedly Helen was no 'political animal', yet her daily contacts at Constable's with two minds such as O.K.'s and F. A. Voigt's —both ardently pro-British Germans, with a passionate interest in public affairs — must have sharpened her realization of the terrifying issues at stake. In a letter simply headed 'Friday', she wrote to Stanley Baldwin again:

My dear S.B.

I sent you a wire this morning in a kind of desperation, after reading Hitler's own phrase at Berchtesgaden: that he would solve the Sudeten affair 'nun der Preis eines Weltkrieges'. I had believed until now that a threat only stiffened our backs. Now I am being silly and quoting *Antony & Cleopatra*—
'I never saw an action of such shame',
and
'I'll bathe my dying honour in that blood
Will make it live again'
and then remembering bitterly that I have always said I cannot see the young men go — *twice*.

Yet if one is not a complete pacifist, one knows that to let a bully threaten and not call his bluff ends in the slavery that John of Salisbury calls 'imago mortis'. And at the Youth rally at the German Embassy two nights ago they got drunk enough to say that they had never dreamt England wouldn't call their bluff — that they weren't ready to take us all on. Chamberlain is a decent man, but he is curiously innocent.

But, dear S.B., I don't want the arbitrament of blood if it can be helped. I do want England to be made to feel that she is a democracy. At the moment, most intelligent people feel that Chamberlain is virtually dictator — that we are a totalitarian state with none of its advantages. It seemed — but forgive the 'female phranzy' — madness to me not to summon a Parliament on an issue like this. I have a horrid fear that Chamberlain is relying on the terrible passivity of the English before a *fait accompli*, though they'll fight like tigers if the issue is before them, still unresolved. The attitude of 'Mother knows best' doesn't survive the nursery: and since the Anglo-Italian agreement no one trusts his wisdom.

Can't you come back, if not as P.M. (though in the Lords you would escape the sheer nagging of the job), then as Lord President, with Eden as P.M. and have a real Coalition cabinet as in the War, with Attlee and Sinclair and *both* Morrisons — the thing has gone far beyond party advantage.

I speak like a fool. I would be better employed translating John of Salisbury's strange wisdom. I'll append a piece of it for your meditation.

There is one beautiful thing — the outraged honour of the young men — not the intellectuals — people like my houseman (who does everything from cooking very nicely to petting the kitten and cutting the grass), and the taximan round the corner, and the stocky little man who came for 'empties' this morning, and whom I waylaid to hear his views. 'I'm a man has got no education, Miss, and maybe I don't know the rights of it. But I'm ashamed to be an Englishman.' I haven't heard that since the Black and Tan stories began coming over to England in 1921.

Anyhow, thank heaven you are home again.

My love and duty always,

Helen.

John of Salisbury goes to you later.

In the event it was Winston Churchill who, a year later, formed the Coalition War Cabinet: it numbered all the men listed in Helen's letter except its recipient, S.B. Meanwhile throughout 1939 the world was watching with bated breath: was it to be peace or war? Helen had no illusions, for Hitler had the mind of the frog that blew itself up to be like a bull, as she put it; she only hoped the explosion would confine itself to Germany. Haunted as always by thought of the transitoriness of all earthly things, her mind besieged by eternity, she went into her garden and gave herself up to meditation. The world had seen it all before — in 410 Hitler's name had been Alaric the Goth, and 40 years later, Attila the Scourge of God. London was Troy, it was Rome, it was Paris or Warsaw, but Europe itself was deathless. This was the whole paradox at the heart of human history, whether of nation or of individual: death the doorway to life, punishment to expiation, sterile destruction to fruitful purification. She found an outlet for her feelings in an original poem — one of the few she ever wrote — a prelude to her many new mediaeval translations 'silted together' from 1939 to 1945 by Hitler's unholy *blitzkrieg*. She wrote to Meg:

> . . . I could not go into the garden without a kind of trance of deep strong delight. The pear was out, and the cherries, and the light was a still gold, as if June were in the heart of April, and I began writing a thing in my head, not finished yet, and very poor, but it will show you what was in my mind —

April 20, 1939
(Hitler is to address the Reichstag on April 28)

> Earth said to Death,
> Give these a little breath.
> Give them eight days to feel the sun,
> To see the limes in leaf . . .
> Give me eight days,
> And I will pour the silence of June
> Into this April noon,
> Wine of October in the vine still curled.
> Then let you come.
> Darkness shall find them sleeping undismayed,
> Who shall make them afraid
> Who saw eternity
> In the brief compass of an April day?

On 3 September at 11.15 a.m. Neville Chamberlain announced that England was already at war, almost immediately the prolonged wailing of sirens sent people scuttling to air-raid shelters, and that night thirty or forty cylindrical balloons rose in the night sky to defend the roofs and spires of London. 'Darling, more than anything I long for you to be here just to share this life with us for one tiny space, and see London dark, and the balloons like the Japanese Day of the Fish blowing in the wind.' Helen was adamant in her refusal to leave London, and next day wrote to reassure Meg:

> As for this small section of your family, O.K., Mollie and me — we've never been so fond of each other or so, in a way, lighthearted. Mollie woke me about 3 a.m. to say the hooters were blowing for a raid. O.K. was strolling about in his dressing-gown, and Rosamund and the little old Quakers sitting side by side like two mice on the kitchen stairs. It all seemed quite ordinary, and yet foolish and strange. So I put on the kettle to make tea, and suddenly O.K. yawned and said, 'Well, if you'll excuse me

I'm going back to bed' — and went upstairs again. It was the one absolute gesture: I feel it has given the tuning-fork note for all future raids.

Both men and women were being called up, stern black-out regulations enforced; food rationing imposed. Mollie has described the effects on the household:

Even after the watershed of September 1939 there were still gay times. Charlie and George (my brothers) with an unexpected 24 hours' leave, Helen dashing out for a bottle of burgundy, and if possible a melon to make it a party. Rosamund looking magnificent in the Wren equivalent of an admiral's uniform also blowing in and giving an excuse for another party. But beginning with the nightmare of effectively blacking out all the huge windows in the house, and the stern A.R.P. wardens saying fiercely that even closed shutters let out chinks of light, and unless the occupants of the top floor mended their ways they would end in jail, it was all a slow descent into the miseries of war. Helen so often with inadequate domestic help or none at all; the sheer drudgery of rationing and queuing for Wugs's rabbit — he would eat nothing else.

In her letter to Stanley Baldwin, Helen had referred — was it with a touch of pride? — to 'my houseman'. Pride goeth before destruction — the Admirable Crichton found time for many pursuits besides cutting the grass and petting Wugs. Let Helen's letters to Meg tell the story:

They have planted two anti-aircraft guns, one pointing down Oppidans Road and the other almost opposite. . . . I am getting in coal and sugar and some tinned things in case of shortage. I ought to go and get a gas mask, and instead I stand and think how to make a little run for hens at the bottom of the garden. Martin (house help) says he will not have to go with the first lot, being completely blind in one eye. O, *what* a life! Poor Martin has just arrived to say that his two small children who lived with a married sister have just been lumped on his small wife who is cook at Clarges St, and has only her tiny room and can't have any children. He is almost desperate and I am bringing them here (5 and 6, only) to sleep on the kitchen divan, and Martin on the wire from the swing seat, till he gets them down to his mother in Cornwall. The married sister was scared about air-raids and went off at a moment's notice to Wales. Martin knew nothing . . . till his distraught wife rang up here to tell him. So we have been making up beds in the kitchen as Martin will have to sleep with them for the time being.

Thursday. In the confusion I lost this letter and didn't get it posted. The infants are dears, but the confusion considerable. You see, Martin must now find a little flat or rooms, and how is he to find them with the infants to look after? Rosamund has rustled up someone from the Over Thirties

who will come and mind them in the afternoon today, and is trying to find
a wealthy lady in Sussex who specializes in giving children holidays, so
that he would have time to turn round. The roof seems inclined to go off
the top of my head.

With considerable help from the occupants of 32 Primrose Hill
Road, Martin found a flat for himself and the children. Some weeks
later, in a letter simply headed *Friday*, Helen wrote an apology for her
long silence:

My darling,
    I was heartbroken to get its sad little letter — the dreadful thing was that
I had mine to you in my bag for days, and never knew it wasn't posted.
Somehow it has been so queer and rather frightening in a way. I didn't see
Martin: O.K. sacked him on Tuesday morning — told him his forgery had
been found out, but that he thought I wouldn't prosecute. I can't, with
those tiny children. I'm beginning to rustle round now and look out, but I
was kind of stunned at first. He had also cheated the accounts again. I've
done nothing but pay outstanding bills, and I haven't the heart to count
them up. He would enter them as paid, you see, and so account for the
money he pocketed. But it's pounds and pounds. And the silly things that
are gone — just like Nelly — dustpan and tongs and brushes and alas 6
silver forks, and — this only discovered last night — the new sewing-
machine. I suppose he has pawned it. . . . I've lost, but it's no use
grousing. I think Shakespeare had been fleeced the same way when he
wrote *Timon of Athens*. Read it, and read the amazing last speech of
Alcibiades — I think, on his grave. He had asked to be buried by the sea
            'where
        Vast Neptune weeps for aye
        O'er thy low grave, o'er faults forgiven.'
I don't quite know what to do next. This Martin business has worried
O.K. a lot, for he more or less engaged him, and thought so well of him.
And it was so proud of its new flat, and its two infants. I think he got
bogged in debt, & that's the trouble.

It was typical of Helen to make an excuse for the culprit and forget
the crime. 'She was a darling,' her niece testifies, 'and her kindness —
she believed every hard luck story, was incapable of passing a street
musician or down-and-out holding out a greasy cap.' Helen's
Foreword to the biblical stories told to Sydney, Jack and Mollie
Martin in childhood and published nearly 40 years later, opens with an
incident from her Cedar Avenue days which can be interpreted as a
paradigm of her whole life. It is written in a prose of limpid simplicity
stamped with the seal of a supreme artist. When G. G. Coulton
sneered at the ornate allusive language of *The Wandering Scholars*,

Helen pointed out that the reader's knowledge was far more involved so long as the allusive writing was interesting enough to make him pursue the allusion and thereby discover a score of other things, than by 'A fat cat sat on a mat' kind of book, which left the reader nothing to do. Someday, however, she told him, she intended to write a solemn study of the fat cat, as one of the tiny masterpieces of English prose. Perhaps the pellucid Preface is her fulfilment of that promise, except that the fat cat has been replaced by a thin dog:

> He was a shabby little dog, and he was thin. He was sitting on the doorstep when I came down one morning, very early, before anyone was up. I think he had been there all night. But he jumped up when the door opened, very hurriedly, and trotted a little way down the path, and then he stopped and turned round and looked at me with big frightened eyes, and began wagging his tail. He did not wag it very hard, because he was so afraid that he was going to be scolded for sitting there, and he didn't dare to say much. But he wagged it a little, because he had just a faint hope that whoever opened the door would not be cross with him, and he did want somebody to like him a little. He had such imploring eyes that it hurt to look at them; and when I got down on my knees beside him and patted his untidy little head he gave a little choked bark that was half a whine, and the tail wagged so hard that all the small body seemed wagging too. But he still looked at me, and his eyes were very hungry. . . .

She goes on to speak of the infinity of God's tenderness and bids her little charges remember 'the next time you are afraid about anything, and the next time you are vexed with yourself and think you are so horrid nobody could love you much, and the next time you feel lonely and out of things, remember that God cares, cares what becomes of you, and cares terribly — far, far more than you would care for a little hungry dog.'

In 1924 when Helen gave financial help to Enid Starkie in Paris, she dismissed the gift — anything she possessed was hers only to be shared, she said. That was her fundamental principle: she felt about money like Omar Khayyam on Vintners:

> 'I often wonder what they buy
> One half so precious as the goods they sell.'

Her frequent acts of kindness cannot be listed because she let not her left hand know what her right hand did. In general, she avoided public social fund-raising but made an exception in favour of the Over-Thirty Association (now called The Over-Forty Association for Women Workers), founded 'to help the large number of unemployed women, many of them elderly and nearly all lonely, who were finding life in London on 13s. 6d. per week a depressing and desperate experience'. She helped Rosamund Tweedy, the Organizing Secretary, and Monica Stiff, a very active member of the Committee, to arrange a charity concert at Londonderry House, during which she read her own poem, *New York City*, and two translations from Latin; the two Hungarian sisters, Adila Fachiri and Jelly d'Aranyi, both famous violinists, and well-known women artists, singers and instrumentalists all gave their services but, from the absence of one name, it is clear that Helen's appeal met with a request to be excused. In a letter dated 'Tuesday evening' she wrote to Dorothy Sayers:

> My dear Dorothy Sayers,
> Muriel Byrne has just rung up to say that there is a chance of Lord Peter saying a word — 1200 to be precise — for the Over Thirty.
> This is to thank you, in case you can, and to say that we are damn nuisances, whether you can or you can't.
> The Over Thirty lives under my nose, so to speak, as Rosamund Tweedy, its organising secretary, is a friend of mine and lives upstairs. But apart from that, I have seen too much of them, before anything was done for them — secretaries that were invaluable once, young ladies behind the counter that lost their looks or their figures, nippies that could no longer be nippy, schoolmistresses that were too expensive for the Burnham scale — but every woman *in* a job knows the pitiful procession of women out of a job who hope that perhaps you could get them one.
> So, if you can do them, my dear, you will have my own personal gratitude, as well as everybody else's.
> In haste,
> Helen Waddell.

The two women had met in 1933 as guests at a dinner party given by Constable's directors, Michael Sadleir and Otto Kyllmann, to discuss publishing prospects. Dorothy was unresponsive, stifled the talk and spoilt the evening: the partners decided on the spot that her metier was commercial advertising, not publishing. Occasional meetings never led to true friendship, and nothing could better illustrate their dissimilarity than their skirmish over English Law in 1942. Since the incident shows that Helen's compassion knew no bounds, it may well find a place here.

In August 1942 six Belfast youths were condemned to capital punishment. As the House of Commons was not in session, the subject could not be fully ventilated, and an appeal to the House of Lords was refused. When the news was made public, Helen passed a whole day in anguish, and towards evening sat down and within five minutes wrote a letter of protest to *The Times*. Otto Kyllmann delivered it by hand at 7.05 p.m. just as the paper was going to press, and by some miracle the Editor found room for it on the leader page next day, Friday, 28 August, under the heading, 'On Belfast murder sentences'. The letters now to be quoted call for no comment, but it must be remembered that the signatory to the *Times*' letter was none other than 'Ulster's Darling'. Before writing it, she had to face the possibility of reprisals — for herself, she cared nothing, but Meg and the family of Kilmacrew in County Down were dearer to her than life. But not dearer than honour. She made the moral choice:

> I write as an Ulsterwoman, jealous for the good name of my province. Six boys, the eldest of them 21, have been found guilty of shooting for political reasons at a patrol car in Belfast and murdering a policeman. They are to be hanged, collectively, on September 2nd. The Attorney-General of Northern Ireland has refused to allow the case to be tried before the supreme tribunal of English justice, the justice to which Northern Ireland has always appealed. Is his case then so weak that it is unable to support the journey to Westminster? And is the memory of a kindly Ulster policeman to become a thing of horror in men's minds, like the memory of Heydrich, thanks to the savagery of his avengers?

A fortnight later she wrote to recount the aftermath to Meg:

> The agony that went into that letter to *The Times* burnt up all the vitality I had: there's something about one's own country that takes the guts out of you. I think I know now what the Frenchmen like de Gaulle feel about France. I've had amazing letters and hardly one that was scolding — a marvellous one from Dean Kerr, and another angelic one from Bob Stevenson, reproaching, but so kindly (he is 77) that I thanked heaven that there were men like him, with his 1,000 factory workers, half of them Catholic and many of them IRA, 'and never a trouble with them', he says . . .
>
> My one real affliction came from Dorothy Sayers who opened up a bombardment which still bewilders me, about the sanctity of a jury's verdict: to which I replied that this was an odd position for the author of *Strong Poison* to take up, and did she really believe that the jury once shut up were like the College of Cardinals selecting a Pope under the direct inspiration of the Holy Ghost? As she is very Anglo-Catholic this enraged her, and I had a succession of bombs about my losing no opportunity of scouting a law of which I could, being Irish, have no conception, and how no Irish person ever understood the majesty of England (to which, however, I had been appealing!) and lost no chance of vilifying it. As we have always been excellent friends whenever we have met, and none of these vexed questions have ever risen, I thought either I had lost my reason or she had — I hoped the latter. But though I really was cut to the heart, I fortunately rang up Muriel Byrne, and Muriel said that though she loved Dorothy, she was liable to go like that on (i) Ireland (ii) Scotland (iii) the

BBC (iv) the mildest enquiry about a point of law on any subject — that Dorothy then became Britannia jabbing her trident indiscriminate-like, and the only thing to do is to come in out of the rain till the fit is over.

So I wrote to Dorothy indicating that I was sorry my anxiety to bring an Irish decision to an English tribunal was of the nature of an insult to English justice, in which I had believed from infancy, and still believed, in spite of its most recent protagonist, Dorothy Sayers.

That actually shut her up, and I, weak but happy, licked my paws and read again this most charming letter from the old Bishop of Norwich, just retired — a cousin of the Sir Frederick Pollock I used to know, the great lawyer. Also a lyric from Nancy Astor, and some others from Ulster people in this country. Stephen Gwynn, just back from Dublin, says the clemency of the N.I. government has made a very good impression there.

A figure at least as poignant as the six reprieved Irish boys, and a great deal nobler, was the young Frenchman, Guy Robin, 'his wife lost in occupied France, and himself with the flaming gaunt passion of the Desert Fathers,' whom Helen befriended in 1940. France's capitulation in 1940, summarized by Max Beerbohm as 'Humilité, Servilité, Lavalité,' caused her intense distress, as her letter to Meg shows:

> I have been so haunted by France, that I went back to Virgil, the fall of Troy, and all the old Fifth column business of the Trojan horse and the tearful refugee who was the traitor. It might be yesterday. I can't think about France. My heart cracks. It is so strange and lonely a thing to have one's mind go joyfully and confidently across the Channel, and suddenly it begins groping in a cold impalpable mist.

As part of her war effort, Helen undertook the uncongenial task of assistant-editor of *The Nineteenth Century*, and it was in this magazine that she serialized month by month under the title *A French Soldier Speaks* the jottings made in a London hospital by Guy Robin, 'a young man whose spiritual ancestry dates from Roncesvalles rather than from the century of Robespierre or of Louis Quatorze'. An undated letter to Meg clearly belongs to the early months of 1940. Typical of a Londoner in the blitz, it tells Meg lightheartedly:

> It's extraordinary how one gets used to noise. You hear the planes going over, bumbling in their clumsy persistent way, rather like a bluebottle, over Primrose Hill, with Edward★ now and then saying in his very loud rude way — 'Swat that fly!' The one mark I left on the December XIX

★'Edward' was a large naval gun among the ack ack guns placed on Primrose Hill. Helen christened him Edward after a *Punch* cartoon in which a fat female in furs led a minute Peke for a walk, above the caption: 'Edward, Edward, you are wearing me out!' Edward spoke for the first time when she was working on the *Lament for Hathimoda*, and incidentally shattered most of the front windows in Primrose Hill Road.

was the quotation on the cover 'For the November Dead.' When
Coventry came, and then Birmingham, my mind went back to the Mass
for All Souls:* 'The souls of the just are in the hands of God, and the
torment of malice shall not touch them: in the sight of the unwise they
seemed to die but they are in peace.' Did I tell you how I want you to
read 'A Free Frenchman Speaks'? I've met him now: dark and young and
sad, with eyes like a lamp; his young wife and mother somewhere in
occupied France. He has not heard from her since the capitulation. He
began talking about the music at Solesmes, where a friend of his at
college has been a monk for years. And then he said suddenly: 'When the
war is won and France is France again, and I go back — if I cannot find
my wife, I shall take vows at Solesmes.' They are the Wild Geese of this
century, these men of De Gaulle's. I don't think he will come through,
somehow, he has that look of being 'absolute for death'. But do read the
opening of the *Free Frenchman* in the November number. It was written
in hospital to ease his heart, and a kind nurse (Lady Brigid Tenison)
found what he was doing, and showed it to a friend of hers, who brought
it to the XIX. I read it one week-end and went off the deep end about it.
Poor boy, the day he came to see me was his thirtieth birthday, so O.K.
took us all four (Mollie was free that day) to the Escargot to celebrate,
and Monsieur Godin made a great fuss of him and made us have drinks
all round, and I think he was happy. But when the photographs came out
of his pocket book, of something enchanting, absurd and French . . . I
felt he *could* have gone back and found her: and refused, for France's
sake. . . . The time this translation takes could always be my own. But it
was something to do for France.

In 1941 Constable published *A French Soldier Speaks* by Jacques,
translated by Helen Waddell. The 'Jacques' was a *nom de guerre*: in the
circumstances of the war, his anonymity had to be preserved. It was
dedicated according to his wish 'A ma jeune femme qui, en France,
m'attend, espère, et prie.' The author, Guy Robin, did not live to see
its publication. On 28 August Helen wrote to her sister:

I've just had a letter from a friend of Jacques, who had had a fresh attack of
pleurisy: on the Friday he had, for the first time since he came to England, a
letter from his young wife, saying that she was safe and well. Ten minutes
after, he had a heart attack, and was dead in half an hour.
      I think, like our own Geo. he died in an ecstasy. One can see how it
happened — the strain of pleurisy with only one lung (the other collapsed),
and the sudden snapping of the long strain of anxiety and dread. And yet I
feel as if a dead weight had gone from me: it is like Lear —
                    'if she but live,
           It doth redeem all sorrows I have felt.'

*H. W. here attributes the Offertory of All Saints to All Souls.

Quite irrationally I feel it is a good omen for our adored France. . . . It is idiotic to take things so to heart. But there was something about that funeral, with only soldiers and strangers, and the tall thin sad-eyed Jacques in that long thin coffin, that broke me, and I have been half-alive, as if the whole grief of Europe was suddenly about one like a tide in Alcuin's phrase,

'so vast the grief,
So universal through the whole wide world.'

And to know that Jacques went out in a sudden glory has transfigured it.

The wreath Helen laid on his grave in the military cemetery in Brookwood was built on a foundation of laurel almost hidden by scabious, roses, and a single white carnation tied with the tricolour, and inscribed:

> For France dead at Roncesvalles
> In the certain hope of a glorious resurrection.

After watching his body lowered into the grave with his commander's last salute, 'Guy Robin — au revoir!' Helen could do nothing for two days until, 'in a sudden pure relief of the spirit', she translated Alcuin's poem to St Michael:

> O Michael, servant of the eternal King,
> Standing upon the citadel of heaven. . . .
> Cease not to help thy feeble folk,
> Until the struggle of this war is spent
> And thy right hand lift us to the palm.

In the *New York Times Book Review* of 8 March 1942, E. K. Rand declared that Guy Robin's book would rank with some of Churchill's speeches, among the great and lasting utterances of the Second World War. His lengthy and deeply moving review concluded with high praise of the chapter on Christmas Eve 1940: 'If we imagine at times that the French lack something of our Christmas festivity,' he assured his American readers, 'we can find out here what we have lost from theirs. Theirs is more than ours a family feast, since it is the day not only of the Holy Child but of the Holy Family.'

In her letter to Meg, Helen speaks of herself as being only half-alive as a result of the young Frenchman's death. Mollie observes of her aunt: 'Helen felt things ten times as intensely as ordinary mortals. Her heights and depths were away beyond the range of O.K. and me. When the German armies swept through Poland her anguish was so intense I was scared — how could anyone suffer so and keep her reason? But once she could write something it was as though she got release.' In her own Translator's Preface to the new volume of mediaeval lyrics that she herself never saw through the press, Helen writes of the ugly winter of 1938–39, full of illness and ill-news, after England and France had prevailed on Czechoslovakia to surrender her western frontier in order to avoid a European conflagration:

Midway in January came the first pale spring Sunday of the year; some of us, thirsty for music, drifted into an afternoon concert. I have forgotten the player's name, and I sat where I saw nothing but the reflection of his hands in the dark mirror of the Bechstein at which he played. I had been brooding, not happily, on the power of physical violence to cripple men's minds, and on this new evil doctrine of enslaving the arts to the State: and suddenly the free movement of those hands against darkness became a symbol.

> Even as a bird
> Out of the fowler's snare
> Escapes away,
> So is our soul set free.
> Rent is their net,
> and thus escaped we.

> I saw the shadow of the player's hands
> Against all Europe.
> Against all time
> I saw the shadow of the player's hands.

In that moment of liberation a forgotten memory of Alcuin came to me, the fragment on the Lombard occupation of Rome that begins: 'By these, by these same chains, O Rome . . .' and ends:
> 'That road is closed to war, whose gate
> Stands open to the stars.'

She decided there and then to abandon all her hopes and dreams of a biography of John of Salisbury and a sequel to *Peter Abelard* and to concentrate her attention once again on the Latin poems of mediaeval Europe:

Their value lies not in the quality of their poetry, but in their courage and their poignancy: indeed in their bare existence. They are like the inscriptions scratched on dungeon walls or prison windows, the defiance of the spirit of man against material circumstance. Alcuin's lament for the sack of Lindisfarne by the Northmen seemed to me when I read it years ago a little trite, and full of ancient platitude; now that the bombers circle over Holy Island, I read it with a kind of contemporary anguish. 'By these, by these same chains' was strong consolation, when the banners of the swastika moved through the streets of Prague.

Boethius' *Consolation of Philosophy*, indeed, is in a different category: in every century men have listened to it, heard in it a kind of angelus rung in the evening of the ancient world. . . . But when the veiled figure stands beside Boethius in the dungeon at Pavia, looking upon him with more than mortal eyes, the moment of recognition is not for him only. Pavia becomes Dachau; the senator's toga a German pastor's dress. 'Whoever he be', wrote John of Salisbury, 'that is willing to suffer for his faith, whether he be little lad or man grown, Jew or Gentile, Christian or Infidel, man or woman, it matters not at all: who dies for justice dies a martyr, a defender of the cause of Christ.'

So it was that the war years determined the choice of poems and the remarkable unity of theme. With her historic sense, Helen knew that in a time of violent transition, continuity with a remembered past was vital and, for Europe, that continuity was essentially Roman. 'Now the sack of Rome', she would explain, 'is a far cry from the Dark Ages but it is the key to them. That inheritance of glory and tragedy was the patrimony of Rome. Hardly one of the barbarians who conquered her but claimed an ancestor who had fought on the losing side at Troy.' So her new book opened with the burning of Troy, and closed with John Milton, the seventeenth-century 'barbarian' saturated with Virgil, Horace and Ovid, who could find no higher praise for the capital of the realm — lit by fire bombs even as Helen was translating his poem — than to address it: *Tuque urbs Dardaniis, Londinium, structa colonis*: City of London, built by Trojan settlers. No fewer than twelve poems of considerable length deal directly with Rome, in circumstances paralleled by the contemporary situation. Thus Claudian's 'Even as the cattle' is entitled 'For France'; Alcuin's 'By these, by these same chains', 'For Vilipuri, Cracow, Prague'; Hildebert's 'No memory is here,' 'The Mood of Vichy'. The presence of the Puritan John Milton among so many mediaeval luminaries may puzzle at first, but he has every right to his place.

When 'Jacques' died in August 1941, Helen used the medium of Alcuin's verse to dedicate an altar to St Michael in his memory. But the thunderbolts of war were to strike much nearer home. Three of her own nephews were already serving in the Forces — Jack, in the Rhodesian Air Force; Charles and George, both engineers, in the R.N.V.R. and R.E. respectively. Helen had always had close affinities with Jack, the little rationalist who, in childish fury at finding his name printed in *Daybreak*, scored it out heavily with a stubby pencil, yet could suddenly seize his aunt's hand, kiss it, and pretend he had done nothing of the kind. A young man full of promise, now married with two children, he worked in Rhodesia in the Forestry Commission before enlisting. Upon hearing the news, Helen wrote giving him the whereabouts of relatives: the Captain G. F. W. Martin is, of course, his youngest brother, who took a bride only two days before leaving England; the rest are cousins:

O my darling, I'm so happy you've got your heart's desire — 'born for extremity and danger'. And I keep wondering where you are, and while it lasted praying that it wasn't at Keven. Mayne — you remember your old friend Mayne — is on his way out, in the R.A.M.C. Ronnie (the rogue Ronnie) is with the Anzacs. Mayne was wondering if ever you three would meet, 'and oh Lord, *what* a blind it would be.' And Peter, Uncle Martin's younger boy, *aet.* 18, is now in England in the R.A.F. I'd have had a finished book to send you, only for being ill. It's lyrics, most of it, some of it lovely. Here's one I did, just when the guns first broke over London, the day of the first great fire at the docks, Sept. 8th, one of the tremendous air fights of the first offensive over England. I got the last two lines in a lull of the guns. It's a 9th century lament for a young abbess, must have been another Heloise.

> Thou hast come safe to port,
>   I still at sea,
> The light is on thy head,
>   Darkness in me.
> Pluck thou in heaven's field
>   Violet and rose,
> While I strew flowers that will thy vigil keep,
>   Where thou dost sleep,
>   Love, in thy last repose.

And this — which is true of Ack and me — from Alcuin:

> There'll come a time when brother speaks with brother,
>   There'll come a time when joy will feast on joy.
> There is a time for all things: now for parting,
>   O Love that knows no end and no alloy.

And this — for a good party:

> Wine it is that gives life pleasure,
> But 'tis naught in single measure.
> Better is it thrice repeated,
> But the fourth is rich conceited.
> At the fifth, the mind's labyrinthine,
> At the sixth, the body's supine.

I wonder where you are. I wonder will you come across Captain G. F. W. Martin, who still thinks nobody like Jack. His wife is enchanting, as gay as a puppy or a kitten, yet heaps of solid sense: adores O.K. — and he returns it. Must stop and get away to office. O.K. sends his love, and

Mollie who is in a new job at Chelsea, much nearer home. I'm hoping to see Momma next month, and Kilmacrew, and Daddy, who becomes more the quintessence of himself and liker Erasmus in countenance every year.

Neglectful but devoted

ANT

And I never had the grace to write to it about a most remarkable cheque. Dear Ack, that is the end of any financial obligation between us, without prejudice, that is, to any future transactions on next leave. But we now start square.

In November, only three months after Jacques' death, news reached Elizabeth, Jack's wife, that he had been involved in a plane crash, and Helen at once wrote to Meg:

Old Ack. No more news yet, and I keep remembering how magnificent and tough he is: and how the other wire I've had in my life — 'Sister dangerously ill' — ended in a darling all pop-eye in bed, and I coming round the door. O Lord, by these things men live. If only I were with you, or you were here. And Daddy. Elizabeth very good and hopeful — says he has been in crashes so often.

O my love, how reluctant one is to suffer.

'When thou passeth through the waters, I will be with thee, and the rivers, they shall not overflow thee.' But you don't *want* to go through the waters, you want the green pastures, and the hens on the Calf Knowe, and Smoky a little dark speck in the far fields, and the gallops of it home, in the dusk, and its race up the apple tree, and its fiendish grin between the boughs.

'For the sword outwears its sheath,
And the soul wears out the breast,
And the heart must pause to breathe,
And Love itself have rest.'

When a telegram announced Jack's death, Helen immediately went to Meg at Kilmacrew. She was back in London for Christmas, dealing not only with work at Constable's, but determinedly putting together her new translations. A letter speaks of her handing each day's work at night to O.K. to page. The lyrics were comfort for her own sad heart and for her family. So she writes to Meg:

Awful busy but doing some really lovely things — suddenly one comes on a fragment of Latin you've copied and haven't translated, and you spend a happy day on it, instead of tidying up what you *have* got. Here's one that Alcuin wrote to Arno of Salzburg — you can imagine what forests and what hills were between Tours and Southern Germany then, and you can take it to yourself from me:

No mountain and no forest, land or sea
Shall block love's road, deny the way to thee.
    Yet why must love that's sweet
    So bitter tears beget,
Honey and gall in one same goblet set?
    Even so, O world, the feet
    Of sorrow follow hard upon delight,
    Disaster overtaketh happiness,
    Joy changeth to a cry.
They will not stay for me: yea, all things haste to night.

    Wherefore, O world,
       So soon to die,
       From us depart.
       And thou, O heart,
       Make haste to fly
Where is delight that fades not,
    The unchanging shore,
That happy house where friend from friend divides not,
    And what he loves, he has for evermore.
Take me, beloved, in thy prayer with thee
Where shall be no estranging thee and me.★

And this, which must have been written at the end of a letter, it's only a fragment:

    Come, make an end of writing and of grieving,
       But not an end of love.
    I wrote this song, beloved, bitter weeping,
       And yet I know 'twill prove
          That by God's grace
    We two shall see each other, face to face,
    And stand together with a quiet heart.★

As always, the returning spring lifted Helen from the Slough of Despond, but when she went into the garden, the sight of the young green that had never failed to enchant her, now spoke of the heaven-haven of eternity. Early in 1942 she wrote to Meg:

The spring is really coming. The older I get, the more convinced I am that matter is not evil, as the Gnostics said, but is maybe a duller vibration of the spirit, so that it is visible. For it isn't the thought of
          'the dreaming garden trees
          And the full moon and the white evening star'
that lifts my heart: it's simply the resurrection from the dead — in one's heart as well as in the clay.

★★See *More Latin Lyrics* pp. 197 and 193, for the final versions of both these poems.

That faith was to be put to the test. On 24 March, four months after Jack's, a telegram announced George's death at Tobruk. Helen's grief found expression as so often in Shakespeare; she exclaimed in the words of Cleopatra's serving-maid,

> The bright day is done,
> And we are for the dark.

The doctor sternly forbade any journey to Ireland: the shock, combined with her grave state of anaemia, had brought her to the verge of collapse, yet half-numbed as she was, she at once worded an insertion for *The Times*, with grace and generosity linking the name of Major G. F. W. Martin, aged twenty-three, with that of his friend from Antrim, Capt. W. McGrath, D.S.O., R.E., who had met his death three weeks before in the hell of St Valéry. Next day she wrote to the family:

> My darling — and my darling Mollie who was his mother too — .
> I can't write. He sits waiting on the settee in O.K.'s room, he walks into the Escargot, he watches O.K. make salad dressing, he stands in the hall getting into his overcoat, always that tilt at the corner of his eyelid, that far-back smiling.
> . . . The wire came about the same time as the last news about Jack, we were still at the office, just about to go home. I did two things which have gone to *The Times*, but I am so scared you will hate them. The notice is just as Daddy wished, but I added two lines from the Greek anthology:
> 'Morning star among the living:
> Evening star among the dead.'
> Then I began writing a note to go under 'Fallen Officers' but the only way I could do it to make it effective seemed to me to link it with his friend. F. A. Voigt said that with one so young, it seemed to him better to dwell rather on the two comrades-in-arms, and somehow I thought Willie McGrath had no one to speak for him. Do forgive me if you think I have let you down.

George, known by his sobriquet 'Wuffles', had been the adored youngest of the family. It goes without saying that, after the fashion of Kilmacrew, the family that remained took his two-day-old bride, Ethel, to their hearts. If J.D. 'the Boss' is given scarcely a mention it is because, like all solid and deep foundations, he held everything together but liked to keep out of sight. Helen was to write of him:

> The one great grief of his life fell on him in his old age: the loss in Africa within four months of two sons; Jack, Coeur de Lion, and George who, at twenty-three, had something of the quality of Sir Philip Sidney. But for the wife whom some of us remember as young as apple-blossom and who

grew beside him like a flowering tree, he would have died of that wound. They saw, with courage, two other children go to fill the broken ranks; if with foreboding, it was not told. If he ever flinched, it was at the sight of an unopened telegram on the hall table. 'Fire', he used to say, 'should consume its own smoke.'

All through the war Helen was working at Constable's, cutting down articles for *The Nineteenth Century*, counting words, measuring lines, ensuring that the articles selected would not exceed the paper allocation. At night she took her turn at fire-watching on Constable's roof, and had to contend with the German blitz by day and night. She was glad when the radio went out of action and she hadn't to listen to the news, for

> O withered is the garland of the war . . .
> And there is nothing left remarkable
> Beneath the visiting moon.

She wrote few letters, but those to Kilmacrew show clearly the direction her thought was taking. In a rarely dated letter on Easter Tuesday, 4 April 1942, she wrote to Meg:

Begin this letter here, for the first page I wrote was a sudden meditation, and you might well ask what I was writing it for — and yet it all belongs. I'll put it last. There never was so strange an Easter.

Dearest, that telegram about Tobruk stands on the mantel shelf always. It was the first thing that brought me out of the tunnel, into some kind of human world with light in it. For I had gone on and on — 'To what purpose is this waste?' And somehow George, with all that fulness of living, mental and physical, and that splendid strength, wasn't unlike the alabaster box. And I suppose because it was Easter, the strange answer, 'To anoint my body for my burying' came to me, and tags of things like, 'To whom it is given not only to believe on Him but also to suffer for His sake.' And the half-realisation that it looks as if the world had always to be saved by someone else's pain and someone else's death — vicarious suffering, whose efficacy we heartily deny when we are young.

    . . . Then darling Ethel's telegram came, and the world went up in glory. For Tobruk is one of the epic sieges, and Fellow was there. I'd always read everything I could about Tobruk, about the shell-ridden gaiety of it, and the absurd concerts given by the different batteries, and the multitude of dogs, pets left behind by the retreating Italians, and adopted of course by our lot, and getting full share of rations. There are two articles in *The Times*, April 1 and 2, about the break-through at the last, how the very last night in great secrecy, the Engineers built bridges across the moat for the tanks to go over at dawn and take the enemy by surprise — and I felt, 'Fellow was there!' Eight bridges, I think, there were, and the tanks were guided in the dark by tape.

The last page of this letter, left unattached, is headed 'Easter Saturday' and runs:

My darling,
    It's very early, and nobody awake: it's been raining and the light is in the drops on the plane tree, and the birds are talking. There's a faint light in the sky, as if the world wasn't yet sure that the grave would even open, and yet in its blind heart knew that it would. My darling, something I read the other day about Christ begging the others in the Garden to sit up with Him, and to pray lest they enter into temptation — 'The spirit indeed is willing' — and that He knew He was himself in extreme temptation, made the whole agony different. You know how I have harped on one's reluctance to suffer. I believe that cry, 'Let this cup pass from me', was the last knife-edge pinnacle of human dread of anguish — mental anguish too, for it was mental anguish at Calvary, even more than physical. I think we harp far too much on Christ's Godhead, make things too easy for Him that way. I believe in the Incarnation, but I believe it was a real incarnation — that the temptations to shortcuts in the wilderness were real temptations, that He was in a sense walking in the world with bandaged eyes, like the rest of us, and that He had to spend those long nights praying, to feel for the hand of God to guide Him.

George Martin's death seems to have marked a turning-point in Helen Waddell's spiritual life. Hitherto she had been acutely conscious of the invasion of Infinity in human life — God's eternity and infinity 'besieged' his creatures, as she put it — but as her Easter morning meditation shows, the infinity of the Godhead was taking more and more markedly the aspect of crucified love. The bright day was done: the disciple was following the Master to Gethsemane and Calvary. When George was killed, Mollie had felt it her duty to rejoin her parents in Kilmacrew, and her going left an aching void in her aunt's heart. Yet with amazing resilience and with all her old fire, she was soon back in her stride. In 1942 she was one of the five women and twenty-two men who contributed (often unpublished) work to *Queen Mary's Book for India*. Helen's entitled *Cyrenaica in the Fifth Century*, 'the first clear spring of Gallic prose, subtle, ironic, and humane', was a translation from the *Dialogues* of Sulpicius Severus. She also had on hand her new translations from Boethius, Alcuin, Hildebert and the rest. But whereas she had immediately found an epitaph for the French soldier 'Jacques', she had as yet raised no memorial to Jack or George, her nephews — a memorial, that is, in words that would last. In July, four months after George's death, she had written to Meg: 'About the memorial — I have a feeling that both Jack and George would loathe a stained glass window, but wouldn't mind a modest brass, just where they used to sit and carve their names: it could be on the lower wall of the pulpit, just on a level with one's eyes as one sits in the old pew.' Her advice was followed, and the memorial unveiled in Magherally Presbyterian Church in January 1943. It was from that pulpit that John Dunwoodie Martin had 'reigned' for no fewer than 54 years until his resignation in 1937. Now, as Senior Minister of Magherally, he stood with his wife and once more addressed his congregation in a speech reported in the Irish press. 'O.K. just off the deep end about Daddy's speech,' Helen at once wrote to Meg. 'It's very like him — the simplicity and the almost intolerable poignancy, masked in restraint. I am so glad he was able to speak, the old lion.' Helen was refused a permit to travel to Ireland, and had to content herself with reports. The Telegraph printed a photograph of the bronze plaques, the portraits of Jack and George by Paul Nietzche, and their father and mother in the foreground. This evoked from Helen a cry of pain and admiration: 'That photograph in the Telegraph shattered me. I can see the portraits are marvellous — but you, you are more marvellous than in any photograph I have ever seen. If I were Nietzche I would put a halo and a Madonna blue veil, and it would be one of the great pictures of the war:

MATER DOLOROSA 1943

I took one look at it, and broke.'

Jack and George Martin, descended from a long line of illustrious Presbyterian forebears, were sons of the Minister of Magherally, whom Helen likened to the Round Towers of his native land, 'inscrutable, indomitable, founded on the rock beneath the green pasture of Down, but lifted up to be aware of far horizons. Scholarship and the land were in his blood, and of the poets Shakespeare and Milton were most often on his tongue.' Milton, a favourite poet with all Presbyterians, was forty-eight years of age when the church at Magherally was founded in 1656. He had lost his dearest friend, Charles Diodati, in 1638 when they were both in their thirtieth year, and had expressed his profound grief in a pastoral elegy privately printed in 1640. It was but natural then that Helen should turn to this Epitaphium Damonis to commemorate George Martin and Willie McGrath who died so young. On 12 August, she wrote to Meg from a house devoid of any domestic help and consequently 'so peaceful, with no one in the kitchen to comfort or cajole or humour':

My days are swifter than a weaver's shuttle, and seem to make the same kind of noise. Somehow the house seems to have had people staying for the night for the last ten days, or else coming for dinner when there wasn't what you could call dinner. To my amazement I really am becoming a kind of cook — in fact Virginia Gildersleeve stopped in the middle of eating lamb and french beans to make an exclamation upon me, as they say in medieval Latin. I did love having her, for she is a grand, dark-eyed woman, elderly but strong and wise and loves laughing. O.K. completely fell for her, and they parted 'O.K.' & 'Virginia'. The last visitor was Hilda Morgan, just back from America, a very thin tired Hilda, but so lovely. Only we sat up talking very late, and I am yawning my head off today.

The really exciting thing for me is that I am working on Milton's *Epitaphium Damonis* . . . for the first time for months and months and months

'Wakens again the ancient mystery,
The madness and the sacred cry within,'

and I am doing really tolerable work again, and the thaw having once set in, I may go on with luck to the book. It is a kind of resurrection: and the odd thing is that it happened all of a sudden on a day of extreme fatigue and depression. I suppose the trough of the wave must be deepest before it begins to rise. Anyhow — the strange thing is that I'm doing it. I seem to be doing it for George — for Wuffles.

The *Lament for Damon*, privately printed simply for family and friends, bears the date 1943 and the dedication: 'To the memory of George Frederick Waddell Martin, Major R.E. Served in the defence of Tobruk 1941   Killed March 17 1942   Aged 23   And of the men, his brothers-in-arms, who died young.' Helen said of it that it was the one poem of Milton's that had real passion behind it, and it is small wonder that she found exciting such passages as:

No tears, no tears for thee, and no more wailing.
I'll weep no more. He hath his dwelling-place.
In that pure heaven,
He hath the power of the air, himself as pure.
His foot hath spurned the rainbow.
Among the souls of the heroes, the gods everlasting,
He drinks deep draughts of joy.

Despite Samuel Johnson's damnation of the form, Helen's introductory note defends the pastoral elegy: 'It is the first movement of grief to cover the face of the dead, and then to cover its own. The countrywoman's apron flung over her head, the Greek pastoral of lament, serve the same instinct: the privacy of grief.' She then propounds a principle that any liturgical reformer should ponder. Johnson had objected to an artificial fiction that precluded grief. 'The truth is, rather, that "fiction", convention, makes room for grief. The traditional language, the ancient symbols, become a kind of liturgy that releases emotion even while it controls it. Behind the unchanging mask of immemorial sorrow a man may speak without self-consciousness, even as in a cathedral there is twilight to obscure distinction and room to mourn.'

After giving expression to his love and grief, Milton had been engulfed for the next twenty years of his life in a 'hoarse sea of noises and disputes'. Helen's next task in 1943 was a political one. Her translation *A French Soldier Speaks* had not gone unnoticed. She was just settling down to a quiet Saturday afternoon when she was rung up by General de Gaulle's secretary. Would she translate General de Gaulle's speech at Tunis on the morning of Sunday, 27 June? They were terribly anxious to have a really moving translation for America. De Gaulle was a born orator. Helen found the speech 'a tremendous bit of work, and the translation not too dusty.' Every moment of that weekend was spent on it, and Helen admitted that the rendering of the last sentence had taken her as long as the rest of it put together:

'To France, to Notre Dame la France, this and this only have we to say today: that nothing is of moment to us, nothing of concern to us, except to serve her.

'Of her, we have nothing to ask, save perhaps this: that on the Day of Deliverance she find it in her heart to open to us a mother's arms and let us weep for joy there: and on the day when death will come to take us, she shroud us in her kind and holy earth.'

Let Helen's letter to Kilmacrew tell the sequel. It is dated 'Thursday, July 9.'

My darlings, I think Bobby, Mrs Warner's cat, has sat on this notepaper on one of his frequent domiciliary visits to me. I have just come back from lunch at the Savoy with the de Gaulles — the General & Madame, who is enchanting. The General I adore — it is difficult not to, as he is so large and rather like a great sad dog. He was very sweet, and said that his speech was very much finer in my English than his French. About 10 of us at lunch, a couple of ambassadors, and a charming Scot, Lord Sempill, who made a sudden speech over the coffee & brandy — and presented de Gaulle with a very ancient ring, and spoke of the ancient bonds between Scotland & France. And then to my stark horror, de Gaulle looked down the table to where I was sitting and said: 'Et Mademoiselle — de quel pays êtes-vous? Veuillez bien nous parler un peu.' Mercifully extremity brings inspiration. I told them that I was Irlandaise: that my country, like France, knew what it was to be enemy to England — 'sweet enemy' — that the wild geese, 'les oies sauvages', had fled after Limerick to the refuge of all free minds,

France: and now, it was the French who were the wild geese, and had
found their refuge in England. For England, horribly inarticulate as she is,
has utterly good a heart: that she has always been in love with France, as a
man loves a woman, delighted by her, but bewildered, never understanding what she is after — 'is that not our power, Madame de Gaulle?'
—which brought down the house. But that it is the woman's business to
understand, to make allowances for the large, blundering, inarticulate
creature: and so must France with England.

A lot of Frenchmen came to me on my departing and spoke with great
emotion many things I did not follow: and the Sempills came up, and I
found she was Sir John Lavery's daughter, and he thinks *The Wandering
Scholars* the greatest book ever written and so on and so on — all the result,
I think, of the excellent cognac. I am sure that was why I was able to talk
French — a little more and I would probably have gone on to Polish.

The letter closes with an admission that was to become a recurrent
refrain: 'I have been a kind of poor creature since I last wrote — flicks
of temperature and profound fatigue, just like old June days in Paris.'
Mollie was no longer at Primrose Hill to ease the burden but, knowing
Meg, Helen never spoke of her own deprivation. Towards the end of
1942 Mollie joined the ATS, and Helen wrote words of wisdom that
stand for all time, to the girl's mother:

Mollie will likely have gone before this reaches you. I am glad for her —
and, my dearest, you will in your heart know a kind of peace, that she is
going to know that goodly fellowship — I don't mean of probably 'orrid
little ATS — but of her war generation:
'Qui n'a pas l'esprit de son âge,
De son âge a tout le malheur.'
If you are not in tune with the spirit of your time, you have all the
unhappiness of your time, and none of the compensations.
. . . I am distressed at the long delay in writing any proper letter, but a
kind of dumbness was on me, as if one went through life on four paws like
a mole. But there, lying in bed this morning, and thinking of the time one
spends in grousing, and hearing the church bells ringing the little triple bell
before the elevation, this preposterous parody of the hymn came to me:
Beloved, let us grouse: Love is of God,
We know it not: it is too high a word.

So Helen was lying a-bed on Sunday morning, listening to the
tower-bell of St Mark's, Primrose Hill, publicly announcing the
solemn moment of the Consecration of the bread and wine at Mass. In
her preparation of the new volume of mediaeval lyrics, she broke her
rule of a twelfth-century boundary-line and trespassed on the
scholastic territory of the thirteenth. Thus she translated the 'Golden

Sequence' of Stephen Langton, *Veni, Sancte Spiritus*, sung to this day in the Mass of Whit Sunday; the hymn to the Blessed Sacrament, *Adoro te devote*; and the Lauds hymn, *Verbum supernum prodiens*, composed by St Thomas Aquinas for the Office of Corpus Christi. It delighted her when Jack's Catholic widow, Elizabeth, told her that her translation of the familiar verse 'O salutaris hostia' had been a revelation to her. Helen stuck the opening verse on her blotter:

> The Word went forth
> Yet from his Father never went away,
> Came to his work on earth,
> And laboured till the twilight of his day.

'The benediction it brings to me is so great, every time a shuffle of papers brings it to light, that I think the book might have some consolation in it for the rest of us,' she wrote. Helen certainly knew the Roman breviary and Missal pretty thoroughly, and few would deny her astonishing familiarity with the Old and New Testaments, her deep personal love of Christ, and a practical expression of Christian faith that can evoke nothing but admiration. This raises the question: How far was her religion institutional? One of her brothers, fearing she would follow the example of her favourite big brother Sambo and turn Papist, invoked John Knox, Martin Luther, Calvin, and Calvin's Jehovah to stop the rot (to gales of laughter from Helen and the family in private session). The truth is that Helen never deviated a hair's breadth from the faith of her Presbyterian forefathers, although as she said, she would have died had she not been able to return and drink deep of Catholic springs of devotion. There is a telling letter to the family at Kilmacrew, giving them news of various relatives. The opening paragraphs are so delicious that it would be shameful to omit them; as always, no date is given:

It's about half past ten at night and it was a good dinner. O.K. is tucked up in bed with his nightlight and no request to be wakened at 7.30 — tomorrow being Sunday: and Wugs has gone out to his club in one of the bombed houses (4 cats — Wugs, Tinker, Snowball, all from the road, and Jimmie from 4 Oppidan Road, go there two nights a week in procession, single file, spend 2 hours there & return at 10 p.m. in the same order). And so, having the house to myself, I converse with my dears.

Brawn, the food of all brave men and kings, came two days ago, and O.K. is in paradise. I have it in the refrigerator, and have that beatific feeling that even if midweek there is no fish except what stinks to heaven, it doesn't matter: Kilmacrew will provide, *has* provided.

Arranged with K.D. to go there last week on Friday. I said about 2.
K.D. said NO: Mother would be coming to lunch, complete with maid to
cook lunch, and come early about 12. So after demur, I agree. I start off,
taking tin of steak and 1 lb sugar, arrive, find Kay in kitchen washing
nappies. Aunt Edith's two maids *hors de combat*, one down with kidney
trouble, the other eczema in hands, so daren't come near baby. I sit in
kitchen. K. says, 'I'm just giving you a boiled egg — you'd as soon have
that as anything?' I say *sure*, but rather wish I had been left to lunch with
O.K. in town and come on afterwards. Kay puts away my casserole of
steak (20 points). Poor Edith arrives with another tin of meat, but says
not coming to lunch, just brought tin — disappears again, looking
longingly at me. I eat boiled egg & toast & tea with Kay. Edith comes
back about 3, looking very weary and unhappy: whispers to me she lies
awake wondering what excuse she could make to get home to Belfast. I
went back with her to her own house, and tried to make her see reason.
And then I had a sudden flash of what was really wrong. I found out she
never went to church. So, like the complete Ancestor, I waded in — it's
really because I know what one's own church means after long absence. I
remember going to communion in the Episcopal church in Paris, because
I could bear it no longer, and whether they would have it or no, I just
went. So I tackled her. Yes, there was a Presbyterian church in Rich-
mond, but it meant changing the bus twice. . . . I said, 'It can't be more
than 10 minutes in a taxi, and you have a kind old taximan on tap. He'll
wait and bring you home.' She disputed, but I was obstinate. I said she
was lost for the psalms, and for that sense of 'Till we *all* come in the unity
of the faith' — that he *might* be a kind minister, and anyhow it was her
duty to go to church (*Me*, that so seldom goes, but I would if . . .) Two
days later, on Sunday evening, she rang me up. 'You were right, Helen. I
had to tell you. And the text was, "O that one would give me to drink of
the water of the well of Bethlehem that is beside the gate." I got my drink
of water — you were right.' My dear, I could have cried. I had to hear all
about the sermon, but all the time I was thanking God that the gallant old
sheep had found its pasture at last.

Helen would certainly have had a meal more to her liking had she
lunched with O.K. in town, for among their circle of friends their
penchant for L'Escargot Bienvenu in Soho was well known. Ralph
Arnold in *Orange Street and Brickhole Lane* comments on O.K.'s love of
restaurants and food and wine, though he ate very little; but a meal
was a ceremony — he enjoyed studying menus and wine lists and
signing chits. During wartime, of course, Helen found the Escargot a
tremendous relief from the strain of providing meals when food was
so strictly rationed; sometimes friends were invited to share their
table. Mollie has described the ritual:

The Escargot was a French restaurant in Greek Street, Soho, owned by

Papa Gaudin, run by son Alex. A long narrow room, five tables to the front, nine or ten at the back, and in between on one side stairs to a basement kitchen (all orders were bellowed down these stairs), and on the other side a small room lined from ceiling to floor with bottles. No one dare enter without the permission of the wine-waiter, Valentine. A very favoured few were allowed in for l'apéritif. Helen and I would perch on an upturned crate with a Martini or sherry. Alex Gaudin, menu in hand, would come in like a whirlwind; torrents of French as Alex waxed lyrical over some exotic dish, but we all had simple tastes and were more likely to choose an escalope de veau, a ragout, fish or an omelette. (It was there I first saw snails being wheedled from their own door by an adroit twist of a fork and swallowed with enormous gusto.) Then began the ritual discussion between Valentine and O.K. — which wine? Was 1934 not a better year than 1927, and so on. Helen usually joined in — she had a very good knowledge of wines. A very special occasion, say George on leave, we would end the meal with cognac, but that was the exception. Occasionally friends or relations who happened to be in London would be there, but most usually it would be only Helen, O.K. and me. Helen seldom gave lunch or dinner parties. The odd one she had to give was more likely to be at the Ivy. O.K. almost always lunched at the Escargot. H. frequently just nipped into a small cafe near Constable's.

A letter about this time to E. K. Rand assures him that Papa Gaudin is keeping some 'Romanée-Chambertin' at the Escargot for the day the war ends, and invites him to come and celebrate with Belle, his lovely wife. She tells him that she has been working on the Regulus Ode of Horace, Paulinus's Lament for Aquileia, Alcuin's for the sack of Lindisfarne, Boethius's in a concentration camp, and assures him he will like the book, almost ready for the press, if Primrose Hill and its litter of MSS don't go up in fire and air one night.

In fact, although the end was not yet, there had come a lull in the bombing, but Londoners were tense in face of the threat of guided missiles: when the secret weapons noisily announced themselves, the Cockneys laughed them to scorn with their pet name, 'the doodle-bugs'. All the same, the six years of war were terrible to endure. Helen's letters to Meg grew fewer and more often annotated 'Found a week later'. If her fifty-fifth birthday was a sample of her normal day, it is no wonder:

I have just found this slip — I didn't know it was in the ration book till I opened it today, and alas nobody has had any good of it: but I believe that one can be given a week's grace so I hurry it back. Your lovely letter came first post this morning — made it a real birthday. And to crown the day, I found my clothes ration book along with Mrs McLeod's account book in the scullery. Also the hens' ration card, which I had been searching for all weekend, turned out to be with Mrs Luff. . . . And finally, the cap-screw of the mincer, lost for a whole day, in spite of turning scullery upside down, was revealed to me in a St Anthony inspiration, as likely to be in the hens' feeding-box, as I remembered unscrewing the cap because of obstreperous fibres of pea-pods. These may seem negative celebrations of a birthday: but as each one of them unrectified would mean long apologetic correspondence with Official Bodies, and laborious chopping for the duration, mincers being now unobtainable, the result is the ecstasy of the absence of pain after endurance of same. I remember being hugely impressed by Stevenson's 'Parsimony of pain; glut of pleasure: these are the alternating ends of youth.' For middle age, I think 'parsimony of pain' is the dominant.

Otto Kyllmann was also becoming thin and wan, got frequent temperatures and constant coughs, although he doggedly attended the office daily. Monica Stiff tells a revealing story: 'Helen was very sensitive to any criticism of O.K. The only time, over the years when we saw each other often, she showed annoyance with me, was when I unthinkingly said, "Why can't O.K. get his own breakfast? William does if I'm out." (Helen had to wait about to get O.K.'s breakfast, and could not get on with her own work until he was fed and despatched to the office.) My question called up a minor storm in Helen: "It is all so different for *you*, William is so much younger than O.K. (he was not, but being tall and slim looked younger than he was), and still in love with you after all these years." It was sad and made me feel very humble.' Was it Heloise speaking? Yet Monica goes on to say that O.K. 'was a darling': 'During the war when I was working in the Chemical Defence Research Department of the Ministry of Supply and my job involved being on night duty at a telephone that could never be left unmanned, O.K. and Helen would meet me during my dinner interval and take me to neighbouring restaurants and generally lighten the dreariness. He was always so kind, and I became very fond of him.'

Helen's own health was steadily deteriorating: any effort was followed inevitably by collapse. Whenever possible she tried to spend the weekends away from London, but hotels were difficult to find. In a letter simply dated Oct. 12 from the Falcon Hotel, Bude, she writes to Meg:

> I am so thankful to be here. I didn't tell you, but the last few weeks I was *awfully* worried about O.K. and so was Rosamund. And you see, I was at the end of my tether myself, and the extra worry up and down stairs with trays. That's why I wrote so poorly; I was so dejected and so awfully tired in body. But I'm taking it easy. It's a lovely kindly hotel — Cornwall is

very like Ireland, even in accent, and there is very good food and amazing
sunsets over the sea. The cruellest rocks I have ever seen, like saw-teeth
running far into the sea, but great stretches of divine sand, with rest for the
mind in gazing at them. But you know, one may as well face it,

> 'So vast the grief,
> So universal through the whole wide world'

that I think sometimes a kind of numbness is on us, that may pass with the
end of the slaughter, but meantime

> 'Out of the day and night,
> A joy has taken flight,
> Full spring and summer, autumn and winter hoar,
> Move my faint heart with grief, but with delight
> No more, O never more.'

Not wholly true, even for Shelley who wrote it.

There is a church close by, with a thin little bell that rings all the quarters
and hours, great company at night, and a vigorous old parson hobbling
about with lumbago and sciatica. Very High, incense and biretta and all the
rest of it, but with extraordinary simplicity in the pulpit, rather like an Irish
priest. And his brief sermon last Sunday was on the Israelites hemmed in
between the mountain and the sea: 'Speak unto the children of Israel *that
they go forward.*' It made me think how much one is content to mark time,
and look back. You remember Keats —

> 'But were there ever any
> Vexed not at passed joy.
> To know the change and feel it,
> When there is none to heed it
> Nor numbed sense to steel it
> Was never told in rhyme.'

But I suppose most things *solvitur ambulando* — 'When he was in the way,
and the Lord met him.' And maybe the quality, the whole quality that one
needs now is what the old trooper said when he came out of the uncon-
sciousness in which he died, and saw for one moment O.K. standing there:
'Faithful, be thou faithful, unto death' — not joyful or efficient or inspiring.

Love, what a jeremiad of a letter — probably because it is finished in the
grey dawn, and the one snag about this otherwise delightful hotel is that to
save staff they have given up morning tea. It is the one thing that will make
the return to Primrose Hill smile upon me — the early descent through the
dark house to where the little boiler sleeps with one red eye open, and Toty
yawns and stretches, and the kettle begins to steam.

Here, one longs for a speaking portrait of Helen during the war
years. Julian Allan,★ a sculptor, asked to describe her, could only

---

★Julian Allan, F.R.B.S., O.B.E. (Mil.) brought about a meeting between Helen
and Evelyn Underhill in her studio in Edinburgh. They made instant friends, but the
outbreak of war precluded any further contact.

reply: 'I would simply say Enchanting: that was always the Helen one met, listened to, looked at. Add to that the living heart, mind, spirit *and* body, with its laughter and Irishness, and the lovely seductive voice, and there she is. There seems no before and after; she is — eternally.' Possibly the figure of Heloise, Prioress of Argenteuil, visiting Gilles (*alias* Saintsbury) in the last pages of *Peter Abelard* is the truest likeness:

> He heard her come into the room . . . Then the door opened. . . . His day had flowered.
>
> She stood for a moment without moving, looking at him, and it seemed to him that some spring of mercy in her overflowed and steeped his heart in its strange dew. Laughter used to well in her, and the light come and go on her face like the broken lights of running water. It was a still face now: the line from the wings of the nose to the side of the mouth should never have been graven so deep — the line that comes from a mouth set not to cry. But the eyes — it was the eyes that opened the gates of mercy on mankind.

Even a chance meeting with Helen Waddell at times resulted in the flowering not of a mere day but of a whole life. Her many acts of compassion are a positive encumbrance to a biographer. There was, for example, Patrick Kavanagh stranded and penniless in a London where loneliness was the only holy thing in the city, or so he thought. In his autobiography *The Green Fool*, he tells of the addresses of two literary people he had been given: the one, a man; the other, a woman. The man was in — but not to him. 'I took a train to the second address. Miss Helen Waddell was in, and in to a stranded poet. She received me as the Prodigal Son was received. It was she suggested my writing this book, and introduced me to the Promised Land.' He does not say that he repaid every penny of the money she lent him; Helen used the cheque to send a needy nineteen-year-old girl with her sick mother to a Brighton hotel for a holiday.

No wonder people loved her. 'Once, coming home from work early,' writes Mollie, 'I was in time to hear Mrs Bernard Shaw scolding her for having too much heart, for wasting too much time on other people's work instead of getting on with her own. A twinkling Helen replied: "But the young are so vulnerable, they need encouragement."'

At the conclusion of a long letter to Meg, Helen refers to a young protégé who was to become especially dear to her. Gremlins had got into a typewriter and played malicious tricks on her obituary for Charlotte Shaw printed in *The Times*: she was in despair:

And on top of it all, I hear from the mother of a youngster I met on the top of a bus — he asking the way to Hachette's from a conductor who naturally didn't know. I told him I was going near and would show him. About 16–17, like a young Keats or Shelley, extraordinarily brilliant dark eyes, and charming manner. We began talking about medieval stuff, said he'd just been reading — did I know it? — and so on, and just as we parted on a street corner I told him I'd written it. Ten days after, this letter came. The boy had been very ill that day (they live in Wiltshire where she has a prep. school), had been on holiday with friends, never said he was in great pain all the time — came home to her, and next morning was taken to hospital. She wanted me to know, for that evening he had been so thrilled when he came home (both he and she liked all my books, she had given him presents of them): and she seemed to find some comfort that he had been happy just before. Now she writes that he is better except that he has lost his memory of the illness — does remember meeting me, and wants to see me again, and they are in town, so I am seeing them both tomorrow.

Her next reference occurs in July 1944:

I have no Mrs Luff, so that I make beds and wash up before I leave Primrose Hill. Christopher Hancock, my young Keats that had the breakdown — came to stay for two nights while being interviewed for a job at the Foreign Office: and he has got it, and is a creature transfigured: adores O.K. (who is already extremely attached to him as to my young brown-eyed puppy), and all seems set fair. He has got rooms, and likes his work, and he has just got a scholarship to Oxford.

She has completely omitted the information that Christopher's mother has supplied:

She asked me to lunch with her in London and then promised that, after he was better, she would help to get him a job while waiting to go up to Oxford (where he had got a scholarship to Worcester College). She was as good as her word for, when Christopher was better, he was installed in the Foreign Office in the Political Intelligence Dept. She had gone to great trouble to get this job for him, in spite of all her commitments.

To the boy's mother, she then wrote: '. . . I know you need the money. Dear, here is a slight contribution towards the exchequer. I wish it could be more. You have a big job, but Christopher alone makes it worthwhile, for he has the most amazing promise, and I hope much that he will come to the full ripening of his gifts after the terrible setback he had last year.' The cheque enclosed was for £150.

Later, Helen wrote to Mollie: 'Christopher Hancock has now left for Oxford, so that I haven't that anxious eager creature coming to the door at weekends wanting the strong succour of O.K.'s kindness and my Universal Auntiness. His job at the Foreign Office was a pretty heavy one for a youngster of 18, editing and getting to press a propaganda weekly they did for France. . . . He can be young at Oxford, and not responsible for anything but himself. But he looked so like Keats.'

Years later, Helen adds the postscript: 'A note from Christopher's mother — that he has got his doctorate at Grenoble, and awarded highest distinction. So Vivien has seen joy at last.'

Helen's second letter quoted above makes mention of Mrs Luff: she and her husband were to play an increasingly important part in Helen's life. Mrs Luff had given her services on and off for some time and, after the Primrose Hill pattern, was soon accompanied by her progeny who ramped all over the house. 'Poor squidges,' said its kind mistress, 'they have only two small rooms at home, and Mrs Luff says they have made a kind of rats' run on the linoleum, because there's so much furniture there's only one way they can go.' So Helen substituted her hen run and the lawn and the beautiful staircase. Then she turned to their father. 'Mr Luff is applying for a job as a postman — has got heart-sick of the street sweeping, and indeed it was a poor job for a man who was a skilled cabinet maker. So I wrote at O.K.'s suggestion to Bashford, who used to be head of their medical service, and it finally wound up with a hearty letter from the Director General, so the Luff family is very happy, if he only passes his medical, and they don't fuss about his being blind in one eye.'

The year 1944 was one long nightmare for Londoners — a throw-back to the heavy raids, the noise, the rubble, the gunfire, and the deaths of 1940–41. Physical resistance was wearing thin. From bed, whither she had retired, Helen wrote to Kilmacrew:

> Why I must always run temperatures for nothing I don't know. I trailed out to Dr James about my ears, but he says that it isn't wax, just being run down and constant sore throats. . . . I turned up old notes on John of Salisbury and reflected that at the moment there is a superficial resemblance between us — 'the pettiness and multiplicity of one's occupation, the controversies by the great ones, the brevity of one's days, and above all one's forgetfulness' — I can't remember the whole passage, but it is word for word the record of my days, and it ends, 'I that had meant to spend my life on things far other.'

She got up, went to Constable's to attack the enormous arrears of work and there collapsed, 'but Dr James very reassuring, said heart all right, only dog tired, take it easy and have a holiday. QUACK. And O.K., who has been vainly trying to find any place in England where one could so much as put a toe in, suddenly said *Canterbury*! It was because they have set to music one of the greatest things in the *Lyrics*: "Phalanx and squadron of the Prince-Archangels", and the Dean asked me to come down and hear it, at a festival on the 16th September. And oh, my darling. I have always craved that you and I should be in Canterbury together — it is the English Chartres. Could you, could you come? There's always room in these old-fashioned hotels for two people to sleep together, and you and I have done that so often. O *do* think of it.'

After the posthumous publication of *More Latin Lyrics* in 1976, Canon J. W. Poole sent the editor a letter which so powerfully illustrates Helen's theme throughout that book, that it may be quoted at some length. Life out of death is the pattern of history, perhaps the pattern of eternity, translated into time:

> I once had the good fortune to meet Helen; and I think you may like to hear about it. All through World War II I was Precentor of Canterbury Cathedral. One evening in 1943, one black-out evening, I heard broadcast by the BBC the First String Quartet of Michael Tippett; and I said to myself, 'This is the man to write music for Canterbury Cathedral choir.' I did not know Tippett, but I wrote to him to ask him to compose a Mass or a Motet for us. He was then Director of Music at Morley College in London. He promised to write for us; but with an honesty that was typical of him he said he could not write a Mass. His place, he said, was among the *pagani*, the young bewildered unbelievers; he must choose some text less committed than the Mass. He would write an Anthem; would I agree to his setting a cooler text? would it do if he chose Plebs Angelica, a sequence in honour of St Michael from *Medieval Latin Lyrics*? Of course I agreed at once; and Michael composed (to the Latin words) a superb Anthem for double choir, a cappella. It is one of the most distinguished pieces of music ever written for an English cathedral choir.
>
> I well remember receiving Michael's manuscript on 2 February 1944. There was an air raid over Canterbury that night, and we took refuge as usual in the cathedral undercroft. It was in that situation that I first looked through the score. All around us, all over Europe indeed, beauty was being destroyed; and now I held in my hand this new beauty, this thing new minted from the mind of a great musician. You will understand my happiness.
>
> Plebs Angelica was sung in Canterbury Cathedral by our own choir in August 1944. It was sung again in the cathedral at a recital by the Fleet Street Choir on 17 October 1944; and Helen came to hear it. As a memento of the occasion she gave me an inscribed copy of her *Epitaphium Damonis*, which she had translated and had privately printed in 1943.
>
> But what I now recall, and wish to tell you of, was a conversation I had with Helen. We were looking together at my copy of *Medieval Latin Lyrics*.

She turned to Peter Abelard's hymn for Saturday Vespers, O *quanta qualia*, and placed the fingers of her right hand over the second quatrain of the second stanza of her translation:

> Where finds the dreamer waking
> Truth beyond dreaming far,
> Nor is the heart's possessing
> Less than the heart's desire.

Meanwhile she turned her face up to mine, and repeated the words in a rapt, quiet voice. I was reminded of Lear's words over the dead Cordelia:

> 'Her voice was ever soft, gentle, and low,
> An excellent thing in woman.'

Who can doubt that in the Everliving she has found her translation verified? Indeed, these four lines are a masterly piece of translation. I incline to place them on a level with her translation of the Lament for Hathimoda which Stanley Baldwin admired: though there is another masterstroke, in the sixth stanza of the same hymn of Abelard's:

> The joy that has no ending
> Of souls in holiday.

In the choir books of Coventry Cathedral (where I was lately Precentor) I wrote alongside this stanza a direction to the singers, *In holiday mood*. So you see how Helen's work casts its influence!

Stringent wartime regulations had prevented Meg's crossing from Ireland, with the happy result that Helen wrote long letters during her fortnight's holiday. In the last of these she tells her of attending a special service for Youth Fellowship in the Cathedral:

. . . to see the procession of young men come up the aisle with their little tin banners for each country — at least half of them dark-skinned — and lay them against the entrance to the choir: and on one of them I saw 'Tokio' and my heart turned over.

I was absorbed in the sermon at Canterbury yesterday, not the Dean, but the Bishop of Croydon, a young man; and at the end of the 'book of words' for that particular service, there was this sentence which I didn't recognise as one of the collects: 'O Lord God, when Thou givest to thy servants to endeavour any great matter, grant us also to know that *it is not the beginning, but the continuing of the same unto the end, until it be thoroughly finished*, which yieldeth the true glory: through Him who for the finishing of Thy work laid down his life, our Redeemer Jesus Christ, Amen.'

And it suddenly came on me that my despairing thoughts about my own small piece of work, the feeling that it makes no difference whether I do it or not — what's the use? — that *there* is the canker in my life, and that not to finish the work I have begun is a sin, what the Desert Fathers called *accidia*, a kind of melancholy that paralysed the soul. 'Whatsoever thy hand findeth to do, do it with all thy might.' It is partly humility, partly fatigue, but I've got to get out of it, and already I have begun to feel a kind of rustling among the leaves.

The leaves, alas, were not the young green leaves of a Second Spring: they were withered and sere as became the November night on which a bomb devastated Helen's dream-house. On 25 November she wrote to reassure Meg:

My dear, it was so strange a thing. You know that like you I am a middling sleeper and given to what they call 'night exercises' in the army. I'd wakened, and finally gone down to prowl and rake the damn boiler. Came back to bed, accompanied by Toty, who seemed to wish for company, put out the light and meditated: then heard a swish, and like any b.f. instead of hauling pillow over my head, sat up thinking, 'Now I'll see the flash'. Then came the indescribable, a sense of rushing tearing fury, a noise that must have been composed of the crash of houses some gardens away, the descent of a lot of my own ceiling, the crash of O.K.'s wardrobe on the floor above, and most of the glass and ceilings in the house, all a strange swoop of sound and rage and shrillness. The incredible thing is that I have often been afraid before, but now not at all. I can only remember a kind of horror at the bestial violence — the rebellion of the sane mind against the beast. It was like a tiger tearing, clawing at the house. And then I said to myself, 'Now the walls will come in', and sat there waiting. And they didn't. And then I put on the lamp, and groped under the bed for my slippers, and cursed my tidy Mrs Kaites who always tucks them into shoe cupboard miles away across the room — now across a sea of mortar and splintered glass. I could now hear O.K. moving, shouting: 'Are you all right?' and going up to Elizabeth Lucas, who was in Rosamund's room (one window and crashed sideboard and hole in partition wall the only trouble there), and on up to Miss Matthews, who met him quite composed, very elongated in a long white nightgown. Meantime I'd followed the ancient custom of making paths for my feet by hurling eiderdown, blankets, cushions as a kind of causeway to the door, and O.K. coming down and again saying, 'Are you really all right?' heard a reassuring, 'All right, but for pity's sake bring me some slippers!' Then we all assembled in the kitchen, and had tea and brandy, and the others went back to bed, but I, as if I were an old hand, decided the one important thing was to clear the glass and rubble out of the kitchen sink, or we'd have a stopped sink for our comfort, and did so. Then I came back to my room and turned on the light, and saw on my pillow the corner of the Adam ceiling resting on its point. It had come down behind me, when I sat up, and in the general roar and rush I had noticed nothing. If I hadn't been a fool and sat up, it would have finished me, for when I tried to lift it off my pillow I couldn't. And if I hadn't been awake — neither O.K. nor Elizabeth Lucas wakened till the crash came, nor the ladies upstairs. So, my heart, I have an odd feeling that Providence intends me to use my useless head a little longer.

I'm telling you this, because I think now you won't be frightened any more.

The loss Helen most regretted was typical of her: 'There are some inanimate things that are a kind of sacrament and symbol, and the loss of them is a loss in life as well as in love. I feel that about the old Chinese script that the V 1 tore to shreds. Something went out of the room when that went. "Here have we no continuing city" — and yet that script and the pear tree belonged to the kingdom of Heaven and the City of God.'

It was too late to sigh as she did, 'A.E. was right. No writer should ever own a house.' She had to endure the inconvenience, the dirt, blacked-out windows that wouldn't open, ceilings that constantly fell, workmen about the place for the next couple of years, a muddle intensified by the necessity of getting down to Constable's to face the awful donkey work of preparing political articles for the press, and shopping during her lunch hour because the shops shut at 4 p.m. The war, Mollie said, did terrible things to Helen, but one thing is certain: it never broke her spirit. Stanley Baldwin teasingly wrote to her once: 'Since the death of Archimedes there has been no such instance of spirit subduing flesh as your working out your problems under a 4.7 barrage on Primrose Hill! It will be a magnificent passage, if given the right hand, when your life comes to be written. But I shan't be there to cheer.'

It is simply not true that Helen produced no great work after *The Desert Fathers*: all during the war she was busy translating some of the greatest things in mediaeval Latin, 'its living and victorious splendours'. Mollie has painted a striking portrait of Helen at work in Orange Street in the black-out of war:

> I would climb the dark stairs of No. 10 and pass through the heavy door to No. 12 and the *Nineteenth Century* office. It was a small room with no windows, and in the middle, Helen would be sitting at a huge desk, a horrible angular desk-lamp shining like a spotlight on her white head and the books and papers scattered over the desk. Dim piles of books and papers rose out of the fringes of the shadows beyond the light, and merged into the darkness. Helen would glance up at the sound of the opening door, her abstracted expression change to one of welcome. 'Mollie, I think I've at last got it to my liking. Listen to this —
>
> O Father, give the spirit power to climb
> To the fountain of all light, and be purified.
> Break through the mists of earth, the weight of the clod,

Shine forth in splendour, Thou that art calm weather,
And quiet resting place for faithful souls.
To see Thee is the end and the beginning,
Thou carriest us, and Thou dost go before
A pause as she finished reading, and then — 'isn't it a lovely last line —
Thou art the journey, and the journey's end.'

After six years World War II came to an end on 6 May 1945. The Battle of Britain had proved that the English of the twentieth century were forged from the same steel as their forebears in the tenth at Maldon; Hitler was merely another Anlaf:

The will shall be harder, the courage shall be keener,
Spirit shall grow great, as our strength falls away.

With tired relief, Helen wrote to Kilmacrew:

It's between 4 p.m. and 5 p.m. and the tension in the street grows every minute . . . . The strange thing is that though there is relief everywhere, there isn't much gaiety. There has been too much killing, too much death. And I find myself remembering,
                    'O hands that made them,
                    Gather the ashes in.'

CHAPTER X

DURING THE AUTUMN years that lay ahead, the travelling and visiting, the friendship and society of Helen's pre-war life in London ceased almost entirely. Her letters became fewer and noticeably graver, possessed perhaps of more spiritual weight and force than ever before, and marked still with abundant common sense and humour, but their quality of aliveness undoubtedly flagged. Their intimacy and naturalness never staled — hers was a temper of mind that could take other people into itself and care for them there, so that no selfishness or ill-temper ever marred her letters, no matter how pressed or oppressed she might feel. But she was swimming against a tide inexorably advancing, threatening, terrifying her. 'There were two Helens,' Mollie has written, 'and while one was content to let day after day drift by, pottering in her house and garden, the other Helen was hag-ridden by the parable of the talents, and her talent lodged with her useless because she wasn't using it. I always thought that the continual tug-of-war and feeling of guilt also had a terrible effect on her, but maybe I'm all wrong.' It was to Mollie rather than Meg that Helen revealed her moods of dejection; in September 1945 she wrote:

> Darling, I never seem to write to anybody. I think more and more I have sunk into John of Salisbury's melancholy when he thought of his life, embroiled in all the hell-broth of religious politics. 'I that had meant to spend my life in far other.' It seems to me that Europe is going deeper and deeper into the cloud — that this demand for four great powers that no man can gainsay is so monstrous it *cannot* come to pass. I began mocking the other day — that the same men who rejected the omnipotent and absolute Trinity are now prepared to accept an omnipotent and absolute Quadrilateral, with the difference that the Trinity was never totalitarian. Extraordinary how *un*totalitarian God's ways are with man — how we are suffered to follow 'the devices and desires of our own hearts'. . . . There are days when you see your life taken out of your hands and cease to struggle. 'Europe is a huge thing within walls', and I suppose having broken my heart over Ireland when I was young, I have been left with a strong belief in the small nations, and what they mean to the European mind.

From girlhood Helen had been prostrated by exhaustion produced by any deep emotional crisis or prolonged mental exertion. After her brother George's death, Maude Clarke suggested their spending a week together at Glencolumkille, the last outpost of Donegal to the Atlantic, on the very edge of the world. 'I don't know that I need it physically so much,' Helen had written to Dr Taylor, 'but my head does. That is the horrible part of a strain. One's body seems iron. I don't faint or collapse or do any of the things that bring you sympathy and release. It goes to my head instead. I don't believe that I'd ever break down physically; it's one's nerves that would go. Sometimes I think this will last until I've learned absolute self-control, past all jangling and irritation and power of being hurt. But I'm not there yet.'

When she began to write stories and publish reviews, Gregory Smith teased her with his usual delightful solemnity about her 'Collected Works'. She laughed at herself, but was quite seriously concerned about the dreadful contrast between 'the few contents I have to show, and the massive promise of the title'. Dr Taylor begged her not to overwork. She replied: 'I couldn't, if I tried. It's a funny sort of brain, mine. It's like the clocks — it gives warning before it strikes. If I have been doing too much, it suddenly sits down, there's no other word for it, and I'm useless for so much as writing a laundry note until I've rested. And that may happen any time — not necessarily at the end of a spell of overwork. I think to the end, I'll either do pretty good work — or no work at all.'

Did Helen ever produce work that wasn't 'pretty good'? Even in the 1940s when she was torn between house, office, and translation, she could demonstrate her keen critical power, her extensive accurate knowledge and nobility of thought, her surprising versatility. She was, as she admits, a 'dishcloth' that year, yet when asked to write a Foreword to a book on education by the headmaster of the Banbridge Academy she, who had shirked any kind of teaching post, immediately came up with this:

> . . . I confess that nothing but local patriotism brought me to the reading of it, having hitherto endorsed what Sir Michael Sadler, the Master of all who teach, once said about books on education — that a curse is on them, no one can ever read them, they are so dull. I began to read the proofs one morning of this June, with the sirens for Alert and All Clear succeeding one another like the arms of a windmill in perpetual lamentation, and the odd little beasts that are the latest invention of the most highly-educated nation in Europe roaring and ranting through a cloudless heaven, then falling silent like a hawk poised over its quarry, before the crash and the scream of the kill. But the spirit of the book that I was reading defied them: reasonable, passionate, humane. I could not lay it down till I had finished

it, and I finished it in an exaltation, the exaltation of Bernard Shaw's greatest, and unrecorded, phrase. It was an argument at lunch on the value of vivisection in medical research. 'The thing is cruel,' said the famous biologist who was defending it, 'but it is a cruel necessity.' 'If it is cruel,' said G.B.S., 'it is not a necessity. If a thing is cruel it is wrong, and if a thing is wrong it is not necessary, it is not even *expedient*. Let men once make up their minds to that, and shut the door — and they will find another. For there is nothing beyond the power of the spirit of man.'

The silence that fell on us when G.B.S. finished speaking came upon me again as I read the last paragraphs of this schoolmaster's plea for the children, for something more than utility in education. 'Education is spiritual in essence and therefore it is the spirit of the thing that counts. You may house your boys and girls in palaces, but this will make little difference unless they are taught by princes.' . . . Once, he went on, prehistoric man trained his sons to the making of weapons that they might survive in the struggle for existence. Then, even in religion, even in science, came the struggle for power. 'If we adopt the utilitarian outlook on education, our aim differs little from that of our ancestors, except that we endeavour to clothe our sons and daughters with an armour of banknotes instead of one of mail. If education is to mean anything at all, the breath of God must sweep through it from the turrets and spires of Oxford to the humblest country elementary school . . . Children, parents, teachers, Ministers of Education, let us desire, imagine, will, and create . . . Let us dream the type that we wish to create.'

The crazy diabolic symphony of power was still vibrant overhead, strange counterpoint to the cry of this passionate dreamer. Then, accepting, transfiguring, harmonising both, the echo of a still mightier singing —

> 'to hope till Hope creates
> From its own wreck the thing it contemplates.'

The whole argument is even more apposite today than when it was propounded; yet however far Helen's adventurous mind explores, she returns always to her point of departure: light out of darkness, life out of death, is the pattern of history, the pattern of human existence.

The ending of the war saw the return of Constable's staff, and set Helen free from the drudgery of *The Nineteenth Century*. 'A fog in the head' as she put it, and 'a bog in the feet' sent her fumbling mind groping for an understanding of life's purpose. 'And then I remember,' she told Mollie, '"Ye have need of patience, that after ye have done the will of God, ye should inherit the promise." I just don't know anything about anything, my dear — I'm become a kind of blindworm, moving by instinct, and I used to think I had some gumption. But I think one moves sometimes only by the pillar of cloud — more often than by the pillar of fire. . . . Sometimes I think that I'll stay at home and lock myself in and go back to the Middle Ages and let the world rip.' She then shows herself as practical in the spiritual sphere as in the domestic, and advises a course that any seasoned director of souls would heartily applaud:

> I am beginning to feel that one, meaning me, is too apt to think that a thing is not worth doing if one doesn't do it very well, and if one's heart isn't in it. The great thing is to do *something*: to recite the Lord's prayer by rote if one's heart is withered like the grass, and incapable of devotion. Only the other day did I realise what a tremendous prayer it really is. Body and soul are so inextricably interwoven that the discipline of *action* may have some power on the spirit, the reluctant slug of a spirit. I remember Momma once said that if you dragged your face up into a smile, it did a little raise one's spirits. Hence perhaps the sacraments. Hence perhaps the Incarnation.

She needed to pin on an artificial smile, for she was dealing with post-war problems of many dimensions: surveyors checking war damage repairs, office pressures, O.K. growing older and wearier, and 15 feet of red brick wall pierced by four large windows, the first stage of a new block of flats, steadily rising just beyond her hawthorn trees at the foot of the garden — fatigue, confusion and rubble, was how she summed up her days. There were weeks when the house was full of workmen rebuilding ceilings and chimneys, and she slept in a different room every night. At the height of the disorder, Nichole Vaudremer arrived without warning from Paris, to stay for three weeks. 'Attached as I am to the morsel,' Helen ruefully wrote to Meg, 'it's like housing a very lively robin . . . chirping at my elbow while I wash potatoes and peel things and chop things, and when one has just come back from the office and started on dinner getting, it is difficult to be genial. But to have lived through the things she has lived through — the hunger, the fear, an hour against a wall in June light, waiting to be shot — one kicks oneself for complaining.' Nichole, a child in 1924 when Helen had been a student in Paris, was devoted to her and after the war tried to visit her yearly.

As permits were no longer obligatory, Helen was able to resume her trips to Kilmacrew, but under altered circumstances. The faces of the two liveliest sons would never be seen again on earth; Sydney, the eldest son, was undergoing treatment for T.B. — the Irish scourge — in a sanatorium; and the Boss himself was ailing. Helen's feelings towards her brother-in-law had suffered 'a sea-change into something rich and strange' since the days of her youth, when she fiercely resented being robbed of her sister. He had never attempted to come between herself and Meg; his home was Helen's whenever she chose to go; shy and reserved, he could not conceal a childlike pleasure when invited to share a picnic with the two inseparable sisters. Gradually Helen conceded that Meg had been right, and soon a relationship of perfect understanding was established between herself and J.D. Towards the end of 1946 it was clear that John Dunwoodie Martin's days were numbered, and Helen went straight over to support Meg. She was present when he died on 5 December, remained for the funeral, returned to London in haste to cosset a disconsolate O.K., wrote for *The Banbridge Chronicle* a tribute to her brother-in-law that was one of the noblest pieces of prose she ever composed, and kept in frequent contact with Meg by letter, entering into her sorrow and strengthening her:

> . . . The life is very far back in you, and is it any wonder after these long years of grief, and strain, and worry about Daddy all the winters: and now the emptiness. But if ever love's cup was full, it was in these last days. I do not think I shall ever see anything so beautiful as you two together. My dearest, you are the heart of the world to so many of us — Mollie and the boys and me — and me too please, says darling O.K. who has just come in. Just now you are only an old piece of strained worn elastic inside. But you have too many people to live for. 'Speak unto the children of Israel that they go forward.' And Daddy will have his crack with Jack and George.

The year 1947 brought a mass of exacting letters and requests for lectures, but one stood out above the rest: Helen was asked to give the W. P. Ker Lecture at Glasgow on 28 October. Refusing all else, she agreed to speak at Glasgow on 'Poetry in the Dark Ages'. What an effort it cost her, can be gleaned from her letters. In April she wrote desperately to Meg:

> *Could* you have us for a while? . . . I've been very dead dog since collapse on Easter Monday, but cheerfuller every day, and above all now that I know I will do Glasgow. . . . I'm thankful that we are getting away so soon, partly because O.K. is so very tired, and partly that I can't do any work — writing, I mean. It's as if I had driven my head so hard that it has sat down on its behind and refuses to get up for anybody. But it's a good lecture, and I see a new book coming out of it — I want to do a really *great* translation of the second book of the Aeneid, Aeneas telling the story of the night Troy fell. It's just London burning.

Not only did Meg welcome and pamper both, but she also went back with Helen to Primrose Hill, and finally sent Mollie to take over the burden of household cares and give Helen the necessary freedom and space to prepare the work. Meg was valiant enough to shoulder alone the work of the farm and the anxiety over Sydney, her eldest son, who in the event was to make a complete recovery from his illness. The sudden release' from tension betrays itself in a letter reminiscent of 'the old Helen':

It's about 7.30 in the morning; nobody awake yet but Wugs who has eaten a hearty breakfast, assisted at my morning tea, and has now gone out into a damp world. I was looking on my desk for a writing pad, and found an old one with a fragment from Alcuin in it, beginning —
'The very days are too full fraught,
The very age of men has changed,
The way they live, the things they do,
    And life flits like a moment.
There's no return of days, or months, or hours, or years.
    They fleet like water flowing from a spring.'★
Darling, I thought you had suffered enough, and there seemed a kind of wantonness in this, which could so easily have been avoided with a little more caution on the doctor's part. But this last letter of yours has a kind of divinity in it — like the Mother of Sorrows that has come through deep and cold. When Charlie wrote that maybe if there hadn't been the false scare about him, it might have gone on for months with Sydney, I could but wonder at a boy so young and so wise. Lord love them both.

I felt Mollie ought to be back with you at once, and was awful worried at me having the comfort of her — for what a marvellous kind spirit it is. Mrs Luff comes back, I hope, tomorrow. And Mollie says I am to let everything rip and just shut myself up with John of Salisbury, till I get it started. I think it will make all the difference, if I even have the papers assembled, and in some order. And I shall renew my Museum ticket, and even when Mollie has gone back, go down and work there for a while, for it is a joy to know that you can look up any reference, and it will get me out of the house, and away from the sight of the torn curtains and the ripped pyjamas. However O.K. is at last getting some new ones, and some new socks. You know the stage when the patch goes on, and the next time it's washed the original rips again at the seam. Just as it says in the Gospels in fact, the rent is made worse.

As always before an important lecture, she spent weeks in pathless and waterless wastes while the days passed in little grains of sand: 'For so long I have been in despair that my mind couldn't get to the heat when it sparks — isn't there some instrument that depends on that? And now at last, it suddenly blew yesterday, and I worked like somebody cutting corn on a hot day. I am completely in collapse today.'

★For the final — very different — polished version, see *More Latin Lyrics*, p. 157.

She was to go North to Edinburgh, stay with Professor and Mrs Vere Hodge, and return home within three days: 'Barbara will go to Glasgow with me, and I'll come back after the P.E.N. party . . . I shall be so thankful when it is all over: it's my wretched head that keeps aching.' She wrote only one letter after it was all over, apologizing for a long silence when she existed in a kind of aquarium:

> I worked most of the way up to Edinburgh on a MS that had been so written and rewritten and bitted and pieced till it looked like a roll of toilet paper — and finally followed Sir Hector (Hetherington) and the Mace-bearer to the platform feeling like Charles I slipping out of the window at Whitehall. But after that it was easy — it's like the panic of stepping off into deep water. . . . I travelled most of Thursday and got back to my ever loving family and a blazing fire. . . . Alas, by Sunday morning my old faithful laryngitis (the laryngitis of exhaustion, as Papa Vaudremer used to say) had clamped down on me, and I thankfully stayed in bed, and am still there.

The W. P. Ker Memorial Lecture was published by Constable in 1948. Almost all the many mediaeval poems quoted in the text were new to the audience — they were the fruit of ten years' work, and never published, except for one or two short lyrics in *The Times*, during Helen's lifetime. Her words had lost none of their magic, her voice none of its music, her personality none of its magnetism, and as usual the lecturer held her audience spellbound. Barbara Vere Hodge reported to O.K.:

> It was a triumph, and I think that everyone who sat in that crowded lecture hall will remember the wisdom and beauty of what she said. It made one glad to see how many of the young ones were there, and to feel them warm to her voice, and respond to the wisdom and renewed hope she gave them. One had the conviction that something undying and eternal was being transmitted to another generation — the essence of that spirit that went with the 'young things gathered up for exile' was being conserved and passed on through the centuries.
>
> Helen came in with such grace and dignity, with W. P. Ker's robes flowing round her and her white hair shining — I am sure he was proud and delighted by the sight of her. For me, it seemed an hour outside time, as if the back and spaces of the hall were filled with shadowy presences — old scholars mingling with the young and living, and all of them sharing the truth and the beauty which Helen presented to them.
>
> It was a great moment in which to share, and I felt honoured.

It was a fitting farewell to the lecture platform: Helen never again appeared on a rostrum, never gave another lecture however much urged to do so. When the Northern Ireland B.B.C. wanted to broadcast an appreciation of herself and her work in November 1947, she replied with some asperity: 'All of me that matters is in the books, which are free for any man's comment.' To Meg she added, 'I *can't stand* this personal touch. I'm damned if I'm going to have a personal write-up. Time enough when I'm dead.'

In saying 'All of me that matters is in the books', was she unconsciously repeating what her new friend, Siegfried Sassoon, always so strongly maintained? 'My real biography is my poetry. All the sequence of my development is there. For me, it is the only thing that matters.' When asked by a B.B.C. interviewer to record his views on the Great War, he had replied: 'One word suffices. *Rats.*'

Helen and he had been drawn into a close friendship and collaboration over his study of Meredith. In 1946 she told Meg: 'Siegfried Sassoon is going to do a life of George Meredith for us — and O.K. is like the warhorse in the Book of Job: looking up letters and thinking of people's reminiscences. Bless it, nothing makes it so happy as the prospect of a great book, which this might easily be.' She saw Sassoon and Meredith as kindred spirits, 'for he had your exceedingly rare power', she wrote to S.S., 'of being completely aware of yourself and, at the same moment, of other people. For *The Egoist* is only half of Meredith. And I think you both know something of what Emily Brontë meant when she said anguish.' The week after the W. P. Ker Lecture, she wrote a letter of such understanding and creative criticism to Sassoon that she there and then became a lifeline thrown out to him at a time of personal crisis and distress:

O.K. will let me see the proofs of the *Meredith*: you have made him happy. The first batch of typescript that I read last May was to me so exciting that it was taken from me. But I have always wanted to talk to you about the problem of his (apparent) flippancy and callousness about the publishing of *Modern Love*. I think myself the reason was this: he *must* publish it. You can't refuse, if you are a human being and a writer, to publish the most truthful thing, and the one thing of genius that you have done, or you'd be the man burying 'that one talent which 'twere death to hide'. But the passionately *private* side of Meredith must somehow protect itself — like the little creatures who try to hide the nest in the heather by fluttering and crying somewhere else. And the only way to do it is the ironic detachment with which he writes about it — his sardonic indifference excepted to its quality as poetry — and a good 'Middle' among works of less weight.

This, at least, is a possible view, and it fits in with the anemone-shrinking sensitiveness that made him understand some of the tortures of the Egoist.

It will be so good to see you, and please God once this bout is over I'll be less Toad-in-a-Hole.

My love and blessing,
Helen.

What is so arresting about Helen's letter is its penetration and probing beneath Sassoon's own egoism. 'She was one who could put life into people,' he said of her, but there were clearly times when she herself stood in sore need of invigoration. She received it during her latter years from her 'dear Rubie', as she always called him, Constable's legal adviser. Steeped in the Bible and in Shakespeare, himself an amateur playwright of no mean order, Harold Rubinstein combined the Jewish ideal of the prophet Micah with the Christian virtues of the Sermon on the Mount. As lawyer, friend and future literary executor, he was ever on the spot to give her expert advice and spiritual support. To him she revealed the despair and disbelief that assailed her as her powers declined and periods of amnesia became more and more frequent; he would then send her gifts of books, his own, to lure her into discussion and raise her spirits.

She went from one doctor to another; they all assured her she was suffering solely from anaemia. 'This blessed anaemia has lifted tons off my mind,' she wrote to Meg. 'For I no longer feel wild-eyed when every circumstance of something that happened last week is with the snows of yester-year. Please God I have not to give evidence in a court of law: only even prosecuting counsel might let me off as one whom God hath afflicted. A very expensive and unbelievably hideous orchid has just arrived from the Dutch barrister who loves my work and hates women. I think he must feel about them as I do about orchids. My love, I seem to myself like the odd creatures in snowstorms inside glass balls, you know the kind. And all the detachéd sardonic side comes uppermost. But oh, not when I think of you, and Kilmacrew, and Sydney and Charlie and my dear dear Mollie.'

Closer at hand than all the rest was Otto Kyllmann. His tender solicitude never faltered. He still attended Constable's daily in the taxi ordered by telephone after the movable feast of breakfast, at midday he lunched at the Escargot, and each evening upon leaving the office, rang Helen up to warn her of his impending arrival. Suddenly, towards the end of 1948, he had a brilliant idea. Experience had taught him that writing gave Helen the greatest release from tension of any kind. Why not put together the best of the stories she had written for children in the pages of *Daybreak* during her student days at Queen's, and he would publish them? Thus was born the exquisite *Stories from Holy Writ* published by Constable in 1949. Michael Sadleir, Ralph

Arnold, O.K. and the whole Constable staff were wild with excitement — 'that strange incalculable gypsy Michael, so bitter and at times so sweet, so impatient of religion' considered the writing as 'something conjured up from the youth of the world', and confessed to O.K. that he adored the early stories, but St Paul 'just crashed him — "Almost thou persuadest me to be a Christian".' When launched, the sales exceeded those of the popular novelist Enid Blyton, to Helen's immense amusement: 'It looks as if the years the locusts ate may turn out the provision for my old age,' she told Meg, and then added: 'There was a marvellous review in, of all places, one of the Catholic papers, but tell it not! However, the Quaker one in *The Friend* would keep the balance of faith.'

That was the last book Helen saw issue from a press under her name. Occasional items saw publication in *The Times*: Hildebert's *Hymn for Whitsuntide* on 4 June 1949; a tribute to Stephen Gwynne, 19 June 1950; the *Lament for Hathimoda* after the death of Elizabeth Lucas, in *The Times* of 19 December 1951; and on 15 April 1954 a translation made some years before of the thirteenth-century hymn, *Adoro devote*, wrongly attributed to St Thomas Aquinas. In 1951 she tells Meg of a visit from Richard, obviously known to both: 'For one thing I shall always bless him. We were talking about translations of Virgil, and I began looking for the proofs of one by an American poet. As I grabbed a heap of papers some fell to the ground, and as I picked it up I found a translation of a prayer by Hildebert of Le Mans, and suddenly the tide came in. I had forgotten it. And behind came a set of translations, and though I felt a little like Swift — "O God, what a genius I had when I wrote that" — the tide began to turn. . . . Did I tell you that Barnard College (the L.M.H. of Columbia) offered me the first Virginia Gildersleeve Fellowship — I think it was 4,600 dollars for the half-year, lecturing at Barnard's.'

Since Helen almost never dated a letter, it is only possible to make a rough guess from her script, but clearly her mind frequently reverted to the collection of translated mediaeval lyrics 'of the graver sort' as she called them, that lay there waiting to be put in order. The postscript to the following runs: 'This should have been posted weeks ago but it had gone underground. Writing soon. Forgive my dirty envelope, can't find another.' As the letter contains an unpublished fragment on Rome, together with a short piece of Alcuin's in a rough draft, it may be well to print it here:

I was seedy for a day or two, but now all bobbish — Rosamund was 'pootlu' in Mollie's immortal phrase, about the same time, but all better now. . . . I have been turning out such a lot of stuff, my own old translations, that I am cock-a-hoop. I didn't think I had forgotten so much good stuff. But I walk warily, not making too sure of anything. It's a queer sensation to come on stuff of the early days of the war.

I don't know if you ever saw this that came out at me the other day — 'Epitaph of Paulinus of Aquileia and Arno of Salzburg':

> Here may Paulinus rest, for ever rest,
> And here let the good Arno lay him down,
> And let no envious heart cross o'er this threshold,
> Friends whom the love of Christ hath joined in one.

And again on Rome:

> Thou has made one fatherland out of many nations,
> Thou hast made thy prisoners thy friends,
> The conquered are thy comrades in the war,
> Thou hast made a city of that which was a world.

> For it was she alone that took
> Her vanquished to her breast
> And cherished all mankind, naming one name.
> In fashion of a mother, not a mistress,
> She conquered men and called them citizens,
> And those that were afar off she brought nigh.

Mediaeval poetry, or literature of any kind, was no longer in the forefront of Helen's mind: she was fully and painfully aware of the gradual failure of her mental powers. At first she buoyed herself up with false hopes — 'Everything all right, only rheumatism: warmth and a long corset will bring it right'; or, 'I think we are both a little discouraged and feeling, in the great phrase of my school friend in Japan, O Masa san, "My intelligence is not working".' She then goes on with determined cheerfulness: 'My darlings, Mrs Luff is back, exactly the same Mrs Luff with a gay apron and a cheerful face, and I think as happy to be back as I to have her. I am still a trifle dazed at the much ado about nothing, but I am quietly going to buy a bottle of Metatone and forget the medical profession. No — I think it was Fersolate that Mollie swears by, and I believe that blessed child must have left me a tin of it, for I just found it in the caravanserai of odd objects on the small old garden table in the kitchen, which is the Cave of Adullam for everything that has no official status. . . . It is the 20th, and a month from now as the crow flies, we'll be in the Heysham train, please God.'

To Kilmacrew therefore Helen and O. K. repaired for Christmas. These visits, a regular feature of the 1950s, were sometimes prolonged for many weeks.

In 1955, under the aegis of O.K. and Mollie, sitting on either side to prompt and encourage, Helen even managed to read part of a paper she had long before prepared, and to add a few of her translated lyrics, for a B.B.C. recording.

To go to a haven where he could have a meal set before him, sit over it for an hour or more as was his wont, simply to talk and satisfy sentiment rather than appetite, content that Helen was safe and sound, must have given O.K. a welcome respite from the gruelling daily round of Primrose Hill Road. But what it meant for Meg to watch, not only Helen's physical deterioration, but what she now knew to be an organic brain failure that must result in the slow disintegration of that sister's very personality, beggars the imagination.

In December 1953, at the age of eighty-four, Otto Kyllmann at last retired from a lifetime of publishing with a minimum of fuss: there was no golden handshake, no elaborate presentation. As Ralph Arnold has put it, one day he was in the office, the next he just was not there — and he never went back. Worried at having lost touch with Helen after the war, Julian Allan called on her about this time:

> I did not see her after the war until much later, & finding myself on a brief visit to London & having to see a sculptor in Primrose Hill, decided to knock on Helen's door. I did. It opened instantly for she was standing behind it. She greeted me in her Irish way, 'My dear, lovely as ever. Come & have tea with me tomorrow.' Alas, I was catching the 10 a.m. train back to Scotland, so could not, but I wish I had —— I was uneasy. I didn't think she knew who I was & lurking behind her in the shadows was a man. Puzzled I left her, feeling that something was very wrong. Now of course, I know who the man was & that her memory had gone. The smile and manner were the same — but I felt sick at heart. . . . One does not want to remember a fleeting sight of so great a creation so tragically being destroyed. She herself never can be, and is eternally unique, for ever enchanting.

It was neither Boethius nor Alcuin nor yet the seventeenth-century Milton, but the Greek Aeschylus, contemporary of Job the Edomite, who wrote in a chorus of the *Agamemnon*:

> Zeus, whose will has marked for man
> The sole way where wisdom lies;
> Ordered one eternal plan:
> *Man must suffer to be wise.*

The woman who, from girlhood, had steadied her soul on the thought of eternity, loved and lived life to the full but walked unafraid of death, was fond of quoting John of Salisbury's *Polycraticus*: 'For we also wrestle with the Angel . . . and the man in whom the love of eternity hath kindled, will go lame in the things of time . . . For not without the anguish of the struggle shall the face of truth be seen . . . nor shall the day break without a benediction.' This 'anguish of the struggle' finds expression in a number of scattered fragments in Helen's late script, meant obviously for Meg: but do they forestall the bewildered human cry: 'To what purpose is this waste?'

> I'm thinking of the road to Emmaus and the sad finality of 'But we trusted it had been He who should have redeemed Israel.' And the strange Traveller's answer: 'O fools and slow of heart to believe all that the prophets have spoken. *Ought not Christ to have suffered these things and to enter into his glory?*'

The next scrap is headed: '(This was written in haste and lost for ten days.)'

> Darling,
>   Only this one question, for I can see what you have been through, with these shallow people who have never known agony.
>   What happened to the frightened broken-hearted men, strangers in Jerusalem, who had seen the Lord they adored nailed up like a jackdaw on the barn door? What happened, that in a few days they were confident and comforted: and that in six weeks' time they were as bold as brass, challenging Church and State?
>   The best proof of Christ's resurrection is the existence of the Christian Church. Sure, they were as scared as rabbits. My darling, I don't know if you have *Lazarus of Bethany* among your *Daybreak*. Because what I have written happened to me, the night George's coffin came, that long coffin, nailed down.
>   I saw that meeting, lying in bed upstairs. I heard the impatience of 'I know that he shall rise again . . . at the last day'. And I heard the answer.
>   I've never doubted since. But I remember St Paul, 'Thou sowest not the body that shall be . . . sown a natural body . . . raised a spiritual body'.

Three of Helen's letters to Kilmacrew are extant, which, from their reference to Miss Pring, her nurse, must have been written in the latter half of the 1950s. They speak for themselves. The last of the three begins on a sheet of blotting paper, and all bear blobs of ink as well as a good deal of scoring out. The admission of having destroyed some of her work explains much. Although for example Dr Taylor wrote weekly for four years, in beautiful cursive script in Indian ink, on paper as tough as vellum, not a single letter of his survives in its entirety. They are all defaced, ruthlessly slashed, any passages referring to Helen herself or her work excised or heavily crossed out. The letters now to be quoted are addressed in the plural to 'My darlings'.

I keep on thinking about my dears, and longing that they lived nearer. I have been very 'cheap skate', slumpish for nothing, but the Parable of the Talents still haunts me, and Wugs says I must get down to it. I rather dread spreading out the documents, but it would satisfy my conscience if I could get a few things on paper. And I was so grateful at what you & Mollie found — or was it Momma? And if I can't find anything, I think I ought to do something about Sunday school — of which I am now so timid.

But first I'll try some of the lovely stuff that I think it was Momma found. It is so easy just to slump and blame the cold. And I think I took a despairing fit and tore some of it up. Enough of that.

Darling, would there be any chance of seeing you — I have a half-dream that you came. But when it's warmer — I wonder if my darlings will get over the water abroad. My dears, will you say your prayers for me, for I sure did very little as regards the Parable of the Talents.

O.K. seems to be rid of so much of his lethargy, so that I have no excoose (sic). But — you remember that lovely close: 'It may be that you will fall, or think you have fallen lower: then serve Him where you are. Still serve Him in the lowest room of all.'

Darlings, forgive this jeremiad, with so much egotism in it. Maybe something will flower again, if it's only dandelions. I can't remember if I blessed you for finding so much new stuff: and O.K. seems a different human being. [P.S. at top of letter: 'I'll write more sprightly tomorrow. Imp.']

Letter 2:

My darlings, I don't know how every letter to you seemed to have got blocked or lost or halved, but at last there is a great lull . . . I am eating like caterpillar, solid munching, and I can go to sleep without any trouble. For so long I felt *This is none of I*. A lot of my letters seemed never to reach you at all.

I still am a very stupid animal, but hearty and stockish. And I have found my fountain pen, your marvellous one, that I loved so much . . . . Dear O.K. seems to be at peace, and keen about his old things, so when the weather is more possible he will be getting around his old friends.

O.K. is marvellously fit, and just as interested as ever. I don't know how long I left you without news of me, but some turned up in the waste-paper basket, but not sent, so I did make some kind of effort to come at you.

So, my dearest dears, forgive all this dimness and neglect. You know how vague you become after a few days: and you will forgive the stupid owl. O.K. wonderfully well, bless him, & Miss Pring. Helen.

Letter 3:

> My darlings, I do hope nobody sent you a worrying message. I was queer in the early morning, but came through all right, and Wugs sleeps happily at the end of my bed. If I could get a few more of the things I want written down, I'd do very well. Don't try to come, my darlings. O.K. is here, God bless him, and Miss Pring so capable and kind.
>
> I don't mean physical comfort — only I'd like to have written more — redeeming the time. I think that goes back in my memory to days at Glandore, for I couldn't *think* how one redeemed time.
>
> I'm so sorry for O.K. with 'the regiment of women' encompassing him. Oh dear, the time I have wasted — if I could have it now. But maybe I'll have a little longer. Don't worry about not getting over. Poor O.K. I am so sorry for him with no man about. I do hope he has gone down to the Savile.
>
> No sense going on like this, but I can hold your hand, and Wugs watches me all the time, very serious-minded.
>
> My darlings, I know you will never forget dear O.K.
>
> Oh dear, if only I were in Ireland — but it simplifies things more as it is.

In a letter to Enid Starkie quoted in *The Mark of the Maker* (p. 188), Nichole Vaudremer (Madame de Praingy) has depicted Helen as she saw her on her last visit in 1952 — a haunting vignette of a Christian following her Master along the Via Dolorosa: 'I see her now as she sat with her hands folded on her knees in her sitting-room in front of a small picture of Christ stumbling under the burden of his Cross. With tears in her eyes, she said: "My cross is very heavy too and is crushing me but, looking at Him, I try to carry it without being too complaining and sorry for myself."' She had once written to a friend whose nephew, after a brilliant war career, had put an end to his own life: 'It's at a time and faced with grief like this that one wishes one was a Catholic, and could cry to the Mother of Sorrows.' One suspects that she frequently did. She loved her nun-nurses in Paris in 1924, and when O.K. was admitted to hospital in the winter of 1956, she obviously hadn't changed: 'Oh dear, if O.K. were himself again,' she wrote to Meg, 'but it's marvellous to know he is getting better. I have fallen for St John and St Elizabeth* — they are so gentle and gay.' After leaving hospital, O.K. and Helen went to spend Christmas at Kilmacrew and returned in the spring of 1957.

Acting on J. H. Newman's principle that suppression of the truth is detestable, and G. K. Chesterton's that nothing is too sacred to be quoted, Meg's diary may now take over the sequence of the next few years.

*Hospital in St John's Wood, London, run by Sisters of Mercy.

1957 April 1–June 19: Helen had bath at 4 a.m. and demanded her breakfast.

Got H. to sign all her books for Victoria College.

Helen disappeared — Billy found her wandering in the bog.

Brice and Doreen (Clarke) here . . . . Nothing can be done. Says she has deteriorated a lot since Christmas.

June 19: My darling went off — such a bewildered darling — it has just broken my heart to see such a change. She that had the world of letters and scholarship at her feet now drifting sadly and aimless. God help her. What has brought her to this, a fate so uncalled for — and so difficult to work with — so changeable — so unlike my Imp. May God be good to her and protect her, and keep poor old O.K. for she would be lost without him now.

1957 December 5–January 30 1958: Helen extremely cross — somehow I feel lost and wandering — I have got so old. God give me grace and strength and courage to look after her and not to faint.

H. is collapsed — back to childhood — even worse. God help me to keep cheery and bright. I am sort of useless & have no courage or hope. Brice will get in touch with H's doctor and suggest a nurse . . .

1959 May 14: Poor old O.K. is gone — died suddenly today. R.I.P. Mrs Luff rang up — says she was with O.K. nearly all day, and promised to stay with him through the night, but late afternoon he held her hand, smiled at her, and died. Helen won't even realize he has gone.

She didn't. She had entered what Peter of Celles in a letter to John of Salisbury called 'the school of the simplicity of Christ.' Meg had asked in deep distress: 'What has brought her to this, a fate so uncalled-for?' to which Helen might have made answer in the words of Peter Abelard's *Hymn for Good Friday*:

> This is that night of tears, the three days' space,
>   Sorrow abiding of the eventide,
> Until the day break with the risen Christ,
>   And hearts that sorrowed shall be satisfied.

Was this also perhaps the unwritten story of 'Heloise now that she is old'? After the publication of the novel *Peter Abelard* in 1933, A.E. told Helen that he had not found her speaking anything through her characters that was not true to the triune nature of man in which body, soul and spirit cry each their own cry, and go their own way, and have no pity for each other. We live behind the clay-shuttered doors of our five senses, and they cheat by so often perceiving only the outer shell. Helen Waddell's life seemingly ceased in the 1950s with the total eclipse of her dazzling gifts of intellect, winning charm, balance and humour, her ripe scholarship and deep spirituality. Mute, unheeding, unfeeling, blind to all beauty, a stranger to the family she had so loved, she sat day after day before a picture of Christ crucified, and in that darkness of soul and body, who shall say what mighty work was being wrought in and by her spirit? Mankind was redeemed by a Man stretched out with hands and feet fastened by nails to a cross.

In a world delirious with the invention of more and more powerful weapons of self-destruction, filled with hoarse noises, with clamour and violence on every side, is it not at least conceivable that the Creator of man should, so to speak, demand hostages to overpass time and space, and to dwell beyond the reach of intellect or so-called psychological awareness, in silent solitude in God's presence? These tithes given to God are called to cease being workers and thinkers, and to plunge instead into the deep silence of their own incommunicable selfhood and spirit to encounter the living God, entirely other yet mysteriously immanent at the inmost centre of every human heart He has created. Such activity has no visible connection with mind or body. As A.E. warned and forewarned Helen: the three component parts of man cry each their own cry and have no pity for each other — but nothing can be so powerful and efficacious in the redeeming of time as the 'activity of rest'. This is that 'power of God made perfect in weakness' which is so often the theme of the Gospels and the Letters of St Paul.

Little remains to be told of Helen's last years. After Otto Kyllmann's death, No. 32 Primrose Hill Road continued to function with Helen, her nurse, a housekeeper and Mrs Luff in occupation, but expenses were so high that finances could not long stand the strain. The thirty years' lease of the house expired in 1962 and the property was needed for development. Why, it may be asked, did Helen not return to Kilmacrew? Because Kilmacrew was no longer the stilled harbour of desire as of old. She was unhappy there, did not recognize it, the name 'Meg' evoked no response. Moved away from the familiar surroundings of her own house, she at once became confused and perturbed. Otto Kyllmann's Power of Attorney died with him, and as Helen was incapable of signing her name, Harold Rubinstein her lawyer had no alternative but to apply to the Courts, and have Helen made a Ward in Chancery; her affairs in future were handled by the Official Solicitor of the Royal Courts of Justice.

At this painful juncture, the family met to decide the course of action. Helen's doctor-nephew Mayne joined them — Maude Clarke's brother Brice was also in constant communication — and Mrs Luff of the smiling face and gay apron who had loved and worked for Helen since 1941, when the latter was in the heyday of her fame, was also consulted. As a result it was agreed that if Dr Hardy Scott (Helen's and O.K.'s doctor for many years) gave her approval — which she did wholeheartedly — Helen should go to the Luffs' house in Camden Town. There she remained, she who had once taken such joy in translating Alcuin's last prayer:

> And now,
> Beside the shore of the sail-winged sea
> I wait the coming of God's silent dawn.
> Do thou help this my journey with thy prayer.

'I can now think of her great soul at rest,' Siegfried Sassoon wrote, 'awaiting release and reward.'

In March 1965 she was admitted to the Whittington Hospital suffering from pneumonia. Mollie went immediately to her aunt's side but received no sign of recognition. Helen Waddell, 'to whom religion was not the mask of desire, but the countenance of that eternity which doth ever besiege our life', died on 5 March 1965.

H.W. to George Saintsbury   4 February 1917

So every fairytale should end happily? I am just remembering that the three in the Japanese lot I did end — not badly, I think, but rather sadly. It is the way of Japanese fairytales to end with a rather sorrowful indefiniteness — they get infinity so — like the line of the headlands on their cheapest little jars.

H.W. to Dr George Taylor   9 April 1918

A scrap of Japanese verse from an old book of my father's that I turned up the other day.

> When I am gone,
> And the house desolate,
> Yet do not thou, O plum tree by the eaves,
>   The spring forget.

INDEX